COLUMBIA UNIVERSITY ORIENTAL SERIES
Volume XXVIII

THE CHUETAS OF MAJORCA

Conversos and the Inquisition of Majorca

by
BARUCH BRAUNSTEIN, Ph. D.

MENNONITE PUBLISHING HOUSE

Scottdale, Pa.

Printed in the United States of America

To Gladys

FOREWORD

In the following study, Dr. Baruch Braunstein has made a very important contribution to the history of the Inquisition. At great personal sacrifice, he went to Spain and to Majorca, there to study the manuscript documents at first hand and thus was able to give us a description of the working of the Inquisition in that island as a basis for a knowledge of the manner in which it functioned in the various parts of what later became the Spanish Kingdom. His chapter on the Chuetas—the 300 families of former "Conversos" living in Majorca almost as a separate community—is most fascinating; and in the six Appendices we have material coming directly from the sources which will be helpful to many students. A very full bibliography of the manuscripts and printed material used is added.

I commend Dr. Braunstein's book most highly to all who may be interested in this subject. Belonging, as he does, to another faith, he has yet successfully striven to be most fair to the Catholic Church.

February 28, 1936.

RICHARD GOTTHEIL,
Columbia University,
New York City.

Salo Baron, of Columbia University, for first suggesting the subject to the author. Many other persons were kind enough to encourage the author in his work and to make suggestions from time to time. Among these are Dr. Homéro Seris, of the Centro Estudios Históricos in Madrid, Don Pedro Sampoll y Ripoll, Don Rafael Ysasi, Don José Ramis de Ayreflor, Don Diego Zaforteza y Musoles, Don Fausto Morrel y Tacón and Don Guillermo Forteza of Palma, Dr. Cecil Roth of London, Rev. Father George B. Ford of Columbia University, and Mr. Louis Wallis and the late Max J. Kohler, Esq., of New York.

Finally the author wishes to record his gratitude to the National Council on Religion in Higher Education, upon whose stipend a part of this study was made, and to Dr. Stephen S. Wise for graciously permitting him to spend a portion of his time for research in Spain on the Bertha Guggenheimer Fellowship, intended for study in Palestine.

BARUCH BRAUNSTEIN.

CONTENTS

ABBREVIATIONS

ACA   Archivo de la Corona de Aragon, Barcelona
AH   Library, Academia de la Historia, Madrid
AHN   Archivo Histórico Nacional, Madrid
BAH   *Boletin de la Academia de la Historia*
BN   Biblioteca Nacional, Madrid
BSAL   *Bolleti de la Societat Arqueológica Luliana*
JQR   *Jewish Quarterly Review*
JTS   Library, Jewish Theological Seminary of America, New York
RABM *Revista de Archivos, Bibliotecas, y Museos*
REJ   *Revue des Etudes Juives*

ACKNOWLEDGMENT

The writer owes a debt of gratitude to many persons, both in the United States and in Europe, whose sincere interest in scholarship and whose kindnesses have been of inestimable value in the preparation of this volume. Of course this does not mean that anyone but the writer himself is to be held responsible for the views and the conclusions expressed in this study.

Thanks are due to the following librarians for their co-operation in the author's search for materials: Don Miguel Gomez del Campillo and Padre Benito Fuentes, the director of the Archivo Histórico Nacional and the head of its Sala de la Inquisición, respectively, in Madrid, Don Salvador Ros of the Biblioteca Provincial, and Don Juan Pons of the Archivo General Histórico in Palma, Majorca, Prof. Alexander Marx of the Jewish Theological Seminary of America, Mr. Roger Howson of Columbia University, Mr. C. Seymour Thompson of the University of Pennsylvania, where the Henry Charles Lea Library is housed. Many doors were opened in Spain through the intercession of Prof. Fernando de los Rios, sometime Minister of Public Instruction and Fine Arts, the United States Ambassador in Madrid, Hon. Claude G. Bowers, the Consul General in Barcelona, Claude I. Dawson, Esq., and Don Javier Lasso de la Vega, of the Universidad Central in Madrid, to whom the author expresses his gratitude. Many persons in Palma, also, gave the author suggestions in his search for the materials of this study. Thanks are due especially to the late Don Francisco Villalonga y Fabregues and his family for allowing the author to peruse the documents in his private library, and to Don Estanislau Pellicer i Navarro for his many kindnesses which materially assisted the progress of this study. Elkan N. Adler, Esq. and Maggs Bros., of London, placed many valuable books at the author's disposal. Thanks are recorded here to Prof. Austin P. Evans, of Columbia University, for his criticism and suggestions, to Professor Earl J. Hamilton, of Duke University, for converting Majorcan money into dollars, to Mr. A. G. Duker for suggestions and for correcting the proofs of the Bibliography, and to Prof. Shalom Spiegel, Dr. Max A. Luria and Mr. Henry V. Besso for occasional suggestions. To Prof. Richard Gottheil, of Columbia University, under whose direction this study was made, the author expresses profound gratitude for reading the manuscript, for making many valuable suggestions and for a multitude of courtesies. Thanks are due to Prof.

INTRODUCTION

The year nineteen-hundred and thirty-four marked the first centenary of the extinction of the Spanish Inquisition. Many books have been written on the subject of the Spanish Inquisition during this last century. Many of them were frankly partisan. They were written to defend the Catholic Church by men who felt that the Church had been held unjustly responsible for those practices of the inquisition which have proved abhorrent to the modern mind. They were intended to answer criticism levelled against the Church. With few exceptions, the literature on the inquisition during the last century has alternated between two battle fronts, carried on by doughty warriors on both sides. A century should have been ample time for cooling all passions and allow for an objective and dispassionate analysis of the Spanish Inquisition.

This author has no such high ambition as writing a complete book on the Spanish Inquisition. His is a very modest task of analyzing a small part of its activities on the island of Majorca and, by so doing, provide the reader, on a very restricted scale, with some understanding of its operations and the scope of its authority.

This author takes the position that the Catholic Church cannot be held solely responsible for the inquisition in Spain. In this work the Church will not be attacked; therefore there will be no defenses forthcoming. For the simple truth of the whole matter is that the Spanish Inquisition was chiefly an agency of the state, and not of the Catholic Church nor of the Papacy, from which it held itself aloof. True, the inquisition needed a charter for its activities from the Pope. This was granted by Pope Sixtus IV, although not without some misgivings on his part that he was forging the inquisition into a tool of the Spanish state rather than, as it had always been, a servant of the Church.[1]

The inquisition was brought into Spain to help make of Spain a unified, national state. Therefore the crown demanded at the very outset that it be a nationalized institution whose personnel be subject to it, and not to the Papacy. Yet it seems natural that some

---

[1] The Pope was so anxious for an inquisition in Castile that he was not unwilling to make the important concession of allowing the crown to appoint and discharge inquisition officials at its sovereign will. The subsequent Bull of the same Pope issued January 29, 1482 showed grave apprehensions that the former one had been drawn without reference to precedent. In it the Pope attempted to reverse himself by taking absolute control of appointments out of royal hands. But with the passing of the years, the Papacy exercised less and less influence over the Spanish Inquisition. Lea, *A History of the Inquisition of Spain*, I, 158, 9 (hereafter referred to as Lea, *Spain*)

writers would oblige the Church to bear the onus for its establishment in Spain because it was a *religious* institution. The state, however, used it as an instrument of governmental policy in making from a heterogeneous Spain a homogeneous, national state.[2] The fact that some high Spanish churchmen—Archbishop Carranza of Toledo and others—were persecuted by the inquisition, which often defied the wishes of Rome, indicates that it was not a creature of the Church. It was rather a servant of the state. The Popes were sometimes openly opposed to it for its cruelty, as well as for the depravity of some of its officials who, it seemed, were more attracted by the spoils arising out of the confiscation of the heretic's property than by the glorious opportunity of saving his soul. At the door of the Church there cannot be laid with any fairness the charges of viciousness and rapacity which the modern mind so abhors in the Spanish Inquisition.

The reader of any book on the inquisition, because of the highly-charged character of its subject-matter, has the right to know at the very outset the point of view of the writer. Let it be made quite clear, then, that this writer, a non-Catholic, is not aiming to defame the Church by writing this volume. When an uncomplimentary adjective is employed to describe the inquisition or its officials, no slur is intended upon the Church. For this writer believes that the Roman Catholic Church cannot be held responsible for the conduct of an institution over which it exercised no control.

If this writer does not lay entire responsibility for the Spanish Inquisition at the door of the Roman Church, neither does he attempt to lay the blame for it at the threshold of the Spanish people. No entire population can be censured for any one institution of the nation. During a great part of the reign of Ferdinand and Isabella,[3] who established the Spanish Inquisition, the crown was seldom interested enough in the people's wishes to convoke the Cortes. Through all the significant years 1492 to 1498, when the policies of the inquisition were formulated, when the Moors were

[2] Professor Salvador de Madariaga writes (*Spain*, pp. 41, 2): "Thus the Spanish Church, while identifying itself with the spiritual interests of the Catholic faith, did not submit to the Roman Church. It was of itself a Church in that for it nationality and religion became one" . . . and "explains why the standard by which the State is unified should not be political nor linguistic, but religious." Sir Charles Petrie, (*Spain*, p. 18): "The Inquisition was always more a secular than a clerical organization and an instrument of policy of State rather than of Church."

[3] The reader is directed to a recent study of Queen Isabella by Father Walsh (William T. Walsh, *Isabella of Spain: the Last Crusader*) for a dramatic, if not altogether impartial, presentation of her life and times, which will also serve to explain her part in the establishment of the inquisition.

finally subdued and many forcibly converted to Christianity, when the Jews were expelled, the crown did not once summon the Cortes in Castile, and only on very few occasions in Aragon.[4] It acted quickly and decisively without putting into motion the cumbersome machinery for discovering the will of the people. The people's will had already been expressed in ways other than through the Cortes, for it cannot be denied that by and large the people favored the establishment of the inquisition. If blame for the inquisition is to be assigned fairly, the best we can do, looking back upon it over the vantage point of centuries, is to assign its establishment to the abnormal character of the times in which it was set up in Spain.

Those were far from normal times. The country was seething with activity, with a superabundance of energy and an excess of heroism. Every Spaniard seemed to be affected by his rulers' energy. Victory invariably brings out these qualities. Granada, epitome of Christian enmity, had been subdued. The spirit of conquest was in the air.[5] Military life afforded the display of precisely those things—pomp, splendor, regalia, noise and drums, a sense of participation in great enterprises carrying an element of risk—which the Spanish temperament craves.[6]

New worlds were being conquered. Horizons opened wider and wider with the new conquests. Then too America had been discovered. If it meant nothing more at that time, its discovery was another manifestation of the destiny of Spain to vanquish the dread of unchartered ocean expanses. In addition, two important kingdoms of Christian Spain had been united through the marriage of Ferdinand and Isabella. These monarchs, once the Moors were vanquished, set themselves to subdue the war-like nobles, pacify the country and place it under centralized control. It was, in short, a period of high enthusiasm and nation-building. What might have seemed impossible of accomplishment in normal times, appeared quite easy and simple to a people flushed by victory and a passion for conquest. There arose a clamor for a unified Christian Spain, to make complete the victory over the infidel Moor. Only a people

---

4 Altamira, *A History of Spanish Civilization*, p. 114.

5 "A people which for generations had lived to fight, whose whole social and political organization had developed out of war, could not lie down to sleep!" Hume, *Spain, Its Greatness and Decay*, p. 1.

6 The Spaniard was not a good farmer or craftsman. Poor and rich alike were lazy. The hidalgos (gentry) would rather starve than ply any trade; all that was left for foreigners. Their pride was so ridiculous that, though in want of food and necessities at home, they "strutted with immense whiskers, broad ruffles without a shirt, and long rapiers, through the streets of Madrid or Toledo." Dunlop, *Memoirs of Spain*, I, 17.

bristling with the excitement of victory could so courageously embark upon the program of an unknown inquisition, an instrument in effecting the unification of a diversified Spain.[7]

The war-spirit in the country, seething with hatred for the Moors, was easily transferred to a campaign for cleansing Spain of all its dissident elements. It was simple to substitute "heretic" for "infidel" as the watchword for a new war. Such a campaign could be undertaken only by a people which had the world at its feet, and which was happily oblivious of the costs and consequences that any sober people might have clearly forseen. Quite obviously, the Spaniards were in such a frame of mind when the inquisition was established.

Only as we look back upon it, however, can we assign its establishment to the abnormal conditions prevailing in Spain. But if we are to judge the institution fairly and without prejudice, it must be judged upon the standards of its own time. The task of the inquisition, from the point of view of its own day, was a praiseworthy one: to save the souls of men when soul-saving was the greatest and noblest human endeavor, and at a time when it was necessary to preserve the unity of the Church and the nation threatened by the forces of heresy and infidelism.

But the task of the inquisition, however praiseworthy, was carried out by men. And men have always been human, no matter how exalted the missions they are to fulfill or the creeds they profess. There have always been unjust, cruel and vindictive men, as there have always been men with noble qualities and fine sensibilities. There were many wise and just inquisitors, trying mightily, according to their mental and judicial horizons, to mete out justice. Contrariwise, some inquisitors were knaves and villains, yielding to temptations for gain and power, such as were easily afforded by the nature of the inquisitorial procedure, as we shall see later on. These functionaries must be judged as men. The institution, with its lofty mission (from the standpoint of its own time), cannot fairly be condemned because some of its officials were avaricious and greedy for gold and power.

It is the hope and ambition of this author that the reader will find an objective and dispassionate point of view expressed in these pages. No offense should be taken, for it is not intended, by any religious or national group for naming, when by reason of the

---

[7] All these things brought about the crystallization of the national ideal of religious unity, expressing itself in the establishment of the inquisition, the expulsion of the Jews, and later in the expulsion of the Moors. Cf. Altamira, *op. cit.*, p. 111.

accuracy and truthfulness of this study it becomes necessary, those motives of men which are not altogether noble. If the reader does not approach these pages dispassionately, but rather expects to find his own prejudices confirmed—the rabidly anti-Catholic a justification for his prejudices against the Church, and the equally rabid pro-Catholic as strong a justification for his own predilections—then he would be wise to read no further. "Granting that the history of the Inquisition will reveal things we never dreamt of," cautions Abbé Vacandard, the Catholic historian of the inquisition, "our own prejudices must not prevent an honest facing of the facts. We ought to dread nothing more than the reproach that we are afraid of the truth."[8] So far as is humanly possible, this book attempts to present an unbiased study of a small part of this vast subject.

A few pages above, the author touched upon the character and extent of this work. It is well at this point to describe it more fully. This is a study of the whole by a careful investigation of one of its parts. This book aims to describe the method, procedure and, in a general way, the effect of the vast Spanish Inquisition, through a study of its major activity on the island of Majorca. It presents with some detail the operations of the Spanish Inquisition with the Jews converted to Christianity—or Conversos, as we shall call them—on the island of Majorca. One of the compelling reasons for bringing the inquisition to Spain was, in fact, to exercise a restraining influence upon Conversos from relapsing into their old beliefs.

There is a special poignancy about the story of the activities of the inquisition in Majorca and the Jewish converts to Christianity—who are today known as Chuetas—which distinguishes it from the activities of the inquisition in other parts of Spain. For today, despite the five-hundred years which have passed since the forbears of the Chuetas were converted to Christianity, they are still an ostracized group in Catholic Majorca. They have not been completely assimilated into the island's life. Nowhere in all Spain has the identity of a small group been preserved so tenaciously over such a long period of time as in Majorca. It is a singular phenomenon that to this day the Chuetas are sometimes referred to as *Judios* (Jews) and *Hebreos* (Hebrews), and denied complete social equality, and sometimes economic opportunity, with the other natives of Majorca.

---

8 *The Inquisition,* p ix (hereafter referred to as Vacandard).

INTRODUCTION

Perhaps the insularity of Majorca has bred a provinciality among its inhabitants which has prevented them from forgetting the Jewish origins of the Chuetas. Perhaps the present condition of the Chuetas is due to the results of the inquisition, one of the chief by-products of whose activity was the disgrace it attached to heresy as treason against God, causing the public to shun the erring person or group. The truth is that all these factors, as well as others, have entered into the unique circumstance of the isolation of the Chuetas. We cannot be sure whether they were admitted fully and freely into Catholic society after their conversion in 1435. Judging from the fact that since the early eighteenth century there were no cases of heresy among the Chuetas—and still they have not been relieved of the stigma of their origins—it may be that they never enjoyed full equality, even before the time of the inquisition. This points to the possibility that the hatred of this people by the Majorcans antedated the inquisition. But it cannot be denied that the inquisition capitalized on this hatred in carrying out its purposes. Since we are dealing with conjectures at this point, we can consider the further probability that the Chuetas might long ago have become completely assimilated and lost altogether as a distinct group, if it had not been for the inquisition. What we see today, however, is that the Chuetas are an isolated group in the island, and there can be little doubt that the inquisition had an important share in preserving their identity, for inquisitorial procedure made them a "marked people."

The first chapter of this work outlines the origins of the inquisition in Europe and later in Spain, together with a survey of inquisitorial procedure, in order to prepare the reader for the activities of the Inquisition of Majorca as it affected the Conversos.

CHAPTER I

ORIGIN AND DEVELOPMENT OF THE INQUISITION

The word inquisition is derived from the Latin *inquirere,* which means to "look into" or "examine." Specifically, it has come to signify the authority of the Church to look into and examine one's religious beliefs. The institution founded upon the Church's power to examine one's beliefs had the right also to determine whether the beliefs held were contrary to those prescribed by the Mother Church, and to mete out punishment according to the offense. The authorization for punishing him whose beliefs were not strictly in accord with those held by the Church—i. e., the heretic—came from the Old Testament, the source of much of the Church's authority. The idolater prefigured the heretic. It was he who worshipped strange and foreign gods, and who led others astray. The idolater in the Old Testament was punished by being stoned to death.[1] When the Church authorities finally approved of the death penalty for heresy, many of them looked for its sanction in the laws of the Old Testament.[2]

Misunderstandings will be avoided if the reader bears in mind the very important distinction between the unbeliever who was subject to the authority and punishment of the Church, and the unbeliever over whom the Church could exercise no authority.[3] Generally speaking, anyone who held beliefs at variance with those of the Church was a heretic, from the Church's point of view. But the heretic liable to punishment by the inquisition, as the agency of the Church, was he who, although a member of the Church, had ceased to believe in the tenets she prescribed. That is to say, only he who was baptized a Catholic and had strayed, or relapsed into his

---

1 Deuteronomy XIII, 6-10; XVII, 1-6.

2 Among them, St Optatus, Bishop of Milevis, in Nubia (4th century), turned to the Old Testament for defending his position in declaring heresy to be punishable by death. He found it in the death sentence meted out to the worshippers of the golden calf (Exodus XXXII, 27-8). Vacandard, p. 1.

3 St. Thomas Aquinas (1225?-1274) wrote· "It is a more serious sin not to perform what one has promised." (Quoted in J Wilhelm's article "Heresy" in the *Catholic Encyclopedia,* VII, 256). This was applied later to new-Christians who had been converted from Judaism, as well as to unconverted Jews Two ways of deviating from Christianity may constitute one a heretic· (1) by the denial of Christianity, as Jews and pagans do, who are technical heretics, or (2) by restricting (or "choosing." which is the original meaning of the Greek word αἱρεσις from which "heresy" derives) one's belief to certain doctrines selected and fashioned, at leisure, and not accepting the full teachings of the Church. (*Ibid.*)

1

former beliefs after having embraced Catholicism, was a heretic, subject to the penalties invoked by the Church. Jews, Moslems and all other non-Catholics, while technically heretics, whose unbaptized souls were destined for the unpleasanter places in the world beyond, were not subject to Church discipline as heretics.[4]

The punishment of death for heresy, which sounds so ominous and brutal on modern ears, was not seriously considered by the early Church Fathers. They taught that the death penalty for heresy as expressed in the Old Testament was too harsh, and that, moreover, the Old Testament laws had been superseded by those of the new dispensation. They argued that St. Paul, who believed that the teachings of the old covenant had been abrogated by the new dispensation through the coming of Jesus, had accordingly changed the death penalty for heresy into the spiritual penalty of excommunication.[5] To the early Fathers excommunication from the Church was sufficient punishment for heresy. They taught that men were to be won to the faith by persuasion and love, not by violence, and that they were to be kept in the fold by the same pacific means. Tertullian (ca. 155-222) wrote: "It is a fundamental human right, a privilege of nature that every man should worship according to his convictions."[6] To St. Origen (ca. 185-254), and to the martyred St. Cyprian (ca. 200-258) also, the harshness of the Mosaic law had been supplanted by the kindliness of the Christian

---

[4] As abettors (fautors or shielders) of heretics, technical heretics might be subject to discipline by the ecclesiastical authorities. The inquisition sometimes demanded that the rabbis, under penalty of death and confiscation of their property, place major excommunication (*herem*) upon their synagogues and not remove it until every member revealed all he knew about the new-Christians subject to the inquisition. When the inquisition in Seville ordered Rabbi Judah Ibn Verga (author of *Shebet Yehuda*, completed by his son in Adrianople, 1554) to place his synagogue under the ban, he fled to avoid compliance with the demand. (Adler, *Auto de Fé and Jew*, p. 60, hereafter: Adler) ; (Lea, *Spain*, I, 168). Pope Alexander V in 1409 thought nothing of having the Jews of Avignon bear a part of the expenses of the Inquisitor of Dauphiné. (Lea, *A History of the Inquisition of the Middle Ages*, I, 532; hereafter: Lea, *Middle Ages*). In 1267 the Jews of Aragon were ordered to bring their copies of the Talmud for examination to the inquisition So the Jews, though technical heretics, were sometimes placed under the jurisdiction of the inquisition.

[5] I Timothy I, 20; Titus III, 10-11; Vacandard, p. 1. I shall quote freely from the pages of the learned Abbé Vacandard. He is a thorough scholar, and cannot be accused of any anti-Catholic bias!

[6] *Liber ad Scapulum* (written as a warning to the Proconsul of Africa, ca. 212), cap. II, Migne, P. L, vol. I, col. 699. Quoted by Vacandard, p. 3. In Apostolic times the doctrine of mutual help was preached: the believer was admonished to assist him who had succumbed to heresy "Bear ye one another's burdens, and so fulfill the law of Christ." (Galatians VI, 2). The misguided believer was not to be treated as an enemy of the faith, but as a deluded person whom it was the duty of good Christians to bring back to his senses, and to the right beliefs. This was the attitude toward heresy characterizing the time before Christianity became the official religion of the Roman Empire Cf. Lea, *Middle Ages*, I, 209.

law.[7] Lactantius (ca. 260-340), among the last of those persecuted for Christianity before it became the state religion, was naturally very sympathetic to the heretic. To him, also, "religion, being a matter of will . . . cannot be forced upon anyone . . . . Nothing is so intrinsically a matter of free-will as religion."[8] The Church doctrine, *Ecclesia abhorret a sanguine* ("The Church abhors bloodshed"), was upheld by leading authorities as sufficient warrant for sparing the life of the heretic.

Many of the early Church Fathers taught that religion is a product of man's free-will, and that only love and never violence can induce men to change their convictions. This is a rather modern attitude toward religion. What occurred, then, which caused the Church to apparently reverse itself and declare heresy a sin heinous enough to be exterminated with utmost rigor, and by death, if need be?

In the first place, during those early centuries, Christianity was itself a heresy. It was therefore apologizing for its own existence when it declared that religion could not be forced, but that it was supremely a matter of the freedom of man's conscience. It was quite natural that a church not yet tolerated should plead for toleration.

Again, up to that time, all discussions on the subject of heresy had been quite academic. No real test had yet come. With the rise of the early heresies—Priscillianism, Manicheism, Donatism—the Christian Church was forced to take a decisive stand. The Church was faced by the realities of heresy and schism, and the principles evolved from academic discussions no longer seemed valid. It was one thing to deliberate about heresy as an academic subject; it was quite another thing, demanding a different technique, to fight off heresies threatening the unity of the Church. The principles laid down for the treatment of these early heresies in the Church largely determined its attitude toward heresy in the succeeding centuries.

The Spaniard Priscillian, together with six of his followers, was sentenced to death by Emperor Maximus in 385. Priscillian was accused of Manicheism and magic, but, according to Abbé

---

7 "For Christians can not slay their enemies, or condemn, as Moses commanded, the contemners of the law to be put to death by burning or stoning." Origen, *Contra Celsum*, lib. VII, cap. xxvi. "But now that circumcision has begun to be of the spirit among God's faithful servants, and the proud and contumacious are slain with the sword of the spirit by being cast out of the Church . . . ." Cyprian, Epistle lxii, *ad Pomponium*, n. 4, Migne, P L., vol. III, col 371.

8 *De Divinis Institutionibus,* lib V, cap xx. (The above three authorities are quoted by Vacandard, pp. 3-5).

Vacandard, he was convicted of the latter crime.[9] His confession was elicited under torture, and scandalous, indeed, were his confessions, as well as those elicited from his accomplices by similar means. A storm of indignation arose protesting the execution of Priscillian and his followers. St. Ambrose, Bishop of Milan, (ca. 340-397) characterized it as a crime. St. Martin of Tours (ca. 316-401) refused to have any communications with bishops in any way implicated in it.[10] One of the Spanish bishops who accused Priscillian and pressed the charges against him was forced by public indignation to leave his diocese.[11] In the light of the widespread indignation it caused among churchmen, to fasten blame upon the Church for Priscillian's death is not altogether justified.[12] He was actually condemned by the secular courts, although with the connivance of some churchmen. The Church might have been relieved of total responsibility in Priscillian's death if it were not that his death set the precedent which the Church followed and condoned by using the principle that the sword of the state should be lifted to protect the interests of the Church. The secular and the religious forces thus joined in an alliance which was destined to continue.[13]

Another heretical sect, the Manicheans, further tested the strength of the Church. The Manicheans, whose center was in North Africa, were accused of unspeakable crimes, and the state determined to put an end to their heresy. Both the Manicheans and the Donatists (another sect in North Africa) were declared by the state to be guilty of treasonable acts, punishable by death. In

---

[9] P. 24 Priscillian was an ascetic and a mystic, holding that marriage and every earthly honor closed the opportunity for continual relationship with God. It is interesting to note that the Council of Toledo (400), fifteen years after his execution, found that the most serious charge which could be brought against Priscillian was a mistake in the translation of one word! The Priscillian heresy survived its founder's death by 200 years, proving again that the blood of martyrs is the seed of a church Some of Priscillian's writings were recently discovered (1885) by G. Schepss (published in the Academy of Vienna *Corpus*, vol XVIII), and have been described as "orthodox and commonplace" E. Ch Bubut's *Priscillian et le Priscillianisme* (Paris, 1909) is the standard work on the subject. Cf. Dom Leclerc, *L'Espagne Chrétienne* (Paris, 1906), ch. III Also· Menendez y Pelayo, *Heterodoxes Españoles*, II, 321 ff ; Adolfo Bonilla y San Martin, *Historia de la Filosofia Española*, I, 194 ff , II, 462 ff.

[10] Lecky, *History of Rise and Influence of the Spirit of Rationalism in Europe*, II, 24-5

[11] Ursatius and Ithacus, the latter deposed, were responsible for Priscillian's plight *Ibid ,* II, 24

[12] Vacandard (p 25) argues that "it is right to attribute .   his death to the action of an individual bishop, but it is altogether unjust to hold the Church responsible"

[13] Heretics, taught St Optatus, were criminals against the state for they disturbed the public peace He quotes the Old Testament for his authority to punish heresy by death (Cf. *supra*, note 2) Leo the Great (Pope from 440-461) assents to this principle in the case of the Priscillians. Cf Vacandard, pp 14, 28

407 heresy was placed upon the same footing as treason, punishable by death, for if treason to an earthly king was requited by death, it was argued, all the more should treason to the Heavenly King be subject at least to the same punishment![14] St. Augustine, opposed to the death penalty for heresy on the grounds that Christian law demanded that men be persuaded and not forced, nevertheless permitted a change in his attitude to allow that force was necessary in bringing sinners and schismatics back to the fold. He felt it was charity and not oppression to constrain men to see good and abjure evil. In some cases, he argued, the death penalty, however much he disapproved of it, should be invoked with all severity against rebellious schismatics.[15]

It must be observed that it was the state and not the Church which took the initiative in declaring the death penalty upon these heretics. Officially, the Church had not declared itself, except insofar as some of its leaders acquiesced in the attitude of the state. Some of them advocated that the power of the state should assist the Church in crushing heresy.[16] Only in 447 can it be said that the Church acquiesced in the state's action of death for heresy when Pope Leo the Great said that he rejoiced in that "the secular authorities, horrified at this sacrilegious folly, executed the author (Priscillian) of these errors, with several of his followers." While he theoretically disapproved of the death penalty for heresy, nevertheless the Pope accepted it "in the name of the public good."[17]

This brings to an end the early period in the struggle against heresy. From the sixth to the eleventh centuries the Church was little troubled with heretics. That is why we pass over a period of five centuries in silence. There were no further important developments in legislation for heretics, for the very good reason that the

---

[14] Innocent III (Pope from 1198-1216) in a letter to Viterbo, dated March 25, 1199, used this argument Cf Vacandard, p 61

[15] *Ibid.,* pp 15-19. Cf also Lea, *Middle Ages,* I, 214

[16] St. Optatus invoked the co-operation of the civil authorities in punishing the crime of heresy by death We have seen that on principle St Augustine (354-430) was opposed to force and to death in punishing heretics, but he, too, yielded to the efficacy of these instruments as acts of charity toward the heretics in breaking down their beliefs Cf. Vacandard, p. 28

[17] *Ibid.,* p. 27. Cf. also Lea, *Middle Ages,* I, 215. Vacandard (p 30, note 1) takes issue with Lea for writing that Pope Leo the Great declared that "if the followers of heresy so damnable were allowed to live, there would be an end of human and divine law;" and further that "the Church was definitely pledged to the suppression of heresy at whatever cost It is impossible not to attribute to ecclesiastical influence the successive edicts by which, from the time of Theodosius the Great, persistence in heresy was punished with death   " Vacandard points out that Lea put into the mouth of the Pope the very words spoken by the Emperors, and that, moreover, there was an overwhelming protest against the death penalty by churchmen Accordingly, he finds that it is difficult to see how Lea can make his assertion of "ecclesiastical influence" in the edicts issued by the state

problem of heresy was not a serious one. We must wait therefore for some threatening heretical movements to arise before we find any evolution of the institution of the inquisition, devoted to the discovery and punishment of heresy. There was then no need for an institution with definite form and procedure to stamp out heresy. Only in the twelfth century the stirring movements which arose brought about the emergence of the inquisition as a distinct ecclesiastical institution. To these movements and to the causes which nourished them we now turn to show, (knowing the background and the principles of the Church) the inevitable growth of the inquisition from medieval times until its beginnings in Spain.

*   *   *   *   *

The beginning of the twelfth century found the world in turmoil. The ideas of the Arabic schools in Spain had already penetrated, with great effectiveness, into the rest of Europe. The Crusades brought Europe into contact with the near-east through the mediation of the Crusaders themselves, who returned to their homes with wider horizons. Heretofore the world had been neatly organized by the Church into very definite compartments. The Church had rigidly controlled all thought in Europe.. But when men began to compare and question and doubt—the inevitable consequences of newer ideas and wider travel—their universe, heretofore so neatly organized, crashed down upon their heads. It precipitated a panic in the Church: the Church's ascendancy had begun to be challenged. The tangible evidence of this revolution was the rise and remarkable growth of sectaries in twelfth-century Europe, threatening the unity of the Church. At the same time, the Church, aware of opposition arising from the dogmas of the sectaries, began to formulate its own more clearly, thus making their violation more obvious to everyone. Dissidents then were more easily to be detected. This provided an early and important step in the development leading to the establishment of the inquisition.

In southern France the authority of the Church was seriously imperilled by the growing strength of the Catharist (or Albigensian) sectaries, whose ascetic life and strict morality quite frequently stood in sharp contrast to much of the dissoluteness of the clergy of the time.[18] The zeal of the sectaries in spreading their dogmas through Europe was a distinct challenge to the supremacy

---

[18] St. Bernard of Clairvaux (1090-1153) paints a distressing picture of the condition of religion in 1147 in the territories of the Count of Toulouse: "The churches are without people, the people without priests, the priests without reverence due them, and Christians without Christ. . . . The voice of a single heretic silences all those apostolic and prophetic voices which have united in calling all the nations into the Church of Christ." (Quoted from Lea, *Middle Ages*, I, 70).

of the Church. It was forced to act, and it acted quickly and resolutely under the leadership of Pope Innocent III.

In 1199 Innocent III addressed a letter to the ecclesiastical and secular officers, as well as to the people, of Viterbo, in Italy. It reads as though the world of that day was in the throes of certain extinction.[19] The advent seemed so close at hand to the Pope that, willingly or unwillingly, he meant to force men to be prepared to meet their Maker. The predilections of men could not stand in the way at such an hour when the end of the world was so imminent. This letter, in effect, was Innocent's call to the faithful. It was also a challenge to the unfaithful sectaries, daily becoming stronger and bolder with the revival of ancient learning and the growth of independent investigation into the mysteries of religion. Revealed religion cannot tolerate such inquisitiveness, for out of it heresy invariably flows. The institution of the inquisition was established at this critical juncture in the history of the Church when every soul had to be saved, no matter at what cost; when the Church was seriously jeopardized in its task of salvation by the rival power of the sectaries.[20]

The modern mind, accustomed to think of religion as a matter of the individual's conscience, may find it difficult to understand this particular conception of religion as a purely objective matter. The Catholic Church in the middle ages took the position that religion was beyond the realm of the free-judgment of the individual. It was a gift of God. It was the duty of the Church to assure its continuity in its pristine form. To keep it and its adherents pure and undefiled was the original purpose of the inquisition. The Church possessed and taught the truth of religion; the inquisition was designed to be its protector.

The inquisition was organized to assure the continuity of the religion of the Church as the pure and authentic revelation. The doctrine of exclusive salvation was responsible for making the inquisition one of the Church's chief agencies in transmitting its authentic revelation unsullied to the coming generations. It fitted admirably into the philosophy of the Church which countenanced nothing outside it. The Church and society were synonymous. The heretic, a rebel against the Church, was also a scourge upon society.

---

19 The essential portions of this letter became part of Canon Law, obligatory for all Christendom. (Read chapter III of Coulton's *The Inquisition*). Catharists were living in Viterbo; therefore the Pope's message addressed to Viterbo takes on added significance. Cf. Vacandard, p. 59.

20 Innocent can not be said to have given definite form to the inquisition; that was done by Pope Gregory IX. But it was he who gave expression to the doctrines at a time which made the inquisition's establishment seem to be a matter of life or death for the Church

As a scourge, he had to be isolated to preserve society from infection and contamination. The function of the inquisition thus follows logically from the philosophy of the Church in the twelfth-century world.[21]

Torn by growing heresies, the establishment of the inquisition seemed to be the only certain way of preserving the Church. It was thus created to meet a very definite emergency, but in its philosophy it was an integral part of the Church and,theoretically existed since the Church's beginnings. Its purpose was to save souls. In the crisis the world was experiencing in the twelfth century, special point was added to its purpose, for it was to save the souls of men at a time when soul-saving was not only the noblest of human endeavors, but was also the most immediately necessary task in redeeming an entire erring and backsliding mankind.[22]

The erring mankind of Pope Innocent's day, against whom he principally directed his zeal, were the Catharist heretics. This is not the place to enter into a detailed description of the movement.[23] It is important for us only because it provided the first compelling reason for the organization of the inquisition. Doubtless coming originally from Bulgaria, where they had been severely persecuted in the tenth century, the Catharists pushed westward over the established trade routes of Europe and finally settled in southern France. With Toulouse as the center of their movement (it is not correct therefore to call them 'Albigenses, after the city of Albi, for they had their origins elsewhere), they spread to northern Spain and Italy.[24] Their doctrines disavowing infant baptism, the eucharist

---

[21] The French Catholic, Bishop Douais, (*L'Inquisition, Ses Origines, Sa Procédure,* Paris, 1906) contends that the Church, in its establishment of the inquisition to exterminate heresy, was fighting the battle of humanity against the sectaries, for among them the Catharists forbade marriage and propagation of the race, and made a high moral duty of suicide

[22] A single Christian society, the *"Republica Cristiana,"* the Church taught, exists, just as there exists only a single Catholic Church; the essential foundations of both are the truths of the Christian religion—as revealed and taught by the Catholic Church. Turberville, *The Spanish Inquisition,* pp. 2, 3 Moreover, the heresy of the time was new to the Church Doctrinal heresy had already been handled, but this heresy "was something more rigorously personal, religious, and more dogmatic" . . . and . . . "had a physiognomy decidedly more social." All the greater reason, therefore, for the Church to be alarmed! Evans, "Social Aspects of Medieval Heresy," in *Persecution and Liberty,* p. 93.

[23] On the Catharist, or Albigensian, heresy see· Paul Alphandéry, *Les idées morales chez les hétérodoxes latins au début de XIIIe siècle,* (Paris, 1903) ; J. J. I. Döllinger, *Beiträge zur Secktengeschichte des Mittelalters,* (Munich, 1890) ; Jean Charles Léonard Simonde de Sismondi, *History of the Crusades against the Albigenses in the Thirteenth Century,* (tr. from the French, Boston, 1833) ; Louis I. Newman, *Jewish Influence on Christian Reform Movements,* (New York, 1925), p. 133ff ; H J. Warner, *The Albigensian Heresy,* (London, 1922).

[24] It is not without interest, since the Inquisition of Spain, which we are to discuss later on, concerned itself with the heresy of Judaism, to point out here that many

and mass, denying the authority of the Pope as continuing the tradition of St. Peter (they believed St. Peter never came to Rome), and the temporal powers of the Papacy and the ostentation of the Church (in contrast to the meekness and poverty of Christ), placed them into direct conflict with the Church. Moreover, their rejection of the right of the state to punish, and their refusal to take an oath[25] (upon which the entire feudal system was based) placed them into direct conflict with the state also. The two-edged sword of Church and state bore down upon them with unremitting severity. The campaign waged against them has come to be known as the Albigensian Crusade, a holy war in which Church and state joined forces to exterminate them.[26] Thus, after comparative freedom for centuries, the Church was again confronted with a strong heretical movement. This time very definite steps were taken which assured Christendom that no longer would heresies be permitted to grow; they would be checked in the bud.

Up to the advent of Innocent III, the heretical Catharists were treated with compassion. That was due, in large measure, to an unwillingness among the princes to persecute them. The bishops, whose task it was to defend the Church against heretics, found themselves deluged by the complexity of their work, which rendered ineffectual their function of bringing heretics to judgment. Their honest difficulties soon brought on indifference to their task as heretic-hunters. The Papacy realized the position of the bishops,[27] and inaugurated, by joint decree with Emperor Frederick Barbarossa in 1184, the Episcopal Inquisition. By this decree, the bishops were instructed to visit, at least once a year, every part of their dioceses where there was any suspicion of heresy. That the bishops did not take this order very seriously may be seen from the fact that when the Lateran Council of 1215 re-enacted it, the penalty for their neglect of duty was the loss of their dioceses. But, as we shall soon see,

---

of the heretical doctrines of Catharism were Jewish in origin Cf Abrahams, *Jewish Life in the Middle Ages*; H. Graetz, *History of the Jews*, (6 vols. Philadelphia, 1891-95, English Translation, hereafter Graetz), vol III, ch IV; also the exhaustive study of Newman, *op. cit.*, p. 133ff.

25 Petrus Cantor, one of the most learned men of the 12th century, also deplored the requirement of the oath, beyond the simple "yea" or "nay" "Why, when a man does keep this counsel of perfection, do we at once denounce him as a Catharist?" *Verbum Abbreviatum*, cc. 80, 127 (Migne, P. L, vol 205, col. 241, 322), quoted from Coulton, *The Inquisition*, p 46

26 For a detailed description of the Albigensian Crusade, in addition to those already cited (*supra*, note 23), see. C Schmidt, *Histoire de la secte des Cathares ou Albigeois*, (Paris, 1849), the standard reference work on the subject. Also, the articles in *Encyclopedia Britannica*, 14th Ed, "Albigenses," (vol I, 528), "Cathars," (vol. V, 31-2, "Waldenses," (vol XXIII, 288-90) ; in Hasting's *Encyclopedia of Religion and Ethics*, article on "Albigenses," (vol. I, 277-87).

27 See part of the letter of Pope Gregory on this subject, quoted, note 44, *below*.

the Episcopal Inquisition was a weak device, giving way to the inquisition of the mendicant orders.[28] The Episcopal Inquisition could not cope with the rise and spread of heresy. Its failure may have been due to the half-hearted measures invoked against the heretics. Pope Innocent III, in his first measures, threatened them with exile and confiscation.[29]

Seeing that his mild measures were ineffectual,[30] Innocent determined, no matter what the cost, to decisively stamp out heresy. Out of his determination, joined with the growth of secular legislation on the subject of the death penalty for heresy, there arose a solution which alone seemed to be a final answer to heretics: to punish them with death.

But it was the secular rulers who first adopted the death penalty for the punishment of heresy, as part of their countries' laws. King Peter II of Aragon was the earliest monarch who, in 1197, adopted the death penalty for heresy.[31] He was followed by Frederick II who included the death penalty in his constitution of 1224 (the penalty of death or loss of the tongue by the discretion of the judge), but it was not until 1231, in his Sicilian Constitutions, that he made the death penalty absolute.[32] It should be noted in passing that Frederick's laws for the death penalty found their justification in the parity of the crime of heresy to treason, (similarly drawn by Innocent III) which made offense to the Divine Majesty a far greater crime than offense to the majesty of the Emperor.[33]

Frederick was influenced in his codes partly by the decrees of the Lateran Councils,[34] and partly by Pope Gregory IX, whom he

---

[28] Vacandard, pp. 119-21

[29] *Lea, Middle Ages,* I, 220   These early measures of Innocent, confirmed by the Lateran Council of 1215, condemned heretics to exile and confiscation of property, and also to perpetual infamy and annulment of all their civil rights, acts, and powers. Vacandard, pp. 58-60, 107. These elements of inquisitorial penalty were also used later to advantage against heretics. But still the death penalty for heretics was not officially invoked, although in Germany many heretics were burned in the 12th century   Lea, *Middle Ages,* I, 220ff (Cf Julien Havet, *L'hérésie et le bras séculier au moyen age jusqu' au XIIIe siècle,* in *Oeuvres,* vol. III, Paris, 1896, pp. 143-4).

[30] The Church's methods for suppressing heresy until the end of the 11th century were kindlier than the practices of the time, when the unruled passions of the mob largely determined that the penalty was invariably death. To this extent Abbé Vacandard and the Catholic scholars of the inquisition are correct Cf. Vacandard, p 63, also A Luchaire, *Innocent III, Rome et l'Italie,* (Paris, 1904), pp. 86-91.

[31] He increased the severity of his father's legislation on this subject which Lea (*Middle Ages,* I, 220) characterizes as "the first secular legislation, with the exception of the Assizes of Clarendon, in the modern world against heresy" More than a half century later, Alfonso the Wise, in his famous code *Siete Partidas,* decreed the stake for Christians who embraced Judaism or Mohammedanism *Ibid.,* p 221

[32] *Ibid*

[33] Vacandard, pp. 107-8

[34] Lea, *Middle Ages,* I, 321.

in turn also influenced. The Pope admonished Frederick to punish heresy, and Frederick obeyed.[35] It was never a one-sided influence, so that the Church cannot altogether shake itself of its responsibility in the death penalty for heresy.[36] Abbé Vacandard frankly admits that the Church cannot be freed of its responsibility in sentencing heretics to death, even though it presumed to free itself from that stigma by "dismissing the heretic to the secular arm," praying that it shall not shed blood. This is obviously a legal fiction, for the Church fully recognized that discharge to the secular arm constituted an order for the execution, an order which the secular arm could not fail to obey. Nor did the secular authorities pay any attention to the formula "mitigating the sentence" by not shedding blood. They knew it was a subterfuge, perhaps inserted to quiet the consciences of the inquisitors who were prohibited by Church law from having anything to do with death.[37]

The penalties for heresy were determined and made almost universal by the energy of Pope Gregory IX, to whom must go the glory and the responsibility for establishing the inquisition as an active arm of the Church.[38] The Episcopal Inquisition failed chiefly because there was no trained corps of men available for the specific functions required to be performed by the inquisition. There arose a need, Lea writes, for "trained experts . . . whose sole business it should be to unearth offenders and extort a confession of their guilt."[39] The mendicant orders (the Franciscans and Dominicans),

---

35 Vacandard, p 113 I purposely quote this Catholic historian for these facts, for in him no anti-Catholic bias can even be presumed

36 Indeed, it was the Church and her dignitaries who were in back of these secular laws, often demanding that the secular ruler swear to exterminate heresy from his territories This flows out of the philosophy of the Church, which held that the interests of the state are subordinate to the Church in the great task of keeping the faith pure Lea, *Middle Ages*, I, 225.

37 Vacandard, pp. 177-81. Attempts were constantly made by Church apologists to justify the apparent contradiction between Church theory and practice Some of these advanced the arguments that (1) "heretics cause their own death by committing crimes which merit death;" (2) the fiction of "releasing the heretic to the secular arm" (*relajado al brazo secular*, the term used in the Spanish Inquisition), was not a fiction but a real release of the responsibility for death from the Church The latter reasoning has held the dominant place in Church apologetics. Some inquisitors, however, assumed the responsibility themselves for the death of the heretic: the Dominican Jacob Sprenger (17th century) speaks of those heretics whom "we *cause* to be burned." And again, there was Inquisitor Cumanus who *caused* 401 heretics to be burned. (Italics mine). Vacandard, p 180, note 1. Cf Lea, *Middle Ages*, I, 223-6. Both the conclusions of Lea and Vacandard are similar in this important matter.

38 Vacandard, p. 115.

39 Abbé Vacandard (p. 121) quotes Lea · "Bishop and legate were alike unequal to the task of discovering those who carefully shrouded themselves under the cloak of the most orthodox observance; and when by chance a nest of heretics was brought to light, the learning and skill of the average Ordinary failed to elicit a confession from those who professed the most entire accord with the teachings of

because of their poverty-vows, special preparation in canon law and theology, and also because of their training as preachers, seemed a providential gift to the Pope in launching an efficient organization. They fulfilled the Pope's hopes in abundant measure. They were responsible, once the general framework was laid, for the inquisition's success. As preachers, they brought the masses over to their side by causing them to hold the heretic in horror.[40] As legalists, learned in ecclesiastical science, they could determine what was orthodox and what heterodox.[41] It was they who interpreted the basic laws and enlarged the framework for the institution which the inquisition became. Because they took the poverty vows, there promised to be no favoritism or jealousy—arising out of the greed for possession—which often marred the effectiveness of the bishop's work as inquisitor.[42]

By 1231 the Monastic Inquisition was already functioning. Pope Gregory issued commissions to the Dominicans, Conrad of Marburg (1231) and Alberic of Lombardy (1232), for the exercise of their office.[43] By 1233 Gregory found it necessary to assure the bishops of southern France that their burdens would be considerably lightened by the assistance the mendicants would give them in warring against the heretics.[44] By this time, the

---

Rome. In the absence of overt acts, it was difficult to reach the secret thoughts of the sectary Trained experts were needed whose sole business it should be to unearth the offenders, and extort a confession of their guilt " Lea, *Middle Ages*, I, 315ff.

[40] The heretic—once he was branded as such by the Church—was a very unpopular person in medieval times, since heresy was considered a heinous offense "The heretic," writes Prof Turberville, "is just as much as the criminal, a rebel and a pariah   ." There are "instances in the late eleventh century and early twelfth century of heretics being lynched by an infuriated mob who regarded the clergy as too lenient." Heresy was "an evil which was looked upon as dangerous to sound morals as well as to sound doctrine—for a corrupt tree brings forth corrupt fruit, and a man who believes falsely will act wrongly " (*The Spanish Inquisition*, p 3) The preaching friars did not have such a difficult job as may be imagined in causing the public to spurn the heretic!

[41] It was a difficult matter to declare what was heresy and what was not. The ordinary layman or priest, ignorant of the subtleties of theology, would have found it very hard, if not impossible, to determine what was heresy. Turberville, *op. cit.*, p 5. "Hear me, my lords," beseeched an ordinary man of the middle ages, attempting to clear himself of the charge of heresy, "I am no heretic, for I have a wife, and cohabit with her, and have children, and eat flesh and lie, swear and am a faithful Christian " Guillemi Pelisso's *Chronicon* (ed by Molinier, p 17), quoted from Coulton, *The Inquisition*, p 46

[42] Lea, *Middle Ages*, I, 318-9, quoted by Vacandard, pp 121-2

[43] In the same year Pope Gregory issued the Bull *Declinante*, ordering the Bishop of Tarragona to discover and punish all heretics in his diocese. The Bull was issued doubtless at the suggestion of the powerful Dominican, perhaps the leading spirit of his Order, St. Raymond de Peñaforte Turberville, *op. cit*, pp 19, 20 This Bull constituted one of the earliest instructions for the inquisition in Spain Cf. Prescott, *History of the Reign of Ferdinand and Isabella*, I, 261.

[44] This was in the letter written April, 1233. Since the bishops were "engrossed in the whirlwind of cares and scarce able to breathe in the pressure of overwhelming anx-

procedure for the inquisition was clearly determined, and dispatched as instructions to the newly appointed inquisitors. Thus there was founded in 1233, the Monastic or, as it is also known, the Medieval Inquisition, the forerunner of the Spanish Inquisition.[45]

We may now consider how the inquisition functioned, and what authority it possessed, which made of it such a powerful ally in maintaining the unity and supremacy of the Church in medieval Europe.

* * * * *

After the inquisitor had decided what community was to be the scene of his activities, he requested the bishop, or highest resident Church official, to order the people to assemble at a specified time and place. An indulgence was the reward for attendance at this assembly. There the inquisitor preached to the people, urging them, as their Christian duty, to hate heresy and the heretic as a menace to the faithful. He admonished them to report to him any information about heretics. Bringing information of this kind to the inquisition was a merit in itself.[46] This rather simple admonition, so necessary for the inquisitor to begin his work, developed later into the Edict of Faith, which was published when the inquisition began its work.[47]

---

ieties, we think it well to divide your burdens that they may be more easily borne. We have therefore determined to send preaching friars against the heretics of France and the adjoining provinces, and we beg, warn, and exhort you, ordering you as you reverence the Holy See, to receive them kindly and treat them well, giving them in this, as in all else, favor, counsel, and aid, that they may fulfill their office." (Lea, *Middle Ages*, I, 329)   The friars were not intended to supplant the bishops in the hunt for heretics   At first they had equal authority with the bishops, but soon the friar-specialists had taken the most important functions away from the bishops   They, and not the bishops, were the presiding officers at the heresy trials   And the bishops soon became, not without their energetic protests, subsidiaries to the friars, who consulted them only on important matters   (Turberville, *op. cit*, pp. 8-9)   Technically, the bishops were co-judges with the friars; only both together could pass upon the sentences meted out   This restriction upon the freedom of the friars soon also became a dead-letter in inquisitorial procedure, for the bishops were perfunctory in the exercise of their duties, leaving all the responsibility upon the friars, who were quick to take advantage of the situation. (Lea, *Middle Ages*, I, 387)

45 On April 20, 1233, the Pope issued two Bulls making the Dominicans responsible for the prosecution of heresy *Ibid.*, p. 328, Vacandard, pp 123-4.

46 Heresy was construed also as failure to bring to the inquisition any tales and gossip concerning heretics, as well as the failure to spy upon heretics and then report to the inquisition. Mr Coulton writes (*The Inquisition*, p. 70) "Gradually there grew up a veritable army of spies of the inquisition, among whom were the 'Familiars' . . . who were recruited from among the lower classes of the population   The people detested the 'Familiars' and were in constant fear of them   The public disfavor they merited was not only a result of their spying, but also because in their actions they were answerable only to the inquisition   They were not subject to the secular courts   It was so easy to impugn heresy upon anybody for 'impeding the officers of the inquisition' that the familiars lorded it over the people." Cf Lea, *Middle Ages*, I, 381

47 The Edict of Faith, published at the inquisitor's discretion, when the public's inter-

The Edict of Faith made it a positive crime for any Christian
to withhold information or knowledge of any suspicious character
whose crimes might conceivably come under the inquisition's jurisdiction. Under pain of anathema—removable only by the Pope or
the inquisition—Christians were ordered to denounce all heretics
to the inquisition.[48]

The community was thus welded into a partnership with the
inquisition in the prosecution of its holy office. But the inquisition
simultaneously summoned every heretic to appear before it within
a specified time—*tempus gratie* (term of grace)[49] it was called
—offering merciful treatment as an inducement for early confession. For surrendering and abjuring their sins under terms of the
Edicts of Grace, which these pronouncements came to be named,
the heretics were rewarded sometime by complete freedom, or more
often by the imposition only of the penance of pious observances, or
by making a pilgrimage to a holy shrine. This was indeed a mitigation from the severe penalties which the inquisition might impose:

---

est appeared to flag, was the instrument through which the inquisition received
information about heretics in the locality in which it operated. At first a simple
matter, later the Edict developed into a document of not inconsiderable size and
importance. That the Christians, upon whom the inquisition called to do their
duty in preserving the faith, had a big job, can be seen from an abstract of an
Edict published in 1696. The following is from Lea, *Spain*, II, 93-4: If anyone
"has known or heard say that anyone, living or dead, present or absent, has done
or uttered or believed any act, word or opinion, heretical, suspect, erroneous, rash,
ill-sounding, scandalous or heretically blasphemous, it must be revealed to the
tribunal within six days. Then follows an enumeration of all Jewish rites and
customs, then similar lists concerning Mohametanism, Protestantism and Illum-
inism; then under the heading of 'Diversas Heregias,' follow blasphemy, with
specimens of heretical oaths, keeping or invoking familiar demons; witchcraft;
pacts tacit or expressed with the devil; mixing for this purpose sacred and pro-
fane objects and attributing to the creature that which belongs to the Creator;
marrying in Orders, solicitation of women in confession; bigamy; saying that
there is no sin in simple fornication, or usury, or perjury, or that concubinage is
better than marriage; insulting or maltreating crucifixes or images of saints; dis-
believing or doubting any article of faith; remaining a year under excommunication or despising the censures of the Church; having recourse to astrology, which
is described at length and pronounced fictitious; being guilty of sorcery or divina-
tion, the practices of which are described with instructive profusion; possessing
books condemned in the Index, including Lutheran and Mohametan works and the
Bible in the vernacular; neglecting to perform the duty of denouncing what has
been seen or heard, or persuading others to omit it; giving false witness in the
Inquisition; concealing or befriending heretics, impeding the Inquisition; re-
moving *sanbenitos* placed in the Inquisition; throwing off *sanbenitos* or non-per-
formance of penance by reconciled penitents, or their saying that they confessed
in the Inquisition through fear; saying that those relapsed by the Inquisition were
innocent martyrs; non-observance of disabilities by reconciled penitents, their
children or grandchildren; possession by scriveners or notaries of paper concerning the above-enumerated crimes. Confessors, moreover, were ordered under the
same penalties, to withhold absolution from penitents who had not denounced all of-
fences coming to their knowledge."

[48] Lea, *Spain*, II, 91; Turberville, *The Span Inq.*, p. 84.
[49] Usually not to exceed thirty days (Vacandard, p. 124), although sometimes longer
(Lea, *Spain*, II, 457). It was also called the Time of Mercy.

imprisonment, exile, confiscation of property, or death.[50] The numbers who came to confess their heresies prove the efficacy of the Edicts of Grace. It was a mutually favorable arrangement, for while it mitigated the punishment which the heretic deserved, it also brought the inquisition information about other heretics, for the inquisition held that full and complete confession, including information about other heretics, alone determined the sincerity of the heretic's confession of his own guilt.[51]

Whose testimony could be regarded as valid? This was a question constantly confronting the inquisition, and one which, by virtue of the character of evidence coming from so many different sources, was extremely important. In the early stages the number of witnesses necessary to make an accusation valid had not as yet been determined, but the witnesses themselves were required to be persons of acknowledged good character. The standards fell, however, and the time came when anyone (including the heretic, excommunicate, homicide, thief, sorcerer, and perjurer) could bring accusation against a heretic.[52] The testimony of a heretic was considered valid for the prosecution, but not for the defense. This illustrates the general decline in privileges which the defendant-heretic suffered.

Witnesses for the defense were very rare, for they constituted under the inquisition "accomplices or abettors" of heresy and, as such, liable to punishment as heretics themselves.[53] This denial of rights to the defense, from the point of view of modern legal procedure, was not considered a denial in trials of heretics, for the reason that the heresy-trial was *not* really a trial, but *an attempt to force the accused to confess a crime which he was certain to have committed.* This principle was the basis of all inquisitorial procedure.

The defense witness, we have seen, was liable for prosecution as an abettor of heresy. In like manner, the counsel for defense

---

50 Lea, *Middle Ages,* I, 371. Sometimes a fine was also imposed. In the Spanish Inquisition the fine took the form of "alms" used in prosecuting the "holy war" with the Moors. (Lea, *Spain,* II, 457). This kind of fine, while more general in the Spanish Inquisition, was by no means unheard of in the Medieval Inquisition Cf Lea, *Middle Ages,* I, 471. In Toledo (Spain) those reconciled under the Edict of Grace (in 1486) were ordered to surrender one-fifth of their property.

51 Indeed, the refusal of the repentant heretic to give information about his accomplices in heresy was proof that he was impenitent; and the impenitent heretic (i. e, contumacious heretic) was technically to be handed over to the secular arm Lea, *Middle Ages,* I, 409.

52 The Church went contrary to the secular law of Frederick II, which declared that heretics could not testify in courts. No less an authority than Gratian (born end of the 11th century) allowed the testimony of both the heretic and the infamous to be accepted in heresy trials. Vacandard, p. 126.

53 *Ibid.,* p. 127; cf Lea, *Middle Ages,* I, 321.

was liable to similar charges. Pope Innocent III forbade lawyers to give the heretic any help or advice.[54] Here, again, the principle enunciated above—namely, the object of inquisitorial procedure was to get the accused to confess to charges of heresy—was advanced as a reason for the patent lack of genuine assistance extended to the accused.

Neither could the accused expect his case to be judged with complete impartiality, for the office of the inquisitor cannot be compared with that of the judge—the impartial and imperturbable legalist who listens to the case and renders his judgment on the merits of the question involved. The inquisitor was rather a "father-confessor," awaiting the confession of the heretic—again on the principle that the heretic was guilty.[55] With rare exceptions, there was strict adherence to the principle throughout the Medieval Inquisition that the accused was to be permitted no counsel.[56] In the Spanish Inquisition, however, the accused was allowed the assistance of counsel.[57] At least it was an attempt toward granting a fair trial. But here, too, it proved to be an ineffectual aid to the accused, because the defense counsel was a member of the inquisition's staff, whose real purpose it was to urge his client to make full confession.[58] Again, the purpose of the inquisitorial process becomes evident as an attempt to bring the accused to make a confession, since the entire procedure assumed the guilt of the accused. The defense, by the very nature of the underlying philosophy of the inquisition, was at best a hopeless task, and at worst a perfunctory routine or a betrayal of the accused to the inquisition. The purpose of the defense is normally to undermine and ultimately prove the falsity of the accusations preferred. But this the

---

[54] Vacandard, p. 127.

[55] Lea, *Middle Ages*, I, 447 Yet the theory of the inquisitor's function held that he could see both sides of the case with equal justice and impartiality!

[56] Vacandard (p. 127, note 2) indicates that Inquisitor Eymeric, a most severe inquisitor, granted counsel to one of the accused who came under him.

[57] The Spanish Courts of Appeals (the *Audiencias*) always had paid-advocates for the poor, and doubtless the appointment of attorneys for the defense arose from this practice Hume, *Spain, Its Greatness and Decay*, p 23

[58] Turberville, *The Span Inq.*, pp 88-9 In the many inquisition processes from the Majorcan tribunal carefully examined by the writer, the defense-attorney was an aid to the accused only in the preparation of his confession. He thereupon urged his client to throw himself upon the mercy of the inquisition When the accused refused to confess, the defense counsel invariably declared he could no longer assist him who was an intractable heretic! It cannot be fairly claimed that the heretic had an opportunity for an equitable defense. That, by the very nature of the inquisitorial trial—which did not pretend to be a trial in the modern sense—was impossible Cf. Lea, *Spain*, I, 482. In the early years of the Spanish Inquisition, the accused had considerable freedom in the choice of his counsel (*Ibid.*, III, 43) Later on, he was allowed a choice only from two or three presented by the inquisition, who were members of its staff, and paid out of its funds. Cf Turberville, *The Span Inq.*, p. 89

defense counsel in inquisitorial trials could not even presume to accomplish. Therefore his efforts were quite useless, even in those cases where he appeared.[59]

Not only had the accused no real opportunity for defense, but the prosecution in the Spanish Inquisition was strengthened by the services of a trained lawyer, called the *fiscal* or prosecuting officer. He was a paid officer of the inquisition who acted upon instructions from the inquisitor. He made the initial request for the trial (in the *clamosa*). He drew up the case for the inquisition, and, in line with the true function of the prosecuting attorney, relentlessly pursued his work through the "presentation of the evidence," the summation of his arguments and the recital of the scandalous and awesome acts of the culprit in the terrifying "accusation," until he finally achieved his victory over the accused, and caused him to be convicted. The tremendous advantage of the inquisition over the accused, who for all practical purposes was denied effective legal counsel, now becomes even more apparent with the development in the Spanish Inquisition of the institution of the *fiscal*, whose avowed purpose it was to assure the conviction of the culprit.[60]

To make matters even worse for the accused, he was not permitted to know the names of his accusers. He was kept in the dark concerning the sources of the charges preferred against him. He was, however, asked to name his mortal enemies, and only if his accusers happened to be among them, was their testimony declared invalid.[61] He was continually admonished to search his mem-

---

59 All interviews between the accused and his counsel were held in the presence of the inquisitor and the tribunal's secretary, thus effectively preventing any mutual interchange of confidences, which feature our modern system. Yet, to be fair, the inquisition's system must be treated on the basis of its own underlying assumptions—as an opportunity for confession, and not as a court of trial, since the accused was presumed to be guilty of heresy from the outset. The procedure demanded that the accused be brought into the proper frame of mind to make his confession. Lea, *Spain*, III, 44, 56-7; Turberville, *The Span. Inq.*, p. 89.

60 Lea, *Spain*, II, 241ff., 479ff., III, 41.

61 Coulton, *The Inquisition*, p 67; Turberville, *The Span. Inq*, pp. 88, 90; Vacandard, p 128. It was a 'shot in the dark' for the accused to attempt the identification of his denouncers with his mortal enemies If the denouncers were named, the accused might have had a chance to prove that they were prejudiced, or advance the argument that they had used this opportunity to square a grudge they had against him, as was indeed the case so often. Moreover, this system precluded any action of perjury against witnesses. An excellent reason for withholding the names of the denouncers was the vengeance which could be exacted from them by the accused or his friends. Boniface VIII (Pope from 1294-1303), who incorporated this practice into Canon Law, expressly stated that the names of the denouncers may be produced when there was no danger in doing so. (Vacandard, p. 128, note 1). But apparently the danger was ever-present for the conduct of the inquisitorial trial precluded any attempt to reveal them at any time. Cf. Lea, *Middle Ages*, I, 438. In the trial of John Huss (1414), some fifteen witnesses declaring against the accused were brought before him. This was a rare practice. (Lea, *Middle Ages*, I, 439; II, 477).

ory for misdeeds and confess them because the inquisition, he was reminded, arrested no one until it was convinced of his guilt. Only when the indictment (*capitula*) was read, did he know precisely upon what charges he was being held.[62]

Through denunciations of the Christian community—who were made to feel it was their duty under the Edicts of Faith—and through the delations of the heretics appearing for special consideration under the Edicts of Grace, the inquisition was usually assured of sufficient information, and its real business of bringing heretics to confession then seriously got under way.

The first step was the arrest of the heretic. The inquisition operated with the utmost secrecy and speed. Otherwise, the suspect might have an opportunity to avoid arrest by flight.[63] Without the slightest warning, the officers of the inquisition seized the heretic,[64] and isolated him from his family, who were often kept in complete ignorance of his fate until the final disposition of his case, which consumed days or years. The prisoner was cast into the inquisition's jail immediately after he was taken from his home. There can be little doubt that the prisons were far from model ones. They were often makeshift affairs, constructed for the time-being until the inquisition could build its own. But these prisons were neither better nor worse than those generally in use during the middle ages. They were often dark, badly ventilated if at all, and, as likely as not, infested by vermin.[65] The accused, once inside

---

[62] Every case this writer examined clearly points this out: the accused was asked whether he knew the nature of the charges against him, for which he was arrested. Invariably there would be a negative reply. He was thereupon ordered to "search his memory" for his sins. Cf. Lea, *Spain*, III, 39.

[63] Flight was adjudged contumacy. The heretic *must* be guilty, it was argued; he was afraid to face the consequences of his sins, therefore he fled. This was the reasoning of the inquisition. Flight was tantamount, therefore, to a confession of guilt. The fugitive was tried, nevertheless, and if found guilty—invariably he was—his effigy was burned in the same way as his body would be burned if he were apprehended (Cf. Lea, *Middle Ages*, I, 403). If he returned spontaneously, he could demand a retrial. Despite inquisitorial vigilance, the fact that many effigies of "ausentes fugitivos" were burned, especially in the early years of the Spanish Inquisition, indicates that the news of impending arrest did somehow leak out in time for the suspects to escape. (Lea, *Spain* I, 183). Or it might have been that the heretics expected imminent arrest, and fled in time to avoid it!

[64] Turberville, *The Span. Inq.*, p. 85. Arrest was invariably followed by imprisonment, although admission to bail, as forfeiture against non-appearance, was practiced only as a great exception during the Medieval Inquisition, and hardly at all in the Spanish Inquisition. Lea, *Middle Ages*, I, 373; Lea, *Spain*, II, 507.

[65] In reading accounts of the incarceration of the heretics during the middle ages in foul holes serving as prison-cells, the modern mind is justly revolted. The secular prisons, however, were in most cases no whit better than the inquisition's prisons; the latter often copied the former. (Cf. Turberville, *The Span. Inq*, p 86) The secular prisons were sometimes used for incarcerating heretics. (Lea, *Middle Ages*, I, 373, 488). In Spain, there are many evidences that the inquisition's prisons were more humane than those of the other jurisdictions At least Ferdinand and Isabella, followed by Charles V, ordered the judges to in-

the prison, was held incommunicado. He was cut off from the outside world. He could not communicate with his family or his friends concerning his case, and they were equally powerless in getting any information to him.[66]

"Following the Roman law," writes Abbé Vacandard, "the inquisition at first recognized three forms of action in criminal cases —*accusatio, denuntiatio* and *inquisitio.* In the *accusatio,* the accuser formally inscribed himself as able to prove his accusation; if he failed to do so, he had to undergo the penalty which the prisoner would have incurred. The *denuntiatio* did not in any way bind the accuser . . . he merely handed in his testimony, and then ceased prosecuting the case; the judge at once· proceeded to take action against the accused. In the *inquisitio* there was no one either to accuse or denounce the criminal; the judge cited the suspected criminal before him and proceeded to try him. This was the most common method of procedure; from it the inquisition received its name."[67]

The *inquisitio,* the form of action which the inquisition finally adopted, placed the accused in a most unfavorable position, while it gave the inquisition untrammeled freedom in the conduct of the trial.[68] As we have already seen, the accused was helpless before his accusers, who, in turn, were practically immune from perjury proceedings. The accused was denied effective counsel. The inquisitor acted as judge, accuser and defender, all in one. The chances for the accused, at the very beginning, seemed utterly hopeless.

spect the prisons weekly. (Lea, *Spain,* II, 509-10). In the beginning, the bishops were expected to build the prisons (Lea, *Middle Ages,* I, 334), but soon special inquisition buildings, housing the inquisition and its prisoners, were built from the fines and confiscations resulting out of the heresy trials (*Ibid.,* 373). Still, in many cases, the inquisition made use of buildings originally constructed for other purposes (such as the Aljaferia in Saragossa, the Castle of Triana in Seville, the Alcázar in Cordova, etc.), and the dungeons with which some of these were already provided were utilized by the inquisition for its prisoners (Lea, *Spain,* II, 510). The Cardinals investigating the inquisition's prisons in Carcassonne revealed deplorable conditions, and took steps to remedy them. The system itself cannot be condemned so much as the men who were given power, and who abused it, but even they were creatures of their environment. Cf. Lea, *Middle Ages* II, 93ff.

66 A modern parallel is that of Alfred Dreyfus who was kept in a state of practical incommunicado during certain stages of his imprisonment. Dreyfus was accused of high treason in 1894. He was not allowed to mention his case or any aspect of his trial See his *Five Years of My Life,* (New York, 1901), p 93. The secular prisons kept prisoners incommunicado when there was a very special reason for such rigor. In the inquisition's prisons, the heretic (was it because his crime was similar to treason?) was always kept incommunicado (Lea, *Spain,* II, 513). But there were many instances when strict discipline was relaxed, and prisoners were somehow able to communicate with their families and friends on the outside (Cf. *below* p. 68, chapter III, note 39).

67 P. 166 Innocent III adopted the *inquisitio* as the recognized method of procedure in inquisitorial cases.

68 *Ibid.,* p. 167.

Moreover, the secrecy of all proceedings effectively closed the door to any hope for him.[69] When he was first cited to appear before the inquisitor, he took an oath to keep inviolately secret everything he saw and heard during the course of his trial. The officers of the inquisition were also sworn to secrecy. Likewise were those persons[70] invited by the inquisitor to hear the evidence, as well as the experts who determined the fate of the accused. Every person connected with the trial, from the jailer to the inquisitor, vowed complete secrecy regarding everything seen and heard.[71]

After swearing to complete secrecy, the accused was asked questions to determine his knowledge of Catholic doctrine.[72] His own background (domiciles, employments, etc.), and the genealogical details of his family were then carefully searched for traces of heresy. Especially was the latter feature important in trials of heretics whose antecedents were Jewish or Mohammedan.[73] From the very first, the accused was enjoined to confess his sins. He was prejudged; his arrest presumed his guilt. From the moment he entered prison, he was importuned to confess his heresies and appeal for pardon. Since his heart might prompt him to make confession at any moment, he was permitted audience with the inquisitor whenever he requested it.[74] A very definite system of interrogating the accused was soon developed and became part of the manual used by the inquisitor, whose purpose it was to show the accused the futility of hiding his guilt.[75] At the most opportune time, in the

---

[69] The secrecy of all the inquisition's actions was one of the chief causes for complaint against it Cf. Lea, *Middle Ages,* I, 406.

[70] "Personas honestas" *Ibid ,* II, 249)

[71] Only very rarely the inquisition set aside the oath of secrecy in its proceedings *Ibid.,* III, 480

[72] He would be asked to recite the Lord's Prayer, the Ave Maria, the Catechism, etc. Cf Turberville, *The Span. Inq ,* p. 87.

[73] In cases I have read the genealogy fills from two to twenty-five folios. The accused was urged to recall his antecedents, as far back as his memory could go, and try to remember especially if any of them had ever appeared before the inquisition

[74] This was called in the Spanish Inquisition the "audiencia voluntaria" (voluntary audience), in contrast to the "audiencia ordinaria" (ordinary, or designated audience), when the prisoner was called at regular intervals, or at the pleasure of the inquisitor

[75] Bernard Gui, one of the most important and active 14th-century inquisitors, placed in his *Manual* a model for interrogating the accused. (It has been recently translated into French· *Manuel de l'Inquisiteur,* 2 vols., Champion, 1926-7). I quote a part of it from Lea, *Middle Ages,* I, 411ff. "When a heretic is first brought up for examination, he assumes a confident air, as though secure in his innocence I ask him why he has been brought before me He replies, smiling and courteous, 'Sir, I would be glad to learn the cause from you.'
"I 'You are accused as a heretic, and that you believe and teach otherwise than Holy Church believes'
"A (Raising his eyes to heaven, with an air of the greatest faith) 'Lord, thou knowest that I am innocent of this, and that I never held any faith other than that of true Christianity'

inquisitor's judgment, the indictment against the accused was presented (in the Spanish Inquisition it was in the hands of the prosecuting officer), and he was forced to reply to it, article by article.
At this point the counsel, in those tribunals where it was permissi-

---

"I 'You call your faith Christian, for you consider ours as false and heretical.
But I ask whether you have ever believed as true another faith than that which
the Roman Church holds to be true?'
  "A. 'I believe the true faith which the Roman Church believes, and which
you openly preach to us.'
  "I. 'Perhaps you have some of your sect at Rome whom you call the Roman
Church. I, when I preach, say many things, some of which are common to us
both, as that God liveth, and you believe some of what I preach Nevertheless you
may be a heretic in not believing other matters which are to be believed'
  "A. 'I believe all things that a Christian should believe.'
  "I. 'I know your tricks What the members of your sect believe you hold to
be that which a Christian should believe But we waste time in this fencing Say
simply, Do you believe in one God the Father, and the Son, and the Holy Ghost?'
  "A. 'I believe'
  "I 'Do you believe in Christ born of the Virgin, suffered, risen, and ascended
to heaven?'
  "A. (Briskly) 'I believe'
  "I 'Do you believe the bread and wine in the mass performed by the priests
to be changed into the body and blood of Christ by divine virtue?'
  "A. 'Ought I not to believe this?'
  "I 'I don't ask if you ought to believe, but if you do believe.'
  "A 'I believe whatever you and other good doctors order me to believe'
  "I 'Those good doctors are the masters of your sect, if I accord with them
you believe with me, if not, not.'
  "A. 'I willingly believe with you if you teach what is good to me.'
  "I. 'You consider it good to you if I teach what your other masters teach.
Say, then, do you believe the body of our Lord Jesus Christ to be in the altar?'
  "A (Promptly) 'I believe.'
  "I. 'You know that a body is there, and that all bodies are of our Lord. I
ask whether the body there is of the Lord who was born of the Virgin, hung on the
cross, arose from the dead, ascended, etc?'
  "A 'And you, sir, do you not believe it?'
  "I. 'I believe it wholly'
  "A. 'I believe likewise'
  "I. 'You believe that I believe it, which is not what I ask, but whether you
believe it'
  "A 'If you wish to interpret all that I say otherwise than simply and plainly,
then I don't know what to say I am a simple and ignorant man Pray don't catch
me in my words'
  "I 'If you are simple, answer simply, without evasions'
  "A. 'Willingly.'
  "I 'Will you then swear that you have never learned anything contrary to the
faith which we hold to be true?'
  "A (Growing pale) 'If I ought to swear, I will willingly swear.'
  "I 'I don't ask whether you ought, but whether you will swear'
  "A 'If you order me to swear, I will swear.'
  "I. 'I don't force you to swear, because as you believe oaths to be unlawful,
you will transfer the sin to me who forced you; but if you will swear, I will hear
it'
  "A. 'Why should I swear if you do not order me to?'
  "I. 'So that you may remove the suspicion of being a heretic.'
  "A. 'Sir, I do not know how unless you teach me'
  "I. 'If I had to swear, I would raise my hand and spread my fingers and say,
"So help me God, I have never learned heresy or believed what is contrary to the
true faith"'
  "Then trembling as if he cannot repeat the form, he will stumble along as
though speaking for himself or for another, so that there is not an absolute form

ble, presented the defense in behalf of the accused. Thereupon a consultation to decide the verdict was arranged: its personnel consisted of the inquisitor, the bishop or his representative, and a group of experts.[76]

In the meantime the accused languished in his cell, and as time passed he grew more fearful of the disposition of his case. Tenure in prison was, in itself, an aspect of recognized inquisitorial procedure. It provided the proper stimulation toward achieving the aim of the trial—the confession of heresy of which the inquisitorial court was certain the accused was guilty.[77]

Was this unfair means? Perhaps it was—from our modern point of view! But the inquisition must be judged on its own presuppositions. The means by which the desired end of confession was brought about were not important. The confession of heresy became the crux of the trial, as well as of the task of the inquisitor. In reality, it was the inquisitor's sacred mission to discover the faith of the accused. The faith of man was such an elusive thing, and it was so difficult to fathom the hearts of men to achieve that end, that every means—fair or foul—were condoned, so long as the desired end of confession was ultimately achieved. This serves to explain the attitude toward torture, for it, too, was only a means toward a noble end![78]

---

of oath and yet he may be thought to have sworn. If the words are there, they are so turned around that he does not swear and yet appears to have sworn. Or he converts the oath into a form of prayer, as 'God help me that I am not a heretic or the like;' and when asked whether he had sworn, he will say: 'Did you not hear me swear?' And when further hard pressed he will appeal, saying, 'Sir, if I have done amiss in aught, I will willingly bear the penance, only help me to avoid the infamy of which I am accused through malice and without fault of mine' But a vigorous inquisitor must not allow himself to be worked upon in this way, but proceed firmly till he makes these people confess their error, or at least publicly abjure heresy, so that if they are subsequently found to have sworn falsely, he can, without further hearing, abandon them to the secular arm. If one consents to swear that he is not a heretic, I say to him, 'If you wish to swear as to escape the stake, one oath will not suffice for me, nor ten, nor a hundred, nor a thousand, because you dispense each other for a certain number of oaths taken under necessity, but I will require a countless number. Moreover, if I have, as I presume, adverse witnesses against you, your oaths will not save you from being burned You will only stain your conscience without escaping death. But if you will simply confess your error, you may find mercy.' Under this anxiety, I have seen some confess."

That the ideas in back of this interrogation did not change radically in the Spanish Inquisition is apparent from the perusal of any "Instruccion" issued by the Spanish Inquisition.

[76] This consultation was called latterly the "consulta de fe."

[77] The prisoner who refused to confess, or confess in full, was remanded to his cell and cautioned "to refresh his memory" The inquisition could afford to wait. That is why cases were protracted over years—until many heretics finally broke under the ordeal of imprisonment, and confessed. Cf. Lea, *Middle Ages*, I, 419

[78] This is really the philosophical basis for the trial in the inquisition. It proceeded logically from its own assumptions Its importance lay in eliciting a confession from the heretic, because of the odium with which heresy was held in those days

Besides ordinary prison tenure, which was one of the methods used to bring the accused to confession, the inquisition might increase the rigor of imprisonment by chaining the accused in a cell· or dungeon, or by putting him on a starvation diet, or both, in order to reduce the stubborn heretic to confession.[79] Spies were also used to elicit information from the prisoner. By subtly insinuating themselves into his confidence, they served as channels through which the inquisition received much valuable information, often resulting in the desired confession of the accused. Jailers and others were used for this purpose.[80]

By far the most effective method used by the inquisition in wringing desired confessions from heretics was the application of torture. It was employed in all cases when the accused refused to make any confession, or when it was felt he was withholding testimony, or when he had made conflicting statements in his testimony.[81] It was the severest method, consequently the last to be

---

With this in mind, the inquisitorial trial, with its obvious tricks and devices designed to "trap" the heretic, begins to have some meaning. The job of the inquisitor, however much we might look askance upon it today, was one which called forth the best in men. "They were doing the work of God!" Moreover, his function was not new; it was a venerable one. The Sicilian Paramo, in tracing the origin of the inquisition, assigns to God Himself the first inquisitor's job, for did He not sit in judgment over Adam and Eve, the judgment which furnished the model for the forms observed in the inquisitorial trials? The reconciliation (the ceremony which reinstated the heretic into harmonious relations with the Church) was the development out of the sentence God meted out to Adam and Eve, the sanbenito (distinguishing garb worn over the clothing of the reconciled) was prefigured in their special garb, and the expulsion from the Garden of Eden was the pattern for the confiscation of property' (*De Origine . . . Inquisitionis*, lib. I, tit 1, 2, 3).

79 A starvation diet of bread and water was considered a most efficacious method of reducing contumacious heretics. (Lea, *Middle Ages*, I, 421, quoted by Vacandard, p. 152).

80 Prescott, *Ferdinand and Isabella*, I, 262, note 1 He quotes as his authority Puigblanch, *La Inquisición sin Mascara*, which must be used cautiously.· It was one of those books written in 1811 for the express purpose of exposing the cruelties of the inquisition, in order to induce the Cortes assembled in Cádiz to suppress its activities (Lea, *Spain*, IV, 404-5) But it cannot be denied that the use of spies was an accepted part of the inquisition's methods. (Cf. Lea, *Middle Ages*, I, 416).

81 Turberville, *The Span. Inq*, p. 91. It is not my purpose to enter into a lengthy discussion upon the moot question of responsibility for the use of torture. It has been one of the most vulnerable spots in the inquisition's armor, exposing it to attacks by all who wished to call it a barbaric institution. Abbé Vacandard himself admits, without quibbling, the Church's responsibility in introducing torture into the inquisitorial procedure. Pope Innocent, in his Bull *Ad Extirpanda* (1252) adopted its use in heresy trials, despite the opposition of the legalist, Gratian, and the Church Fathers before him Lea (*Middle Ages*, I, 421, quoted by Vacandard, p. 149) found the first instance of the use of torture in secular jurisprudence in the Veronese Code of 1228, and in the Sicilian Constitution of Frederick II (1231) The introduction of torture came about through a renewed interest and study of the old Roman Law, although, as Vacandard points out (pp. 149, 152), it was not altogether unknown in southern Europe, and Tanon (*Histoire des Tribunaux de l'inquisition en France*, pp 362-73) recalled that the ecclesiastical tribunes of Paris made use of it before its adoption in Innocent's Bull of 1252. Still the con-

applied, in evoking confessions. Yet its certainty, and the speed with which it brought the desired results, made it a constant temptation for inquisitors to use more frequently than perhaps was necessary. For example, in the examination of the Inquisition of Carcassonne by cardinals sent there to correct alleged abuses, it was found that torture was employed habitually to extort confessions.[82]

But what revolts the modern mind perhaps even more than the application of torture, is the apparently complete detachment with which the "torture audiences" have been recorded by the scribes, who wrote into the cases every gruesome detail of the proceedings.[83] But again, perhaps the consciousness of the holiness of the inquisition's task so pervaded their minds, that the aspects of the scene which repulse the modern mind were transfigured by the character of their work. They were conscious that it was God's work they were doing! The heretic was guilty: that was the fundamental presupposition. And by any means, foul or fair, he must be brought to make his confession in order that his soul might be relieved of its guilt.[84]

The accused was brought into the torture chamber, and was asked if he wished to confess. The sight of the torture instruments was often adequate stimulation to make the desired confessions. If the prisoner refused, he was stripped and bound; and once again he was asked to confess. At every stage of the process he was urged to confess. If he persisted in refusing, he was placed upon the torture instrument,[85] and as the torture was being applied he was again

---

science of the Church was revolted by the use of torture and the Church's canons forbade any cleric, on pain of being declared irregular and unfit for his holy functions, from having any part in the torture-process, or from being present during its application This impediment was lifted in 1256 by Pope Alexander IV, who allowed inquisitors to absolve each other and thus remove their irregularities. Lea, *Middle Ages,* I, 422.

[82] *Ibid.,* I, 423

[83] Few records of the torture proceedings have come from the records of the Medieval Inquisition, but the records of the Spanish Inquisition contain the full account of the "audiencia del tormento." Every gasp, whisper, shriek, and every appeal for mercy has been faithfully recorded.

[84] Cf Turberville, *The Span. Inq ,* p. 93 Vacandard (pp 205-6) writes: "We do not deny that the zeal of the Inquisitors was at times excessive, especially in the case of torture. But some of their cruelty may be explained by their sincere desire for the salvation of the heretic. They regarded the confession of suspects as the beginning of their conversion. They therefore believed any means used for that purpose was justifiable."

[85] A number of torture instruments were used. Among them were:
(1) the *rack*: "a triangular frame on which the prisoner was stretched and bound, so that he could not move. Cords were attached to his arms and legs, and then connected with a windlass, which, when turned, dislocated the joints of the wrists and ankles." (Vacandard, pp 152-3)
(2) the *strappado,* or vertical rack, called also the "garrucha" in Spain. "The prisoner, with his hands tied behind his back, was raised by a rope attached to the

urged to confess. If he confessed while being tortured, or if he indicated a willingness to confess, the omnipresent secretary took down his confession which, according to inquisitorial procedure, the accused had to confirm before another day had passed if it was to

---

top of a gallows, or to the ceiling of the torture chamber; he was then let fall with a jerk to within a few inches of the ground. This was repeated several times. The cruel torturers sometimes tied weights to the victim's feet to increase the shock of the fall." *Ibid.*, p. 153, cf. Turberville, *The Span Inq.,* p 94.

(3) the *aselli* or water-torture "The prisoner was placed on a sort of a tresle, known as the 'escalera,' or ladder, with sharp-edged rungs across it, his head lying lower than his feet, in a hollowed-out trough and kept in position by an iron band round the forehead. Cords which cut into the flesh were twisted tightly round the arms, thighs and calves. The mouth was forcibly kept open and a strip of linen was forced into the throat, water being poured through this from a jar, so that throat and nostrils were stopped and a state of semi-suffocation was produced." *Ibid.*, p. 95.

(4) the *cordeles* and *garrotes* The prisoner was adjusted "by a belt or girdle with which he was swung from the ground, his arms were tied together across his breast and were attached by cords to rings in the wall. For the trampa or trampona the ladder in the potro had one of its rungs removed so as to enable the legs to pass through; another bar with a sharp edge was set below it and through this narrow opening the legs were forcibly pulled by means of a cord fastened around the toes with a turn around the ankle Each *vuelta,* or turn given to the cord, gained about three inches; five vueltas were reckoned a most rigorous torture, and three were the ordinary practice, even with the most robust. Leaving him stretched in this position, the next step was the mancuerda, in which a cord was passed around the arms, which the executioner wound around himself and threw himself backward, casting his whole weight and pushing with his foot against the potro. The cord, we are told, would cut through skin and muscle to the bone, while the body of the patient was stretched as in a rack, between it and the cords at the feet. The belt or girdle at the waist, subjected to these alternate forces was forced back and forth and contributed further to the suffering This was repeated six or eight times with the mancuerda, on different parts of the arms, and the patients usually fainted, especially if they were women. After this the potro came in play. The patient was released from the trampa and mancuerda and placed on the eleven sharp rungs of the potro, his ankles rigidly tied to the sides and his head sinking into a depression where it was held immovable by a cord across the forehead Three cords were passed around each upper arm, the ends being carried into rings on the sides of the potro and furnished with garrotes or sticks to twist them tight; two similar ones were put on each thigh and one on each calf, making twelve in all The ends were carried to a *maestra garrote* by which the executioner could control all at once These worked not only by compression but by travelling around the limbs, carrying away skin and flesh. Each half round was reckoned a *vuelta* or turn, six or seven of which was the maximum, but it was usual not to exceed five, even with strong men Formerly the same was done with the cord around the forehead, but this was abandoned as it was apt to start the eyes from their sockets." (Lea, *Spain*, III, 20-1). This method was one of the most widely used in the Majorcan Inquisition. At each *vuelta* the victim, suffering terrific pain, would cry for mercy and relief. In the Spanish Inquisition the public executioners administered the torture and the instruments used were those ordinarily employed in the secular courts. Lea (*Spain*, III, 18) writes. "The inquisition thus had no special refinements of torture and, indeed, so far as I have had opportunity of investigation, it confined itself to a few methods out of the abundant repertory of the public functionaries" The Spanish Inquisition employed a physician on its staff. who was in attendance during the torture to determine whether the culprit was fit to endure the torture, and for how long. In Spain the "audiencia del tormento" did not occur frequently, in the cases I examined extending over a long period of time Apparently the inquisition was not prone to admit that it used torture frequently, and out of respect to public feelings, doubtless, it was not mentioned in the public recitations of the trial at the *Sermo,* or auto de fe. (*Ibid.*, III, 32).

be valid. If he remained obdurate despite the torture, the culprit was remanded to his cell and the torture was ordered simply "continued," thus effectively nullifying a merciful provision in inquisitorial procedure that the accused could be tortured only once.[86]

The accused might be tortured both in the capacity of an alleged heretic, and as a witness (in *caput alienum*). The latter grew out of the fact that the inquisition did not regard a heretic's confession sincere, as we have seen, unless he gave complete information about his accomplices in crime.[87]

The inquisition foresaw that the death of the accused might possibly result from torture. Against this eventuality it protected itself. It argued that the fault fell squarely upon the accused, who was forcing the inquisition into doing something which his voluntary confession of the truth would have made unnecessary.[88]

Men have long regarded the application of torture to human beings to evoke confessions of their religious beliefs as a relic of barbarism. But throughout the middle ages and well into modern times the ideal of religious unity has been so strong that dissidents have been forced to suffer. The odium modern men have of torture should not be placed upon the Catholic Church alone, if for no other reason than dissidents under other religious jurisdictions have been forced to suffer similarly for their religious ideals.[89]

The next step in inquisitorial procedure, after confession had been duly made, was the imposition of the sentence upon the heretic. But since the inquisition was not to be compared to any ordinary court, where retribution was demanded for crimes committed, technically it did not pass sentence. It was a court whose task it was to save souls, and to point out where the way to salvation lay, therefore it had no power to inflict punishments. It was *a pen-*

---

[86] This provision is to be found in the Instructions of 1484 He who revoked his confession made under torture was held by the authorities to justify even a third application of torture, although the eminent authority, Simancas, did not countenance such an act. *Ibid*, 28.

[87] I have met with many instances of additional torture justified on these grounds. However it is put, the fact is that the *same* person was tortured, although on separate grounds Cf Coulton, *The Inquisition*, p 68; Turberville, *The Span. Inq.*, p 94.

[88] This interesting formula occurs just before the "audiencia del tormento" in the cases I have examined *Ibid.*, p. 95, note 1

[89] Thus Michael Servetus was burned in Calvinist Geneva for his views, which were heterodox there. And today, since men are being punished in Germany (which wants to establish a co-ordinated state—the medieval ideal of a unified state) because of the accident of their birth, or because of their religious and political ideals, it should not be difficult for the contemporaries of this movement to understand a similar movement of years ago, actuated by motives perhaps higher than its exemplar today.

ance, theoretically speaking, and not a sentence, which the inquisition imposed upon the heretic in order to dissuade him from sinning again. The Church was a loving mother, eager to welcome back her wayward children. The inquisition, therefore, only imposed a chastisement or expiation for sins. This was the theory of the penal functions of the inquisition.[90]

It is difficult to imagine that in the inquisition, regarding itself as infallible as the faith it strived to uphold, there would be any acquittals.[91] Reluctant as the inquisition was to announce an acquittal, during the Spanish Inquisition there were records of many acquittals.[92] To avoid embarrassment for the inquisition, the device of "suspension" was discovered, which simply allowed matters to stand as they were, if no additional testimony adequate for conviction could be produced. Thus "suspension" saved the infallibility of the inquisition, while it left the accused in the predicament of being neither wholly free nor convicted; at any time his case might be reopened.[93]

With these exceptions, the inevitable sequel to confession was the sentence which the inquisition imposed upon the penitent heretic as a condition for readmission, or reconciliation, to the Church. The sentences fell into three categories: (1) Pious observances, such as pilgrimages to shrines of saints, or to Palestine as a Crusader, or incarceration in some monastery for instruction in the faith, constitute the lesser penalties.[94] (2) Humiliating penalties included

---

90 This theory is in accord with the purpose of the inquisition · to bring the heretic back to his senses, and to the Church The penitent heretic who had incurred only light suspicion of heresy was freed, beside his "penance," with an "abjuracion de levi" (a light abjuration) . with his face turned to the crucifix and with his hand touching the Gospels, he swore that henceforth he would detest heresy and cherish the Catholic faith alone. If he incurred a "heavy" suspicion of heresy, he was abjured with an "abjuracion de vehementi," an awesome ceremony in which he agreed to perform his penance or be treated as a "relapsed heretic"—for whom the penalty was the stake without a new trial. Cf. Turberville, *The Span. Inq.,* pp. 99-101. For the theory of the penal functions of the inquisition, see Lea, *Middle Ages,* I, 459-62.

91 For the inquisition, as we have seen, made arrests after it believed it was sure of the guilt of the accused In the Medieval Inquisition acquittal was hardly ever practiced, on the grounds that it barred future proceedings in the event new evidence came to light Lea, *Spain,* III, 105.

92 I have seen the records of many cases acquitted by the Suprema sitting in Madrid, passing upon all the sentences of the tribunals

93 This is a good illustration of the inequality of the accused before the inquisition Lea, *Spain,* III, 109.

94 There were many varieties, limited only by the fertility of the inquisitors' minds During the middle ages pilgrimages to shrines of saints was a commonplace measure for requiting sin, which the priests often invoked for a sin revealed in the confessional. Flogging was an inevitable accompaniment of these "lesser penalties," which, in the Spanish Inquisition, often included a period of exile from the here-

"the wearing of the crosses," which came to be called the *sanbenito,* a special garment with crosses on the front and back which the heretic was required to wear as part of his penance.[95]   (3) The severest punishments were imprisonment and death, reserved for the impenitent or relapsed heretic.[96]

In addition, each sentence carried with it one of the severe penalties imposed by the inquisition—the confiscation of the property of the accused. At the time of the arrest, a notary made a careful inventory of the culprit's belongings.[97] The inquisition, operating on the assumption that arrest implied guilt, often carried out confiscation of the property in advance of conviction.[98] "Actual confiscation," writes Abbé Vacandard, "took place in the case of all obdurate and relapsed heretics abandoned to the secular arm, with all penitents condemned to perpetual imprisonment, and with all suspects who had escaped the inquisition; either by flight or by death."[99] Flight presumed guilt, and the property of the fugitive was duly confiscated and his effigy burned. It was the same with the prosecution of dead heretics. Their bodies were exhumed, for they were not allowed to lie buried in consecrated ground. With great solemnity the mortal remains of dead heretics were burned, and

---

tic's village, town or district. Although considered a "light" punishment, such penalties might easily ruin the culprit's business or profession Cf. Lea, *Middle Ages*, I, 464-7 Turberville, *The Span. Inq.,* p. 100.

[95] This garment was called sanbenito (saco bendito; in Spanish also "zamarra"), for it was an adaptation of the habit worn by penitent monks It was a sleeveless gown of linen or cotton. When worn by an impenitent heretic, it was decorated with a red cross surrounded by flames, devils, demons and serpents. When worn by a penitent heretic, it had crosses, usually of saffron, sewed transversely on the garment. The sanbenito was matched by the "coroza" (conical-shaped headgear made of the same material) For a further description of these garments, see Lacroix, *Military and Religious Life in the Middle Ages and at the Period of the Renaissance,* p. 437ff

[96] The relapsed heretic is he who, though once reconciled to the Church, falls into heresy a second time, for which the stake was the penalty. As a matter of fact, heretics have been known to be reconciled a second, and some even a third time [In the Majorcan Inquisition, the records reveal third reconciliations: Antonia, the wife of Ferrer Pratz, was reconciled: (1) March 26, 1490, (2) July 1, 1491, and (3) June 23, 1509 AHN *Rel. de Causas de Fe,* libro 1, 866, fols 32, 60 v(erso)]

[97] Turberville, *The Span. Inq.,* p. 104

[98] *Ibid ,* p. 105; cf Lea, *Middle Ages,* I, 507.

[99] Pp. 202-3. Lea (*Middle Ages,* I, 507-9) has gathered so many exceptions to this statement that we are inclined to believe that confiscation was likely to have occurred more frequently—determined pretty largely by the "time and temper of the inquisitor." The Council of Béziers in 1233 ordered "confiscation for all reconciled converts not condemned to wear crosses." A later Council of Béziers (1246) and of Albi (1254) "prescribed it for all whom the inquisitors should penance with imprisonment" Finally, legalists admitted that imprisonment need be the only criterion for confiscation, and even to this rule many exceptions developed.

their property confiscated.[100] A large part of all cases of the inquisition were posthumous trials against dead heretics.[101]

According to Roman law, forfeiture of the traitor's property —and the heretic was classed with the traitor—occurred when the crime was committed.[102] The inquisition therefore regarded the property of heretics *as confiscated when they began their heresy.* How great an uncertainty this placed upon business relationships! No one could be sure of the complete orthodoxy of his business colleagues. Since heretics could make no valid assignments, he who was unfortunate enough to hold their property when arrested— regardless of how many hands it passed through—was forced to return it, or make restitution therefor. The prosecution of dead heretics made it doubly hazardous for business, for the property technically was confiscated whenever they began their heresy, and, no matter in whose possession it chanced to be after their death, he was forced to relinquish it. Vacandard, quite correctly, gives the credit to Lea for developing the "money side" of the inquisition, for Lea first showed how great were the hardships which confiscation imposed upon "thousands of innocent and helpless women and children thus stripped of everything," and upon "all classes in the business of daily life."[103]

In dividing the confiscated property the determining factor was not always the law, but the strength of the inquisition. According to the Bull *Ad Extirpanda,* it was to be divided equally among the local authorities, the inquisition and the bishop.[104] But when the bishop's functions in punishing heresy were finally appropriated by the Monastic Inquisition, his share of confiscations was allocated for the Papal Treasury.[105] With the growth in power by the inquisition, it pocketed most of the confiscations for itself. In

---

[100] Cf. Vacandard, p 203, and note 1, quoting the Chronicle of Pelisso, one of the first inquisitors of Albi· "This was done with much solemnity. The bones and even the decomposed body of the heretic were carried through the city streets at the sound of a trumpet, and then burned The names of the dead were read out, and the living were threatened with a like fate if they followed their example" ("De cimeteriis . . . extumulati . . . et ossa eorum et corpora fætentia per villam tracta et voce tibicinatoris per vicos proclomata et nominata dicentis· Qui aytal fara, aytal perira . . . "

[101] Eighty-eight cases out of the 636 tried by Inquisitor Bernard Gui were posthumous Vacandard, p. 203.

[102] Lea, *Middle Ages,* I, 520

[103] Vacandard, p. 204. Cf Lea, *Middle Ages,* I, 501-24. Frederick II and Pope Innocent IV decreed that children could inherit their fathers' property if they informed against them to the inquisition. Pope Gregory IX rejoiced when he heard that fathers denounced their children, children their parents, wives their husbands, and even mothers their children' Vacandard, p 246.

[104] Lea, *Middle Ages,* I, 509.

[105] *Ibid.*

the Spanish Inquisition, the confiscated property was at the sole disposal of the Royal Treasury. However, the inquisition's power often determined what portion should go to the Royal Treasury.[106]

The inquisition enriched itself through confiscations. In fact the desire for persecuting heretics seemed to languish when confiscations were not forthcoming.[107] Many inquisitors, like many secular rulers, were perhaps more avid of prosecuting heretics when the latters' property was known to be valuable.[108] It must be remembered that men operated the inquisition, and among them were always some who were moved less by the ideals they presumably served than by the monetary gain their positions brought them.[109]

For the heretic who abjured his sins the inquisition kindly offered reconciliation to the Church and, through imprisonment, the opportunity to pay penance for his sins. The theory of the medieval Church demanded perpetual imprisonment for the heretic—originally a similar penalty for the penitent as well as the

---

[106] A case in point is that in the Majorcan Inquisition, when the Conversos' property was confiscated in 1678. Charles II commanded the viceroy to look after the king's interests by getting inventories of the property. To this the inquisition caustically rejoined that this was solely its own jurisdiction· sequestered property was its own sacred trust until finally confiscated When the final accounts were made, the king was given a pittance as his share of the spoils Cf. *below*, pp. 68-9 The inquisition had become an *imperium in imperio!* Archivo de Simancas, *Inquisición*, lib 69, fols. 2, 8. The communications are dated August 8th, and August 29th, 1678 (From the records examined by the writer in the Henry Charles Lea Library, University of Pennsylvania, Philadelphia) Cf. Lea, *Spain*, IV, 512.

[107] Vacandard (p. 204) concurs with Lea that the confiscations were "the stimulant of pillage."

[108] The Inquisitor Nicolas Eymeric writes mournfully. "In our days (14th century, Aragon) there are no more rich heretics, so that princes, not seeing much money in prospect, will not put themselves to any expense; it is a pity that so salutary an institution as ours should be so uncertain of its future." Langlois, *L'Inquisition d'après des travaux récents*, (Paris, 1902), pp. 105-6.

[109] Bernard Gui paints a portrait of the ideal inquisitor which the Church authorities, it may be presumed, would have preferred, rather than many of the unjust men who were sitting in the seats of the inquisitors· "He should be diligent and fervent in his zeal for religious truth, for the salvation of souls, and for the destruction of heresy. He should always be calm in times of trial and difficulty, and never give way to outbursts of anger or temper. He should be a brave man, ready to face death if necessary, but while never cowardly running from danger, he should never be foolhardy rushing into it. He should be unmoved by the entreaties or the bribes of those who appear before his tribunal; still he must not harden his heart to the point of refusing to delay or mitigate punishment, as circumstances may require from time to time In doubtful cases, he should be very careful not to believe too easily what may appear probable, and yet in reality is false; nor, on the other hand, should he stubbornly refuse to believe what may appear improbable, and yet is frequently true. He should zealously discuss and examine every case, so as to be sure to make a just decision . . . Let the love of truth and mercy, the special qualities of every good judge, shine in his countenance, and let his sentences never be prompted by avarice or cruelty." Vacandard, p. 131. (Cf. *supra* pp. 20-2, note 75, in which a part of Gui's Manual is quoted, for an illustration of how he practically sought to carry out these high ideals).

impenitent heretic—on the grounds that the heretic had forfeited all claims to compassion. Yet the Church's infinite goodness spared the heretic his life.[110] It was manifestly impossible to carry this theory into practice when the numbers of heretics arrested could no longer be provided with prison accommodations.[111] In practice, therefore, sentences of life-imprisonment were reduced, and sometime commuted into pilgrimages or wearing the sanbenito.[112] In the Spanish Inquisition, so far had practice departed from theory, that the authority, Simancas, writing in the sixteenth century, reported that the sentence of "perpetual prison" was generally understood to mean three years, and "irremissible prison," eight years.[113]

The severest penalty of all meted out the heretic was death by fire.[114] It has already been indicated that the Church technically had no hand in the death penalty, but its abhorrence of blood and its "relaxation to the secular arm" were actually legal fictions which the Catholic scholar Vacandard admits do not absolve her from blame.[115] The death penalty was reserved for the impenitent heretic,[116] the

---

110 Vacandard, p 110

111 To avoid openly departing from the theory, the inquisitors delayed seizing heretics unless some special reason—flight, or relapse—made it necessary that they be imprisoned. Sometime, heretics condemned to imprisonment were confined to their own homes until their terms expired, or until prison accommodations could be made (as in Toulouse in 1237). Lea, *Middle Ages*, I, 485-6.

112 Vacandard, pp 194-5.

113 The word "perpetual" had taken on a very definite connotation in prison sentences meted out by the inquisition. Thus one record reads · "perpetual prison for six months." Lea (*Spain*, III, 160) is brought to admit that "the real infliction was therefore much less severe than it appears on the records."

114 Some inquisitors interpreted the verse quite literally "If a man abide not in me, he is cast forth as a branch, and is withered; and men gather them, and *cast them into the fire, and they are burned*" (Italics mine.) St. John XV, 6 Cf Vacandard, p 177.

115 Vacandard (pp. 177-81) prefaces his discussion of this subject: " . . . to free the Church from all responsibility in the infliction of the death penalty" is "truly an extremely difficult undertaking"

116 The impenitent heretic (*negativo*) he who refused to admit his heretical practices. Since arrest by the inquisition was tantamount to guilt, anyone who *refused* to confess was adjudged "impenitent" or contumacious, and released from the protection of the Church—i. e, "relaxed to the secular arm." As a matter of sober fact, many good Catholics went to their death rather than confess to heretical practices which they had doubtless never committed Obviously Llorente's figure (9/10 of those condemned by the inquisition were good Catholics) is far from the truth (Turberville, *The Span Inq.*, p. 110). In the Spanish Inquisition the *negativo* suffered the most dreadful death of being burned alive. Abbé Vacandard argues that impenitent heretics should not be put to death, according to principles of "Christian charity and gentleness." For with the death of the heretics, there was no possibility at all of their conversion, thus robbing the inquisition of its chief purpose! This penalty cannot be defended except on the authority of "the old law" (Old Testament), "whose severity, according to the early Church Fathers, had been abolished by the law of Christ." (Vacandard, p. 238) . . . "Neither rea-

relapsed heretic,[117] and for him who had made incomplete confession,[118] or persistently refused to swear on oath.

The sentences were read at the *Sermo* or *Auto de fe* (Act of Faith)—the only public ceremony of the inquisition. This spectacle, intended to place the public assembled in awe of heresy and of the inquisition's power, was also made to represent the drama of the Last Judgment Day. It was a demonstration of grand proportions. In the Spanish Inquisition, the auto de fe proved an admirable setting for the new king to swear an oath of allegiance to the inquisition.

The prisoners wearing sanbenitos—by which the public recognized their penalties—crowned with *corozas* (conical hats) and holding lighted candles, the effigies of the fugitives, and those of the dead (also their exhumed bones) carried by porters: all of this together made an unforgettable impression. After a sermon extolling the faith and the importance of the inquisition, the sentences were read.[119] The unfortunates condemned to death were delivered to the secular arm and taken to the communal execution grounds (*brasero* or *quemadero*) for execution. Thus, contrary to

son, Christian tradition, nor the New Testament call for the infliction of the death penalty upon heretics." (*Ibid.,* p 239)

[117] The relapsed heretic was he who had once been reconciled to the Church, and yet, despite his solemn abjurations, returned to (or *relapsed* into) his former heresies. (On more than one occasion heretics were reconciled alive two or three times Cf. *supra* p 28, note 96) The relapsed heretic was sentenced to death Even then he had the opportunity to be "penitent," which merited him, in the Spanish Inquisition, the lesser penalty of being garrotted before cremation Historical fact is again on the side of the inquisition, in its mitigation of the harshness of the death penalty of those whose abjuration was proved fraudulent by their relapse into heresy In the early years of the inquisition, imprisonment was held by Pope Gregory IX (in 1233) and St. Raymond de Peñaforte (in 1242) to be a sufficient penalty for the relapsed heretic The inquisitors soon became the final judges and they, too, it must be recorded in their favor, felt that imprisonment was enough—a leniency comparing favorably with the harshness of public opinion of that time But by 1258, Rome had decided that relaxation was the only proper penalty for relapse Yet the prisoner could be given absolution and communion, if he repented, even at the last moment! This placed the inquisitors, as Vacandard observes (p. 238), in the embarrassing position of professing to believe in the sincerity of the repentance of the heretic (by virtue of granting him absolution), and yet sending him to the stake. "To condemn a man to death who was considered worthy of receiving the Holy Eucharist," Abbé Vacandard affirms, "on the plea that he might one day commit the sin of heresy again, appears to us a crying injustice " *Ibid*

[118] He who refused to confess all the inquisitors thought he should confess, fared worse in the Spanish Inquisition, where he was subject to death, than in the Medieval Inquisition, where he would have escaped this penalty. Cf. Turberville, *Th Span. Inq.,* p. 110.

[119] The sentences were read· (1) *con meritos·* reciting with great detail the sins of the accused (which proved to be a "popular education in vice" . .   Lea, *Spain*, IV, 510) ; or (2) *sin meritos* a recitation of the crime, without any detail. Sometime the readings of the sentences alone took up most of the day, and the spectacle, beginning in the early morning, was prolonged into the night. Executions of the sentences, such as flogging, imprisonment, exile, galleys, etc, were put into effect on the morning following the auto de fe (*Ibid.,* III, 219-20)

popular imagination, the burning of heretics was not a part of the auto de fe which was officially closed when the burnings took place. In Spain, the public spectacles were called *autos publico de fe,* in contrast to the by far greater number of *autos particulares,* the private autos, held in the Churches or in the audience chambers of the inquisition. The auto was the climax of the trial. It attracted immense throngs of people, who were granted indulgences for their attendance. They took place usually on Sundays or holidays. The printed accounts (*relaciones*) of the many large autos de fe were broadcast and found a wide reading public.[120]

*   *   *   *   *

From the many allusions already made to the Spanish Inquisition, it is clear that, contrary to popular belief, it was the heir of the Medieval Inquisition. Nevertheless, the Medieval Inquisition was in a moribund condition in the fifteenth century when Ferdinand and Isabella, the Catholic monarchs of Spain, adapted it to the special needs of their country, and so gave it a new lease on life. How they adapted it, and what part it played in the final realization of their dreams for a unified Spanish state, will now be briefly discussed.

When, in 1469, Ferdinand and Isabella were married, they entered upon one of the most trying and difficult careers of any sovereigns. Their country was in civil war. Only seven years later, with their victory in the Battle of Toro, March 1, 1476, the rival party led by Beltraneja (much disputed whether she was the legitimate daughter of King Henry the Impotent) was finally crushed.[121] Thereupon they turned their attention to the constantly warring nobility, who were keeping the country in a state of perpetual siege.[122] In the Cortes of Madrigal, shortly after the victory at Toro, the desire of the sovereigns that central administration of justice be placed in their hands, in addition to the general vindication of royal prerogatives, was made unmistakably apparent. Not only did they ask for power to administer justice, but they

---

120 Much of our information comes from these "relaciones." The great Madrid auto de fe of 1680 was minutely described by Joseph del Olmo, Secretary of the Madrid tribunal It was the occasion for a painting by Rizzi, now hanging in the Prado Museum, Madrid. Similarly, Padre Francisco Garau's *La Fee Triunfante* gives us much information about the activities of the Majorcan Inquisition.

121 For a good account of the state of Spain just before and during the early years of the reign of Ferdinand and Isabella, read Prescott, *History of the Reign of Ferdinand and Isabella,* chapters I-V. The opening chapters of Father Walsh's *Isabella the Catholic* provide a popular presentation; similarly Rafael Sabatini's *Torquemada,* (London, 1913), p. 76ff.

122 Merriman, *The Rise of the Spanish Empire,* II, 3, 4, 48-9, 98-9, (hereafter · Merriman).

set into motion the machinery to strictly enforce it, recognizing that only thereby could internal peace be achieved. Isabella travelled through the country and helped to pacify it by bringing many of the robber-noblemen to justice. The nobility had to be broken if the crown was to become the supreme power in the land.

Spain lacked a strong, centralized government capable of welding its heterogeneous groups into a unified nation. The new sovereigns recognized this deficiency and set about to supply it. Their marriage, itself, had brought two Spanish kingdoms under one control. Moreover, the sovereigns wisely utilized the widespread hatred against the common enemy, the Moors, in their campaign of unifying the Christian peoples of Spain.

In those early years, everything pointed toward the realization of the sovereigns' great ambition to convert the feudal monarchy that Spain was, with the power of the crown at the mercy of the nobility, into an absolute, centralized and unified state, with its power and life issuing from the crown itself. Those early years constituted a warlike period. The feebleness of the available police power forced Ferdinand to reorganize the armed brotherhood (*Santa Hermandad*), which was used chiefly to bring the defiant nobility to terms. In order to bring about a semblance of national and political unity, the sovereigns were also forced to amass strength and influence by accumulating money, and by bringing as many parties and classes as they could over to their side. These internal conditions suggest one explanation for the emergence of a revitalized inquisition on Spanish soil, as a tool in the hands of the monarchs.

The inquisition was brought into Spain to solve its religious problem. The character of the institution was such that it worked remarkably well into the sovereigns' plans for bringing the country under their absolute control. To Christian Spain, the religious problem always seemed a formidable one. As early as the Council of Elvira in 313, and until the Moors invaded the country in 711, fulminations against the Jews and the exercise of Judaism occupied the Councils of the Churches, reaching their climax in the persecutions under the converted Aryan, Reccared, and his successor, Sisebut (589-620). By the time of the *Reconquista* and the capture of Toledo (1085), the decrees against the Jews, although on the statute books, had become dead-letters, because most of the Jews were then living in the Moorish states. But with the increase of Jewish population in Christian Spain, the problem again reasserted itself.[123] After the power of the Moors was effectively broken in

---

[123] For a discussion of the various enactments against the Jews in Spain, see Amador

the battle of Las Navas de Tolosa (1212), the Jews became the subject of much unfavorable legislation. The Crusaders, coming into Spain for the battle of Las Navas, brought their sectarian zeal with them and encouraged a growing native ill-will against the Jews. This ill-will found the climax of its expression in the fourteenth century with the destruction of the Jewish communities in Navarre (1328), the revulsion against Jews allegedly responsible for the Black Plague (1348),[124] their loss of the crown's patronage with the ascendency of Henry de Trastamara (1369-1379), and finally the riots of 1391 which spread through Spain and the Balearic Islands.[125] Baptism alone could save the lives of the Jews. Therefore, as a result of these events, there emerged the class of new-Christians, Marranos or Conversos, who took the place which Jews had heretofore assumed in the religious problem of Spain. They were no longer restricted as Jews, but free as Christians to aspire to whatever heights their native abilities might elevate them.

The new-Christians or Conversos constituted the chief cause for the establishment of the inquisition in Spain.[126] Scandals arising out of their secret practice of Judaism provoked the Church to vigorous action. The masses joined in the clamor against them, for it was evident that these people, hitherto Jews and now nominal Christians, still pursued their old businesses, only now with the added impunity which the Church's protection afforded them.

That many Jews who were converted to Christianity sincerely accepted their new religion cannot be denied. The high positions they attained in the Church—some as exalted as bishops—are in-

---

de los Rios, *Historia Social, Politica, y Religiosa de los Judios de España y Portugal,* I, chapters II, III, IV, (hereafter : *Judios de España*) , Graetz, III, 43-52, 513-15; Margolis and Marx, *A History of the Jewish People,* (Philadelphia, 1927), chapters XLV, LVIII.

124 The Jews were accused of occult powers They were held responsible for the plague since it did not appear to ravage them 'as much as it did the Christian population. The Jews were alleged to have poisoned brooks and wells. Despite the Bulls of Pope Clement VI, which prohibited Jews from being killed without proper trial (and later defending the innocence of the Jews against these preposterous charges), they were slaughtered mercilessly. Cf. Graetz, IV, 100ff.

125 Amador de los Rios (*Judios de España,* III, 646-9) has made two compilations: (1) Massacres of Jews from 1013 to 1482, with the motives therefor; (2) Massacres of Conversos from 1449 to 1531 They are well worth study, for they tell cryptically the sad history of the Jews in the peninsula under Christian domination —both as Jews and as converts to Christianity. The causes for the riots were many. The ill-will the people had against the Jews was whipped into a frenzy by the priest Ferrand Martinez, confessor to the Queen Mother Doubtless jealousy of the wealth and positions which Jews held was a contributing factor. Many Jews were tax-farmers—a precarious business which always brings down scorn and hatred upon the heads of those who engage in it, be they Jews or Christians.

126 As has already been pointed out, the inquisition was an instrumentality in the hands of the sovereigns to force the population into a unity, and unity of faith (to be achieved by the inquisition) was considered the first essential of good government. Cf. Walsh, *Isabella the Catholic,* p. 164.

dicative of their sincerity.[127] But the masses of converts undoubtedly became Christians in order to save their lives. Motives no nobler than their own skin-saving can hardly be attributed to many of the converts. Rooted in the traditions of Judaism, which dominated every moment of their lives, it is not surprising to find that the insincere converts returned increasingly to their former faith.[128] Moreover, the Catholic Church did not exert herself to educate the neophytes. Thus, a strong inherited tradition, uninfluenced by Catholic teaching, made their adherence to their former faith almost inevitable. In some instances, Jews were bribed to accept baptism. Obviously such as these could not long remain sincere followers of any faith.[129]

The forces leading up to the inquisition will not be estimated properly unless it is understood that the sentiment of the people changed after 1391: up to that time there was only a religious hatred against Jews;[130] after that time it changed to a race hatred

---

[127] Pablo de Santa Maria (the former Rabbi Solomon haLevi) became bishop of his native city (Burgos), and served in the Council of Regency of Castile (Roth, *A History of the Marranos*, p 19, hereafter · Roth). His son Alfonso who followed his father's footsteps as Bishop of Burgos, was one of the delegates to the Church Council of Basle (1431-43). He was largely responsible for its anti-Jewish enactments (*Ibid.*, p. 24; Graetz, IV, 245). Pedro de Santangel, a member of the Jewish Chinillo family of Calatayud, was Bishop of Majorca (1464-6). (Roth, p. 22; Villanueva, *Viage á Mallorca*, vols XXI, XXII of *Viage Literario a las Iglesias de España*, hereafter Villanueva; XXII, 81). Many of the Conversos and their immediate descendants became some of the most virulent enemies of the Jews! The zeal of the apostate is notorious, and in some cases his zeal in persecuting members of his former religious group is accounted as evidence of the sincerity of his conversion Thus Pablo Christiani, a convert from Judaism, debated as the representative of Christianity with Rabbi Moses Nahmanides at the Disputation of Barcelona (1263). (Graetz, III, 597-8). Many important personages in Spain were converted Jews, or descendants of Jews from their maternal or paternal side. Thus the mother of King Ferdinand was reputed to be a member of the Jewish Henriquez family! (Roth, p. 24). The 15th-century *Libro Verde de Aragon* is an exposition of the Jewish antecedents of many noblemen Another book (*El Tizon de la Nobleza Española*), similarly demonstrative of how many Spanish noblemen had Jewish blood in their veins, was written in the 16th century by the Cardinal Francisco Mendoza y Bovadilla

[128] Cf Graetz, IV, 309ff. for some of the practices of the new-Christians · "They washed the heads of their infants after baptism   . . . They observed Jewish rites and customs, either from piety or from habit .   .   They took no account of the origin of their conversion, which had been accomplished with fire and sword .   "

[129] The riots of 1391 spread through Spain to Majorca, where a number of Jews were tempted to accept baptism by the promise of receiving 2,000 libras (ca $1,500., see *below* p 69, ch III, note 44), as a reward for their apostasy After their conversion, they demanded the money, but never received the proffered bribe Such people, selling their faith to the highest bidder, and duped in addition, cannot be said to make the finest kind of believers, nor can they be expected to hold any high regard for the religion of those who deceived them! Llabres, "La Conversion de los Judios Mallorquines en 1391," *BAH*, XL, 1902, 152-4

[130] Isabella did not believe the antipathy between Jew and Christian was racial. She interpreted it as a difference in religion alone, which conversion could permanently and effectively remove Cf. Walsh, *Isabella the Catholic*, pp. 153-4

which no amount of immersion could wash away. New-Christians shared with Jews in the contumely in which they were held by Christians. In Toledo the *Sentencia Estatua* deprived new-Christians of their rights as members of the Christian Church! Pope Nicholas V, in Bulls of 1449 and 1451, condemned the *Estatua* and pleaded for equality of the new-Christians as members of the Mother Church, but to no avail. The temper of the people could not be changed by Bulls of the Pope. The passion for *limpieza* (blood that is free from taint of Jewish or Moorish strains) lent point to the people's hatred for the Conversos. The latter had *mala sangre* (tainted blood) in their veins, a reason strong enough for depriving them of privileges. Thus a powerful economic motive made reasonable—and even necessary—the ousting of Conversos from their positions, into which the gentry wished to place themselves. This fact, coupled with the Church's hatred of the insincere converts, reduced the opportunities for the converted Jews. It was a vicious cycle: hatred of the new-Christians by the old-Christians forced them into their former faith; this in turn brought out the hatred which the Church held against them for the insincerity of their conversion.

The acrimony and hatred of the old-Christians burst forth against new-Christians and Jews alike in riots throughout Castile. The Franciscan Friar Alfonso de Spina (d. ca. 1491), Rector of the University of Salamanca, brought together in his book *Fortalitium Fidei* all the malicious legends and scandals circulating over Europe about Jews and their baptized brothers. He, together with the Court-Chronicler Bernaldez, inflamed the people against the Conversos as perverters of the true Christian faith. To the mind of the Christian, the inquisition was the logical solution for the religious problem of Spain. It was not a spontaneous conclusion, but the inevitable result of a long historical development in Spain. Indeed the process of the inquisition, it was realized, would provide a more orderly method of dealing with heretics than heretofore: when the public took the law in its own hands, and killed them off with utmost impunity. From the point of view of the sovereigns, the inquisition would be of assistance in restoring public order and security.

The sovereigns, it cannot be doubted, also saw that the faith was being perverted and, as "defenders of the faith," felt it was their sacred duty to meet the problem. Even in 1451, before their time, Pope Nicholas V had delegated inquisitorial powers to high ecclesiastical dignitaries in Castile, and Pope Sixtus IV had already sent his legate there to exercise the powers of the inquisition. Both

attempts failed, due in great measure to the unsettled conditions of
the country and to the lack of centralized authority necessary to
enforce the inquisition.

Both Ferdinand and Isabella were statesmen enough to see
that the inquisition would inevitably be established in Spain. Isabella, as a devout religious person, doubtless would have favored
it, regardless of what it meant to the crown. Ferdinand was not as
devout as his consort but was perfectly willing, if Machiavelli is
to be believed, to use religion as a pretext for the attainment of his
political ambitions.[131] Even if they had desired to oppose the inquisition, it is to be very seriously doubted that they would have succeeded, because of the temper of the people. Both of them were
sensible enough, however, to see that the inauguration of the inquisition would make the ecclesiastical forces their allies. Besides, they
realized that the confiscations arising from its processes would enrich them and give them greater opportunity for victory over the
infidel Moor and the defiant noblemen.

So it was that a combination of forces, all unconsciously working hand in hand, secured the establishment of the inquisition for
Spain. Intense national pride made all dissident elements superflu-
ous and even injurious to the ideal of complete national unity. Toward the ambition of creating a unified Spain, the Church brought
its missionary zeal of converting thousands to the dominant faith.
It was these, in turn, who created the serious problem of heresy.
The Church, reflecting the feelings of the people, was aroused when
it became evident that the quondam Jews still held important posts
and were increasing their power by virtue of their privileges as
Christians. The economic motive added fuel to the flames of hatred, now transformed from a religious into a racial hatred of the
Jews, both converted and unconverted. These forces, added to the
ambitions of the sovereigns in creating a strong, centralized authority, assured the establishment of the inquisition for Spain.

Whatever finally determined the sovereigns to solicit a charter from Pope Sixtus for an inquisition just at the time they did,
cannot be stated with certainty. However, due to a suspicious prox-
imity in dates, it may be that the "Judaic celebration on Good Friday, 1478" by the Conversos of Seville, where the monarchs chanced
to be, supplied the immediate reason for the inquisition. The Papal
Bull establishing it bears the date of November 1, 1478.[132]

131 Some scholars believe that Ferdinand, like Isabella, took a great delight and interest in the inquisition out of religious motives Ferdinand was, to be sure, its guard-
ian-angel! Cf David S Schaff, *History of the Christian Church*, (New York,
1910), V, 541.
132 Doubtless this was the celebration of Passover—the *Seder* on March 18, 1478.

The Pope hesitated in granting the Bull because it placed in the Spanish crown all control over the inquisition. The Bull gave power of appointment and dismissal of the inquisition heads to the crown, a power heretofore exclusively enjoyed by the Pope. The Spanish crown, jealous of its authority, was interested in establishing the inquisition as a national institution, subject to it for its powers and privileges.[133] Five years after the Pope granted the Bull establishing the Spanish Inquisition, he gave the sovereigns his permission to create a fifth council of state whose exclusive business it was to supervise the inquisition. This decisively cut off any Papal interference in the operations of the Spanish Inquisition. The Council of the Inquisition was named *Consejo de la Suprema y General Inquisición* (more often called simply the *Suprema*). A post unknown in the Medieval Inquisition—the inquisitor-general—was created to be the active head of the Spanish Inquisition. Thus the new inquisition in Spain, at its very foundation, was organized as a royal council, and, like the other councils, completely dominated by the crown, to which it was alone responsible. It became a national institution reflecting the zeal and ambition of its organizers.[134]

(The *Seder* is the meal and service which takes place, traditionally, the first two evenings of Passover) Roth, p. 40; Turberville, *The Span. Inq.*, p. 41. Lea (*Spain*, I, 156) gives the date as March 28, 1478.

[133] Already somewhat earlier there had arisen some friction between the crown and the Papacy in the matter of nominating bishops to the territories conquered from the Moors The former demanded full power to nominate them, and finally gained a victory over the Papacy Hume, *Spain, Its Greatness and Decay*, p. 15.

[134] For a discussion of the independent inquisition set up by Spain, see Lea, *Spain*, I, 172ff ; Madariaga, *Spain*, p 41ff , Roth, p 40ff ; Turberville, *The Span. Inq.*, pp. 22, 52ff. Because of the peculiar set-up of the Spanish Inquisition, the eminent Catholic historian, Lord Acton (*Correspondence*, I, chapter XV, in his review of "A History of the Inquisition of the Middle Ages," by Henry Charles Lea, appearing in the *English Historical Review*, 1888) believed that "the later (Spanish) Inquisition . . . is not so much a prolongation or a revival as a new creation . . ." (p 555). Yet Lord Acton never denied that its practice and procedure sprang directly from the Medieval Inquisition of which it was, by that token, heir. The sovereigns were jealous of their power and demanded that the inquisition be free from Rome How this worked to the detriment of many prominent Spaniards is perhaps best illustrated by the case of Villanueva, Secretary of State for Aragon under Philip IV (1605-65). The Pope's two briefs ordering Villanueva to be tried in Rome were disregarded. Only after some years, when the case had become something of a "cause célèbre" in Europe, the Pope refused to be put off, but by the time the papers of the case reached him, Villanueva had died. The trial stretched over thirty-two years! (Lea, *Spain*, II, 133ff., Turberville, *The Span. Inq ,* p. 65ff.) Neither did the inquisition stop at the highest ecclesiasts, indicative of its defiance of Rome This is best illustrated by the case of Bartholome de Carranza, Archbishop of Toledo, who had gained the ill-will of Inquisitor-General Valdés The case clearly was one to save the skin of the Inquisitor-General, who raised the scare of Protestantism in Spain, and accused Carranza of heresy! Though a close friend of King Philip II, and a well-known figure in Europe, Carranza was tried as a Protestant heretic, and, so powerful was the inquisition, that it ignored the protests of the Council of Trent (1562-3) and the anathemas of the Pope. The Pope demanded that Carranza be tried in Rome, yet he seemed

Having traced briefly the background and the forces which brought the inquisition to Spain, we now turn to the contribution which this book hopes to make to the general subject of the inquisition. One of the sixteen tribunals[135] established by the Spanish Inquisition was that of Majorca, in the island's chief city of Palma. Its function was to protect Catholicism by bringing to trial all heretics throughout the Balearic Isles, which, together with Majorca, included Minorca, Ibiza, and a few sparsely inhabited rock-bound isles nearby.

The remainder of this book deals with the activities of the Majorcan Inquisition in relation to the Conversos—to those Jews who embraced Christianity, and to their descendants. It is a study based upon a first-hand and an extensive examination of a large number of original documents, in the form of inquisitorial processes and manuscripts which, for the most part, are being revealed to the public for the first time.[136]

---

powerless against Philip, who refused to yield. Finally the latter yielded, and Carranza was sent to Rome. But the tactics of the Spanish Court and the Inquisition caused interminable delays, and finally a third Pope came into the celebrated case After seventeen years had passed since the trial had begun, Carranza was condemned by the Pope to certain penances That he was not set free was a surprise to all Europe. But the condemnation under Pope Gregory XIII was doubtless the result of pressure brought to bear from Spain There are some grounds for the suspicion that Carranza was put out of the way, as an impediment to Spanish policy. Clearly, it was a triumph for the inquisition. Lea, *Spain,* II, 46ff.; Turberville, *The Span. Inq.,* pp. 60-5.

[135] Barcelona, Canary Islands, Cordova, Cuenca, Granada, Logroño, Llerena, Madrid, Majorca, Murcia, Santiago, Saragossa, Seville, Toledo, Valencia and Valladolid. (For other tribunals established during the long life of the inquisition in Spain, see Lea, *Spain,* I, 541-55).

[136] In his researches, the author found a considerable number of documents dealing with other phases of the Majorcan Inquisition's activities. They may be published at some future time.

CHAPTER II

AN EPOCH IN THE MAJORCAN INQUISITION

According to an anonymous manuscript entitled: "Origin of the Inquisition of Majorca," in the National Library of Spain, at Madrid, the inquisition began operations in Majorca in 1232.[1] Thus it was established a year prior to the foundation of the Medieval Inquisition (1233).[2] Its early beginnings in Majorca are attributable to Raymond de Peñaforte, the Aragonese Dominican, who prevailed upon Pope Gregory to appoint inquisitors for Aragon.[3] Majorca, being at the time a part of Aragon, benefitted by the Pope's action, for it was served by the inquisitors who served Aragon. In 1262, when the kingdom of Majorca was formed out of the Balearic Isles, Cerdagne and Roussillon,[4] a separate tribunal of the inquisition was organized for the newly constituted kingdom. Yet the island of Majorca had no special tribunal of its own; all its business was transacted through a commission receiving delegated powers from the heads of the inquisition residing in Cerdagne and Roussillon.[5] This condition existed for many years despite the Majorcans' urgent pleas for the need of a special inquisitor

---

1 *Apuntes para la historia General del Santo Oficio de Mallorca*, (Cuerpo de Manuscritos, BN), (hereafter · *Apuntes*), apparently served as the original basis for the *Origen de la Inquisición de Mallorca* (also in the Cuerpo de Manuscritos, BN). The title "Apuntes" (Notes) indicates that it was the framework for the "Origen," which is also the more comprehensive title So far as the author is aware, these original works are being quoted for the first time, heretofore having been unknown The date (1232), marking the beginning of the inquisition in Aragon, is based upon the Bull *Declinante,* issued by Pope Gregory IX, which authorized the search for heretics The anonymous author doubtless knew of this Bull when he fixed the beginning of the Inquisition of Majorca as 1232. Cf. Lea, *Middle Ages,* II, 163

2 Cf. *supra,* pp 11-13 Turberville, *The Span. Inq.,* p. 8.

3 The inquisitors were already active as early as May 26, 1232, as a result of Peñaforte's petition Lord Acton (*Correspondence,* p 555) believes Peñaforte's influence brought about the organization of the inquisition, attributed to Pope Gregory IX. As the leading Dominican of his day, he was doubtless responsible for the place his Order had in the execution of the inquisition. Cf. Lea, *Middle Ages,* I, 302; *Encyclopedia Britannica,* XII, 381; also Maycock, *The Inquisition from its Establishment to the Great Schism,* p. 227.

4 *Cerdagne:* (in the Pyrenees) a county in southwest France and northwest Spain, its territory now divided between the French department of Pyrénées Orientales, and the Spanish provinces of Gerona and Lerida *Roussillon·* (adjacent to, east and somewhat north of Cerdagne, in the Pyrenees) a county in southwest France, now part of the department Pyrénées Orientales

5 *Historia General del Reino de Mallorca* (hereafter · *Hist. Gen*), III, 360; cf Lea, *Middle Ages,* II, 177. Even from its organization in 1232, the heads of the tribunal governing Majorca lived in Cerdagne and Roussillon, so that no change in the inquisition was effected with the organization of the new Kingdom of Majorca.

of their own to combat the scandalous heresies rampant on the island.[6]

We have no record of any inquisitor functioning in Majorca during the first century of the inquisition. The earliest known inquisitor exercising his office in Majorca was the Friar Ramon Durfort, who was already serving in 1332, and who continued in office until 1343.[7] We have a record of four more Dominicans (Jaime Domingo, Pedro Rippe, Pedro Tur and Bernardo Pages), serving the inquisitor's office in Majorca until 1413, when an independent tribunal was finally set up to function exclusively for Majorca. The schismatic-Pope Benedict XIII was responsible for this change, appointing Guillermo Sagarra as the first inquisitor for the independent Majorcan tribunal.[8]

From that time until the new inquisition was founded in Majorca in 1488, seven inquisitors followed Inquisitor Sagarra.[9] Doubtless the most outstanding of them was Antonio Murta (1420-1436), who took an important part in the final conversion of the Jews of Majorca in 1435.[10] In the decade before the new inquisition was established on the island, the Inquisitors Merola and Garcías[11] had reconciled sixteen Jewish heretics.[12]

The purpose of the inquisition in Majorca, as elsewhere in

---

[6] Perhaps of equal importance with the heresies they complained of as reason for the need of an exclusive inquisitor for the island, was the pride and independence of the Majorcans, who rebelled at any outside jurisdiction. They refused, for example, to appear on the mainland to be tried, at the request of the queen-regent, and Alfonso V agreed (1439) that this old privilege could not be set aside. Lea, *Spain*, I, 266, *Hist. Gen* III, 360. The ruler of the island was much concerned at this time with reducing to vassalage some of the petty kings and lords in North Africa, and could not trouble himself with other matters. Merriman, I, 305

[7] Paramo, *De Origine . . . Inquisitionis*, lib II, tit. 11. Lea, *Middle Ages*, II, 177. I have compiled a list of the Inquisitors of the Majorcan Tribunal, from various sources · Appendix I

[8] *Hist. Gen* I, 101-2; III, 361-2. This decree was promulgated March 18, 1413, when Benedict was attending the famous Disputation of Tortosa, in which Geronimo de Santa Fé engaged some of the leading rabbis of Spain in an effort to prove the errors of Judaism, and thereby gain converts for Christianity. Cf. Lindo, *The History of the Jews of Spain and Portugal*, pp 209-15; Graetz IV, 209ff.

[9] See Appendix I.

[10] *Hist. Gen.* II, 653. See *below* p 43, note 16

[11] Lea (*Spain*, I, 266), following only the text of *Hist Gen.* (III, 362) without apparently consulting the notes in volume II of the same work added by later editors (among them the noted historian Bover), makes no mention of Friar Rafael Garcias, elected inquisitor in 1484 (*Ibid.*, II, 653). Lea suspected that Inquisitor Merola "as inert as his brethren elsewhere . . . was probably stimulated to greater energy by the prospect of removal, for in 1487 the number (of reconciliations) rose to eight." Merola had been superseded by Garcías, and it was under Garcías that the activity increased.

[12] Heretics, i. e, accused of having reverted back to their former faith of Judaism In this study we are calling them simply Conversos The sixteen were reconciled four in 1478, one in 1482, two in 1485, eight in 1487. AHN *Rel. de Causas de Fe*, libro 1, 866, fols 52, 52v.

Spain, was to solve the problems arising out of the emergence of the class of new-Christians or Conversos.[18] The Conversos arose in Majorca as a result of the riots of 1391,[14] the preaching mission of St. Vincent Ferrer (1413-1414),[15] and the calamity of 1435, which marked the official end of Judaism on the island.[16] Many

---

[18] Stringent laws were decreed against Jews, making ready converts out of those who were anxious to avoid these restrictive, anti-Jewish laws. [For some of this legislation, see Kayserling, *Die Juden in Navarra, den Baskenlandern und auf den Balearen*, (hereafter Kayserling), p 161ff, cf *Tratado del Origen de los Smagogas, y Judios de esta Isla de Mallorca*, etc, (hereafter. *Tratado.*), I, cap. 10]. Priests were apparently overly-anxious to take advantage of the few willing to be converted, for the Jewish community of Majorca asked immunity of the ruler (James II) from the proselytizing zeal of the clergy, and a decree (dated April 4, 1305) forbade any priest from entering the Jewish quarter upon any pretext whatever, unless accompanied by an officer. (The text of the decree is to be found in Villanueva, XXI, 165ff.; cf *Tratado*, I, cap 15)

[14] The riots broke out in Palma August 2, 1391 Originally being a struggle between the peasants and the city-folk, which provided causes for many revolts in Majorca, it finally spent its fury upon the Jews Merriman (I, 498ff.) and Altamira (*A History of Spanish Civilization*, p 101) provide good discussions of these social wars. (Cf. Graetz, IV, 171; Kayserling, p 164, also Quadrado's *Forenses y Ciudadanos*) Some 300 Jews were killed as a result of the riots. For an excellent description of the Jewish quarter in Palma in 1391, see Quadrado's "La Juderia de la Capital de Mallorca en 1391," *BAH*, IX, 1886, 294-312. It has recently (1931) been republished in pamphlet form.

[15] It is not insignificant to note that preceding Ferrer's visit to Majorca the oppressive decrees, promulgated by King Ferdinand I of Aragon in 1413, were put into effect. They were copied from the *Ordenamiento de Doña Catalina* of Castile in 1412, and were intended to make the lot of the Jew (as well as of the Moor) almost insufferable Laws of this kind assisted materially the proselytizing efforts of Ferrer. The *Ordenamiento* prescribed wearing of distinguishing badges by Jews on coarsestuff garments; prohibitions against shaving or cutting the hair round, leaving the country, practicing as physician or surgeon, working in any of the numerous trades, fraternizing with Christians in any way and even in selling provisions to Christians. Of greater importance perhaps, was the deprivation of the Jews' own jurisdiction of their courts, long enjoyed by them in Spain; henceforth they were subjected to the civil and criminal jurisdiction of the Christians The twenty articles of the *Ordenamiento* are in Amador de los Rios' *Judios de España*, II, 496ff.; Villanueva, XXII, 51-2 Padre Villanueva made a copy of the *Ordenamiento* for his book out of the copy found in the Archives of the Convent of the Padres Predicadores, in Palma *Ibid*, 258ff; cf Graetz, IV, 202ff; cf also Furio y Sastre, *Memorias para Servir a la Historia Ecclesiastica . . . de Mallorca*, p. 109ff

[16] It was the oft-repeated story that brought tragedy to the Jews of Majorca · a story current throughout Europe (Prescott, *Ferdinand and Isabella*, I, 267); that the celebration of Passover demanded the Jews show their contempt for Christianity by desecrating its holy symbols, sacrificing Christian children, and using their blood for the Passover ceremony (a fiction which still holds sway in some dark corners of the modern world, but which a number of Christian scholars, including Hermann Strack, in his book, *The Jew and Human Sacrifice*, London, 1909, conclusively disproved), as well as rehearsing the crucifixion upon some unfortunate. In Majorca in 1435, the Mohammedan servant of a Jew was alleged to have been inflicted with all the torture and pain of "the passion" by the Jewish community The rabbis and leaders of the Jews were arrested by the bishop, and cast into prison. The governor demanded their transfer to his jurisdiction. The priests thereupon took quick advantage of the situation, preaching that the Jews would surely find immunity at the governor's hands. Finally, a court composed of Dominicans and Franciscans, employing torture (the means in current use for extracting confessions) condemned the confessed-perpetrators to death. It was in these proceedings that the Inquisitor Antonio Murta played an important part.

Jews fled from the island after the events of 1391, to be followed
by more fugitives after the riots of 1435. For even after the Jewish
community in Majorca ceased to exist officially,[17] some of the recent
converts managed to escape, despite the law of 1413 prohibiting
flight.[18] There can be no doubt, therefore, that among the many
who accepted Christianity some thought it wiser to yield to the
storm, and accept baptism, then to watch for their opportunity to
flee from the island and re-embrace their former faith.[19]

_____

(Graetz, IV, 246-7, *Hist Gen*. II, 653, also *supra*, p 42) Graetz writes that one
of the Jews, Astruc Sibili, came forward to denounce the leaders of the crime,
which he admitted as having actually taken place Perhaps to gain immunity for
himself, or because he may have been at odds with some of the leaders, and using
this opportunity for revenge, he accused the whole community as accomplices in the
horrible crime (He was also condemned) *Judios de España* (III. 85) does not
mention this incident, following Padre Garau, *La Fee Triunfante*, p. 102ff,
Hist Gen, III, 384ff., and *Cronicon Mayoricense*, (hereafter Cronicon), p 158.
The name Astruc Sibili, in these accounts, occurs as one of the condemned rabbis
The Jews fled to the hills, but were promptly apprehended Their flight was construed as guilt. Finally, the condemned Jews accepted baptism, and by so doing,
their sentences of burning at the stake were commuted to hanging. The Jewish
community followed their leaders, and accepted baptism; thus the entire community of some 200 souls becoming converted (Graetz, IV, 247) The people were
deeply touched by this show of piety and (so fickle is the public) changed its attitude toward their new brothers-in-the-faith, and demanded that the condemned
Jews be freed! It was a victory for the faith, and the priests encouraged the people
in demanding a pardon for the condemned men The governor finally yielded, and
a great celebration marked the official close of the Jewish community of Majorca,
which had existed for over a thousand years. (In addition to the references mentioned, see Zimmels, *Die Marranen in der Rabbinischen Literatur,* pp 84, 94-5)
In honor of this conversion, the large candelabra of the Jewish synagogue was
presented to the Cathedral in Palma, where it may still be seen, over the main altar.
Cronicon, p 158; Villanueva, XXI, 118-9 In the Cathedral's treasury may be
seen the "Torah Crowns," used in synagogues, but now embellishing the staffs carried in solemn procession in the Cathedral Cf the author's article in *B'nai B'rith
Magazine*, March, 1934

[17] On March, 10, 1436 a decree was promulgated forbidding the exercise of Judaism
on the island, as well as the establishment of a synagogue, or the sojourning of
Jews on the island for a period not to exceed fifteen days, under penalty of confiscation of property. In Majorca, Judaism was declared illegal fifty-six years
earlier than on the mainland. 'The island-chroniclers boast that the Jews of Majorca as a community were the first in all of Spain to be converted to Christianity Cronicon, p 158; Colin Campbell, tr. of *Hist Gen* in abbreviated form. *The
Ancient and Modern History of the Balearick Islands,* p 254

[18] The sixteenth provision of the Law of March 20, 1413 (the flight of so many following the riots of 1391 made this law necessary) prohibited any Converso from
leaving Majorca. *Tratado,* I, cap. 22. See also Fajarnés, "Emigracion de los judios
y conversos de Mallorca después de la matanza del Call," *BSAL*, VIII, 1899-1900,
55-7.

[19] Many, like Simon ben Zemah Duran (1361-1444), who later became one of the
foremost rabbinical authorities of his day, fled with his father from Majorca to
Algiers after the riots of 1391 Graetz, IV, 199 (He is the author of *Responsa of
Rabbi Simon Ben Zemah Duran Sefer Hatashbetz,* a collection of questions
placed before him by Jews from all parts of the world, and his replies thereto
based upon Jewish law. This kind of literature is rich in hints and suggestions of
the social, religious and economic life of the Jews in the period in which it was written. See Epstein, *The Responsa of Rabbi Simon B Zemah Duran as a Source
of the History of the Jews in North Africa*). Unlike Duran, a great number of Jews
allowed themselves first to be converted, and then they tried to escape, just as

Due to the lack of exact information, and to the constant migrations, it is difficult to estimate with certainty the number of Conversos who remained on the island. St. Vincent Ferrer has been credited with converting more than 20,000 Jews in Majorca.[20] This figure is patently an exaggeration.[21] The Jewish historian, Professor Graetz, estimated that two-hundred persons, comprising the entire community, were converted to Christianity when Judaism officially ceased to exist on the island (1435).[22] Those Conversos originating from the earlier conversions of 1414-15 doubtless increases the figure suggested by Graetz. However, somewhere between the two estimates lay the truth. When the early records of the new inquisition are examined, it is found that five-hundred and sixty Conversos were reconciled during the first three years of the inquisition's operations.[23] Obviously there were more Conversos in Majorca than the number reconciled. Inadequate as they are, in view of so little exact information, we must be satisfied with these intimations of the number of Conversos in Majorca when the inquisition began its work. It was with these and their offspring, for the most part, that the inquisition busied itself.

The new inquisition began its operations on the island with a clean slate in 1488 when two inquisitors were appointed to replace

---

there were a considerable number who accepted baptism because it was the easier way out of a difficult situation, or because they were bribed into doing so. (See Llabres, "La Conversion de los Judios Mallorquines en 1391," *BAH*, XL, 1902, 152-4: cf *supra*, p 36). The tendency to make martyrs out of *all* Jews in this period is patently an historical error, and cannot be substantiated in every instance by facts, for the Jews were human beings, subject to the noblest as well as to the lowest impulses. The rabbis invariably welcomed back into the Jewish fold the *Anusim* (i e, those *forced* into conversion) The degree of *force* entered largely into the discussions. Was deprivation of property and food tantamount to actual physical force, and death the only alternative in case of refusal? Duran, an eye-witness to what Jews had endured in Majorca, was disposed to a liberal interpretation He argued that the converts should not be deprived of their rights as Jews, unless their *voluntary* apostasy was verified and established. Duran's contemporary, Isaac ben Sheshet, would admit them into the Jewish fold only when they presented *proof* of their strict adherence to Judaism; a most difficult matter under the circumstances of those times *Responsa of Rabbi Isaac Ben Sheshet Barfat,* questions 4, 5, 11, 12; cf Epstein, *op. cit.,* p 30, note 46 Duran lavished his attention upon his brother-Jews in Majorca, before 1435, urging them to remain true to Judaism by disassociating themselves from the Conversos, exhorting them to observe the laws of equity as well as the dietary laws *Responsa of Rabbi Simon Ben Zemah Duran Sefer Hatashbetz,* p 14, parag 44, p 28b, parag. 227

20 *Hist. Gen*, III, 390
21 Graetz (IV, 206) writes that "Ferrer's mission to the *Jews of Castile and Aragon* is said to have resulted in not less than 20,500 forced baptisms" (Italics mine). In the 17th century Palma had 6,000 inhabitants (AHN *Processos de Competencias,* legajo 1719, 11, fol. 2ff) In the 18th century *Censo Español* (Conde de Florida-blanca, Imprenta Real, 1787), Palma had a population of 57,024 persons.
22 Graetz, IV, 247, *supra*, note 16.
23 That number is not considerably decreased by the double reconciliations which occurred in some instances. AHN *Rel. de Causas de Fe,* libro 1, 866, fols. 1-91v

the former one in office.[24] They began their work inauspiciously, for they reconciled, with the customary trial-procedure, only four Conversos.[25] But an Edict of Grace, issued immediately upon their assumption of office and in effect for two years, was most efficacious. It brought three-hundred and thirty-seven Conversos to the inquisition pleading to be forgiven for their errors, and asking to be reconciled to the Church.[26] The Edict of Grace placed in the hands of the inquisition names of other heretics, denounced by the newly-reconciled as their accomplices. That the inquisition made good use of this information we may judge from its extensive lists of reconciliations and relaxations.[27]

In the year 1489 the inquisition relaxed fifty-three Conversos to the secular arm,[28] an early harvest of denunciations.[29] All of the relaxed, save five, were fugitives from the island, and accordingly were burned in effigy. Their flight was sufficient evidence of their guilt, and should they ever have been seized, their bodies would have been forfeited, in the same way as their effigies had already been burned.[30] We have a record of only one Converso unfortunate enough to meet her fate in this way: relaxed in effigy on October 28,

---

[24] Pedro Perez de Munebrega and Sancho Martin were the inquisitors appointed with the inauguration of the new inquisition Appendix I.

[25] Lea (*Spain*, I, 267) records sixteen reconciliations My documents record only four · two August 13th, and two August 16th I think Lea has erred in this instance, for I have looked over the documents from which he derived his information (at the Henry Charles Lea Library, University of Pennsylvania), and I can discover only four reconciliations (through customary trial-procedure, in contrast to those reconciled through Edicts of Grace) for 1488 Cf. AHN *Rel. de Causas de Fe*, libro 1, 866, fol. 52.

[26] *Ibid.*, fols. 1-32; Amador de los Rios (*Judios de España*, III, 252, note 1) quoting Arnaldo Albertí (*De hereticis*, lib. VI, quest. 12a) writes that the Edict of Grace was effective for two years Only after its expiration does Amador de los Rios place the *real* beginning of the operations of the inquisition. Yet, as a matter of fact, the commonly accepted procedure was for the inquisitors to issue an Edict of Grace *immediately upon assuming their office.* Cf. *supra*, p. 14ff Amador de los Rios adds that the number of reconciliations in Majorca was equal almost to those in Castile!

[27] That the Edicts of Grace were effective may be assumed from the request of the Conversos that they be discontinued, because they brought them so much harm through the many denunciations which filled the prisons of the inquisition Lea, *Spain*, III, 274.

[28] A compilation of the number of Conversos (as well as others) reconciled and relaxed may be found in Appendix III. (For the complete lists of reconciliations and relaxations, faithful transcriptions of the documents of the Majorcan Inquisition, see Appendix II)

[29] AHN *Rel de Causas de Fe*, libro 1, 866, fols. 92-4v.

[30] Antonio Vidal was the first fugitive to be burned in effigy under the jurisdiction of the new inquisition. Together with his parents, he had been apprehended by the inquisition once before. It appeared that escape was the choice of the whole family. Antonio's father was also burned in effigy at the auto de fe of May 11, 1493 *Ibid.*, fols. 92, 97v; cf. also Jacobs, *An Inquiry into the Sources of the History of the Jews in Spain*, p. 124, Item 1682.

1489, she was burned in person the following May.[31] She was not
the first to be relaxed in person by orders of the inquisition, however. A poor tailor from Valencia has that doubtful distinction:
he was burned in person on July 11, 1489.[32] He was one of the
five mentioned above who was not tried as a fugitive; three in addition to him were relaxed in person, and the fifth, a dead heretic,
was exhumed and her bones cremated with her effigy.[33]

In its early years the new inquisition concerned itself a great
deal with condemning fugitive heretics. Their trials produced the
confiscations of their property. Here, as with the processes against
the dead, the descendants were naturally disturbed, for the convictions which invariably resulted robbed them of their means. To
meet this contingency, there arose the expedient of compositions,
approved by the crown, which, for a sum, insured the descendants
against confiscation of the property of an absent or dead heretic.[34]

In addition to fifty-three relaxations, the year 1489 brought
ten reconciliations, also a result of the denunciations made by those
reconciled under the Edict of Grace.[35] In the midst of all this activity, the inquisitors were removed—for which action no reasons
have been given[36]—and a native Majorcan (Juan Ramon) was put
in their place in 1489.[37] We find that he was also supplanted in a
short time, for the following year the inquisition was headed by
Juan de Astorga.[38]

It was under Inquisitor de Astorga that eighty-six additional
Conversos were reconciled on March 26, 1490, under the terms of
the Edict of Grace issued two years previously.[39] In all, four-hun-

---

31 Aldonza, the wife of Matheo Funcar. AHN *Rel. de Causas de Fe,* libro 1, 866, fol. 93v.
32 Gabriel Llop *Ibid.,* fol. 92.
33 Graciosa, the wife of Guillermo Vives. *Ibid.,* fol. 92v
34 Lea, *Spain,* I, 236, 267-8 In Alberti's report of the "Time of Mercy" in 1490 (see *below* p 49, note 43), the device of "compositions" was referred to. It seems that it was no new method even then!
35 AHN *Rel de Causas de Fe,* libro 1, 866, fols. 53, 53v.
36 Perhaps because they were so active! The Conversos may have complained, and they may have been able to effect a change—a change which, as we shall see, was not to their advantage. Another plausible conjecture in explaining the change may be in the reaction of a strongly individualistic people to an institution whose heads were "foreign." (Cf *supra* p. 42, note 6) The inquisitors accordingly were replaced by a native Majorcan, in an effort to cater to local sentiment
37 See Appendix I
38 *Ibid.*
39 There were eighty-seven reconciliations in all, under this date; one of them was that of Brianda, a Moorish slave, the first non-Converso to be reconciled in the new inquisition AHN *Rel. de Causas de Fe,* libro 1, 866, fols. 32-9v. Lea (*Spain,* I, 267) estimated ninety-six reconciliations, a number which my records do not confirm

dred and twenty-four Conversos came forward to be reconciled under the advantageous terms offered by the Edict of Grace. These
figures point conclusively to the fact that the Conversos themselves
believed they were no longer immune from the new inquisition.
Nor could they ignore it, as they had ignored the earlier tribunal.
That is why they pressed forward to make the best of the difficult
situation in which they found themselves. Denunciations from
those reconciled under the Edict of Grace continued, for in the
same year (1490), fifty-six Conversos were reconciled through
customary trial-procedure,[40] while thirty-six were relaxed, eighteen
in person.[41]

It is to be observed that in 1490 there were forty-six more
reconciliations through customary trial-procedure than in the
previous year. This increase is significant, for it indicates that the
Conversos had begun to realize that voluntary self-accusation,
through the Edict of Grace, placed them in a precarious situation
by making them liable for the death penalty in case of relapse. The
figures are eloquent of the chances some of the Conversos were
willing to take: they would risk the harsher penalties in the customary trial-procedure on the chance that they might escape arrest,
rather than voluntarily indict themselves and denounce others
through the Edict of Grace.[42]

It was also in Inquisitor de Astorga's régime that the Edict of
Grace issued in 1488 had expired. Apparently impressed by its
results he sought to promulgate another one. Accordingly he issued
the *Tempus Gratie* (Time of Mercy), with the special permission
of the king and the inquisitor-general, which allowed heretics to become reconciled "with a moderate pecuniary fine to redeem their

---

[40] AHN *Rel de Causas de Fe*. libro 1, 866, fols 53v-7. In addition to these Conversos, one Miguel Jorda, an Englishman, was reconciled for "Lutheran heresy"(!),
bringing the total reconciliations up to fifty-seven. How there could have been
Lutherans before Lutheranism was born is a problem which only the inquisitors can settle! The first case of Lutheranism in any tribunal of the Spanish Inquisition was that of Archbishop Carranza (cf. *supra* p 39, note 134) which dragged on for years after 1559. The chances are that the error in our records comes
from the fact that they were copied from the original case-records by scribes just
when the "Lutheran heresy" was making itself felt, and they probably ascribed
to it any case when the reason for its prosecution was difficult to establish. Cf.
Lea, *Spain*, III, 411ff.

[41] AHN *Rel. de Causas de Fe*, libro 1, 866, fols. 94v-6. Among them was Aldonza,
the wife of Matheo Funcar, already referred to (*supra* p. 47, note 31) as having
been relaxed in effigy October 28, 1489 and in person May 31, 1490. Thus the
actual number of *new* relaxations for the year was thirty-five

[42] "The confessions under the Edicts of Grace are pitiful reading," Lea (*Spain*, II,
459) writes. The blame for heresy was invariably transferred to the shoulders of
others—husbands, wives, mothers, fathers, and children were not excluded. "The
Edict of Grace was of little benefit to the New Christians," Lea (*Ibid.*, p. 460)
avers, but "it was of the utmost service to the Inquisition."

lawfully confiscated property." Under terms of the Edict of Grace, heretics were reconciled without confiscation of property. Under the special consideration extended through the Time of Mercy, they were given the opportunity to save their property by a fine—property which should have been "lawfully confiscated" since they had not confessed in the first Edict of Grace.[43] In our records, the Time of Mercy is nevertheless referred to simply as the second Edict of Grace.[44]

That there was a sincere "begging for pardon" by the heretics is amply proved by the great number of reconciliations made during the time of the second Edict of Grace (1491-1493).[45] Four-hundred and forty-six were reconciled under the Edict's terms,[46] all save one[47] being Conversos. It must be pointed out that these were not all new reconciliations. Of the four-hundred and forty-six, only one-hundred and thirty-six were reconciled for the first time.[48] The remainder, three-hundred and ten, had already been reconciled under the first Edict of Grace. They had relapsed into their old heresies—their desire for reconciliation anew was evidence of that —yet they were dealt with kindly and readmitted as a token of special favor and mercy. Relapse, according to the laws of the inquisition, merited death. Had it taken full advantage of its own power, the inquisition might have brought death upon at least these three-hundred and ten who had relapsed. That it did not, is some evidence of the inquisition's mercy. When, therefore, the inquisition is accused of a total lack of humaneness, some incidents—this is one among many—can be pointed to as examples of its compassion.[49]

---

[43] Arnaldo Albertí (1480-1545) is the source of this information. *Repititio Nova*, fol. cxlii, 4ff. (This is a rare book I examined it in the Henry Charles Lea Library, University of Pennsylvania)

[44] AHN *Rel. de Causas de Fe,* libro 1, 866, fol. 2.

[45] Cf. Lea, *Spain,* I, 267 There were no reconciliations at all made through the regular trial-procedure in 1491 (AHN *Rel de Causas de Fe,* libro 1, 866, fol. 57), and only four in 1492, one of whom was a Moorish slave, the second Mohammedan-heretic in the annals of the new inquisition of Majorca Many more cases of Mohammedan-heresy were destined to come before the inquisition in the following years, as a result of the forcible conversion of the Moors to Christianity in Cordova, Granada, and Valencia. Cf Geddes, *History of Expulsion of the Moriscos,* Bover, *Biblioteca de Escritores Baleares,* I, 9-13, and Lea, *The Moriscos of Spain,* pp 82-110.

[46] AHN *Rel. de Causas de, Fe,* libro 1, 866, fols. 2-48 Cf. Lea (*Spain* I, 267) and Cronicon (p. 194) who count 424 reconciliations. My records give the higher figure.

[47] Brianda, the slave See *supra,* note 45

[48] Really 135 Conversos, when Brianda is omitted. This includes eighty-four on July 30, 1491, and one on October 13, 1492. AHN *Rel de Causas de Fe,* libro, 1, 866, fols. 39v-48. Cf. Lea, *Spain,* I, 267, and Adler, p. 135

[49] "The canons pardoned the heretic but once," Lea (*Spain,* III, 48) writes, and "if after reconciliation he was guilty of reincidence, there was no mercy for him on

Yet there will be some who will insist that the Conversos' money, coming into the inquisition's coffers as a result of this special Time of Mercy, was the real reason for the inquisition's apparent mercy.[50] Here, again, the inquisition had every right, according to its laws, to confiscate the entire property of the heretics. That it chose to levy a fine upon the property and not claim all of it as its own, is another example of its compassion.

Juan de Astorga, who exercised his office so diligently, was replaced by Gomez de Cienfuegos,[51] and he in turn by Pedro Gual, a native Majorcan, in 1493.[52] With the latter, the reconciliations under the two Edicts of Grace were brought to a close. The inquisition, from his time on, was destined to continue without the support of Edicts of Grace. From his time, it may be said, the inquisition was firmly established in Majorca; its prosecutions resulting chiefly from the abundant denunciations made by those already reconciled. On May 11, 1493, forty-seven Conversos were burned in effigy and four in person, at what was one of the most elaborate autos de fe yet arranged by the inquisition on the island.[53] In addition to these relaxations, two were reconciled at the same time.[54] Save for two reconciliations in the following year (1494),[55] Inquisitor Gual apparently had finished his work, for in 1495 he was replaced by Nuño de Villalobos, who remained at the helm of the inquisition for a period of five years.[56] During his time one-hun-

---

earth" .   but "it should be said that the Spanish Inquisition did not always enforce this cruel precept" Lea's testimony in this matter is final (he cannot be judged as a partisan of the inquisition). He continues to write· "In the later periods second reconciliations were by no means infrequent, and 'even in the earlier time, men sometimes shrank from the holocausts which the strict enforcement of the rule would have caused   " Cf also Adler, p 99 Not only were there second reconciliations in Majorca, there is a case of third reconciliation! (See *supra* p 28, chapter I, note 96).

[50] The pecuniary results amounted to 1500 gold ducats. Cronicon, p. 194 (If we take the ducat to be worth about $2.28, the total fines were about $3,420)

[51] Appendix I

[52] *Ibid.* The temper of the Majorcans must have made it difficult for others than natives to head the tribunal, and an increasing number of native Majorcans led the inquisition as time went on (Cf. *supra* p 42, note 6)

[53] AHN *Rel. de Causas de Fe*, libro 1, 866, fols 96v-8v.

[54] *Ibid ,* fols 57, 57v Among the relaxed occurs the name Juan Alexandre Adret, "Medico" (physician) ; among the reconciled the name Juan Allesandre Adret, "Jurista" (jurist) The name Adret was not an uncommon one, it would not be unusual for two men to bear the same name. Adret was the family name of the famous Rabbi of Barcelona, Solomon ben Abraham ben Adret ("Rashbah," 1245-1310). Cf Graetz, III, 618ff

[55] AHN *Rel de Causas de Fe,* libro 1, 866, fol 57v One of the two was a native of Castile During 1493 a devastating plague ravaged the island, the fifth of its kind recorded (See the report of the plague by the Chronicler Terrassa, Cronicon, p. 195).

[56] Appendix I.

dred and thirty Conversos were tried, ten of whom were reconciled and one-hundred and twenty were relaxed.[57] Of this number, only one person was actually sent to the stake,[58] one was disinterred and her bones cast to the flames,[59] and the remaining were burned in effigy. As late as the close of the fifteenth century, therefore, after the island inquisition had been functioning for twelve years, the numbers of relaxations in effigy continued to grow. That is indicative of the great numbers of Conversos who had managed somehow to effect their escape from the island, despite threats of laws and dire consequences to follow if the inquisition apprehended them.

From the inquisition's establishment in Majorca (1488) until the end of the fifteenth century (exclusive of the Conversos reconciled under the Edicts of Grace), three-hundred and forty-six cases had come before it, resulting in two-hundred and fifty-seven relaxations and eighty-nine reconciliations. That the inquisition's work was overwhelmingly concerned with Conversos may be seen from the fact that during the same period only four other cases came under its purview. Although the majority of the relaxations were executed in effigy (the accused were fugitives), the confiscations of their property went on just the same. Apparently these confiscations were lucrative, for not only were the expenses for a host of officials paid from them, but the crown ordered that some of its debts be paid out of their proceeds.[60] The growing income of the island inquisition moved the crown to assign a bonus to its officers, as a token of recognition of their good work.[61] The end of the fifteenth century clearly brought to a close a period of great

---

[57] AHN *Rel. de Causas de Fe,* libro 1, 866, fols 52, 57v-8, 98v-103v. (An example of how the MSS we have at hand can correct many mistakes · Bartolomé Jaume is quoted in Cronicon, p 197, note 1, as having recorded the burning of "la muller den Rafael Tudela" for heresy, in 1500 In reality, Dolça, the wife of Rafael Tudela was burned in the auto de fe of August 6, 1495 AHN *Rel. de Causas de Fe,* libro 1, 866, fol 99).

[58] *Ibid.,* fol. 103v : Beatriz Villanova on January 30, 1499, and with her, at the same time, the only other person committed to the stake (during the five-year régime of Villalobos) was also burned—Antonia Prats. for the charge of "invoking demons." This is not the same person as Antonia Prats (*supra* p 28, chapter I, note 96), for the latter was reconciled for a third time more than ten years after this date (on June 23, 1509).

[59] Berenguer Arnau, on June 14, 1497. AHN *Rel. de Causas de Fe,* libro 1, 866, fol. 100v

[60] King Ferdinand in 1499 ordered the Majorcan tribunal to pay 450 gold ducats to the receiver of the Valencian tribunal, and fifty florins to his favorite nunnery at Calatayud. Lea, *Spain,* I, 268

[61] 3,000 sueldos (ca. $112.00) to the inquisition's receiver, and 100 Majorcan libras (ca. $751 00) to a notary of the tribunal. Moreover, to informers who reported that property liable to confiscation had been concealed, an offer of 50% of the property's value was given. *Ibid.*

activity and efficiency in the island inquisition, which, as we shall see, was destined to be excelled only by its activity in the late seventeenth century.

The year 1500 was a blank year for the inquisition—doubtless because the island was absorbed in the suffering of a widespread famine[62]—for no reconciliations or relaxations were reported.[63] But in the following year the inquisition relaxed in person seven Conversos to the secular arm. For the entire first decade of the sixteenth century, while the results were not so large as the previous decade, the inquisition's records reveal an abundance of relaxations of Conversos. In this ten-year period (1500-1509), one-hundred and six, in all, were dispatched to the flames.[64] This number is less than half that for the period previously discussed (1488-1499), but unlike the relaxations of that period (which with few exceptions were executed in effigy), in this period out of the one-hundred and six relaxations, forty-six were executed in person. While a considerable number of fugitives are still represented by these figures, by this time the inquisition was unmistakably beginning to send living men, and not mere effigies, to the flames. That change was a significant one and continued in the following years. Of the forty-seven Conversos who were reconciled[65] in the same period (1500-1509),[66] two were Portuguese.[67] Four friars succeeded one another as the inquisitors during this decade.[68]

---

[62] So severe was the famine, that days passed when only six ounces of bread was apportioned to each man! Cronicon, p 220

[63] AHN *Rel. de Causas de Fe,* libro 1, 866, fols 58, 103v.

[64] *Ibid.,* fols. 103v-8 None other than Conversos were relaxed! Only in the reconciliations, do we find non-Conversos.

[65] In addition to the reconciled Conversos, two persons (Andrena Tonis and Isabel, the wife of Jayme de San Marti) were reconciled on charges of fautorship of heresy (assisting and abetting Jews and Jewish heresy)—a charge which naturally fell under the jurisdiction of the inquisition *Ibid ,* fol 59v

[66] *Ibid.,* fols. 58-61.

[67] The Portuguese Inquisition was not established until 1536 A great number of Jews were forcibly converted there, under unusual circumstances, in 1497. The Jews, instead of being permitted to depart from Lisbon, as King Manoël had promised, were caught and baptized without respect to their own wishes. Their baptism was accomplished to satisfy the contract giving the daughter of Ferdinand and Isabella in marriage to Manoel, which demanded that there be no Jews in Portugal. Two years after the forcible conversion, a law forbidding Conversos to leave Portugal, without royal consent, was promulgated. Luis Hernández and his wife were among those who managed to get out of Portugal The Majorcan Inquisition reconciled them, and since we have no further record of them, they doubtless lived out their days in peace The standard work on the Portuguese Inquisition is Herculano, *Da Origem e Estabelecimento da Inquisição em Portugal.* See, also, Lea, *Spain,* I, 140ff., Roth, p. 54ff.

[68] Francisco de Oropesa, Guillermo Caséllas [notable for his fight against the followers of Raimon Lull (ca 1235-1315), the island's mystic and missionary], Juan de Loaysa, Juan de Anguera. Appendix I

From 1510 to 1519 relaxations of Conversos increased in number. In this decade one-hundred and twenty were relaxed to the secular arm, only five of whom, it should be observed, were relaxed in person, the remaining one-hundred and sixteen were relaxed in effigy.[69] Forty-nine Conversos were reconciled in this period,[70] during which three inquisitors served as heads of the tribunal.[71]

From 1520 and onward there was a marked decline in the energy and efficiency of the island inquisition. For example, in 1521 and 1522 twenty-nine Conversos were sentenced to relaxation (only one in person[72]), following which for eight years there was not a single relaxation,[73] until 1530, when six effigies were burned.[74] Six more effigies were burned the next year (1531) ;[75] at the same time one Converso was relaxed in person. Finally, in 1534 another Converso was relaxed in person[76] and one in effigy,[77] and in 1536 two more were relaxed in effigy. Thus from 1520 to 1536 forty-six relaxations of Conversos took place, three in person and the remaining forty-three in effigy. From 1536 until 1675 the records are altogether free of relaxations of Conversos.[78] So that for almost a century and a half the island inquisition did not sentence a single Converso to relaxation, either in person or in effigy. That this marked a period of respite, not alone for Conversos, but for all others under the inquisition's jurisdiction, becomes apparent when we find that only seven persons were relaxed, on all charges, during this period.[79]

---

[69] AHN *Rel. de Causas de Fe,* libro 1, 866, fols. 108-13 In contrast to the number of Conversos relaxed, only two others—a Mohammedan in effigy, and a blasphemer in person—were relaxed

[70] *Ibid.,* fols 61-4v. Only two non-Conversos were reconciled in this period—one for relapsing into Mohammedanism, and another "por diversas herexias" (for various heresies).

[71] Juan de Anguera continued as head from 1506 to 1512, when the Dominican Pedro Vicente Alemany succeeded him in 1512, serving for four years. He, in turn, was succeeded by another Dominican, Juan Navardu, who remained its head until 1520. Appendix I. [Juan Navardu was called to Perpignan (Roussillon) in 1524 (Lea, *Spain,* I, 552) ; but we find him at the head of the Majorcan tribunal again in 1534.]

[72] AHN *Rel. de Causas de Fe,* libro 1, 866, fols 113v-14v

[73] Excluding the relaxation of Gondislavi of Montalegre, Castile, in person for being a "contumacious Lutheran," on December 4, 1523 *Ibid.,* fol. 114v.

[74] *Ibid.*

[75] *Ibid.,* fols. 114v-15.

[76] Isabel Costanza—relaxed in person for being both a relapsed Judaizer, as well as a relapsed witch· "Por Judia y sortilega hechizera relapsa." *Ibid.,* fol. 115.

[77] *Ibid,* fol. 115v.

[78] I use for my authority the inquisition's records, themselves, which we have been constantly consulting in this study the *Relaciones de Causas de Fe,* from the Archivo Histórico Nacional, in Madrid. For a list of these records consulted for the purposes of this study, see the Bibliography Manuscript Sources

[79] AHN *Rel. de Causas de Fe,* libro 1, 866, fols. 115v, 116 Cf Appendix III

The record of reconciliations for this period reflected the same apathetic condition of the tribunal. During the years 1520 to 1579 only thirty-eight Conversos were reconciled, twenty-five in the period 1520 to 1525, four in 1530, four in 1531, two in 1536,[80] one in 1544, and finally two in 1579.[81] It can be said with justice that the inquisition was only a shadow of its former lusty self.[82] This is reflected in the fact that when, in 1549, its two important offices of prosecuting attorney and receiver of confiscations became vacant, the inquisitor-general could see no necessity for filling them. More than a half century later (1618), the inquisition was forced to petition for financial aid from the crown, describing its condition as deplorable.[83] Weakened by unending conflicts of jurisdiction with the civil and ecclesiastical authorities (the latter upheld by the seldom-taken recourse to Rome in 1642), as well as with the Military Orders, its important functions of discovering and punishing heresy suffered greatly.[84]

We have now come to an end of an epoch in the activity of the island tribunal. For nearly a half century after its beginning in 1488 (1488-1536), it concerned itself almost exclusively with Conversos. During all these years it tried only thirty-three cases of non-Conversos, representing both reconciliations and relaxations. In order that the reader may gain some idea of the inquisition's operations in the first epoch of its activity with Conversos, we recapitulate: two-hundred and twenty were reconciled (exclusive of

---

80 Of these, one reconciled was a friar "por Judio y Moro," for practicing both Judaism and Mohammedanism! *Ibid*, fols 64v-76

81 In addition to the two Conversos reconciled—Maria Diez and Bartholome Lopiz—another Converso—Graviel (Gavriel?) Burgos—was sentenced to "spiritual penances" in the auto de fe of June 4, 1581 for "suspicion of heresy." *Ibid.*, libro 1, 860, fol 29v Concerning one of these—Bartholome Lopiz—we have a little more information of the charges against him than we have had for those above Lopiz was charged with uttering blasphemous remarks He believed, for example, that "there was nothing more in the world than birth and death   .   except observing the Sabbath on Saturday, when candles were lighted, and refraining from eating pork in observance of the Mosaic law " He was "a poor, old man of seventy, and considering his full confession of the Mosaic law, he was let off with an easy penance." *Ibid.*, fols. 1, 1v

82 It must not be thought, however, that the inquisition had fallen into desuetude, altogether, for from 1579 to 1675 (during which long period not a single Converso was reconciled or penanced in any way by the inquisition) some 887 cases came before it! These figures have been collected from original inquisitorial records, which apparently have not been utilized before. (Obviously Lea did not know of them—at least he did not use them—for he came to the conclusion that the tribunal was inert during these years *Spain*, III, 305, 6) These cases did not bring much income into the inquisition, comparable to those in past years, through confiscations and fines, because they were cases of poor people and priests (solicitations) for the most part. AHN *Rel de Causas de Fe,* libro 1, 860, containing 312 folios, *Ibid.,* libro 1, 861, containing 478 folios!

83 Lea, *Spain,* II, 437; III, 305

84 *Ibid* , I, 268, 499; III, 504.

the Edicts of Grace, under whose lenient terms five-hundred and fifty-nine were reconciled[85]), five-hundred and thirty were relaxed, eighty-one of whom were relaxed in person. It is significant to point out what is already patent from these figures of relaxations—thus correcting the false impression abroad that death and apprehension by the inquisition were synonymous terms—that during this period only little more than fifteen percent of all relaxations were "in person." It is necessary, if the inquisition is to be fairly judged, for the term "relaxation" to be qualified by "in effigy" or "in person." Otherwise the reader might infer that every .relaxation in the Spanish Inquisition actually brought death with it. A wholly distorted picture of the inquisition's activities would result unless the reader bears in mind the important distinction between the two kinds of relaxation. It is for this reason that great care has been exercised in all the figures used to make this distinction very clear.

We have not been able to give the reader detailed information concerning the specific charges preferred by the inquisition against the Conversos. That is so because our sources of information have been general in character, giving only the name of the culprit, the charge, and the date and the disposition of the case, in one line or at best in a few lines. We have not had at our disposal details of each case. Therefore the information presented up to this point has of necessity been general in character. From this point on, however, beginning with 1675, we have detailed information for almost every Converso arrested. Hundreds of individual cases or inquisitorial processes have been preserved (each one often filling hundreds of folios), and have been carefully examined for the purposes of this study. Out of these case-records our information has been derived for the last portion of this book. Precisely because we have had the good fortune to discover these case-records, the remainder of this work will naturally be more interesting, because a more complete and adequate picture will be presented to the reader.

_____

85 The *total* number of reconciliations through the Edicts of Grace was 870, but of these reconciled one was a non-Converso, and 310 were reconciled for a second time. Through the first Edict of Grace 424 were reconciled, and through the second Edict 135 *new* Conversos (not reconciled before) ·were included, making a total of 559 *persons who were actually reconciled*

CHAPTER III

THE HEYDAY OF THE MAJORCAN INQUISITION

Events Leading to the General Arrest of the Conversos

We have observed that for more than a century the island inquisition had been practically free from cases involving Conversos. It might appear, therefore, that the crimes of which they had been accused by the inquisition—practicing or believing in their former faith of Judaism and urging others to observe it—had been stamped out by the middle of the sixteenth century. That would be an untenable conclusion. The sudden increase in trials of Conversos, commencing with 1675, is conclusive proof of the fact that there remained a considerable group, descendants of those Jews embracing Christianity in 1435, who remembered and observed some of the beliefs and practices of the old Mosaic law which years before they had promised to abjure.

Yet it seems absurd on the face of it to believe that the inquisition was not aware that a small group in the island's population was persevering in its Jewish observances. For the truth is that, although no Conversos came before it in many years, the inquisition did not at any time abandon its search for them. Neither did it content itself with the work of extirpation achieved by it in former times. Thus on March 2, 1624, the tribunal issued an Edict of Faith which commandeered the assistance of all citizens into the service of the inquisition as spies and informers against heretics.[1]

To make sure of its effectiveness, the Edict of Faith recited the various ceremonies and rites by which the Conversos, among the other enemies of Christianity listed in the Edict, might be detected. They observed Saturday as Sabbath, slaughtered their fowl according to the ancient Mosaic law and, also in accordance with it, kept three fast-days each week. They celebrated Passover. They recited a special blessing on Friday evening over wine.[2] They threw their nail- and hair-trimmings into the fire, and recited appropriate Jewish benedictions for the rite. The Edict revealed

---

[1] *Nos Los Inquisidores Apostolichs contra la Heretica Pravitat y Apostasia en la Ciutat, Diocesi y Regne de Mallorca.* Printed Inquisitorial Edict of Faith, signed by two officials of the Majorcan tribunal JTS This Edict was promulgated. we see from the notation on the margin of fol. 4, at the behest of the Inquisitor-General

[2] They recited the *Baraha* (I quote from the Edict, fol. 2) · " . . . prenent la taça de vi en la ma, dient certes paraules sobre aquell donant a beure a cade hu un glop."

that the Conversos invariably ate meat during Lent and all other days upon which Catholics avoided it. They recited Psalms but never concluded their recitation, as did the Christians, with "Gloria Patri et Filio et Spiritui Sancto." They still awaited the coming of the Messiah, and observed many "fasts of pardon." For forty days after a child was born among them, they refrained from entering a Church. They took care to circumcise their males and give them "Jewish names." When a death occurred among them, they turned the corpse to face the wall, washed it with warm water, dressed it in a new shroud, placed coins in its mouth, and emptied all the water standing in jars—all in observance of the Mosaic law. For a whole year after death, the immediate family of the deceased ate only bread and olives, abstaining altogether from meat.[3]

The Edict was announced with impressive ceremonies, and public excommunications and anathemas were invoked against those who refused to obey it. Though it gave complete information for discovering heretics, and invoked penalties for those who disobeyed its orders, the Edict was a failure, at least to the extent that it brought no Conversos to the inquisition.

Still another document reveals that the presence of the Conversos in Majorca was not altogether unknown to the inquisition. This document, drawn up by the inquisition's prosecuting officer in 1674, was a severe indictment of the Conversos (called "Hebrew Nation" in the document). It accused them on various grounds, but chiefly as perpetrators of "scandalous Jewish heresy."[4] It is a fascinating record, alleging to disclose the life, customs and habits of the descendants of those early Jews who had not been assimilated to the Christian life of the island, even after more than two centuries since their conversion in 1435.

The document was prepared at the behest of the Suprema, in its instructions dated July 13, 1672. It accused the Conversos upon thirty-three distinct charges. After their conversion some intermarried with "true Catholics," the document reads, but old-Christians would no longer marry them since they were held in such universally-bad repute. The Conversos themselves chided those who married outside their group, holding them in even lower esteem than that in which they held Christians. The Conversos were secretive and clannish, never admitting outsiders to their conversations or into their society. Their children carried names of saints and martyrs of the Old Testament. Each Converso carried the sign of the tribe of Jews into which he was born, and marriages with

---

[3] *Ibid.*, fols. 1-2v

[4] AHN *Processos de Fe*, legajo 1709, 1, pieza 3, fols. 5-8v. This important document is reproduced in Appendix IV, as "The Indictment of the Conversos."

persons of inferior tribes, although descendants of Jews, were regarded as degrading. Their homes had no pictures of the Holy Family, but only those of Old Testament saints. They looked disdainfully upon Catholics, calling them Canaanites and rabble, and revelled in cursing them. The Conversos avoided intermarriages with Catholics, offering huge dowries even to strangers so long as they were of their own faith. When this was not possible, they arranged consanguinous marriages while their children were still young. They sealed their marriage-contracts in cemeteries in order to keep them secret. They sold only those commodities in which weights and measures had to be used—in order to make sure that good Catholics would be cheated. They did their utmost to procure high Church offices to be able to scoff at the Church with impunity. They executed their own laws. When a murder occurred among them, they concealed it and dealt with the culprit according to Mosaic law. They collected alms among themselves for their own poor. They sent large contributions to a synagogue in Rome (where one of their own constantly lived), which served as a refuge for those who fled from the island. They gathered together secretly at stated intervals. They ate neither pork, nor food prepared with it, even though they occasionally bought some of the prohibited food to deceive the people, but reselling it at the first opportunity. They ate only certain kinds of fish and portions of meat, in accordance with their laws, and bought live fowls which they slaughtered in their own way, accompanied by appropriate ceremonies. They observed Saturday as their day of rest, but, simulating to work thereon, they escaped detection. They refused the ministrations of priests when one of them died. All these things were going on to the great scandal of good Catholics, the inquisition tribunal reminded the Suprema, asking, in conclusion, that the extermination of Jewish heresy begin at once and cleanse the island.

Thus it is obvious that the inquisition was aware of the existence of Jewish heresy in Catholic Majorca. The reason that its extermination was not undertaken immediately after the Suprema received this severe indictment of the Conversos can only be conjectured. Perhaps the power of the "Hebrew Nation" was strong enough, through bribes strategically placed or through personal friendships with the inquisitors, to momentarily turn the inquisition's attention away from them. For the inquisitor of the time, as we shall have occasion to see, was not above reproach. Whatever may have been the reason for postponement, the Suprema took no action, and the carefully-prepared indictment was allowed to remain a dead-letter in its archives.

Early in July of the same year (1672), some startling evidence was presented to the inquisition. Certain Jews of Leghorn, it was reported, had made "inquiries concerning the Jews who lived in Majorca." When the interrogated remonstrated, saying "there are no Jews in Majorca, all are Catholics," the Leghorn Jews replied that there were "Jews in Majorca—as faithfully Jewish as those living in Leghorn!"[5] The inquisition was told that the Jews of Leghorn were referring to those people who lived on the "Calle del Sayell, the descendants of converted Jews, known variously as *Fortezas, Aguilones, Tarongines, Corteses, Picones*, in fact almost all of those who lived on the streets named *Sayell, Bolseria* and *Plateria*."[6] Such knowledge must have been general to have made its way over the sea to Italy!

In the following year (1673), the inquisition received additional information of the Conversos' heresies. This information came from a priest[7] who had obtained it from the confession of a servant-girl of one of the Conversos. The servant had described the "Jewish ceremonies" as she had seen them in her master's house: the fasts and feasts which Catholics did not observe; the preparations made to properly usher in the Sabbath on Friday evening. No food was cooked on Saturday in her master's house. Special precautions were taken against eating pork and in the use of lard in preparing food. Live fowls were always on hand, and they were slaughtered by the use of a "special knife."[8] Those were patently Jewish practices which the girl had confessed, and the priest accordingly reported them to the inquisition. Her charges were verified by the confession of another servant-girl employed in the homes of Ana Sureda and Pedro Onofre Cortes.[9] When the latter and his wife wanted to slaughter a fowl, they concealed themselves from their servant. (Yet they never apparently were successful in hiding themselves from her, for she described the ceremony with great detail.) They would usually go up to one of the rooms on the top

---

5 The Majorcan Juan Pablo Ferragut had stopped off in Leghorn on his way home from Rome, and he it was who had had the conversations reported with 'some of the Jews of Leghorn' He spoke of this quite freely upon his return to the island, but he died before the inquisition called him to testify His cousin reported the conversations.

6 These streets are still inhabited by the descendants of the Conversos. *Sayell* is now called *Jaume II*. Cf. Zaforteza, *Ciutat*. AHN *Proc. de Fe*, legajo 1708, 2, fols 9v-10; *Ibid.*, legajo 1708, 5, pieza 2, fol. 5.

7 The Jesuit Father Antonio Clapes, who reported the confession, was a *calificador* of the tribunal See *below* p. 62, note 17.

8 AHN *Proc. de Fe*, legajo 1708, 2, fol. 7ff.

9 Both were Conversos, names we shall encounter farther on. *Ibid.*, fol 3vff., *Ibid.*, legajo 1705, 5, fol. 1ff

floor of the house, she narrated, where a pan filled with ashes was
placed to catch the blood of the slaughtered fowl. Once the ritual was completed, they discarded the pan. Only occasionally they
were careless and left it for the maid to clean. The maid observed
the identical ceremony when she served in the household of Ana
Sureda.[10]

The Suprema, when notified of the additional information, ordered that the girls be re-examined according to the minute instructions which it dispatched. But the Suprema's reply was considerably delayed: the instructions were not received by the Majorcan
tribunal until almost four years later. Can we say that some influence obstructed the action of the Suprema? Whatever prompted
this postponement we do not know. But we do know that a number
of Conversos were promptly apprehended upon the receipt of the
Suprema's instructions in 1677. The fact that their arrests followed
so soon after it received the instructions showed a ready desire on
the part of the local tribunal, at any rate, to act without delay.

The island inquisition, meanwhile, was busying itself with
other matters absorbing much of its time and energy. A party of
Jews fleeing from Oran[11] (North Africa) to Leghorn were apprehended by the inquisition's officers who searched boats in the harbor
of Palma to prevent the smuggling of Jews, heretics, and heretical
literature into Catholic Majorca. The policy of the inquisition was
to question every Jew on board. If they admitted that they had been
baptized, they were seized and their property confiscated.[12] Among
the seventeen Jews on board the boat was one Alonso Lopez, a lad
of sixteen or seventeen who, because he spoke Spanish fluently, was
held under extraordinary suspicion. In normal times, perhaps, the
Jews would not have been imprisoned or subjected to any special
scrutiny, so long as they did not set foot on Spanish soil. But those
were not normal times, and the inquisition made its procedure more
severe because many Conversos were fleeing to answer the summons
of the half-crazed but compelling figure of the false Messiah, Sabbatai Zevi, who claimed he was divinely appointed to lead his people

---

[10] *Ibid.*, fol. 3v

[11] Oran was captured by Spanish arms under the fighting-Cardinal Ximines, in 1509.
From Oran the few Jews who remained were expelled (April, 1669) by order of
the Dowager-Regent, Maria Ana of Austria, upon the solicitation of the Inquisitor-General, the German Jesuit, Johann Everardt Nithard Cf Graetz, V, 169;
Lea, *Spain*, I, 310, Merriman, III, 21ff

[12] The Viceroy of Majorca was at first reluctant to yield to the request of the tribunal
that the Jews be imprisoned, for it seemed to him that they carried no prohibited
articles, save perhaps two packages of sealed letters written in (what he thought
was) Hebrew AHN *Proc. de Fe*, legajo 1708, 16, pieza 2, fol. 1v

back to the promised land, according to the mystic compilations, in the year of deliverance (1666).[13]

The traveller's genealogy, history of his past life, destination, etc., etc., were scrutinized by the inquisition. If he were a Jew, then, because of the troublesome times, he was incarcerated under some pretext until the Suprema advised his release. Accordingly, the seventeen Jews were examined and, after some time spent in the inquisition's jail, all but young Lopez were ordered to go on their way. Lopez was detained and closely questioned. At first he denied he was ever baptized but finally, through the inquisition's methods of delay and secrecy, admitted that he was born and baptized in Madrid, later living in Malaga, and finally going with his father to North Africa. It was in Oran that father and son were formally initiated into Judaism and circumcised.

Long before Lopez had confessed his Christian background, however, the inquisition had received incriminating evidence of his heresies from the tribunals of Granada, Madrid and Malaga.[14] The crew of the boat testified that Lopez had eaten, prayed, slept, and generally consorted with the other Jews on board; that had Lopez cared to be a Catholic, the crew said, the other Jews would not have molested him. Further evidence showed that he had arranged to marry a young Jewess of twelve, as soon as they would reach their destination.[15] His cell-mate also informed the tribunal that Lopez was a "proud follower of the Mosaic law," which he had vowed never to forsake.[16] During the summer of 1673, distressed and anguished by tedious months spent in the inquisition's jail, young Lopez, who protested again and again before this time that he was a Jew and desired to remain a Jew, finally con-

---

13 Cf. Graetz, V, 118ff ; Lea, *Spain*, III, 303; Margolis and Marx, *A History of the Jewish People*, p. 558ff.

14 AHN *Proc. de Fe*, legajo 1708, 16, pieza 1, fol. 21; *Ibid.*, pieza 2, (unnumbered folios). Exchange of information between the tribunals enhanced the effectiveness of the inquisition's work A perusal of the annotated replies from the tribunals shows how seriously the inquisition took this interchange of information.

15 It was not an uncommon practice, in times of exile among Jews, for child-marriages to be arranged During the exile from Spain, in 1492, children of twelve and thirteen were married Indeed, it was a common practice for Jewish girls to marry as early as twelve, and for boys in their eighteenth year, the latter according to the Mishnaic regulation· *Pirke Abot*, V, 24; cf Herford, *Pirke Abot* (New York, 1925), p. 144 But during the time we are concerned with, there was an additional reason for early marriages arising out of the widely-accepted notion that the Messianic era could come only when all children originally designed by God had had an opportunity of being born! The souls, created by God in the beginning of time, had to be united to earthly bodies before the Messiah could appear Such an idea became almost universal in the time of Sabbatai Zevi, one of the pseudo-Messiahs Cf. Abrahams, *Jewish Life in the Middle Ages*, 184ff.

16 AHN *Proc. de Fe*, legajo 1708, 16, pieza 1, fol. 25v.

fessed his heresies and asked for mercy. Even then he refused to surrender his belief in Judaism, and when the disappointed council ordered him back to his cell, he protested: "For the love of God, for the love of God, forgive, forgive, for I am innocent," for he was not able to cease being a Jew and become a Christian!

In response to the inquisitors' questions about the Jewish ceremonies, Lopez described them fully. He told them, among other things, that the Jew observed the Sabbath as a remembrance of the day upon which God rested from the creation of the world. In the various audiences with the theologians[17] Lopez was often confounded by their superior arguments. Often the inquisition felt he would surely submit, just as many rabbis and great men among the Moors had already recognized the greater excellence of Christianity and had forsaken their old faiths. Only the devil, it seemed to them, could blind him to his errors! After a long session with the theologians, Lopez was wont to cry out in the manner of a half-crazed man obsessed by one idea: for him it was good enough to remain a Jew, and no power could move or convince him to be anything else![18]

When the theologians advanced the prophecy of Isaiah (chapter XIV, verse 7), for proof that the conception of the virgin was fulfillment of the old law, Lopez remained unmoved. "There can be no birth without a male," he retorted. He stoutly denied the assertion that the Messiah had already come, monotonously responding all the while that "he was a Jew, a son of Israel and that he waited for the Messiah."[19] To improve his stubborn soul, the inquisition instructed him to read Friar Luis de Granada's book, and remanded him to his cell.[20]

Lopez remained an incorrigible heretic, despite the twelve audiences with theologians, demanded by inquisitorial procedure. The inquisitor, impatient with the heretic's stubbornness, convoked a *Consulta de fe* which, on January 10, 1674, voted for his relaxation

---

[17] He had these audiences before *calificadores*: learned theologians, forming a commission of experts, who determined the seriousness of the charges, and decided whether the actions and the words of the culprit amounted to heresy or suspicion of heresy. Thus the function of *calificación* was important enough to determine the whole future of any given case before the inquisition. Cf. Lea, *Spain*, II, 263ff., 485ff.

[18] AHN *Proc. de Fe*, legajo 1708, 16, pieza 3, fols. 8v-13

[19] *Ibid.*, fols. 13v-16

[20] The mystic Luis de Granada taught the great spiritual value of *Recojimiento* (abstraction of mental prayer). He was long under suspicion by the inquisition as an "alumbrado" (a sect which taught that the highest spiritual union with God could come through exhaltation) The books of Luis de Granada (*Guia de Pecadores, De la Oración*) were prohibited by the *Indexes* of 1559 and 1583. As the years passed, his works became so innocuous to good Christians, that the inquisition used them as text books of the Christian faith, and recommended them, as in this case, for the conversion of a stubborn Converso. Cf. Lea, *Spain*, III, 17, 530.

as an impenitent heretic. The decision was approved by the Suprema on the thirteenth of the following month.[21] For another eleven months he was confined to jail, before the sentence was finally executed. In a great auto de fe, on Sunday, January 13, 1675, he was burned alive at the *quemadero,* at the Gate of Jesus, outside the city-walls. The execution took place, despite the bishop's request that it be postponed for two days allowing him an opportunity to work for the unfortunate's conversion.

Lopez was burned at one of the most solemn autos de fe ever witnessed in Majorca. It made a profound impression upon the populace to see a man burned to death, for the first time in the memory of most of the islanders.[22] More than thirty thousand persons jostled one another in the Plaza del Borne, Palma's most spacious square, anxious to see the spectacle at close range. In addition to the execution of Lopez, the effigies of six fugitive Portuguese Conversos were burned.[23]

---

21 AHN *Proc. de Fe,* legajo 1708, 16, pieza 3, fols 20, 20v.

22 "No ai en Mallorca ni en la memoria de los nacidos ni en la tradición de los pasados otro exemplar de aber quemado en ella hombre vivo"   *Brebe descripción y noticia del Auto general de fee,* etc, fol. 95v.

23 The same extensive platform used in the auto de fe of 1645 was again used in this auto de fe. (The auto de fe of 1645 in Majorca has received no attention in this work because there were no Conversos in it) I quote from the account of the auto de fe cited in *Anales Judaicos de Mallorca·* "Un auto general tuvo la Santa Inquisición en Mallorca en este mismo año de 1675 El dia 13 de diciembre del año antecedente se publicó el dicho auto de fe de este modo· Iban montados a caballo muchos familiares saliendo de la Casa de la Inquisición accompañadas de las trompetas y tambares publicando el Auto General para el día 13 de enero de este año de 1675, que se habia de celebrar en la plaza del Borne. El mismo dia á las once de la mañana iban en coches el Señor Inquisidor Fiscal, el canónigo Juan Bautista Desbach, un secretario del Tribunal, el Señor Pedro Antonio Zaforteza, el Señor Juan Odon Desclapés, y otros á convidar al Señor Virrey, Obispo, Cabildo, y Jurados para el auto de dicha dia Hicieronse cadalsos en el Borne, como se hicieron en el año 1645 El de los Inquisidores arrimordo á la casa del Señor Jurado Sureda, el cual tenia cinco gradas, despues proseguian diez ó doce gradas : á cada lado del descanso habia como un pulpito con sus tapetes, violados para leer las sentencias y predicar A la parte derecha de este cadalso había otro para los Jurados y demas Regimiento, y al lado de este otro para las señoras. A la otra parte para el Cabildo, y á la parte de adentro para los eclesiasticos A la parte de adentro para los eclesiasticos. A la parte de la casa del Marqués Dameto otro cadalso para los jueces de la Audiencia, y consecutivo otro donde se colocó el altar En estas gradas habian de estar los penitenciados, y un toldo puesto que comprendía todos los cadalsos Se puso estacada en el Borne para que no pudiesen entrar coches Junto al dosel de los Inquisidores había una tribuna dentro del terrado de dicha casa de Sureda para el Virrey, y a la parte junto a la ventana de la cuadro de dicha casa, otro tablado mas alto que el de los Inquisidores con dosel de brocado para la vireina lo que permitieron los Inquisidores para darlo gusto siendo así que jamas se había practicado tal cosa Todo el teatro estaba entapizado de damasco carmesi y tapices Delante del altar había un carredor que salia en medio del teatro para presentarse alli los penitenciados cuando si les leía la sentencia La Casa de la Inquisición estaba entoldada, y toda la plazuela con unos arcos de arrayan, damascos y cuadros en las paredes, y sobre la puerta un letrero que decía "Docebo iniquos vias tuas, ed impii ad te convertentur." Todas las calles por donde había de pasar la procesión se limpiaron y pusieron cortinas en las ventanas El dia 12

The Conspiracy of 1678

It can be said with certainty that no single incident precipitated the general arrest of Conversos which took place in the year 1677. Of course, conviction of the seven Conversos in the auto de fe of

de enero á las 2 de la tarde empezó la procesión en la Inquisición, y se formó del modo siguiente: Yba delante el Señor Don Francisco Cotoner con el pendon del tribunal, cuyos cordones llevaban dos caballeros, seguianse despues todas las comunidades y parroquias con sus cruces cubiertas de morado, á escepcion de la de la Catedral, seguianse los familiares con antorchas encendidas, despues seguian los pages artistas y hombres de honor, los caballeros, consultores, y calificadores, todos con velas encendidas, y ultimamente iba el canónigo Don Diego Desclapés con alba pluvial, llevando la cruz, acompañado del veguer y del Revdo Bartolome Llado, luego seguiantos con bonetes vestidos de negro, el canónigo Juan Bautista Desbach, fiscal del tribunal, acompañado del alguacil mayor y de un secretario Dirigióse á las dos de la tarde por la Plateria, plaza y calle d'en Morey, palacios del obispo y del Virrey por Santo Domingo, calle de los Verins, Mercado, Carinur, Santa Magdalena y S. Jaime llegó al Borne á puesta del de Sol Estaba formada allí la compañia de los doscientos, los conventos y las parroquias se retiraron. Toda la noche ardieron cirios en el altar y linternas delante la cruz verde Tocada media noche, quatro dominicos, quatro observantes y quatro carmelitas que velaron en el altar empezaron los matines, y concluidos laudes celebraron misa, de tres en tres en el altar que se componia de tres angulos y duraron hasta el dia. El dia 13 de enero á las 6 de la mañana concluidos y los dibinos oficios en todas iglesias á las 6½ en la casa del tribunal se empezó á componer al acompañamiente Iban delante muchos hombres de la compañia de los doscientos, seguíanse seis estatuas de sentenciados, despues los penitenciados acompañados de los familiares y pages. Fueron los penitenciados 33 á saber 6 en estatua, dos de los cuales murieron recocidos y sus mugeres que eran penitenciadas llevaban la estatua del marido, todos traían el nombre escrito, de los cuales habia un mozo de 19 años, natural de Madrid, como se continuará con los demas á lo ultimo de esta relación. Despues de estos venian los familiares á caballo con muchos caballeros convidados, las honestas personas y calificadores, tambien montados, los religiosos observantes y los consultores. Seguíanse despues los ordinarios Don Diego Desclapés, ordinario de Tarragona y el P Mesquida, ordinario de Mallorca, religioso agustina, a quienes acompañaban los canónigos Ripoll y Rotger, despues el Señor Inquisidor Rodriguez, y á su derecha el Virrey, y á su siniestra el jurado mayor, y á estos seguian los demas caballeros y magistrados. Delante los jueces ordinarios iba el canónigo Juan Bautista Desbach, fiscal del Santo tribunal con el pendon del mismo, traian los cordones Don Leonardo y Don Francisco Cotoner, dieron la misma vuelta que la otra procession Llegados al Borne á las 8½ tomaron á sus asientos, el fiscal se sentó bajo del inquisidor, el secretario Fabregues fué a recibir el juramento de Virrey y jurados, y luego empezó la misa el introitó con música Dichos los Kiries el P M F. Pedro Roig domecilo (tal vez el original desía dominico), y calificador, predicó media hora, cantó la misa el P. M. Vives, mercenario, tambien, calificador Concluido el sermon, se empezaron á leer las sentencias, y por su orden cada reo estaba en medio del teatro, á medio dia se leyó la de un judio, y fué relajado al brazo secular, cerca las tres de la tarde firmo la Audiencia la sentencia de ser quemado vivo por no querer reducirse, y acompañado de muchos religiosos y PP. de la Compania, fue conducido al Losa de la puerta de Jesus, y sentado sobre un cadalso dide fuego el verdugo á mucha leña que habia bajo de él y en breve quedó consumido. Leyeronse las demas sentencias que se concluyeron á las 8 de la tarde, prosiguió la misa cantada que quedó concluida á las 9 fueron concluidos los penitenciados a la Inquisición . . . Hubo 6 relajados y quemados en estatua por judaizantes contumaces, pero eran portugueses y se habian escapado de este reyno Alonso, alias Jacob Lopez, natural de Madrid, de edad 19 años, cristiano nuevo originario de Portugal (sic), judaizante, contumaz, fué relajado en persona á la justicia y brazo secular, y quemado vivo en valle de la puerta de Jesus con las estatuas de los 6 fugitivos. El Sr. Arzobispo, obispo D. Bernardo Cotoner, pidió al Virrey 2 dias de tiempo para la conversión de aquel infeliz, á lo que contesto era preciso que luego se ejecutase la sentencia, por las pocas esperanzas que habia de

1675 quickened interest among the islanders for an intensified search of heretics. Indeed, some writers believed that the eyes of the inquisition were opened only by the discovery and punishment of these Conversos.[24] The Suprema apparently was not so easily excited by the alleged growing danger of heresy on the island due, perhaps, to the fact that the culprits were not native Majorcans.

If there was a growing movement to ferret out heresy by the inquisition, there was also a quickening of spirit and a growing enthusiasm for the worthwhileness of the Mosaic law among the Majorcan Conversos. They had seen Lopez sacrifice his life for it! His stoical death created a mood of martyrdom among them. It stirred dormant longings and memories. The influence of Lopez's death upon them was attested in a tradition among some Catholics that the Conversos had seized the "martyr's heart for a relic."[25] Pedro Onofre Cortes, one of the prominent Conversos, in speaking to another Converso of Lopez's "martyrdom" reflected the sentiment of the whole community: "Lopez had died serving his God, and he who died for his God would surely be crowned in heaven."[26]

On August 18, 1677 the Majorcan tribunal received instruc-

---

su conversión, no habiendose convertido en tanto tiempo y con tantas instancias de la Inquisición. Los reos por su orden son los siguientes (I name only the Conversos) :

Relajados a la justicia secular y quemados

Gaspar Rodriguez,	portugués fugitivo, por judio, quemado en estatua.				
Isabel Mendez, muger de Gaspar Rodriguez	"	"	"	"	"
Lazáro Rodriguez	"	"	"	"	"
Isabel Gomez	"	"	"	"	"
Antonio Moldonado					
Doña Beatriz Pereira, muger de Antonio Moldonado	"	"	"	"	"

Alonso, alias Jacob Lopez, hijo de Abram, madrileño, por judio, pertinaz, relajado y quemado vivo

Despues de medio dia el Inquisidor D Juan Bautasta Desbach, costeó una comida a la nobleza en siete mesas de trienta cubiertas cada una puestas en el Borne delante los tablados · al Virrey, Arzobispo Cotoner, y Audiencia, se les llevó la comida a sus catafales (y el sacerdote celebrante como la pasaría hasta la noche). Por la tarde hubo helados y chocolat. Pasaron de 30 mil personas que habia en el Borne para ver esta función que importó á los reales cofres entre tablados y petrechos 4,000 ducados.

The above report also appears in the Cronicon (pp. 469-71), in Catalan. A very interesting reference to this event occurs in Piferrer and Quadrado, *Islas Baleares,* p. 537ff. Cf. also· AHN *Rel. de Causas de Fe,* libro 1, 866, fol. 116; *Tratado,* II, cap 11; Garau, *La Fee Triunfante,* (hereafter· Garau), p. 175; *Relacion de los Sanbenitos que han puesto y renevado esta año de 1755, en el Claustro del Real Convento de Santo Domingo,* etc, (hereafter· *Relacion*), fols. 2, 10. There were seven Conversos relaxed out of a total of thirty persons penanced and reconciled for various charges in this famous auto de fe.

24 *Tratado,* III, cap. 11
25 Which appears ridiculous since the victims were burned to ashes.
26 AHN Proc. de Fe, legajo 1705, 15, fols. 113v, 139v " . . . quien muerte por su Dios, en los Cielos es coronado . . . ."

tions from the Suprema to act upon the testimony of the two domestics, which we have already discussed above.[27] A week later (August 25th), one of them was re-examined and her story was practically the same as she had recited it four years before.[28] Thereupon, on the following day (August 26th), an order for the arrest of Pedro Onofre Cortes, "a descendant of Jews, a native and resident of this city (of Palma), of the Calle del Sayel," was duly signed by the inquisitor.[29]

On September 14th the Suprema confirmed the arrests of both Cortes and his wife, ordering at the same time the sequestration of their property.[30] A month elapsed before they were apprehended. Finally, on October 13th, Cortes was imprisoned. There were doubtless valid reasons for this additional delay. The inquisition bided its time, while the Conversos went on practicing their heresies, apparently without too much discretion.[31] They celebrated the Day of Atonement—*El Dia del Perdon*—on the tenth day after the new moon of September with the usual formalities, giving the assurance that it was an annual event.[32] It was observed in the garden of the militant Converso, Pedro Onofre Cortes. Although he was the first to have been arrested, the very same day he entered the prison he was joined by his wife and son and three other Conversos.[33]

The work of the inquisition, so long delayed, had now begun in earnest. Skilfully the inquisition drew out from the six imprisoned Conversos all they knew of the extent of the heresy.[34] With this information arrests followed in rapid succession: two on No-

[27] *Supra*, pp 59-60. The instructions were dated July 20, 1677, thus scarcely a month had elapsed between their issuance in Madrid, and their receipt in Majorca. AHN *Proc. de. Fe,* legajo 1705, 15, pieza 1, title page, fols. 2v, 3; *Ibid,* legajo 1708, 5, title page, fol 1 Contrast this with the lapse of almost four years consumed for a similar purpose, *supra,* p 60

[28] AHN *Proc. de Fe,* legajo 1705, 5, fols 2, 3

[29] *Ibid,* fol 8 This was not the first arrest of Conversos, it must be observed. For on May 14th of the same year, Ana Sureda, the mistress of one of the informing maids, was ordered to be arrested The Suprema's approval of the arrest came August 18th, in the form of a careful re-examination of the witness. Pedro Onofre Cortes, in this way, became the first Converso actually to be taken into custody by the inquisition in this period

[30] *Ibid.,* legajo 1705, 15, fol. 9

[31] "In 1677 or 1678 a meeting, held in a garden outside of the city, attracted the inquisitor's attention. It was designated as a synagogue, and *doubtless there was some imprudence.*" (Italics mine). Lea, *Spain,* III, 306.

[32] AHN *Proc de Fe,* legajo 1705, 5, fol. 2; *Ibid.,* legajo 1708, 5, fol 12ff.

[33] *Ibid,* legajo 1712, 3, fol 1 Among them were Miguel Cortes de Francisco and his wife, and Ana Sureda. That 'the inquisition's procedure was effective enough to cause denunciations, even among the members of a family, is evident from the early denunciation of Melchor by his brother, Pedro Onofre Cortes. When Melchor bewailed his lot, asking who could have accused him before the inquisition, his brother Pedro confessed that he had!

vember 9th, two on November 20th, and finally, within somewhat more than a year after the first arrest (October 13, 1677), two-hundred and thirty-seven Conversos had been seized by the inquisition.[35] The prisons, lacking accommodations for such large numbers, overflowed.[36] The island was thrown into turmoil. The natives stood aghast that persons with whom they had daily come into contact were really "abominable heretics," like those burned a few years before. Another victory of the first magnitude had been scored by the inquisition![37] That year has been remembered in the annals of the island as "the Conspiracy of 1678" (*la Complicidad del año 1678*), to which the inquisition records refer with unusual frequency.[38]

The Autos de Fe of 1679

The trials growing out of the Conversos' arrests continued for more than a year and a half. During this time the prisoners, herded in the crowded jails, tasted for the first time the suffering that adherence to their secret faith brought them. All their yearnings after martyrdom were dissipated in the darkness and foulness of the prisons. Rather a mood of expediency characterized their testimonies before the inquisition.

The crowded prison conditions gave the Conversos ample opportunities for taking counsel together, and for evolving some plan that would free them from the nightmare of the inquisition. By constant interchange of information among those imprisoned, and between them and their coreligionists on the outside (through the medium of well-bribed jailers), the general policy decided upon

---

35 The names of the 237 Conversos arrested were compiled by the inquisition for its own record, which was entitled: "Testimonio que consta por los procesos de la complicidad de los Judaisantes de la calle del Sayell, Bolseria y Plateria, en quanto a los escrutinios de los susodichos." AHN *Proc. de Fe,* legajo 1712, 3, año de 1680, 8 fols.

36 *Ibid.* Before these arrests, the slow business of the inquisition permitted the warden of the inquisition's prisons to live in his own house, at some distance from the inquisition. After these arrests, he was ordered to move to the secret prison of the inquisition, now enlarged to accommodate the prisoners. The inquisition purchased the property adjoining it—in great measure confiscating it, if we are to believe the efforts made by the owners to forestall the sale, because of the low price paid—and used it for its prisons, only later to demolish it and build the magnificent palace of the inquisition in a style "so sumptuous that it passed for one of the finest in Spain." (Lea, *Spain,* III, 307).

37 It must not be supposed, however, that every Converso was arrested. One of them envied his coreligionists who were not in custody, although they were as ardent in their faith as he was. There are some records of bribes paid to keep Conversos out of prison. One Converso paid an official of the inquisition 100 reales for the immunity of each member of his family. But so few Conversos escaped the general arrest, that for the next decade the fortunates were singled out and Conversos asked one another how they had succeeded in averting it! AHN *Libro Becerro,* 1, 65, fol. 21ff; AHN *Proc. de Fe,* legajos. 1708, 20, fols. 13v, 14; 1710, 1, fol. 55ff.

38 *Cronicon,* p. 143; *Tratado,* III, caps. 12-15.

was to confess only a very limited amount of information, and denounce one or two accomplices—just enough to avert suspicion of complicity. Their plan was successful.[39] Until the scheme had begun to work smoothly in the early part of 1678, the Conversos' confessions varied considerably. After that time, they were practically duplications of one another. This is clear from what transpired in the audience-chamber of the inquisition. For a time after his arrest, Pedro Onofre Cortes staunchly held to his faith in the law of Moses. Somewhat later he vehemently affirmed his love for Catholicism and begged for mercy—because, he said, he wished to live and provide for his unfortunate family![40] Raphael Valls was at first branded a contumacious heretic, and he adamantly refused to make confession of his heresies. Suddenly he revealed to the astonished inquisitors that God had given him the light to see his faults! He prostrated himself before the tribunal, begged for clemency, and promised to be faithful to Catholicism thereafter.[41] Soon after her imprisonment in November, 1677, Raphael Valls' wife also asked pardon for her sins and transgressions.[42] Many other Conversos followed them in confessing their sins and begging forgiveness.[43] The Conversos, both inside and outside the inquisition's prisons, came before the tribunal with carefully laid plans which kept the inquisitors ignorant of much that had actually taken place among the secret followers of the Mosaic law.

The triumph of their scheme did not, however, release them from the confiscation of their property, which reached the amount of almost one and a half million pesos (more than one and a quarter

[39] Many of the messages between those in and those outside the jail were carried by one Jayme, the slave of the prison's warden (Jayme was later imprisoned and punished by the tribunal) During this imprisonment (and the one which followed in 1688), Juan Merino, the inquisitor's coachman, was also a medium of communication with the outside (He was also imprisoned and punished by the inquisition, although not before he had accumulated a good-sized fortune in money and jewels which the Conversos gave him as gifts for his trouble). Through messages circulating among those in the prisons, they knew what was going on at all times, even though they had taken a pledge to "keep secret everything they saw and heard, until the final disposition" of their cases AHN *Rel. de Causas de Fe*, libro 1, 865, fols 180, 188v 196v, 360, 389, 390, 392, 404v, 406v, 408v, 424v. JTS *Proc. de Fe*, legajos · 3, 18, fol 209 , 3, 19, fols. 37v, 61

[40] AHN *Proc. de Fe*, legajos · 1708, 2, pieza 2, fol 3v ; 1710, 1, fols. 11, 30, 30v.

[41] *Ibid* , legajos · 1705, 15, fol 140; 1708, 4, fols. 4v, 64 The Inquisitor Rodriguez de Cossio Barreda may have favored Valls because of loans the latter was alleged to have extended to him Some records indicate that when it appeared that Valls' stubbornness would bring upon him the penalty of death by burning, the Inquisitor sent Valls a note through Valls' son, expressing his great concern. Whereupon Valls made his confession, and pleaded for mercy ! It was even rumored that the Inquisitor was of Jewish stock, because of his friendship for Valls. *Ibid* , legajo 1705, 5, fol 26v No evidence of his Jewish antecedents has been found

[42] *Ibid* , legajo 1708, 4, fol. 6v.

[43] *Ibid.*, fol. 8v.

million dollars). This was a phenomenal sum for such a small tribunal, and as early as 1678 King Charles II ordered the viceroy of the island to supervise the confiscation to insure his proper share. Thereupon ensued a struggle between the king and viceroy, on the one side, and the inquisition on the other. But the king was beaten. He finally received only 4⅔% of the confiscations, and not the customary 33⅓% to which he was entitled.[44]

Confiscation of property of the merchants—a class which the Conversos largely constituted[45]—threatened to cripple the industry and trade of the island.[46] This is attested by a memorial addressed

---

[44] Archivo de Simancas, *Inquisición,* libro 69, fols 1-5, 69, 70v, 156, 563 (consulted in the Henry Charles Lea Library, Univ of Pa) Cf Lea, *Spain,* I, 335; IV, 512; Coulton, *The Inquisition,* p. 74 , also Fajarnés, "Cartas Reales sobre las laudemios de los bienes confiscados á los judios de Mallorca," *BSAL,* VIII, 1899-1900, 94. The king, in a letter of May 20, 1678 (he was wise enough even at this early date to recognize that fat confiscations would result from the arrests of the Conversos), ordered his viceroy to take charge of the confiscations But it was not an easy matter The viceroy was first told that the process of confiscation was solely the inquisition's rightful prerogative, and he was denied the inventories of the confiscations. The Suprema took a hand, instructing the tribunal to protect itself by censures, and even by excommunications, if the viceroy threatened further action. The letter addressed to King Charles II by the Suprema was a stinging rebuke, couched in language which might have been proper in addressing an inferior, but not the king! The inquisition's argument was clear its laws demanded that the properties confiscated by it must remain under its jurisdiction, and to permit of their secular control would be a profanation of religion ! When all the accounts were settled, the island inquisition reported that, after the costs for making the arrests, feeding the prisoners (cf *below* p 76), and maintaining its officials had been deducted, scarcely anything remained from the confiscations of the impoverished heretics ! Actually, the king received some 52,000 pesos, and beside 18,000 pesos spent on the fortifications of the island, the remainder went to the inquisition's coffers Yet the Suprema assured the king that he had been given such a large sum only because of the affection felt for him. The confiscations yielded 1,461,276 pesos (ca $1,244,418 00) According to Lea (*Spain,* III, 306) the confiscations yielded 1,496,276 pesos, according to Taronji, *Algo Sobre el Estado Religiosa y Social de la Isla de Mallorca* (p 242, following *Tratado,* III, cap. 16, and *Anales Judaicos de Mallorca,* see Appendix V, p 190) 1,491,276 pesos. I use the lesser amount (Cronicon, p 435) All money-values quoted in this work have been converted into dollars by the formula suggested by Prof. Earl J Hamilton of Duke University. From a contemporaneous MS (no. 6731, Cuerpo de Manuscritos, BN), he discovered that the Majorcan dinero was equal to the Castilian maravedí. Extensive researches brought Prof Hamilton to the conclusion that a U. S. bushel of wheat was worth 319 4 maravedís in 1686-1690 If we consider the present price of wheat as $1.00 per bushel, the approximate modern value of the Majorcan currency mentioned in this work may be found by reducing the amount into maravedís, and dividing the resultant sum by 319 4. The following table may be useful for finding rough equivalents

1 dinero (1 maravedí) = $0 003131
1 sueldo (12 maravedís) = 0.037572
1 libra (240 maravedís) = 0.751440
1 peso (272 maravedís) = 0 851632

[45] The confiscations included not only real estate, but also merchandise, jewelry, furniture, and all kinds of movable property. In the late 15th and early 16th centuries there were some surgeons, physicians, and lawyers among the Conversos But, with the diminishing opportunities for entering guilds, the Conversos turned almost exclusively to what was open to them, and became traders, merchants and shop-keepers, which fields they soon held completely

[46] Some notion of the wealth confiscated, indicative of the Conversos' widespread

to the crown in June, 1679 by a distinguished Majorcan nobleman, the Count of Montenegro, who complained against the wholesale confiscation of the Conversos' property, because it constituted a great menace to the island's commerce. In addition, the taxable property was being reduced through confiscation, thus causing the community to suffer further, and only continuing hardships, the Count admonished in his memorial, would come to the island with the exportation of the confiscated wealth.[47]

Significant as they are, the figures for the confiscated property do not reveal the actual value of the property seized by the inquisition. During those years the inquisitor was Francisco Rodriguez de Cossio Barreda, a profligate and an unscrupulous man. He used every trick and ruse to enrich himself out of the heretics' property.[48]

holdings throughout the island, may be gathered by examining the *Libros Becerro* (the "Registry Books"), listing all the confiscations, compiled by the advocate and archivist of the tribunal, upon the order of the Inquisitor-General. Three *Libros Becerro* are in the Archivo Histórico Nacional · AHN *Libros Becerro*, 1, 64, 65, 66. Two additional *Libros Becerro,* but duplicating much of the same information, are in the private library of the late Don Francisco Villalonga y Fabregues of Palma. Cf Fajarnés "El Santo Oficio y los compradores de bienes de judaizantes," *BSAL,* VIII, 1899-1900, 34; and "Sobre la venta de ropas que fueron de los judíos mallorquines," *BSAL,* VII, 1897-1898, 412

[47] ACA *Inquisición de Mallorca,* Consejo de Aragon, legajo 973. "Señor: Los bienes . . . que se han confiscado a los Penitenciados llegaron a suma de un millon de Reales de á ocho, para aquel Reyno es muy considerable cantitad y porque si el empleo, y consumo se sacasse fuera resultaria en gravissimo daño y destrucción del comercio que antes se conservava en el con las haziendas, y dineros de esta gente, y los derechos de la Universidad padecerian notable detrimento resolvio el grande y general consejo embiar á los Reales pies de Vuestra Magestad el Conde de Montenegro paraque representassa esta y otras materias de suma importancia para la conservación de aquella Isla, y suplican sea Vuestra Magestad favorcerla en la expedición dellas como mas fuere del Real Servicio del Magestad beneficio y restauración della El Conde en el memorial refiere que los bienes confiscados por la Inquisición consisten primeramente en 14,305 libras Mallorquines de á siete Reales cada libra que pagava de censos cada año la Ciudad y Reyno de Mallorca; diez mil libras de renta cada año de censos impuestos sobre diferentes villas y gremios de aquel Reyno; seis mil libras de renta cada año de censos impuestos sobre bienes de partes del mismo Reyno. Otros bienes raizes y heredades desta gente cuyo valor casi llegara á veinte mil libras Mallorquinas. Noventa casas . . . en buen sitio para comercio y trato que aunque el tiempo que los Penitenciados las poseian eran mucho valor, oy no se puede afirmar lo que valdran. Que el dinero de contado, joias, mercaderias, muebles, y azeites no se puede con fundamento dezir el valor . . y algunas cantidades que tienen de credito contra diferentes personas del aquel Reyno, y se juzga que todas estas perdidas y caudal importara un millon de Reales de á ocho . . . . Mandara lo que mas fuere de su Rl. Servo. Madrid, 22 de Junio del 1679."

[48] Rodriguez resigned (or was deposed) soon after charges were preferred against him. The charges were of such imposing nature that the Suprema was forced to take cognizance of them. His indecent living had become a public scandal, and the reputation of the inquisition had suffered thereby. AHN *Pleitos Civiles,* legajo 2, 18 (This legajo contains 39 bundles of documents, each bundle containing from 4 to 5 folios, all devoted to this case). Rodriguez's name does not appear after 1680 in the expense accounts of the tribunal sent to the Suprema, nor in the cases and correspondence of the tribunal. AHN *Rel. de Causas de Fe,* libro 1, 864, fol 222v. Actual dismissal of an official of the inquisition was almost unknown, according to Lea (*Spain,* II, 224), yet Rodriguez was relieved of his office! The

In public auctions, arranged by the tribunal's receiver for confiscated property, the inquisitor and his friends managed to buy the desirable items at a fraction of their real value. At a prearranged signal—sometimes the inquisitor wiped his nose with his finger, or waved his hand in a certain direction—the auctioneer declared the bidding closed and announced the article sold to one of the inquisitor's henchmen. If this plan was not successful, a number of Rodriguez's minions—among them the jailer, surgeon and other officers of the inquisition—strategically placed themselves in the crowds, urging, and threatening if necessary, that no competitive bids be made. The inquisitor then made purchases at his own price.[49] A brazier worth sixty libras, for example, which would surely have brought forty libras under free bidding, was bought by the inquisitor for almost nothing. A valuable painting of St. Augustine was auctioned off so quickly that the merchants did not even have a chance to bid for it. The auctioneer afterwards admitted, when called to testify before the inquisition, that he was working under strict orders from the inquisitor. The deceitfulness and chicanery of Rodriguez outraged the populace, and he was finally relieved of his office.[50]

Not infrequently pieces of the confiscated property were exchanged for ones of inferior value before the auction, the difference in value accruing to the inquisitor and his accomplices. The friend of a Converso testified that he went to the auction in order to buy a donkey from the confiscated estate. In place of the young and strong animal he knew, he was stunned to see that a decrepit and trembling animal was put up for sale; he was sold for five libras, whereas the original would have easily brought twenty-five libras. Similar incidents occurred throughout those years, proving that the actual worth of the confiscated property was perhaps much more than three or four times the sum realized by the inquisition. The inquisition's officers were enriched by the confiscations, while the Conversos kept complaining—perhaps not without reason—that it was because of their wealth and not for their heresies that they had been arrested.[51]

---

names of officers of the inquisition in league with Rodriguez have been blotted out of the documents of this case

49 AHN *Pleitos Civiles,* legajo 1689, 7   AHN *Proc. de Fe,* legajo 1710, 1, fols 11v, 12, 45.

50 Rodriguez went so far as to take out from the confiscated property some 900 ells (an ell=2 to 4 feet) of goat's-hair cloth, for which the island was famous, and gave it to one Francisco Mesquida who sold it in Madrid   The merchant made a gift of a diamond ring to the receiver of confiscations to show his appreciation

51 In fact, one witness believed that the desire of the Conversos to flaunt their wealth and fine clothes had brought on the arrests   The Conversos' attitude is quite com-

The Conversos were not stripped of all their property, however, for they arranged to conceal part of their possessions. This is not surprising when one considers that they had lived on the island for generations, and counted many trustworthy friends among the old-Christians, who, if not anxious, surely were not unwilling to help them shield a part of their property from the inquisition.

To some priests, especially to those who maintained a warm dislike for the inquisition,[52] they surreptitiously carried their jewels and gold for safe-keeping during their imprisonment. They assigned notes to many priests and made them their fictitious creditors, thus allowing for claims to be made upon the confiscated property. Some placed parts of their fortunes in the hands of the Jewish merchants of Flanders, and of Italy, and elsewhere with whom they carried on trade. Others did not trust mortals, and buried their wealth under charcoal bins, in caves and graves. Some had the boldness to sew jewels into the buttons they wore on their clothing during imprisonment, bribing the examining officer when he became suspicious.[53]

When they were freed from the inquisition and asked for the return of their property, they found that, in most instances, they had misplaced their trust. The greater number of the priests emphatically denied that they had ever made themselves parties to defraud the inquisition. A curate of Santa Eulalia, the parish church of the Conversos, who had received valuables to the amount of three-hundred libras, threatened to denounce the owners to the inquisition when they requested them. Another priest who had been entrusted with a sack of jewelry and pearls told the Conversos that he had turned it over to the inquisition. They fared somewhat

prehensible Their bitterness was increased when they saw that a string of beautiful pearls belonging to one of them had been taken out of the confiscations and, before an inventory was made, had been presented to the handsome wife of the inquisition's secretary by the inquisitor himself.

[52] The Conversos "might well deem themselves secure, especially as the churchmen were free in their denunciations of the tribunal. In 1668 the inquisitor complained to the Suprema that the priests of the episcopal party talked of the inquisition as a secret heresy, and that it was a den of robbers which should be abolished . . . ." Lea, *Spain*, III, 306. In this atmosphere it was not difficult to find many who were willing to help defeat the purposes of the inquisition

[53] The prisoners were thoroughly searched when they entered the inquisition's prison The "escrutinio," written into every case-record examined by the author, contains a minute description of the prisoner—color of eyes, hair, general appearance, distinguishing marks, etc. (as in our jail-procedure today). The clothing worn by the prisoner was also carefully described—as to color, material, etc., and every item the prisoner took into jail with him (bedding, linens, etc.) was very studiously written into the record. To have avoided detection of precious stones worn on their persons, after such a rigorous examination, is tribute to the Conversos' ingenuity, or bribes, or both!

better at the hands of a canon of the Cathedral, who returned ten out of two-hundred libras left with him. It was either naiveté or sheer stupidity on the part of the Conversos that prompted them to give the secretary of the inquisition for safe-keeping a number of bills of exchange on Rome and Madrid, explaining to him that he surely understood the heavy penalties confiscation brought, and would therefore want to help them. He returned ten reales, claiming the remainder of the sum as charges for commutation of the sanbenito and prison term of one of the Conversos.[54]

Obviously the Conversos suffered great losses by their arrest. Those formerly rich, one of them lamented, were now poor.[55] Their houses were taken away. Their merchandise, by which they earned a living, was confiscated. Their business was cut off. In addition, they were burdened by the sanbenito, which they were forced to wear publicly, and thus placed in a decidedly inferior status to others in providing for a livelihood.[56] The Suprema was importuned by many petitioners, begging release from the contumely of wearing the sanbenito in public for, they alleged, it prevented them from earning enough to feed their starving families![57]

The confiscation of their property was not the only punishment meted out to the Conversos by the inquisition. Since this constituted their first offense as heretics, they were permitted to become reconciled to the Church (reconciliation was also considered a punishment), from whose benign care they had strayed. In addi-

---

54 But perhaps it was not altogether naiveté when one recalls that the chief interest of Inquisitor Rodriguez in prosecuting heretics was his personal enrichment. It was only after the trials and confiscations of so much wealth that the priests and others who thought the inquisition was "a den of robbers" (*supra* p. 72, note 52) believed it would be more advantageous for them to sing another tune!

55 AHN *Proc. de Fe,* legajos: 1705, 15, fol. 140; 1710, 1, fols. 14, 15, 16, 17, 19, 21, 24, 54v. AHN *Rel. de Causas de Fe,* libro 1, 865, fols. 148, 285, 428, 431v, 438, 439, 440; *Ibid.,* libro 1, 866, fols. 161v, 165.

56 Not without reason, therefore, that King Philip II regarded the sanbenito "the severest infliction" imposed by the inquisition. Lea, *Spain,* IV, 527.

57 One such petition, for example, dated July 15, 1679, contains the prayer of Augustin Honofre Cortes to the Suprema to allow him either to discard his sanbenito for the nine months remaining in his sentence, or to return part of his wealth confiscated by the inquisition. He pleaded for at least the privilege to discard the sanbenito, in view of 1,600 libras which the inquisition had confiscated, his entire fortune and patrimonial estate, for with the sanbenito it was impossible for him to earn a livelihood for his wife and family. Another Converso, Pedro Juan Fuster, frantically appealed to the Suprema for some relief and help, since his property had been confiscated by the inquisition. At the age of fifty, with obligations to feed his four children, he was suddenly thrust into almost abject poverty. He pleaded with the Suprema that at least a portion of the value of his estate be returned to him . . . . "only forty-seven libras and ten sueldos be returned to him, which would be adequate to maintain and educate his family . . . ." On November 3, 1702 he went to Madrid to press his claim. It seems that either the Suprema granted his request, or his patience was exhausted, for we have no further evidence that he asked for relief again. AHN *Pleitos Civiles,* legajo 1689, 7.

tion, they were imprisoned for a specified length of time—depending upon the enormity of the offence and the extenuating factors, such as immediate and voluntary confession. Finally, they formally abjured their heresies, and promised henceforth to remain loyal and obedient sons of the Church.[58]

The sentences were pronounced at five impressive autos de fe, in the spring of 1679, held at the Dominican Church of Palma. The first took place on Sunday, April 16th, with fifty reconciliations. It was similar to the others in that it consumed most of the day, beginning at seven in the morning and ending at six in the evening. The reading of the sentences to the culprits, who stood bareheaded, with lighted candles in their hands before the assembled multitude, was followed by the recitation of the lengthy and formidable abjuration of their heresies. A special attraction featured the first auto de fe. With a multitude at their heels the inquisitors went outside the city walls to a place near the public execution grounds, and demolished the house where the Conversos held their religious services for the Great Fast, and plowed up the garden with salt. A stone column, inscribed with the reason for the demolition, was placed there to serve as a warning and example.[59]

---

[58] AHN *Proc de Fe,* legajo 1708, 2, fols 85, 87, 87v.

[59] *Ibid.,* legajo 1705, 5, fol 10; cf. Cronicon. p 472; Lea, *Spain,* III, 129 For the text on the column, see Appendix V, p 187. I quote the report of this auto de fe from *Anales Judaicos de Mallorca*
"El mes de febrero de 1678 fueron presos por la Inquisición 200 descendientes de judios. Dia 16 de Abril de 1679, segunda dominica de Pascua, el tribunal de la Inquisición celebró auto publico de fe en la igelsia de Sto Domingo. Empezó á las siete de la mañana, y duro hasta las seis de la tarde Se demolió la casa y jardin donde judaizaban y enseñaban las ceremonias judaicas, los 50 reos de este auto, lo cual estaba cerca la Puerta Pintada (called by the Arabs Bab-Al-Kofol The Gate of Litharge. Latterly it has come to be known as Puerta de Santa Margarita, and is situated at the end of Calle de San Miguel, adjoining the Hospital Militar, in Palma. Cf. Zaforteza, *Ciutat,* pp 20, 25, 27). Los reos son los siguientes ·
1. Raphael Piña, de 38 años, condenado en habito y carcel por dos años, con confiscación de bienes.
2 Isabel Marti y Forteza, de 80 años, habita y carcel por tres años y confiscación de bienes
3 Isabel Marti, de 30 años, habito, carcel perpetua, y confiscación
4. Isabel Cortes y Forteza, de 20 años, habito, un año carcel y confiscación
5. Isabel Marti, de 50 años, habito, tres años, carcel y confiscación
6. Isabel Bonnin y Valls, 34 años, habito y carcel perpetua.
7. Isabel Marti y Cortes, de 50 años, habito y carcel dos años
8. Isabel Marti y Forteza, de 45 años, habito y carcel perpetua
9 Isabel Marti, doncella de 28 años, hija de Rafael Marti menor, tres años carcel
10. Francisco Marti, soltero de 22 años, dos años carcel.
11 Gabriel José Cortes, de 37 años, dos años carcel
12 Gabriel Cortes de Francisco, de 41 años, *Id*
13 Francisco Bonnin, de 40 años, *Id*
14. Isabel Cortes, de 30 años, muger de Miguel Cortes, carcel perpetua
15. Catalina Aguiló, de 44 años, muger de Juan Antonio Cortes, dos años carcel.
16 Magdalena Piña, de 26 años, muger de Francisco Bonnin, un año carcel.
17. Beatriz Cortes y Forteza, de 30 años, muger de Miguel Cortes, un año carcel.
18 Francisco Tarongi de Rafael, de 67 años, tres años carcel

On the following Sunday, April 23rd, the second auto de fe
was held, with fifty-two culprits. A week later, April 30th, another
auto de fe took place, with sixty-two culprits. The fourth auto de fe
was held on May 3rd, with forty-six persons, many (from the age
of thirteen to seventeen) were graciously permitted by the inquisition to be relieved of their sanbenitos immediately after the
sentences had been pronounced. The final auto de fe was held on
Sunday, May 28th, with eleven Conversos.[60]

After the autos de fe, the prisoners were placed in the inquisition's newly-acquired penitential prisons. In the prisons, some

19. Maria Forteza y Cortes, de 50 años, tres años carcel.
20. Margarita Marti y Sureda, doncella de 18 años, habito, carcel y confiscación de
bienes.
21. Margarita Aguiló y Marti, de 19 años, un año carcel
22. Margarita Marti y Cortes, de 33 años, muger de Pedro Onofre Cortes, dos
años carcel
23. Bartolome Baltasar Marti, de 42 años, dos años carcel.
24. Francisco Bonnin y Pomar, 57 años, muger de José Bonnin, tres años carcel
25 Ana Cortes y Sureda, de 24 años, Id.
26 Bartolome Forteza, de 46 años, Id.
27. Juanot Forteza, de 39 años, dos años carcel.
28. Leonor Bonnin y Piña, de 25 años, un año carcel
29. Leonor Cortes y Marti, de 60 años, Id.
30. Margarita Marti, de 26 años, dos años carcel
31. Juan Antonio Cortes de José, de 45 años, carcel perpetua
32. Pedro Onofre Cortes de Guillermo, de 40 años, carcel perpetua
33 Juana Ventura Terongi, de 26 años, un año carcel.
34. Agustin Antonio Cortes, de 64 años, carcel perpetua
35. Antonio Marti, de 67 años, tres años carcel.
36. Rafael José Tarongi, de 52 años, Id.
37. Rafael Cortes de Alfonso, de 35 años, dos años carcel.
38 Rafael Baltasar Marti, de 30 años, un año carcel
39. Quiteria Marti y Aguiló, de 37 años, dos años carcel.
40. Teresa Cortes y Aguiló, de 42 años, Id.
41. Miguel Tarongi de la Volta, de 52 años, carcel perpetua
42 Margarita Marti y Sureda, de 35 años, Id.
43 Miguel Cortes de José, de 35 años, Id.
44 Rafael Valls, de 39 años, carcel perpetua irremisible
45. Miguel Marti del Arpa, de 37 años, dos años carcel.
46 Margarita Tarongi y Marti, de 47 años, Id.
47. Miguel Pomar, de 57 años, un año carcel
48 Miguel Forteza, de 46 años, dos años carcel.
49. Juan Marti, de 46 años, carcel perpetua irremisible.
50. Baltasar Joaquin Marti, de 23 años, un año carcel
Todas eran de la Calle de Sagell. Del 23 dia mismo mes y año salieron al auto
52 personas por judios judaizantes. Dia 30 de los mismas salieron 60. Dia 3 de
Mayo, 49. En 28 del mismo salieron 13. Esto y las demas circunstancias de estas
autos consta en el libro impreso titulado La Fee Triunfante.
(According to AHN Rel. de Causas de Fe, fols. 76-89v, five autos de fe took place).

60 According to the figures of Cronicon (pp. 434-5, 472), 219 Conversos were reconciled in these autos. The number reconciled, according to the Relacion (which cites
only four autos), was 173: 40 in the first, 41 in the second, 47 in the third, and 45
in the fourth. (AHN Proc. de Fe, legajo 1712, 3) Kayserling (pp. 181-2) and
Michel. (Histoire de Races Maudites, II, 35-6) have figures similar to Cronicon, Lea (Spain, III, 306), and Tratado (III, cap. 12-14). A contemporary of the
events, Padre Garau, reported that "more than 212" were reconciled in the autos
de fe (p. 24). In the last auto de fe, May 28th, two renegades, beside eleven
Conversos, were reconciled

of the Conversos, despite their solemn abjuration of the Mosaic law, continued to observe its rites and ceremonies. Many fasted there, just as they did at home. Upon one pretext or another they refrained from eating pork. The women prepared the meals for their husbands and families, as they did at home. They often gathered together and, led by Raphael Valls and Pedro Onofre Cortes and others, prayed to the God of Israel. They discussed the law of Moses and its observances, and for the first time many of the Conversos listened to their leaders expound the principles of their secret faith. The ignorant were taught its prayers and observances. A spirit of unity and fellowship in a sacred cause, in the face of a common enemy, inspired them, and in the penitential prisons they were welded together into a strongly unified group.

In the penitential prisons, also, there arose among the Conversos a strong sentiment for leaving Majorca. They knew they would no longer be immune from the harsher penalties of the inquisition, if they persisted in practicing their secret faith. Yet they had no desire to forsake it, despite their promises. They had a profound trust that the God of Israel, who had performed so many miracles in olden times to free His oppressed people and smite their persecutors, would also help them in their plans to flee from Majorca to a land where they could live freely as Jews. The thought of escape warmed their hearts, and in the penitential prisons their plans assumed definite form.[61]

From all reports their stay in the penitential prisons was far from unhappy. They enjoyed many liberties. They could bathe in the sea, and they were given the freedom of the city to earn enough for their food—for the inquisition had already adopted the economy measure of refusing to support its prisoners. They had been imprisoned for terms varying from six months to the "irremissible prison" term of three years. During their stay the penitential prisons were full of activity. Wandering minstrels came to amuse them. The warden of the prisons supplied a violin and a guitar, some books, pens, ink and writing-paper, only warning prisoners in advance of the coming of the inquisitor or the prosecuting officer so that they could quickly conceal everything. So lax was the discipline in the penitential prisons that they were referred to as "a house of diversion."[62]

---

[61] AHN *Proc. de Fe,* legajos 1708, 20, fol. 7, 1710, 1, fols 20v, 28, 35, 39, JTS *Proc. de Fe,* legajo 3, 19, fol. 11.

[62] The penitential imprisonment must have been a very pleasant and profitable time for the warden of the prisons, for a few years afterwards he looked back to those "good years, when he, the physician, and the prisoners had had such pleasant times together." He enriched himself out of the bribes from the Conversos for over-

The Faith Triumphant

The Conversos found upon their release from prison that, like criminals in all times and places, they were vigilantly watched and their goings and comings carefully scrutinized.

To continue the practice of their secret faith was practically impossible under the alert eye of the inquisition. They made a serious appraisal of their position, and concluded that its only solution lay in flight. On the one hand they were impoverished. Unfortunately, a drought had impaired crops and, added to the increase in prices, made living very difficult for them. On the other hand a sinister hatred arose against them as the responsible parties for the rise in prices and the suffering it entailed. If they had not permitted themselves, the people complained, to fall into the hands of the inquisition through the exercise of their "accursed beliefs in the decadent law of Moses," their wealth would not have been confiscated, and money would not be scarce, causing prices to rise and the poor to starve!

Public confidence and good will, so necessary to merchants, had virtually been shattered. In fact, the public looked upon the Conversos as scourges, with whom no decent Christians could carry on intercourse. When driven to the Cathedral to hear the sermons, under the lash of an inquisition's officer, they ran the gamut of invective and imprecation. They wanted nothing more than to shuffle off the nightmare of public hatred, suspicion and shame. Flight was the only avenue left open to them. Therein lay their salvation.

Accordingly they made plans for their expatriation. They decided that they would leave the island in small groups, so as to be less noticeable, and assemble in Barcelona, Valencia or Alicante, ports on the east-coast of Spain nearest Majorca. There they would wait for the others to join them for the voyage to some place "where they could live freely as Jews." They could go to many places. Nice, Marseilles, Flanders, London, Leghorn, Rome, Alexandria, and Smyrna, were among the refuges considered. Beginning in 1682 their expatriation began with small groups leaving on a prearranged schedule.

---

looking—or encouraging—lax discipline, and for failing to discover the gold and the precious stones his prisoners carried on their persons (Cf *supra* p. 72, note 53). He was reported to have amassed from four to six thousand reales. During the succeeding years (1688-91), some of the Conversos testified that they believed the Inquisitor-General was in league with the warden and shared in his bribes! The constant complaint, running through the testimonies of the Conversos, was· "We were arrested by the inquisition only because of the money its officers mulcted from us, and not because we were believers in the law of Moses!" This is, of course, a one-sided opinion of the matter. AHN *Proc. de Fe*, legajo 1710, 1, fols 11, 37-43.

Officers of the inquisition were bribed to procure the necessary licenses, insuring their departure with greater facility. It was said that one of those recently reconciled had received permission to go to Rome on the pretext of taking his orders for the priesthood, but in reality had gone there to join the congregation of Jews which the Conversos were alleged to support.[63] The family of Gabriel Carlos Cortes escaped to Nice.[64] Juan Antonio Cortes, his family and others, totalling twenty-five persons, also went to Nice, by way of Barcelona, on the pretext of seeking a livelihood, but once there, they observed the Mosaic law freely.[65] Francisco and Guillermo Terongi, disciples of Raphael Valls, fled to Alexandria, by way of Valencia, to live as professing Jews.[66] A group of families including those of Raphael Valls, his brother-in-law, Raphael Augustin Pomar, and Miguel Terongi, had arranged to leave for Valencia early in 1683. They were to remain there for a short while before proceeding to a place where they could live freely as Jews. Their departure was postponed by the arrest of Ana, Raphael Valls' daughter, (February 6, 1683).[67] Raphael Joachin, a son of Raphael Valls, in advance of his party in Valencia, returned to Majorca when he received the news of his sister's arrest. He too was thereupon seized by the inquisition.[68] Guillermo Vizente, the son of Pedro Onofre Cortes, succeeded, however, in reaching Barcelona, and finally going to Leghorn, where he proclaimed himself a Jew. Augustin Cortes de Alfonso went by sea directly to France. Thus, the Conversos' plan for expatriation was in large measure being successfully executed.[69]

---

[63] This Converso was Gabriel Piña. *Ibid.*, legajo 1709, 10, pieza 2, fol. 5ff.; AHN *Rel. de Causas de Fe,* libro 1, 865, fol. 22ff., 188v, 280. JTS *Proc. de Fe,* legajo 3, 18, fols. 25, 64. Cf *supra,* p. 58

[64] AHN *Proc. de Fe,* legajo 1710, 1, fol. 37v.

[65] *Ibid.,* legajos 1708, 4, fols 47v, 59-60; 1709, 1, pieza 2, fols. 1-10; 1709, 3, fol. 94; 1713, 9, fol. 4. AHN *Cartas,* legajo 1, 857, fol 296. In a letter to the Suprema, dated November 16, 1691, the tribunal recalled the escape of Juan Antonio Cortes (de Joseph) and a party of twenty-five, because in 1686 the tribunal received advice from the Cardinal of the Duchy of Savoy, reporting that all these fugitives who had openly declared their allegiance to Judaism were detained in prison by the Bishop of Nice for relapsing into Judaism. The Cardinal now asked that the records of their trials before the Majorcan Inquisition be forwarded to Rome, where they were to stand trial.

[66] AHN *Proc. de Fe,* legajo 1711, 20.

[67] *Ibid.,* legajo 1708, 4, fol. 156.

[68] AHN *Rel. de Causas de Fe,* libro 1, 865, fol 249.

[69] AHN *Proc. de Fe,* legajos. 1705, 15, fol. 22; 1713, 1, fol. 47. Fifteen additional fugitives were listed in the tribunal's report to the Suprema (December 11, 1688), all of whom had been reconciled. (AHN, *Rel. de Causas de Fe,* libro 1, 864, fol. 431ff.; also *Ibid.,* libro 1, 865, fol. 234ff.; and Garau, pp. 77, 83). They were: Raphael Joseph Marti, and his wife, Isabel, Raphael Balthazar Marti, Juan An-

On its side, the inquisition continued its vigilance and arrested many Conversos during the time they were trying to carry their plan of expatriation into effect. The records of the inquisition show how active the tribunal was during those years. Its prosecution of the dead, alone, provided sufficient work to keep its officers occupied. In the seven-month period between August, 1681 and March, 1682 ninety-five prosecutions of deceased Conversos had been undertaken.[70] On October 8, 1683, the tribunal forwarded to the Suprema abstracts of posthumous proceedings against one-hundred and seventy-five Conversos.[71] But the prosecutions of the dead did not prevent the inquisition from continuing its prosecution of living heretics. Thus one Converso was publicly reconciled on July 27, 1682, and in the same year two more (reconciled once before) were suspended.[72] The following year another was absolved of his heresies,[73] and four were imprisoned.[74] In the same year (1683), as we have seen, two children of Raphael Valls, (Ana and Raphael Joachin), were seized. In September, 1685 Pedro Onofre Cortes was ordered arrested; a month later his case was suspended.[75]

Notwithstanding greater vigilance by the inquisition (whose effectiveness was then enhanced by the leadership of two inquisitors),[76] the Conversos continued their surreptitious observance of the Mosaic law. Because they were more carefully watched, they performed only those ceremonies which could be celebrated in the strictest privacy. Through Pedro Onofre Cortes' confession, we learn that the last celebration of Passover, including the slaughtering of the Paschal lamb with his "special knife," occurred in the

---

tonio Cortes, Miguel Geronimo Pomar, Margarita Marti, Miguel Cortes, Beatriz Forteza, Melchor Aguilo, Margarita Aguilo, Jacinta Cortes, Joseph Andres Cortes, Gabriel Melchor Marti, Leonor Cortes and Catalina Aguilo.

70 AHN *Rel. de Causas de Fe,* libro 1, 864, fols. 181-203.

71 On that date the tribunal's secretary wrote the following letter to the Suprema, sending with it the abstracts of the cases· "Remitimos a V. A en 43 hojas utiles una relación de ciento y setenta y cinco sumarios contra tantos difunctos que han resultado testificados del delito de Judaismo por los reconciliados en la complizidad desta Inqqon   " *Ibid.,* fol 236 Then follows the abstract, called· "Relación de Causas de difuntos de la Inqqon de Mallorca por abecedario." *Ibid.,* fols 237-79v. This material sent to the Suprema by the Majorcan tribunal is the source of our information on this point Yet Lea (*Spain,* I, 306) doubts that any proceedings against dead heretics took place at the time since "there would have been no profit in looking up ancestral heresies."

72 AHN *Proc. de Fe,* legajo 1710, 15, fols. 1-5; AHN *Rel. de Causas de Fe,* libro 1, 864, fol. 211

73 Raphael Forteza AHN *Proc de Fe,* legajos 1709, 10, pieza 1; 1710, 5, fol 1

74 Juan Baptista Diego Marti, Raphael and Ursula Forteza, and Juana Bonin. *Ibid.,* legajos· 1708, 4, fol 56; 1709, 10, fol 3

75 *Ibid.,* legajo 1705, 5, fol. 11.

76 Juan Bautista Desbach and Francisco Baca de Lederma. Cf. Appendix I.

spring of 1687. Again, all the Conversos participated in the Great Fast in September of the same year.[77]

They met together in various homes, and these "secret meetings," as they were called by the Conversos, exerted great influence upon their morale. In the "secret meetings" their intellectual leaders discoursed upon Old Testament prophecies. They encouraged them by reciting the miracles of the past, and led them in prayers, said with ever-growing feeling and hopefulness. In these meetings the escape of Conversos was customarily revealed to the group. They each came to feel, through these meetings, a stronger sense of community responsibility. How grieved was the entire community when one of them was imprisoned! With what joy and happiness they welcomed the news of a safe departure, and with what eagerness they greeted the notice of safe-arrivals of the fugitive groups! In these meetings, also, sales of the fugitives' properties were arranged, with the minimum loss to their owners. If necessary, fictitious notes were written against the unsold portions of the estates, in order to thwart the inquisition when proceedings for confiscations were attempted. These "secret meetings" may be characterized as the heart of the Conversos' communal life in the years between 1680 and 1688, marking the interval between their first and second imprisonment by the inquisition. The Conversos believed that they were outwitting the inquisition. Indeed, with the passing of the years, their plans for expatriation might have been successfully concluded had not an untoward incident occurred.[78]

Unfortunately, one of the Conversos turned traitor to his group, frustrated his brothers' plans, and bewildered them into losing their heads at the critical moment: thus making them an easy prey of the inquisition. He was Raphael Cortes de Alfonso. Some Conversos believed that the onus of the perfidy should have fallen on the inquisitors because they were alleged to have bribed Raphael into informing against them. But the fact is that Raphael had very good reasons to denounce them, without the added inducement of bribes. The Conversos had ostracized Raphael for marrying an old-Christian. Not one of them, not even his mother—so strong was the feeling—had congratulated him upon his marriage. Apparently he had a weak mind—he was called *Cabeza-loca* (Crazyhead)—and it occurred to him that denouncing the Conversos would alone be adequate revenge for the insults he suffered at their

---

[77] AHN *Rel. de Causas de Fe*, libro 1, 865, fols 295, 302, 302v; *Ibid ,* libro 1, 866, fol. 198.

[78] AHN *Cartas*, legajo 1, 857, fol. 68; AHN *Proc. de Fe*, 1708, 20, fols. 4, 9v, 10v; AHN *Rel. de Causas de Fe*, libro 1, 864, fol 451

hands. Accordingly, he confessed to a priest—who was an officer of the inquisition—that Pedro Onofre Cortes was trying to win him back to the Mosaic law.[79] (From what we know of Pedro's zeal for his secret faith, there can be little doubt of the truth of this accusation.) Pedro had spoken to Raphael at great length of his hatred for Christianity, and of his great love for the law of Moses, through which alone salvation would come. He told him in great detail of the method of circumcision, the *sine qua non* of membership in the Jewish group. Pedro was alleged to have said that the sorrow and persecution of the Conversos came upon them justly as a penalty for forsaking the true faith: the God of Israel had duly punished them for their backslidings! Raphael also told the priest of Pedro's unbridled anger when he married an old-Christian. It was Pedro who brought on this ostracism by the Conversos! In the blindness of his rage, Cabeza-loca saw in his erstwhile teacher the symbol of the entire community. At the priest's request he wrote down with great care the text of his conversations with Pedro. At last he had his revenge upon Pedro, he thought, for he had denounced him as an incorrigible Converso![80]

Cabeza-loca died before the incriminating papers were transferred to the priest. The latter thereupon took them from the dead man's house, and immediately turned them over to the inquisition. It acted upon the information without any delay. Pedro Onofre Cortes was forthwith arrested, but his case was suspended by the Suprema.[81] The news of the betrayal by Cabeza-loca threw the Conversos into consternation. The suspension of Pedro's case did not allay their fears; they assumed it was the inquisition's ruse for gathering additional information. Bewildered and fearful, they held "secret meetings" more frequently. Ignorance of what Cabeza-loca's papers actually contained added to their confusion. They felt certain, however, that he had denounced the entire community to the inquisition. They were sure of impending imprisonment, and so they hastened their plans for escape from the island. Instructions were given Raphael Valls' son to make all the necessary arrangements for the flight. Weeks stretched into months, but an opportunity for departure did not present itself.

---

79 This confession took place July 28, 1685, before the Jesuit Father Sebastian Sabater, in the Church of Monte-Sion, a former synagogue of the Jews!

80 AHN *Proc. de Fe,* legajo 1705, 5, fols. 19, 23-30v Cabeza-loca himself did not escape the inquisition! He was tried posthumously and his case was suspended (December 10, 1692).

81 *Ibid.,* legajo 1705, 15, pieza 2 (the order from the Suprema is on the unnumbered folio, dated October 23, 1685). Three months elapsed between the initial confession to the priest and the suspension of the case.

Their dread was somewhat eased when the inquisition made no further arrests. In September, 1687, however, a new inquisitor (Joseph Hualte) was added to the tribunal. With enthusiasm and energy he launched into his new work, and began to prosecute Conversos on the basis of evidence previously received. Cabezaloca's papers again figured prominently. Other evidence, including that of Raphael Crespi Cortes, submitted two years earlier through his father-confessor, was also pressed into the service of the inquisition.[82]

To the leadership of the tribunal another inquisitor (Pedro Guerrero de Bolaños) was added in 1688. Under Inquisitors Hualte and Guerrero de Bolaños the Majorcan Inquisition attained its greatest effectiveness and became one of the best known tribunals in all Spain. The first result of their work was the imprisonment of Pedro Onofre Cortes (February 11, 1688), followed by that of his wife and son (March 4th).[83] These arrests precipitated a panic among the Conversos who feverishly laid new plans for flight.

It was at that moment that fate seemed to favor them. An English vessel was anchored in the harbor, and its captain was promptly engaged to transport a group of them. The amenable captain was pledged to absolute secrecy. He surely knew that his prospective passengers were escaping, or the conversations held surreptitiously on board the vessel and in the houses of some of the Conversos would hardly have been necessary. Final plans were laid with utmost caution. Unlike the many previous flights, this time a substantial number of Conversos, fearful of their fate if they remained, were escaping at the same time. It was perilous and they knew they ran grave risks, but the alternative of imprisonment by

---

[82] *Ibid.*, legajo 1705, 5, fols. 19-21v; AHN *Rel. de Causas de Fe*, libro 1, 866, fol. 117. Raphael Crespi Cortes, a native silversmith of Palma, was reconciled in the famous auto de fe of 1680 in Madrid (described by Joseph del Olmo, an eye-witness to the proceedings, in his work, *Relación Histórica del Auto General de Fe que se Celebró en Madrid este año de 1680*, p. 221). After serving in the penitential prison in Toledo, he returned to Majorca to find that he was regarded as an outcast among his own people for living as a Christian He ate lobsters, and other foods forbidden by the Mosaic law! Pedro Onofre Cortes took it upon himself to chastise him, and to teach him at the same time the elements of the *true* faith. Raphael refused to listen to instruction and went his own way to find that the Conversos had ostracized him. In 1685 he told his confessor that certain people of the Calle del Sayell were observing Judaism. Although the priest reported the conversation to the tribunal at once, no action was taken until the new Inquisitor Hualte summoned Raphael Crespi Cortes to the tribunal for a thorough examination, in the course of which he denounced Pedro Onofre Cortes as a confirmed observer of Jewish practices Raphael himself perished as a penitent heretic in the auto de fe of May 1, 1691. AHN *Rel. de Causas de Fe*, libro 1, 866, fol. 117.

[83] *Ibid.*, libro 1, 864, fol. 444v; *Ibid.*, libro 1, 865, fols. 183, 277; JTS *Proc. de Fe*, legajo 3, 18, fol. 100.

the tribunal strengthened their resolve to take the chance. Bags of food and clothes were secretly placed on board the vessel a few days before that eventful Sunday evening, March 7, 1688, when they were scheduled to flee. With outward calmness, a group of women and children left their homes early that evening for what appeared to be an innocent stroll into the country. By prearrangement they met their men-folk outside the city-walls, and together they went to a designated part of the harbor where they boarded a launch for their vessel. Happily, it seemed no one was any the wiser, and the most dangerous part of their escape, under the cover of night, had been completed.[84]

Despite repeated attempts, the boat was unable to leave the harbor because a fierce storm had suddenly arisen, preventing its sails from being lifted. The elements seemed to conspire against them, and, after six hours of anguish on board the vessel, they returned to land! Yet they hoped their secret had been undisclosed, and stealthily they returned to their homes. The vigilant ear of the inquisition had been awakened, however, and its officers awaited them. Between the early morning hours of two and three on Monday, March 8, 1688, they were cast into prison.[85]

This calamity crushed the Conversos. Their morale and cohesion, so strong up to that time, was immediately broken. In the early dawn of the morning of their arrest the brother-in-law of Raphael Valls made a complete confession of the whole affair, and of his own part in it. He testified that the Conversos had fled only to escape "false testimony against them which would have made them prisoners of the inquisition." He knew that they had been stubborn in refusing to believe in Jesus Christ, who had caused the storm to arise, preventing their departure. Surely, then, Jesus was more powerful than the God of Israel, whom he had already forsaken! Denunciations rapidly wove a net around all Conversos, both those who had participated in the frustrated flight and those who had remained at home. Arrests began immediately after March 9th and continued for the next few years until every member of almost all the Converso families, including children from the ages of eleven to thirteen, was finally brought to the inquisition.[86]

---

84 AHN *Cartas*, legajo 1, 857, fols 58, 59 JTS *Proc. de Fe*, legajos: 3, 18, fols. 5, 5v, 7; 3, 19, fols. 10v, 13; 6, 2, fols. 5-6v Cf also Kayserling, "Die Juden auf Mallorca," *Jahrbuch für die Geschichte der Juden und des Judenthums*, I, 1860, pp. 67-100.

85 "Die Juden auf Mallorca," *op. cit.*, p. 69.

86 AHN *Rel. de Causas de Fe*, libro 1, 865, fols. 48ff. 101-2, 152, 210v, 294v. Onofre Cortes, 12 years old, Margarita Bonin, 10, and her sister, Magdalena, 12, Fran-

The trials dragged on for three years. Little additional information of Jewish practices was received, beyond that which the inquisition already had. Audience after audience revealed the misery of the prisoners. The weak confessed immediately and freely. The strong loosened their tongues only when the instruments of torture cut into their flesh.[87] Many were tortured, some perishing from its effects. The strong among them could not be moved—whatever the manner of inquisitorial delay and torture—to forsake their belief in the God of Israel. A spirit of martyrdom hovered over the trials during those years. The Conversos were well aware that death was the inquisition's punishment for relapse into heresy. Confession and contrite repentance merited death by garrotting, although the fire was not cheated, for the body was thereupon thrown into it, while contumacious heresy carried with it the terrifying fate of being burned alive. That was more than many of the strong-hearted could bear, and some confessed their heresies to save themselves from this ordeal. But the horror of torture did not avail to cause Pedro Onofre Cortes and Miguel Valls, brother of Raphael Valls, to forsake their secret faith. It was only after they had been notified of the penalty they must suffer that they begged for forgiveness and thereby avoided the agony of being burned alive.[88] Isabel Cortes, who spoke so brazenly and audaciously before the inquisitors, also lost her courage and died a penitent heretic.[89] Only three of them—Raphael Valls, his

---

cisco Bonin, 13, together with other children were detained because they accompanied their parents on the attempted flight. They were kept in the custody of the inquisition, in the house of one of the familiars, until their release on June 21st. In spite of the unanimous testimony that, as children, they knew nothing of the purpose of the flight, they were arrested. Raphael Cortes, only 14 years old, was sentenced to reconciliation. He appeared in the public auto de fe of May 19, 1690, and sentenced to one year imprisonment, and to confiscation of property! It is interesting to note that one of the witnesses who testified to the youthful culprit's beliefs in the Mosaic law was the 12-year-old Francisco Vizente Terongi!

[87] *Ibid.*, fols. 163, 166; AHN *Proc. de Fe*, legajo 1708, 23, fols 4v-8; JTS *Proc. de Fe*, 3, 19, fols 14-17 The ghastly "audiencia del tormento" reveals the pitiable shrieks of the victims brought to a frenzy from the pain of the torture-process. Minutely and painstakingly each word and gasp was written into the records by the omnipresent scribes. There are innumerable cases of those who remained contumacious ("negativo") until the first turn of the "right thigh for a period of 2½ hours;" or until "the second turn of the left thigh," when the attending physician reported that the victim had "lost her senses," or until the "second turn of the left leg for more than ½ hour" before the delirious sufferers would confess, and beg for mercy and forgiveness (Cf. *supra* pp. 24-5, chapter I, note 85).

[88] Garau, pp. 49ff., 56 Pedro Onofre Cortes remained a contumacious heretic until he was notified, four days before the auto de fe, that he must die by being burned alive. Miguel Valls, also, remained contumacious until he heard his sentence read in the same auto de fe. Both confessed and saved themselves from being burned alive.

[89] AHN *Rel. de Causas de Fe*, libro 1, 865, fol. 153. The short digest of Isabel's trial

disciple Raphael Benito Terongi, and the latter's sister Catalina Terongi—remained to the last impenitent and contumacious heretics, whose fortitude no device of the inquisition was able to crush. They alone, of all those tried by the inquisition during the years 1688-1691, were burned alive.[90]

Extenuating circumstances, together with fines totaling some twenty-four hundred libras, mitigated the punishment of twenty-four relapsed Conversos to abjuration of their heresies.[91] The records for confiscation of the Conversos' property show that all they had concealed during their first imprisonment had come into the hands of the inquisition with their second imprisonment.[92]

---

lists the "many blunders and extravagances she made before the inquisitors" before she finally accepted Christianity (". . . que los Christianos crehen en un Dios hecho por manos de hombre que tiene ojos, y no ve, oydos, y no oye, boca, y no habla, manos, y no palpa, pies, y no anda, y que han compuesto una ley a su modo porque con esto comen, y tienen estimacion, y los SSres Inqqres y Secretarios tienen buen salario conque se sustentan pero que los Christianos bien conocen que la ley que el dios de Israel dio a Moysen es la verdadera, y que a la hora de la muerte crehen en la ley de Moysen, y con esso se salvan y que si leyeran la Biblia, y no se entre estubieren en rondallas fueron todos judios, pero que lo han trabucado todo, y que los mandamientos tambien los han trabucado, porque el tercero mandamiento en la ley de Moyses dice que se guarde el sabado y en la ley de los christianos se manda santificar las fiestas, y dijo al Sor. Inqor que tenia tapado el entendimiento, y que si dios embiara un Angel ya conoceria el error en que estava . . . ."

90 AHN *Rel de Causas de Fe,* libro 1, 866, fol. 118v.

91 AHN *Cartas,* legajo 1, 857, fol. 60v. In a letter to the Suprema, the Majorcan tribunal reported that the confiscations were so meagre that it feared it would not be able to meet the expenses involved in keeping the prisoners in the jail of the inquisition! The complaint sounds ominously similar to the one made in 1679 Cf. *supra,* p 69, note 44, also *supra,* p 76).

92 AHN *Libro Becerro,* 1, 65, fols. 571-616, *Ibid ,* 66, fols 113-558; AHN *Juntas de Hazienda,* libro 1, 869, fols 182-479; *Ibid ,* 870, fols 3-7 The balance reported in the tribunal's treasury in February, 1688, before the imprisonments began, was 619,087 libras, 11 sueldos, 4 dineros, after which it increased as follows:

1688					
March	621,257 libras*	16	sueldos†	4	dineros‡
October	637,947 "	2	"	6⅔	"
November	643,867 "	10	"	7⅔	"
December	646,639 "	17	"	⅔	"
1689					
July	658,736 "	9	"	1½	"
August	660,408 "	13	"	13	"
September	667,747 "	4	"	6½	"
October	668,571 "	3	"	7½	"
November	669,477 "	15	"	6½	"
December	673,231 "	15	"	½	"
1690					
February	676,372 "	12	"	8½	"
April	678,631 "	3	"		
June	679,189 "	12	"	½	"
August	681,556 "	5	"	4	"
October	683,062 "	12	"	6	"
December	687,173 "	18	"	11	"

The three years of trials resulted in four autos de fe, which took place in the spring of 1691 in the Dominican Church.[93] The first was held on the third anniversary of the frustrated flight (March 7th). Stage and scaffolding were erected in the Dominican Church to accommodate the nobility, clergy, officers of the inquisition and twenty-one Conversos, who were to formally hear their fate.[94] No capital sentences were announced, but spectators crowded the Church, and overran into the streets surrounding it. The severest sentence was pronounced upon Raphael Valls' son, Raphael Joachin, who, beside having formally abjured his errors and gravely warned and censured like all the others, was condemned to seven years in the galleys, in addition to permanent sanbenito, imprisonment, confiscation of property, and two-hundred lashes.[95] The other two sons of Raphael Valls, Francisco and Miguel, were condemned to sanbenito and to imprisonment for two years. Pedro Onofre Cortes' wife, Juana Miro, was condemned to perpetual sanbenito

---

1691						
January	690,031	"	19	"	4	"
March	691,306	"	3	"	2	"
June	694,797	"	15	"	3	"
December	703,124	"	3	"	3	"

*1 *libra*=$0.7514. †1 *sueldo*=$0 0375. ‡1 *dinero*=$0.0031. Cf *supra* p. 69, note 44. A perusal of the stout *Libros Becerro* is strong substantiation of the fact that the Majorcan tribunal had not given an accurate report of its financial standing to the Suprema. (Cf. *supra*, note 91.)

[93] The Jesuit Padre Garau wrote his reactions as an eye-witness to the autos. His book supplies contemporary evidence, supplementing the records of the inquisition, themselves, which are our chief source. In his account, he gave vent to all the bitterness, hatred and venom which he had in his heart against "the perfidious Jews, who, though punished time and again by the wrath of God, were adamantly stubborn to the true faith" Padre Garau's book has been one of the chief weapons in the hands of the enemies of the Conversos. Very few copies of the original edition (1691) are extant. The Majorcans believe that they were all bought up by those who were villified in it. Perhaps, for a similar reason, so few copies of the second edition (1755) are today available. A third edition was published in Palma in 1931. It is full of faults and should be used by the scholar with the greatest caution Constant reference to the two earlier editions are essential for accurate information. For example, the name Joseph Aguilo (no. 3 in the account of the third auto de fe, May 6th) is altogether omitted in the third edition. Raphael Agustin Pomar occurs in the third edition as Raphael Aguilo Pomar. None of the errors which crept into the second edition (1755) were corrected in the third edition. thus the date of the fourth auto de fe is July 2nd, not June 2nd (although the date is given correctly at the head of the list of persons participating in it; p. 111 in the second edition, and p. 83 in the third edition). Obviously, then, the new edition cannot be taken as a manifestation of any renewed scholarly interest in an old book (which was the reason advanced by its publisher to the author for the new edition)! Cf pp. 125, 131, 133

[94] AHN *Rel. de Causas de Fe*, libro 1, 866, fols. 90v-1v. Four non-Conversos increased the number to twenty-five persons in the first auto de fe.

[95] Permanent imprisonment usually implied a period of three years. There were cases of sentences "to perpetual prison for six months." Cf. Lea, *Spain*, III, 59. The lashes were administered on the public streets of the city. (For "perpetual prison," see *supra*. p. 31, chapter I, note 113).

and imprisonment, in addition to the confiscation of her property.[96]

The second auto de fe, celebrated on May 1st, far outstripped the first both in importance and grandeur. For it the Dominican Church was more brightly adorned than before. The culprits—twenty-one of them—were led out of the inquisition's prisons into the Church, to hear pronounced their fate of death-by-fire. The contrite confessions and manifestations of their regret for being heretics, however, mitigated the severity of the sentences, and they were ordered to be garrotted before being burned. They were forthwith turned over to the secular arm for the execution of the sentence. For this purpose a huge brasero, eighty feet square and eight feet high, with twenty-five stakes, was erected in an uninhabited section, about three miles from the center of the city, at the foot of

---

[96] AHN *Rel de Causas de Fe,* libro 1, 866, fols 90v-1v, Garau, pp. 36-44, *Relacion,* pp. 27-9. The following Conversos were sentenced in the auto de fe of March 7, 1691·

1. Gabriel Cortes, hijo de Raphael Cortes, dfo, y de Isabel Cortes, alias la Moyaneta, 21 años de edad   His sentence was read "con meritos" (see *supra,* p. 32, chapter I, note 119). He formally abjured his errors, was gravely warned and censured, and then reconciled. He was condemned to sanbenito and prison for one year and to confiscation of his property
2. Geronima Pomar, 59. *Id.*
3 Francisco Valls, hijo de Raphael Valls y Isabel Bonin, 24 *Id,* with two years of sanbenito and prison
4. Miguel Valls, hijo de Raphael Valls y Isabel Bonin, 21 años. *Id.*
5 Raphael Joaquin Valls, hijo de Raphael Valls y Isabel Bonin, 28 *Id,* with 200 lashes, and seven years in the galleys.
6 Francisca Cortes, hija de Agustin Cortes de Raphael, alias Brugea, y Isabel Terongi, 18. *Id,* with one year of sanbenito, and imprisonment.
7 Beatriz Cortes, muger de Pedro Juan Terongi, alias el Conde, 21. *Id,* with two months prison
8 Juana Miro, muger de Pedro Onofre Cortes de Guillermo, alias Moxina, 28 años *Id,* with perpetual sanbenito and prison.
9 Juan Antonio Pomar, 60 *Id*
10 Juanot Cortes, hijo de Pedro Onofre Cortes de Guillermo, 23. *Id.,* with a threat that should he attempt to escape from the island, he would serve in the galleys for 10 years, and his property would be confiscated.
11 Onofre José Cortes, hijo de Raphael Cortes, dfo, y Isabel Cortes, alias la Moyaneta, 25. *Id.,* with two months sanbenito and prison
12 Leonor Cortes, hija de Raphael Cortes, dfo., y de Isabel Cortes, alias la Moyaneta, 22 *Id.,* with two years of sanbenito and prison.
13. Leonor Cortes, hija de Agustin Cortes, dfo, y de Mariana Moya, 22 *Id*
14 Miguel Crespi Terongi, 24. *Id*
15. Leonor Valls, muger de Juan Pico, 60. Abjured *de levi,* sentenced to exile from the city of Palma, but within the island, at the discretion of the tribunal, fine of 200 libras, gravely warned, censured, and denounced
16 Onofre Aguilo de Onofre, 61. *Id.*
17 Francisco Marti, alias Verdet, 37. *Id.*
18 Pedro Juan Aguilo de Pedro, 40. *Id.*
19 Onofre Cortes de Melchor, alias Don Juan, 52. *Id,* with a threat that should he attempt to escape from the island, he would serve 10 years in the galleys, and 200 ducats fine
20. Isabel Cortes, muger de Francisco Marti, alias Verdet, 32 *Id.,* with a fine of 500 libras.
21 Catalina Terongi, alias la Tia Grossa, viuda de Ramon Marti, 72 *Id,* with a fine of 200 libras.

the hillside of Bellver Castle. It was close enough to the city to be accessible, yet far enough removed for its inhabitants to avoid the stench from the burning of human flesh. The site overlooked the spot from which those doomed to die had three years before attempted to escape. The Jesuit Father Francisco Garau, eye-witness to the scene, jubilantly declared that the Conversos were meeting the fate predestined for them: "they had been saved from the perils of the water only to perish in the fire!"[97]

Notwithstanding the tremendous heat of the day, a crowd estimated at thirty-thousand persons followed the procession outside the city where the brasero stood.[98] There the culprits were garrotted and burned in a grand holocaust. It was accounted a triumph for the faith, since all of the Conversos, heretofore contumacious heretics, had forsaken their belief in the Mosaic law and had accepted the Christian faith. Among them was Pedro Onofre Cortes, the staunch defender of the Mosaic law, who was finally persuaded to find salvation in Christ. So sincere was his conversion that he refused to surrender an image of a crucified Jesus which he carried to the stake. Protesting her faith in Jesus, another Converso was heard to pronounce the name of Jesus as she expired at the last turn of the garrote.[99]

[97] Garau, p. 31, cf *Anales Judaicos de Mallorca,* IV, cap. 32 (see Appendix V).

[98] James Stanhope, the British Minister at Madrid, complained in a letter to his father, dated May 5, 1691, from Palma, that he "could get but very ill accommodations, by reason of the concourse of people which are here at this time to assist at the Auto de Fe, which began this week, for Tuesday last there were burnt here twenty-seven Jews and heretics, and tomorrow I shall see executed about twenty more; and Tuesday next, if I stay here so long, is to be another *Fiesta,* for so they entitle a day dedicated to so execrable an act   The greater part of the criminals that are already, and will be put to death, were the richest men of the island, and owners of the best houses in this city" Stanhope, *Spain under Charles the Second,* pp 16-17

[99] AHN *Rel. de Causas de Fe,* libro 1, 865, fols. 147-96, *Ibid.,* libro 1, 866. fol. 116vff ; Garau, pp. 41-61. The following died in the auto de fe.
1 Pedro Onofre Cortes de Guillermo, 55 años de edad.
2. Miguel Valls del Campos, de Minorca, 39.
3 Francisca Cortes, muger de Onofre Aguilo de Onofre, 48
4. Catalina Pomar, viuda de Raphael Marti menor, alias del Arpa, 71.
5. Isabel Cortes, viuda de Raphael Joseph Cortes, alias la Moyaneta, 55.
6 Catalina Bonin, muger de Raphael Agustin Pomar, alias Xotento, 36
7 Mariana Cortes y Moya, viuda de Agustin Cortes mayor, 59.
8 Teresa Cortes, viuda de Onofre Aguilo de Pedro, 55
9 Isabel Marti, muger de Juan Bautista Marti, alias Verdet, 40
10. Raphael José Cortes de Agustin, alias Filoa, 60
11. Ana Marti, viuda de Agustin Salvador Cortes, 49.
12. Raphael Crespi Cortes, alias Villa, 43.
13. Onofre Cortes de Agustin, 31.
14 Maria Forteza, viuda de José Cortes, 50
15. Isabel Cortes, muger de Miguel Alejos Cortes, 40.
16 Isabel Bonnin, muger de Raphael Valls, 43.
17 Francisca Forteza, viuda de Geronimo Terongi, 39.
18. Raphael Agustin Pomar, alias Xotento, 39

In the third auto de fe, celebrated on May 6th, sentences were pronounced upon twenty-one Conversos: fourteen burned in person and seven in effigy. Of the latter, four were executed posthumously, two died in prison, and one was a fugitive heretic. Of the former, eleven were mercifully sentenced to be garrotted before being burned; the remaining three were sentenced to be burned alive. This was the most extraordinary auto de fe of them all, for in it Raphael Valls, Raphael Benito Terongi and Catalina Terongi were sentenced to be burned alive as contumacious heretics. It was the most elaborate of the four autos de fe, and attracted greater numbers of people than the others, for the reason that human nature—no matter how advanced it be—is somehow deeply attracted by the promise of witnessing death.[100] The most distinguished persons of the island, including the viceroy and other dignitaries of state and Church, gave the occasion the prestige of their presence. That the auto de fe was a scene of deep pathos has been attested by the newly-appointed governor of Milan—on his way to assume his post —who was so deeply touched by the tears and apparent piety of one of the condemned Conversos that he petitioned, but in vain, for her life.[101]

The greatest interest in the auto de fe centered in the person of Raphael Valls, the reputed "rabbi" and leader of the Conversos. Many attempts were made to convert him to Christianity. Crucial Biblical passages were interpreted by learned theologians determined to make him see the light, but he was not convinced. The arguments of the far-superior scholars did not cause him to forsake his faith, however much he may or may not have been misguided in his beliefs.

Raphael Valls, Raphael Benito Terongi and his sister, Catalina, had boasted of stoic insensibility to whatever pain and suffering they might be forced to endure because of their faith. But Padre Garau—we must allow for his bias—painted a picture of the most abject misery which accompanied the deaths of these who presumed to be martyrs to their beliefs. Raphael Valls, he testified, was very weak; his strength gave out soon after the fires were lighted. His entrails burst open, and burning like a hot coal, he

---

19. Melchor Joseph Forteza, alias Menjus, 36.
20 Francisca Cortes, muger de Gabriel Cortes de Agustin, alias Capalt, 63.
21. Violante Marti, viuda de Onofre Cortes, 61.

100 Havelock Ellis (*Soul of Spain*, London, 1908, pp. 24, 26) noted especially the "sombre violence of the Spanish temperament" and "the insistent fascination of death" upon it.

101 Isabel Aguilo, for whom he petitioned, was burned. AHN *Rel. de Causas de Fe*, libro 1, 866, fol. 118v.

died the death of Judas! Raphael Benito Terongi appeared to Padre Garau as a dupe. He was a stupid lad who had neither wisdom nor intelligence, but only a passionate faith that everything his master had taught was the ultimate truth. He, too, fought the flames, Padre Garau reported. He even succeeded in freeing himself from the steel band which clasped him to the stake, but just at that moment, he fell sideways into the fire! His sister, Catalina, who had piously vowed to throw herself into the fire, shrieked to be set free when the flames began to singe her.

These victims died with a terrible expression upon their faces and with the utmost fury in their eyes, Padre Garau wrote, so that for days afterward the people spoke to one another of their miserable death. They were not like Christian martyrs, Garau insisted, for the faces of Christians were calm and serene, their eyes mirroring the assurance and the justice of the cause for which they had sacrificed their lives. Not so these Conversos, who were merely stubborn and unreasonable, and who in their death revealed the fury of lost souls.[102] Yet others who witnessed the holocaust must have been deeply impressed by the manner in which they died—it

---

[102] *Ibid.*, libro 1, 865, fols. 138-47, 196-219, 226-43v; *Ibid.*, libro 1, 866, fols. 118-19v; Garau, pp. 72-8; *Relacion*, pp. 4-7. The names of those executed in the auto de fe follow:

Relaxed in person
1. Miguel Marti del Arpa, 50 años de edad.
2. Raphael Ventura Cortes, hijo de Raphael Cortes, dfo., y de Isabel Cortes, alias la Moyaneta, 19
3. Joseph Aguilo, hijo de Onofre Aguilo de Pedro, y Teresa Cortes, 35.
4. Isabel Pomar, viuda de Francisco Bonnin, 71.
5. Isabel Terongi, muger de Agustin Cortes de Raphael, 43.
6. Isabel Marti, muger de Bartolome Terongi, alias el Conde, 42.
7. Juana Cortes, viuda de Bartolome Forteza, alias Menyus, 58
8. Margarta Terongi, hija de Raphael José Terongi, alias Felos, y Francisca Terongi, dfos., 29.
9. Beatriz Cortes, muger de Melchor José Forteza, alias Menyus, 28
10. Violante Forteza, muger de Raphael José Cortes, alias Filoa, 53.
11. Isabel Aguilo, muger de Pedro Juan Aguilo de Pedro Juan, 28.

Relaxed in person and burned alive
12. Catalina Terongi, muger de Guillermo Terongi, alias Morrofes, 45.
13. Raphael Benito Terongi, hermano de Catalina, y hijo Raphael José Terongi, alias Felos, y de Francisca Terongi, dfos., 21.
14. Raphael Valls, 51.

Relaxed in effigy, with their bones
15. Leonor Cortes, muger de José Marti de Francisco, alias Bruy, 63 (Died in prison).
16. Leonor Marti, viuda de Raphael Geronimo Cortes, 72. (Died in prison)
17. Agustin Cortes, 65.
18. Margarita Marti, viuda de Miguel Terongi de la Volta.

Fugitives, relaxed in effigy
19. Francisco Joseph Terongi, hijo de Raphael José Terongi, alias Felos, y Francisca Terongi, dfos.
20. Guillermo Tomas Terongi, hermano de Francisco
21. Agustin Cortes de Alfonso, alias Formatje

should be pointed out as a corrective to Garau's testimony—for the three have been celebrated as martyrs and heroes in ballads which the islanders have chanted until very recently.[103]

The final auto de fe took place on July 2nd. It was unpretentious and tame in contrast to the former three. Twenty-three Conversos were sentenced: seventeen were penanced and reconciled for a second time; three who died in prison during 1678 were also reconciled; one was burned in effigy and two in person.[104]

---

[103] Gabriel Alomar, in his "Prologo" to Estrugo's *El Retorno a Sefard,* p 8, Roth, p. 96; cf the poem written by Francisco Pelaya Briz, in *Calendari Catalá del any 1870,* Barcelona Kayserling (p 184) quotes the following stanzas, chanted by the islanders

En Valls duya se bandara
Y en Terongi's pano
En sos Xuetas derrera
Qui feyan se processó.

Com es foch li va arriba
A ses ruas des calsons,
Li deya "Falet, no't dons,
Que te carn no's cremera

Y venia gent d'Evissa
Pajesos d'Arta, d'Andraix
Porque es dia sis de maix
Ferren se saccoradissa.

The expression "Falet no't dons" is used of one "obstinate in his opinion," according to the *Amales Judaicos de Mallorca,* IV, cap. 32 (Appendix V, p. 190). The same source has the following text: "Felet no't dons que no mos cremerán a noltros, si no á sa roba."

[104] AHN *Rel. de Causas de Fe,* libro 1, 865, fols 220, 226, 240-2, 305-10v, 338-71v.; Garau, pp. 83-9; *Relacion,* p. 29. The names of the victims in this auto de fe follow:
Relaxed in person
1 Francisca Marti, alias Verdet, 58 años de edad.
2 Magdalena Forteza, muger de Gabriel Piña, alias Cap de Olleta, 73.
Fugitive, relaxed in effigy
3. Miguel Forteza, alias Butzeta.
Reconciled in effigy
4. Leonor Forteza y Valls, viuda de Gregario Forteza, 75 (when she died in prison in 1678).
5. Mariana Miro, muger de Raphael Ventura Cortes, 43 (when she died in prison in 1678).
6 Miguel Piña, 26 (when he died shortly after imprisonment in 1678).
Reconciled with various penalties
7 Geronimo Cortes, hijo de Gabriel Cortes de Agustin, alias Capalt, y Geronima Marti, dfos., 31. Gravely warned and censured, and condemned to three years in the galleys and fined 200 libras
8. Ana Aguilo, muger de Raphael Cortes de Gabriel, 36. *Id.* Condemned to exile in a city of the kingdom, 200 lashes and fined 100 libras.
9. Isabel Marti del Arpa, hija de Raphael Marti menor del Arpa, dfo., y Catalina Pomar, 40. *Id.* Condemned to exile for three years within the kingdom, 200 lashes and 200 libras.
10 Ana Marti, hermana de Isabel, 34. *Id.* Condemned to exile for one year within the kingdom, 200 lashes and 200 libras
11 Margarita Marti, 38. *Id* Condemned to exile for three years, 200 lashes and 200 libras.
12. Raphael Cortes de Gabriel, alias Capalt, 42. *Id.* Condemned to exile for five years, 500 libras and a penalty of ten years in the galleys in case of default.
13 Miguel Geronimo Aguilo, 37. *Id.* Condemned to confinement on the island, and 200 libras, with the penalty of ten years in the galleys in case of default.
14 Juanot Nicolas Marti, hijo de Miguel Ramon Marti y Francisca Pomar, dfos, 40 *Id.* Condemned to exile for two years, one year from Palma and three

In all, eighty-six Conversos were condemned in the four autos de fe of 1691.[105] Of these, forty-six were women, proving conclusively to the inquisition that the Mosaic law appealed only to weak and ignorant women-folk, and never to the strong minds of intelligent men.[106] Before the end of 1691, the inquisition had tried, in addition, thirty-nine Conversos, whose cases were finally suspended.[107]

---

leagues around it, and the other year at the tribunal's discretion, within the confines of the island, 400 libras and a penalty of ten years in the galleys in case of default

15. Gabriel Nicolas Marti, 50 *Id* Condemned to exile for two years within the confines of the island, 500 libras and a penalty of ten years in the galleys in case of default

16 Bartolome Cortes de Alfonso, 41. *Id* Condemned to exile for four years within the confines of the island, 500 libras and a penalty of ten years in the galleys in case of default.

17 Isabel Pomar, viuda de Raphael Marti del Arpa, 37 *Id* Condemned to exile for two years outside Palma, but within the confines of the island, 500 libras and a penalty of 200 lashes in case of default

18 Miguel Piña, hijo de Gabriel Piña, alias Cap de Olleta y Magdalena Forteza *Id* Condemned to a fine of 500 libras, and three years in the galleys

19 Margarita Ana Piña, 28 *Id*. Condemned to exile for one year from Palma and four leagues around it, but within the confines of the island, 100 libras, and a penalty of 200 lashes in case of default.

20 Juana Ana Marti, muger de Raphael Nicolas Forteza, 32 *Id*. Condemned to confinement within the island, 500 libras fine and a penalty of 200 lashes in case of default

21 Raphael Bonnin de José, 39. *Id*. Condemned to three years of exile within the island, 200 libras fine and a penalty of ten years in the galleys in case of default

22 Isabel Marti, viuda de Agustin Antonio Cortes (for relapse into Judaism in 1689) Sentenced to confiscation of property, ten years of exile from Palma. She was dispatched to the village of Campos, where she died a few days after arrival

23. Pedro Juan Bernardo Forteza, alias El Pages, for relapse into Judaism. Sentenced to be confined two years to the village of Sineu, for instruction in Christianity, with a penalty of four years in the galleys in case of default

The last two (22, 23) do not appear in Garau's record I found notices of them in "Relaciones de Causas de Fee despachados en la Inquisicion de Mallorca, en los años de 1691 y 1692," (AHN *Rel. de Causas de Fe,* libro 1, 865, fols. 242, 326v).

[105] At the same time only four non-Conversos were sentenced, showing that the inquisition's business during this period was chiefly with Conversos.

[106] Garau, p. 80ff

[107] The activity of the inquisition should not, therefore, be judged alone upon the figures of those condemned in the autos de fe The following cases were suspended· Margarita Marti, alias Porra, Isabel Marti, viuda de Pedro Baltazar Marti, Ana Cortes, muger de Juanot Sureda; Quiteria Marti, viuda de Bernardo Aguilo, Gabriel Cortes de Agustin, alias Cap-alt; Leonor Cortes, hija de Gabriel Cortes de Agustin; Juanot Forteza; Francisca Forteza; Miguel Aguilo, hijo de Honofre Aguilo de Pedro; Raphael Aguilo, hijo de Balthazar Joachin Marti; Isabel Terongi, viuda de Francisco Aguilo, Gabriel Piña, alias Cap de Olleta; Isabel Forteza, hija de Raphael Diego Forteza; Leonor, muger de Miguel Piña, Raphael Forteza; Francisca Cortes, viuda de Raphael Diego Cortes; Pedro Juan Terongi; Isabel Valls, viuda de Juan Baptista Forteza; Isabel Cortes, viuda de Miguel Angel Cortes; Juan Baptista Forteza; Miguel Melchor Cortes; Leonor Marti, viuda de Gabriel Juan Forteza; Clara Cortes, viuda de Thomas Forteza; Agustin Joachin Cortes, alias Billa, Joseph Marti de Francisco, alias Bruy; Melchor Cortes; Bartholome Baltazar Marti, alias el mal-ric, Cathalina Forteza, muger de Bartholome Baltazar Marti, Quiteria Cortes, muger de Bernardo

The Mosaic law was effectively crushed, and all desire to practice it was burned out of the hearts of even the most fearless Conversos. In the years which followed, the Conversos and their descendants—then already called Chuetas[108]—looked back to the year 1691 as the darkest in their history.

The year 1691 marked the apogee of the Majorcan Inquisition. Its great work now lay in the past; it was content to rest upon its laurels. Its achievements from 1691 onwards served only to maintain its position.

In the following years the tribunal had its hands full with the trials which arose out of denunciations by those arrested before 1691. No capital punishments were meted out after 1691; most of the cases were suspended. In 1692, for example, the cases of twenty-one Conversos (five already dead) were suspended. Among these cases were those of three living Conversos who had plundered the houses of their coreligionists, immediately after they had left them on the fateful night of March 7, 1688. They were dealt with leniently—although a portion of the property they stole was re-

Aguilo, Cathalina Aguilo, muger de Miguel Marti; Gabriel Thomas Cortes, alias Billa; Juana Cortes, muger de Gabriel Çortes de Francisco; Juanot Sureda; Isabel Cortes, muger de Pedro Juan Aguilo de Pedro; Isabel Marti, viuda de Jayme Cortes de Agustin; Violante Marti, viuda de Raphael Bernardo Cortes; Francisca Marti; Gabriel Carlos Cortes; Augustin Alfonso Cortes.

108 *Chuetas,* by which name the Conversos' descendants of Majorca are called up to this day, despite the prohibition in Royal Decrees against its use (see *below* p. 126), occurs first in the cases of the inquisition, beginning with 1688. In the many cases and documents of the years previous to 1688, which the author has examined, no trace was found of the use of this name. In accordance with inquisitorial procedure, after the administration of the oath the names of the culprit's antecedents were requested. He was asked whether any of them had ever come before the inquisition. After 1688, one finds that the invariable answer to this question was that the antecedents were "de casta y generación de Chuetas de la Calle del Sayell." By 1688 the name "Chueta" was already in common use in the communications of the tribunal to the Suprema (AHN *Cartas,* libro 1, 857, fol. 68). The Conversos were calling themselves by the name "Chuetas" (or "Xuyetas"), indicating that it had been in current use for sometime or they would not have used it as freely as they did. Moreover it could not have been a word with such ugly and vile connotations, as so many scholars think it is, for them to have applied it to themselves. Thus Kayserling (p 180) looks upon it as the diminutive of *chuya* (pork or pork-eater). Similarly, one of the Chuetas took it to mean this (*Revista Ilustrada,* año II, p. 622). Michel (*Histoire des Races Maudites,* II, 312-3) also interprets the word in allusion to the Conversos' abhorrence of pork. Also, Roth (p 384) believes it derives from the word *chuco,* the Spanish equivalent of the French *chouette,* an expression used in calling a dog. This author agrees with Gabriel Alomar, in his prefaces to George Sand, *Un Invierno en Mallorca,* (p. xx) and to Estrugo's *El Retorno a Sefard* (p 9) in his derivation of the word Chueta from *Jueto* or *Jueu,* Catalan and Majorcan words for "Jew." The people contemptuously used the diminutive form, thus expressing their feelings for the scorned people. The authoritative *Diccionario de la Lengua Española de la Academia Española* correctly attributes the origin of the word Chueta to the Majorcan *Jueu.* The Chuetas were commonly referred to as *Individuos de la Calle,* or ghetto-folk (for example in the Royal Decrees—see *below* pp. 125, 6, chapter VI, notes 13, 14— they are referred to: "los Individuos vulgarmente llamandos de la Calle.") Not infrequently are they called *Hebreos* and *Judíos*

stored to the inquisition—because one of them had given the inquisition notice of the Conversos' flight. So we see that another Converso had turned traitor against his own group by having informed the inquisition of the attempted escape.[109]

In the following year (1693), nine additional cases of Conversos were suspended.[110] The year 1694 brought the suspension of fourteen more, eleven of whom were dead.[111] In 1695, of the twelve cases tried, only one dealt with a living Converso: she was admitted to reconciliation although she had relapsed into heresy a second time. The eleven were posthumously tried,[112] condemned as relapsed heretics, and burned in effigy.[113]

Thus the prosecution of Conversos in the seventeenth century was finally closed.[114] The Conversos were decisively subdued, but it should not be imagined that they were exterminated. They continued to live on, and some additional records attest the determination of the inquisition to keep them in constant fear of the renewal of its prosecutions. Although few Conversos came before the inquisition in the following years, its memorable victory over them was kept alive through the permanent display in the Dominican Church of their sanbenitos, proclaiming their crimes. The sanbenitos were preserved with the intention of perpetuating the infamy of the heretics. The sins of the fathers were thereby visited upon their innocent offspring, who were constantly petitioning for the removal of these galling remembrances of their antecedents' misdeeds.[115] That the display of the sanbenitos might not lose its effect, in 1699 the island's inquisitor ordered that all those representing the condemned since 1645, especially those of 1678 and

---

[109] AHN *Rel. de Causas de Fe*, libro 1, 865, fols. 432, 432v; JTS *Proc. de Fe*, legajo 6, 2, fols. 3-4v

[110] AHN *Rel. de Causas de Fe*, libro 1, 866, fols. 124-68v (from the "Relacion de las causas de Fee despachados en esta Inqqon. de Mallorca el año passado de 1693"). In the same year, in addition to Conversos, eleven non-Conversos were tried, reconciled and penanced.

[111] *Ibid.*, fols. 173-200v. In this year six non-Conversos were tried by the inquisition

[112] The confiscations arising out of the deceased persons' property "amounted to considerable quantities," according to the report of the Inquisition of Majorca to the Suprema, September 27, 1695. AHN *Juntas de Hazienda*, libro 1, 870, fols. 215-397.

[113] AHN *Rel de Causas de Fe*, libro 1, 866, fols. 203-56v AHN *Votas y Sentencias*, libro 1, 1161, which contains the report of the conditions of the Majorcan tribunal sent to the Suprema, September 27, 1695 Cf. *Relacion*, pp. 7, 8. Eight non-Conversos were tried this year.

[114] Michel, *Histoire des Races Maudites*, II, 35-7; *Tratado*, III, caps. 17-24; *Anales Judaicos de Mallorca* contains an interesting account of the "Vicissitudes of the Conversos in the 17th Century" (reproduced in Appendix V).

[115] They offered the authorities huge sums of money to destroy the sanbenitos. Michel, *op. cit.*, II, 38.

1688-1691, be renovated and repaired, and the missing ones replaced. The Suprema itself was much disturbed over the delay of the tribunal in assuring the permanency of the sanbenitos, especially since the names and crimes of the heretics appearing on them had been erased by time.[116]

---

[116] The cost for this renovation was between 400 and 500 libras. We have seen that Philip II (*supra* p. 73, note 56) considered the sanbenito one of the most effective punishments meted out by the inquisition. (Cf. Lea, *Spain*, III, 169ff.). The former inquisitors were apparently too busy and they overlooked the Suprema's order (dated April 1, 1693) for their renovation and replacement. It was only in 1699 that the thorough and industrious Inquisitor Ibañez discovered this order and put it into immediate effect. AHN *Cartas*, legajo 1, 857, fol. 128.

CHAPTER IV

THE "JEWISH CEREMONIES" OF THE CONVERSOS

What were the specific ceremonies of the Mosaic law for which the Conversos had been condemned? There were many of them. As one peruses the extensive list of Jewish ceremonies which the inquisition alleged they observed, one cannot help but marvel at the number of them they remembered and practiced; a fact made all the more marvellous by the circumstance that almost two-hundred and fifty years had passed since the observance of Judaism had been declared illegal on the island. The historic memory of the Conversos was amazing. Many of the Jewish rites and ceremonies were cherished all the more because they were proscribed, and were passed on from father to son as part of a cultural legacy, as an occult bond linking them through the generations.

In coming and going on their missions of trade (to Marseilles, Nice, Rome, Leghorn, Alexandria, Smyrna and elsewhere),[1] the Conversos not only were inspired by actual contact with Jews to continue their adherence to Jewish practices, but they brought back to their families books with which to educate them in the Mosaic law. Pedro Onofre Cortes received one of such books which Raphael Valls had smuggled into Majorca. It contained the daily prayers, in Hebrew and Spanish, also the prayers for the new moon and the fasts and other holidays of the Jewish religious year. At first reluctant to admit how he acquired the book, at length he confessed that Raphael Valls had brought the book from some foreign city.[2] His testimony was confirmed by another Converso who told the inquisition that one of her friends owned many books on the subject of the Mosaic law, presented to him by "Raphael Valls, who lives near the inquisition, and who makes many voyages outside Majorca."[3]

These imported books exerted a tremendous influence upon their beliefs. Pedro Onofre Cortes, for example, admitted that the inspiration he received from one of these books, brought by Raphael

---

[1] One Converso described to another certain Jewish ceremonies he had seen observed among the Jews in Leghorn. The description of these ceremonies soon became the common property of all the Conversos AHN *Rel de Causas de Fe,* libro 1, 865, fol 429v

[2] AHN *Proc. de Fe,* legajo 1708, 2, fol 31v. In another place (*Ibid,* legajo 1705, 5, fol. 8) he admitted that he had arranged with Raphael Valls to testify he bought the book from a stranger, in case any questions were asked.

[3] *Ibid.,* fol. 58.

Valls from a "place where the law of Moses is observed," provided the explanation for his long attachment to Judaism. It implanted in him strong doubts about the validity of Christianity. Pedro testified that in certain passages in the Old Testament, to which this book referred, God alone was commanded to be worshiped, while Christianity was idolatrous, for in it others beside God were objects of veneration and worship.[4]

The Conversos attempted to adhere to the Jewish dietary laws which, perhaps more than any other part of Judaism, publicly stamps one an adherent of the Mosaic law.[5] They argued that the eating of pork may be acceptable to idolaters, but they were the descendants of those Jews who under Moses had forsaken idolatry when they disavowed the worship of the golden calf! They utilized all human ingenuity to avoid detection in the observance of the Jewish dietary laws, admittedly a most difficult task. Pork was forbidden in their diet, likewise scaleless fish, all types of crabs, turtles, hares and similar animals.[6] They used oil exclusively for frying in order to avoid animal-fats, and in time the use of oil came to be a mark of identification of the Converso.[7] Meat from which

[4] *Ibid.*, legajo 1708, 2, pieza 2, fol. 4. These ideas were strengthened by his reading of books entitled *Flos Santorum, Monarchia Ecclesiastica* (by Friar Geronimo Ramon), *Almenera de la Luz,* a book of examples and spiritual exercises for the observer of the law of Moses, together with the Bible, which he often read with Raphael Valls. (Cf. AHN *Proc. de Fe,* legajo 1705, 15, fols 1v, 9). Cortes also consulted the *Remillete de Flores* for the prayers which he frequently recited (Cf *Ibid.,* fols. 17, 18) Other books read by the Conversos for inspiration and knowledge of the law of Moses included *David Perseguido,* and *Espejo de Consolación* Raphael Valls burned the books which supplied the heretical literature for his family when the arrests of 1677 began (Cf. also *Ibid.,* legajo 1715, 5, pieza 1; *Ibid.,* pieza 2, fol. 116; AHN *Rel de Causas de Fe,* libro 1, 865, fols 177, 223, 223v, 257v ; *Ibid.,* libro 1, 866, fols. 198, 200ff.).

[5] Their meticulousness in observing the dietary laws was doubtless a hang-over from earlier times, for Rabbi Simon ben Zemah Duran, the native Majorcan who fled after the riots of 1391, remarked that the Majorcan Jews observed the laws of ritually clean food (*Kashruth*) to the neglect of the laws of equity. Cf. Epstein, *Responsa of Rabbi Simon B. Zemah Duran* etc., p. 43.

[6] The mother of a Converso's servant who brought bacon to her daughter was startled to learn how strenuously the mistress objected to it, prohibiting its preparation in her kitchen (Cf. AHN *Proc. de Fe,* legajo 1708, 5, fol. 6v). There is a tradition on the island that the Conversos, in order to outwardly show their loyalty to Christianity, cooked pork outside their houses, in an effort to persuade the populace that they had lost every attachment to Judaism. Thus to them the *sine qua non* of Jewish observance was loyalty to the dietary laws, the practice of which was indeed extremely hazardous (Cf Roth, p. 178). Because of the danger involved, the Conversos soon realized the folly of making the dietary laws the essence of Judaism, and their leaders propounded the doctrine that Judaism was a matter of the heart. Into the heart it would be difficult, they reasoned, for inquisitors to peer!

[7] In reply to the question of his servant, Pedro Onofre Cortes said that only since the time of the pestilence had he used oil (olive oil was plentiful on the island and is still one of its chief products) when the use of lard had made him very sick. Roth, p. 179: (Cf. Dr. Roth's documented article: "The Religion of the

the blood had not been drawn was also a forbidden food. It was
ordered to be first washed thoroughly, and then salted. (It is extraordinary that this rite was practiced among Conversos.) If the
animal was not slaughtered according to Jewish ritual, they desired
at least to prepare the meat according to the ritual.[8] They baked
their own bread, throwing a piece of fresh dough into the fire, according to traditional Jewish usage, praying that God will cause the
dough to rise.[9]

The Conversos bought live fowls and slaughtered them according to their own laws.[10] A special knife for this purpose was
concealed in the house of Pedro Onofre Cortes, and was constantly
being borrowed by the neighbors who never asked for it by name,
but said cryptically: "lend *it* to me."[11] Not everyone, however,
could use the "ritual-knife." Special functionaries (*shochtim*:
trained and recognized as ritual-slaughterers) went from house to
house and performed the slaughtering, which was always accompanied by appropriate benedictions.[12]

The Conversos wanted to observe Saturday as their Sabbath.
In the detailed instructions for the observance of the law of Moses
which one of the Conversos wrote into his will, the Sabbath was
recommended for observance "as the chief holiday of the law of
Moses."[13] In honor of the Sabbath all corners of their houses were
scoured. All linens were changed, and their homes took on a festive atmosphere. The men changed into their holiday clothes, and
the women adorned themselves with their holiday finery, and with
cosmetics. A special meal was prepared for Sabbath eve, which in-

---

Marranos," *JQR*, XXII, 1931, 1-33); AHN *Proc. de Fe*, legajos· 1708, 2, fol. 6;
1708, 5, pieza 2, fol. 3; 1709, 4, fol. 52

[8] *Ibid*, legajo 1708, 2, fol. 57: "que no se avia de comer sangre ni carne que tuviesse
sangre y la mandaba lavar muy bien, que no tuviesse sangre, y la ponian en
sal . . . ."

[9] "Dios la haga crecer a la masa." ("May God make this dough increase.")

[10] AHN *Proc. de Fe*, legajos: 1708, 5, pieza 2, fol. 4; 1709, 3, pieza 3, fol 18; 1709, 4,
fols. 7v, 21. Among a half dozen live fowls a Converso purchased, one had come
dead. The mistress of the house forthwith sent it to a Christian! Live fowls were
kept in the house and slaughtered as required.

[11] *Ibid.*, legajos: 1708, 5, pieza 2, fol. 3; 1709, 3, pieza 3, fols 5, 21v.

[12] *Ibid*, legajos: 1708, 2, fols 17v, 57; 1709, 14, fol. 8 A pan of ashes or sand caught
the blood. I doubt very much if they actually decapitated the fowl, as Dr. Roth
suggests in "approximating the ritual regulations," but actually slaughtered it according to the methods of Jewish ritual (Cf. Roth, p 179) The benediction recited was. "Bendito tu Adonay, nuestro Dios, Rey del mundo, que nos santificó
en sus mandamientos y nos encomendó la degolladura." When the blood was covered with the ashes or sand, the following was recited "Bendito tu Adonay, nuestro
Dios, Rey del mundo, que nos santificó en sus mandamientos y nos encomendó la
cobertura de la sangre." (See Appendix VI, Benedictions 18b, 18c).

[13] AHN *Proc. de Fe*, legajos 1708, 2, fol. 57; 1709, 10, fol 3 (The will of Ana Sureda's father).

variably included fish, so that a domestic remarked that she knew when Sabbath came "by the odor of fish in the house."[14] The lamps, newly-cleaned in the Sabbath's honor, were lighted with ceremony, precautions being taken that new oil and fresh wicks insured their burning from Friday sunset until Saturday sunset.[15] In time, the Sabbath-light came to be one of their insistent Jewish memories.

No food was prepared on the Sabbath; it was cooked on Friday before sunset. The Conversos strictly adhered to the traditional Jewish custom of eating on Sabbath only the food prepared the day before. If nothing had been prepared in advance, they contented themselves with the simple fare of bread and olives. They excused themselves from cooking on Saturday by explaining that they were very busy in their stores, being the day the country-folk came to the city to buy.

They ushered in the Sabbath (at sundown Friday) with a prayer, praising the power, the omnipresence and the mercy of the God of Israel. This benediction was dedicated to St. Tobit, for they prayed that God might lead them as He had led St. Tobit, out of sorrow and blindness into happiness and light.[16] From a book called the *Remillete de Flores,* their treasure-trove of prayers, the Conversos copied and memorized the prayers and, fearing detection, threw the manuscript into the sea. One of the Friday evening prayers which they recited from the *Remillete de Flores* was entitled *Recibimiento del Sabat* (the Spanish for the Jewish prayer *Kebalat Shabat,* "Welcoming the Sabbath"), and was written in Hebrew. Another Hebrew prayer from the same source was the *Idus,* (which beyond all doubt was the *Kiddush,* the prayer sanctifying the Sabbath-wine) recited before the meal ushering in the Sabbath. They said the *Idus* prayer "with a cup in hand, and after drinking a little (wine) out of it, the master of the house gave it to his wife to drink. All this was done in accordance with the instructions of the book, in remembrance of the practice of the Jews

---

14 *Ibid*, legajo 1708, 5, fol 5. Pedro Onofre Cortes bought the best fish on Friday; an egg omelet was substituted if fish was not available.

15 *Ibid.*, legajo 1709, 3, fol. 29v "Quando enciendan el candil, dixese 'Alabado sea el nombre de Dios'" ("Blessed be the name of God"). But Lea (*Spain,* III, 301) doubts that the Conversos were so careful· "lamps might be lighted on Friday night, but it sufficed to light one and let it burn till it went out." Moreover, Lea (*Ibid.*) did not discover that the Sabbath was enough of a holiday for the Conversos to change into clean clothes· "the changing of body linen is rarely alluded to." In our records, however, the Conversos invariably changed into a complete new wardrobe for Sabbath, as well as for the other holidays they observed.

16 St Tobit, with St. Raphael and St Esther were "the patron saints" of the Conversos. (Cf. Roth, p. 171). See Appendix VI, Prayer 4.

who, upon leaving the synagogue on Friday evening, went to their homes and recited this prayer with a wine-cup in hand, allowing all the circumcised to drink of it."[17]

In addition to the Sabbath, the Conversos observed with punctilious regularity some of the fasts prescribed by the Mosaic law. The most important of these was the Day of Atonement, which they called variously *El Ayuno del Perdon* ("the Fast of Forgiveness"), or *El Ayuno Mayor* ("the Great Fast"). It was the most solemn holy day of their religious calendar, which even the very old among them observed, although their age exempted them from the rigor of the minor fasts. Like all other holidays and fasts, its observance began with the appearance of the first evening star, and continued until the following evening, again with the appearance of the first star. During the fast day they abstained completely from food and drink for twenty-four hours. At the time of the Great Fast they prayed to God to forgive them their sins, great and overburdening as they were, and beseeched Him never to forsake them, for He alone was their source of strength and their refuge in their secret and furtive lives.

Just before the beginning of the wholesale arrests in 1677, the Conversos observed the Day of Atonement in the garden of Pedro Onofre Cortes, and most of them managed to be present, so important to them was this holy day. Only a very few were left behind in their stores and houses to ward off any suspicion.

The description of the ritual for the Great Fast comes to us from many sources, which agree even to minutest details. After they had assembled, one of their own, acting as the leader, asked if they wished to pray according to the customs of the fast day. They replied that they all desired to pray. Thereupon the leader turned to the appropriate prayers in the book, and recited them in a loud voice, after which they repeated them. The prayers opened with the words, *Osana, Osana,* but they were not able to remember much more for, the Conversos reported, the prayers were in a strange language (doubtless Hebrew). The men covered their heads with handkerchiefs, reminiscent of the prayer-shawl used by Jews. Before the Services for the Great Fast ended, the worshippers begged

---

[17] "Tambien leia otra que se intitula *Idus* de recibimiento de sabat, lo qual decia con una taza en la mano, y haviendola dicho bevia un poco, y dava de bever a la . . . su muger, y esto lo hazia porque el libro lo decia, y que los hebreos quando salian de la Sinagoga de viernes por tarde por celebrar el Sabado devian en su casa esta oración con una taza de vino en la mano y davan de bever á los sircunstantes . . ." AHN *Proc. de Fe,* legajo, 1705, 15, pieza 3, fol. 5v. This is testimony of one of the Conversos, and this ceremony is similarly described in the Edict of Faith (*Nos los Inqdores . . . op. cit.,* JTS, fol. 2) showing, at least in this instance, how accurately informed the inquisition was about their Jewish ceremonies. Cf. *supra* p. 56, note 2.

forgiveness of each other, kissing one another's hands in token of their mutual forgiveness.

The Great Fast was the climax of three fasts which occurred during the first ten days following the appearance of the new moon of September. The first two were observed within two or three days of one another, the first of which was the Fast of Gedaliah. It was preceded by a meal consisting simply of fish. The meal which preceded the Great Fast, however, was little short of a banquet. It consisted of chicken and the finest of foods, arranged with the greatest ostentation. In honor of this holiday (as well as for the others they observed), the Conversos persisted in their ancient custom of using new salt. In honor of the Great Fast, also, the entire house was thoroughly cleaned, all clothes and linens washed, each person freshly bathed, dressing himself in his choicest garments. The uniqueness of the Day of Atonement impressed itself upon the minds of the Conversos so that it remained, even for the most lukewarm among them, the one abiding memory of their Jewish past and ofttimes the last thread of contact with it.[18]

Next to the Great Fast in religious significance was the Fast of Esther, which, according to their reckoning, fell on the eleventh day after the new moon of March. The traditional joyous aspects of the festival were forgotten by the Conversos. Only the rigor of the fast which Queen Esther had ordered for the salvation of her people impressed itself upon them.[19] With more than orthodox severity, the Conversos abstained from food for three days for the Fast of Esther. So strongly did this fast appeal to their imaginations, that very often they forced the children to observe it also, moderated of course for their tender constitutions by permitting them to eat on the middle day of the three-days' fast.

It is small wonder that the Fast of Esther appealed so strongly to them, for they felt that the circumstances of the story were parallel to their own conditions: Esther had kept her faith and her people a secret, yet she never forsook the faith of her fathers, and, when summoned to meet the crucial test of revealing her religion to the king, she did not flinch. Her bravery and courage inspired them. If the heroine appealed to their imaginations, so did the villain of the story, the wicked Haman, the symbol of the Jews' enemy. God would save them, for they reposed their confidence and faith in Him, the Conversos believed, although enemies surrounded them, in the same way as He had saved His people from the hands of

---

18 AHN *Proc. de Fe*, legajos· 1705, 5, fol 2, 1705, 15, fol 3; 1708, 2, fols 30v, 32, 32v, 56, 58v, 65v; 1711, fol. 5.
19 Book of Esther IV, 16.

Haman. The three-days' fast having ended, they refreshed themselves by bathing, and clothed themselves with clean garments "in memory of the marvels which the God of Israel had done in liberating the children of Israel, and in honor of the freedom and triumph of the Jews over Haman." The meal served upon the eve of the fast and at its close was simple, consisting only of fish, peas, and spinach. At the conclusion of the fast, the Conversos again asked one another's pardon by kissing hands and saying: "God will pardon us as He has pardoned the patriarchs."[20]

The austerity of Catholicism, added to their own pitiable spiritual state, produced self-mortification in the character of the Conversos—an attitude foreign to traditional Judaism. Therefore the fasts attracted their attention and impressed themselves upon their memories. As the generations passed by, the joyousness of the festivals, which in Jewish tradition complemented the fasts, was forgotten, and only the sombreness and the self-mortifying elements of the fasts remained, because the latter more nearly reflected their own morbid souls.

In addition to the two important fasts, their religious calendar had other minor fasts. They observed the "Fast of Lentils" in July, doubtless in memory of the destruction of the Temple in Jerusalem. The meal ushering in this fast consisted of lentils and hardboiled eggs.[21] On the eve of Passover some of them observed the "Fast of the First-Born", preceded by an elaborate meal prepared with great care, and served on a very large and beautifully-appointed table. The oldest son was carried into the banquet room in the arms of his father, in allusion to the original reason for the celebration of this fast.[22] Other Conversos observed the first day following the appearance of the new moon (*Rosh Hodesh*) with a fast.[23]

In addition, many observed voluntary fasts on Monday and Thursday, and sometime also on Sunday or Wednesday. These were observed as fasts of penitence, a mood which constantly afflicted the Conversos who tortured themselves by the dreary thought that they were living in apostasy of their faith. That was reason enough

---

[20] AHN *Proc. de Fe*, legajos: 1705, 15, pieza 2, fols 3, 3v; 1705, 15, pieza 3, fol. 2, 1708, 2, fol. 55v; JTS *Proc. de Fe* legajo 3, 18, fol 101v.

[21] AHN *Proc. de Fe*, legajos: 1705, 5, fol. 9v; 1708, 2, fol 56; JTS *Proc. de Fe*, 3, 18, fol. 75. In their own minds the historical reason for observing this fast had become muddled and confused, so that one Converso said he kept it in memory of Saul (?) who had sold his birthright to Jacob for a lentil-pottage! Mourners' fare consisted of eggs and lentils, according to Jewish tradition. *Bab Talmud· Baba Bathra*, fol. 16a

[22] Exodus XIII, 2, 11ff. AHN *Proc de Fe*, legajos 1705, 15, fol 7; 1708, 2, fol. 22v

[23] *Ibid*, legajo 1705, 5, fol 2v.

for their fasting; they were convinced that out of it atonement would come for their sins. They observed the voluntary fasts also in order to invoke God's protection upon Conversos in the prisons of the inquisition. The recurring frequency of these fasts made necessary more than ordinary precautions, so that in our records reports like these recur: they "fasted with great simulation and deceit, seating themselves at the table but not eating a morsel"; "some took food to the top floor of their houses upon one pretext or another, but it was later found untouched"; "some left their homes at mealtime alleging an urgent mission, saying that they would take their meal elsewhere"; "others sent their servants away in order to avoid detection from their peering eyes."[24]

The Jewish festival-cycle was practically supplanted among the Conversos by a succession of fasts. Indeed, some festive occasions in the religious calendar were changed into fasts to mirror the Conversos' sombreness and sense of sinfulness. But they remembered the Feast of Tabernacles as a festival. It was described as "the days of wandering in the desert when the Jews lived in booths." . . . "Two or three days after the Great Fast come seven continuous days of festival", they were taught, "in which one ought not work, but abstain by complaining of severe headaches, or the like. During these feast-days one should kill the fowl himself, allowing no one else to do it for him."[25] Although Purim (they called it the "Fast of Esther") retained, even for them, the joyous memory of the liberation of the Jews from the hands of their enemies, they observed it by fasting.

The Conversos celebrated the Passover festival, also, whose historical background appeared peculiarly like their own. They, too, were living in bondage, like their progenitors in Egypt. "God has castigated us," said one of them, "because we have become idolaters, like the Jews in Egypt." They anticipated that another Moses would arise to lead them out of their house of bondage into a land of promise.[26] They prepared the Paschal Lamb in strict accordance with the Biblical injunctions, and roasted it whole. They

---

24 *Ibid*, legajos· 1705, 5¡, fol. 2v, 1705, 15 fol 5v; 1708, 2, fols 4, 7v, 18, 20v, 55v; 1708, 5, pieza 2, fol 4¦.

25 *Ibid.*, legajo 1708, 2, fol 56. (From the instructions in the will of Ana Sureda's father)

26 So strong had the historic memory of the slavery in Egypt taken root in the minds of these people that the first of the Ten Commandments became a most important doctrine in the law of Moses, which, they claimed, the Christians had forsaken "Thou shalt love only *Adonay,* thy God, He who brought thee out of Egypt and given thee freedom, and delivered thee out of the hands of Pharaoh" ("Adorarás solo Adonay tu Dios aquel te sacó de Egipto, y te dió la libertad, y te sacó de manos de Pharaón") JTS *Proc de Fe,* 3, 18, fols 46v. 176

ate also a sort of unleavened bread during Passover, despite the danger which its use might visit upon them. (When leavened bread was served at the table during Passover, the Conversos laughed and refused to eat it; whereupon some member of the family produced unleavened bread which was consumed with great gusto!) The large feast alluded to above, on the eve of the "Fast of the First-Born", came, with the passing of years, to take the place of the *Seder* meal and service, traditionally observed the first two evenings of Passover.[27]

It was only natural that the Conversos would take advantage of the great incidents in human life—birth, marriage, and death—to teach and emphasize the observances of the Mosaic law. The first religious ceremony after birth was baptism, and their infants were all baptized, as all other Christian children. There are no indications in the records that their male children were circumcised, despite the allegations made by the inquisition. That kind of attachment to the Mosaic law courted certain disaster. Many of the Conversos, however, were convinced that circumcision alone insured fealty to the God of Israel; some saying that the uncircumcised could not be good Jews. An adjustment to circumstances necessarily had to be made. The comforting formula was therefore developed that God did not demand circumcision, so long as they "circumcised their hearts with good deeds." For the bolder spirits this offered no real solution. Pedro Onofre Cortes wanted his wife to perform the rite upon him and refrained from carrying it out "only because of natural shame." We have a record of only one circumcision among the Conversos: Raphael Benito Terongi, who performed the rite upon himself with a small piece of glass while in the inquisition's prison.[28]

---

[27] AHN *Proc. de Fe*, legajos: 1705, 5, fols. 3-5; 1705, 15, pieza 1, fol. 7; 1705, 15, pieza 3, fol 118; 1708, 2, fol 60v; JTS *Proc de Fe,* legajo 6, 2, fol 10v. The prayer: "El uno: el Gran Dios de Israel . . . ." (Appendix VI, Prayer 10), is part of the traditional Passover liturgy, but we have no indication that the Conversos recited it during the Passover season.

[28] AHN *Proc. de Fe*, legajos, 1705, 5, fol 27v; 1705, 7, fol. 4v; 1705, 15, pieza 3, fols. 32, 63. They knew that circumcision was the distinguishable sign of the Jew, and the testimony of many of them clearly shows that it aroused great arguments among them. But caution prevailed over enthusiasm, and with the one exception, they contented themselves with "circumcising their hearts with good deeds" "Circumcision, of course, was out of the question; it was too compromising and there was no one to perform it unless some zealous youth might betake himself to France or to Italy for the purpose." Lea, *Spain*, III, 301; similarly Roth, p. 174. For the only other instance of circumcision (beside that of Raphael Benito Terongi)—and here we are not certain—Raphael Joachin Valls was accused by enemies denouncing him to the inquisition of circumcising his three sons, although there is no definite proof that he performed the rite beyond the alleged circumstantial evidence that they died when very young (See *below* p. 120).

With the approach of puberty each girl was instructed in the special Mosaic laws of purity and cleanliness. During the menstrual period the girl was admonished against eating cooked foods. After the eight-day period had passed, she was ordered to bathe in a warm solution of wild marjorom and salt. The menstrual period of the married woman made her incommunicable to her husband. After the birth of a child, the mother was held by the Conversos to be incommunicable for two months, at the close of which period she was ordered to bathe in a solution similar to that used after the menstrual period.[29]

The marriages of the Conversos were performed in conformity with Catholic ritual. Nevertheless, they secretly concluded their marriage arrangements (as they were accused of doing) and sealed them with a "Jewish oath," made usually in their gardens or at the cemetery, before the graves of their dead. Originally, following the conversions of the Jews, from 1391 to 1435, there were a number of intermarriages between Conversos and old-Christians. In the latter part of the seventeenth century, however, the feeling against the old-Christians increased (they were called "Canaanites," the traditional enemies of the ancient Jews), and those among the Conversos who married old-Christians were scorned and ridiculed, and stamped as renegades. As group-consciousness grew among the Conversos by the operations of the inquisition, a similar exclusiveness grew among the old-Christians, who increasingly refused to intermarry with them. It was a mutual exclusiveness which, with the passing of the generations, divided Majorca and tended to segregate the Conversos and their descendants from the rest of the people of the island.[30]

The small group, living within the larger and more powerful one, seeks to maintain its integrity at all cost. The Conversos went to tremendous effort in assuring their group-integrity. Thus Raphael Valls went to extreme means in safeguarding the solidarity of his group by teaching that only those with untainted Jewish blood could find salvation through the God of Israel. His teaching accordingly forbade any intermarriages between Conversos and old-Christians. A fierce antagonism awaited him who married outside the group, for he was thus flouting the desired group loyalty and

---

29 AHN *Proc. de Fe,* legajo 1708, 2, fol. 61v. Biblical legislation ordained that the menstrual period makes a woman unclean for seven days (Leviticus XV, 19ff). The bath in marjorom and salt was the substitute among the Conversos for the ritual-purification bath (*mikveh*). The Biblical legislation for women in childbirth is to be found in Leviticus XII, 2ff. For a full discussion, see the Tractate *Niddah* ("The Menstruant"), 6th division of the *Mishnah.* [Cf. Canon Herbert Danby's fine translation of the *Mishnah,* (Oxford, 1933), p. 745ff.].

30 AHN *Proc. de Fe,* legajo 1709, 3, fol. 109

cohesion. So carefully was the hatred of the renegade nurtured a-
mong them, that the Hebrew word *Malshin* (slanderer or denounc-
er) was contemptuously applied to him as late as the close of the
seventeenth century. Humiliation also awaited the offspring of the
intermarried, the Conversos calling them mulattos and half-
breeds.[31]

Such hatred inevitably engendered bitterness by the outcasts
toward their former group. Often, to make matters worse, the
immediate family completely disowned those who intermarried,
and, in pursuance with traditional Jewish custom, mourned for
them as though they were dead. Their parents, brothers, and sis-
ters would not suffer themselves to come near them. These discon-
tented and isolated persons, so ignominiously thrust out from their
group and family circles, very often proved to be the worst enemies of the Conversos, because they knew their life intimately
enough to be effective slanderers. One of these, we have seen, denounced the Conversos to the inquisition.[32]

A chasm separated Conversos from old-Christians; but among
the Conversos themselves divisions obtained. They constituted a
number of "tribes," and it was considered a breach for any member
of a "higher tribe" to marry a member of an "inferior tribe."
(Here, again, the allegations against them were true.) Memories
of the three-fold division of the Jews into priest, levite, and ordinary Israelite, doubtless had its revenge in making divisions within
the group, causing no little suffering to bold transgressors of the
hard and fast classifications.[33]

It was not unusual therefore that the Conversos were meticu-
lous in the marriage alliances of their children, often arranging
them when the parties to the marriage were still very young. The
old-Christians accused them of entering into marriage alliances with
foreign Conversos. This was manifestly a fabricated allegation for
suspicion was too strongly focused upon them to bring any foreigners into an island community, which always regarded the stranger
with suspicion. One part of the accusation, however, is correct:
the Conversos demanded credentials to assure them that the prospective bride or groom was a believer in the Mosaic law before the
marriage was consummated. Those whose reputation as faithful
Conversos was firmly established were considered the best prospective alliances, often bringing handsome dowries. Only by such

31 "poma y presech"
32 AHN *Proc. de Fe,* legajos· 1705, 5 fols 6v, 7, 15; 1709, 1, pieza 3, fol. 29, 1709, 3, fol 5, 1709, 8, fol. 4; 1709, 9, fol. 1v Cf. *supra* pp. 80, 81.
33 AHN *Proc. de Fe,* 1705, 5, fols 12-15.

care practiced through the generations could there be assurance of the continuity of their beliefs and ceremonies.[34]

Death inevitably turned the Conversos inward in contemplation of the genuine worthwhileness of life. They felt an assurance that those who had observed the law had passed on to their great reward. In the house of death the Conversos gathered and spoke of "the goodness of the deceased," (a cryptic expression meaning his adherence to the Mosaic law). To the bereaved family the leaders of the group spoke comfortingly of the bountiful mercy of the God of Israel, and of the reward the deceased had merited for believing in Him. It was generally known that a priest was never present during the final hours to administer the last rites (as the old-Christians alleged). In consonance with Biblical usage, they turned the faces of their dead toward the wall. They closed all the windows of the house of death. They washed the corpse with water and ointment, in observance of the Jewish rite of *taharah* (the ritual laving of the body), and clothed it in a clean shroud. After the interment had taken place, a day of fasting was observed. No food or drink was served for eight days in the house of mourning, and during the same time no meat was eaten by the immediate family, to make sure of the observance of the dietary laws at least for that period. The immediate family did not change garments for a month following the death.

The entire community of Conversos went into mourning for the death of one of its members. Not one of them ate meat until the body was interred. All prepared food was put aside for another day. If a death was announced before mealtime, the master of the house ate no meat, "saying in dissimulation that he had to leave on an urgent mission." He ate, instead, the funeral fare of rice and oil, customary among the Majorcan Conversos. If the news of death came during the night, a strict fish diet was observed the following day. Thus, at least at the time of the death of one of them, the entire community attempted to observe the dietary laws, as token of their bond of Jewishness with the deceased.[35]

These ceremonies left a deep impression upon the minds of the children. They stood out as the most vivid memories in their life, transcending in importance and in endurance any formal instruction

---

34 *Ibid.,* legajos · 1705, 5, fol 7; 1708, 3, fol 3; 1709, 8, fol. 4; AHN *Rel. de Causas de Fe,* libro 1, 865, fol 408

35 AHN *Proc. de Fe,* legajos · 1708, 2, fols 8, 10v, 13v, 14, 61; 1708, 5, fols. 2, 4; 1709, 1, pieza 3, fol 3; AHN *Pleitos Civiles,* legajo 2, 1689, fol. 24v. Cf. Roth, pp. 189, 190
It was said that they buried their dead unlike old-Christians inside the Churches, but, like Jews, in virgin soil outside the Churches near a stream of fresh water AHN *Proc. de Fe, legajo* 1709, 1, pieza 3. See Appendix IV, p. 185

they received. The parents recognized this fact and when they felt
the child was old enough to guard with secrecy what he saw and
heard, he was allowed to witness and participate in these ceremonies.

The problem of introducing the children into the teachings of
the secret faith was difficult and trying for the elders. They were
faced by the dilemma: to introduce them at too early an age might
place the whole family in danger because of some bit of childish
prattle; to introduce them after they had reached the age of discretion might be too late to make any lasting impression. Although
no age for introducing the offspring into the secret practice of Judaism is uniformly indicated in the records, there is sufficient evidence
to show that it was close to the traditional age of *Bar-Mitzvah* (the
rite celebrated at the end of the thirteenth year, when the boy becomes an adult Jew).

Some children were introduced into secret Judaism at twelve,
others at thirteen or fourteen; there being no defined age limit. Ordinarily, the girls were taught at puberty, when they were first told of
the Mosaic laws of purity to be observed during and after the menstrual period. It is not uncommon, however, to find that some parents waited until the marriage arrangements had been completed to
tell their children that they must observe the Mosaic laws, often
securing at the same time a pledge that it would be taught to their
children. At some time or another the father (or the mother) summoned the child to tell him of the Mosaic law which he was henceforth expected to observe, for "it was the one true faith through
which alone he could obtain salvation."[36] In this way all their
knowledge of Jewish observances was passed on from generation
to generation. Their secret religious heritage, thus committed to
the keeping of the coming generation, consisted of the Jewish fastdays and festivals, the dietary laws, the few fragmentary prayers
and benedictions, the traditions of marriage within the group, and
the theology and the stories of the patriarchs and prophets of the
Old Testament.[37]

---

[36] This is a constant refrain running through all the documents, often occurring as
frequently as two and three times on some folios.

[37] The case-records and documents provide almost numberless references to the problem the Conversos faced in teaching the Mosaic law to their children In this instance, as in the other problems discussed above, I shall content myself with only
a few references, which might be multiplied endlessly at will AHN *Proc. de Fe*,
legajos· 1705, 5, fols 6, 8v; 1705, 15, pieza 3, fols. 9, 140v; 1708, 2, fols. 55-60,
1708, 4, fol 4v; 1708, 20, fols 7, 20; 1709, 8, fol 4, 1709, 9, fol 1v; 1709, 10, fol 2,
1715, 5, fol. 2v. AHN *Rel. de Causas de Fe*, libro 1, 865, fols. 156, 161v, 169, 186v,
194v, 200v, 246v, 250v, 260v.

In case any question or doubt arose concerning the law of Moses, Pedro Onofre Cortes and Raphael Valls, the two leaders of the secret community, were consulted. They were the recognized teachers of the Mosaic law. The Converso who grew skeptical of the law was sent to Cortes, who invariably allayed his doubts and strengthened his devotion to secret Judaism. Cortes was called "the theologian." He was deeply jealous of his faith, and so anxious was he to propagate it that he dared to return to his native village to convert the laborers there to his beliefs. Raphael Valls was regarded as the head of the community (the "rabbi"), the source of guidance and knowledge. During the secret-meetings of the Conversos, Valls was always the dominating presence who moved and inspired the people by his wisdom and courage, exhorting them to persevere in their observance of the Mosaic law, no matter how great were the sacrifices it demanded.[38]

While it is remarkable that the Conversos remembered as much as they did, in many ways they fell short of observing the law of Moses in its entirety, or in its purity. The ideals and the basic theological doctrines of their secret faith were shot through with generations of Catholic influence. It is not, therefore, a complete surprise to find that the Conversos' confession of faith was not the traditional Jewish declaration of the unity of God: "Hear, O Israel, the Lord our God, the Lord is One," but, in the pattern of the Catholic Church, the insistence upon the salvation of the soul of the individual. Indeed, the great difference between the observant Catholic and the Converso lay in the source of salvation: the former believed salvation lay only in the law of the Church, the latter only in the law which God gave to Moses. The essence of the secret religion of the Conversos was that salvation came only to him who firmly believed in the Mosaic law. The attainment of salvation by the individual alone, it must be observed, negates the whole traditional Jewish concept of the interests of the whole community as against those of the individual.[39] Judaism at basis is a socialized faith; Christianity an individualized one. Little did the Conversos realize that they were disavowing the very spirit of the faith they so eagerly wanted to observe.

---

38 JTS *Proc. de Fe*, legajos: 3, 18, fols. 50, 50v; 3, 19, fol. 57v It was said only of Raphael Valls that he knew the 613 precepts of the Mosaic law! He was doubtless the most erudite among them; therefore he was called the "rabbi."

39 "The idea of salvation for the individual was indissolubly linked with the salvation of the people." Moore, *Judaism*, (2 vols, Cambridge, Mass., 1927), II, 312. Cf. Kohler, *Jewish Theology*, (New York, 1928), pp. 5, 6 For a discussion of the "individual" in Judaism, see Schechter, *Some Aspects of Rabbinic Theology*, (New York, 1910), pp. 76-9

Through their ignorance the Conversos also broke away from the traditional emphasis of Judaism against the worship of saints, when they prayed to St. Raphael and St. Tobit to deliver and succour them. What was important to them was that their prayers and aspirations reach God. If this communication could be effected only by means of saints (so strongly intrenched in them was Catholic doctrine), then they employed saints, so long as the saints mediating between them and God were Jewish, and not Christian saints!

The crux of their secret Jewish theology was the salvation it offered the individual's soul by virtue of his belief in the Mosaic law. From it flowed a multitude of affirmations for them adequate enough to invalidate the arguments advanced by Catholicism. Thus the Conversos argued that Christ was a man like other men. He was born of a woman like all men, therefore Christ must be mortal, and no mortal could be God. Neither could God and man together become God. They could not believe in God and Christ, they insisted, nor in God, Christ and the Holy Ghost. They found it beyond their human power to believe in three Gods! In this way they tried to dispose of the arguments of Catholic theologians.

To the Conversos the Messiah had not yet come, nor would he come, they believed, until the Hebrew people (of which they considered themselves a part) had made penance for their sins. When the Messiah appeared, the Jews would be freed from their bondage and, under his leadership, return to the land of promise. They were acquainted with the prophecies of Daniel and often set them up as the bulwark of their hope in the future coming of the Messiah—who would appear in God's good time, when He alone would pierce the mystery which was hidden and sealed away in His book. The fifty-third chapter of Isaiah's prophecy, when used as proof that the man of sorrows was Christ, left them unconvinced. They applied the idea of "the servant of the Lord" to the Jewish people who, like themselves, were being despised and rejected of men. Christians said that the Jews deserved punishment as the crucifiers of Christ. Rather it was the Jews, the Conversos believed, who were the suffering and crucified people.

The Conversos looked upon Christianity with suspicion, for they held that true religion was wrought only by God, while Christianity was a product of men's hands; for were not the images of its God and saints made by human hands? Indeed, they often pitied the Christians who were blind to the folly of worshipping idols, images of stone and wood, which the laws of Deuteronomy expressly proscribed. What idolatry and sinfulness, the Conversos remonstrated, to worship images when God had created the world and all the images, and He was greater than the entire world, which was only a manifestation of His power! God's infinity could not be compressed into an image, for He was omnipresent, and no one could see His face. The Conversos scoffed at the Christian God, "which has eyes but sees not, feet but moves not." The Conversos felt sure of their ground in retaining at least this much of their Jewish legacy: an almost instinctive revulsion against idolatry.[40]

Of all aspects of Christianity which appeared ludicrous to the Conversos, there was none more than the power possessed by the priest, a mere mortal, to grant forgiveness for the sins of other mortals—as though he were God and not a mere man himself. Among the clergy of the time there were some dissolute and indulging priests (the inquisition always had some cases of *solicitation* by priests during the confessional before it), giving them, they thought, ample validity for their arguments. Catholic priests led a wicked life because they were denied the right of marriage, the Conversos believed, but "Jewish priests" were always allowed to marry! God alone, and not mortal man, could forgive other mortals. He alone was beyond all temptations, while the priesthood was subject to human frailties, which disqualified it for its God-like function.[41]

Prayers

Strongly binding the Conversos to their secret beliefs was the sense of security they felt coming from communicating with their God through prayer. They employed Catholic prayers, very often with only slight modifications and omissions, in praying to the God of Israel. In addition, they recited the penitential psalms as "Jewish prayers" by omitting the "Gloria Patri et Filio et Spiritui Sancto" at the close, as the old-Christians had alleged. It made little difference what one said in prayer, so long as the intention of the prayer was to communicate with the God of Israel. Indeed any words spoken in prayer, the Conversos were convinced, would be

---

40 JTS *Proc. de Fe,* legajo 3, 18, fols. 162, 163. Idolatry figures as one of the three cardinal sins (adultery, idolatry, shedding of blood) which the Jew must shun, even at the expense of his own life Cf. Schechter, *op cit.,* p. 205 "One who renounces idolatry is called in Scripture a Jew." "The rejection of idolatry is acknowledgment of the whole law" Moore, *op. cit ,* I, 325, note 1

41 AHN *Proc. de Fe.* legajos: 1705, 5, fol 3; 1705, 15, pieza 3, fols 64, 129; 1708, 2, fols 31, 57, 63v; 1708, 2, pieza 2, fol 5v; 1708, 5, fol. 6v; 1711, 7, fols. 1v, 31v. AHN *Rel. de Causas de Fe,* libro 1, 865, fol 401. "The Christians are consoled by their confessors," remarked one of the Conversos, "but we do not need the consolation of confessors We console one another." We have seen that (*supra* pp. 72, 73) priests took bribes from Conversos, offering them in return help and immunity from the inquisition Their opinion of them was not enhanced thereby!

acceptable to God, if the worshipper *intended* that the prayer reach Him. These were some of the subterfuges employed by the Conversos, making it possible for them to augment their small repertory of prayers.

The Conversos were constrained to pray for they were conscious of their own weakness and impotence against the overpowering odds in the environment, and they instinctively turned to their God for strength and support. Their prayers were supplications for help. Enemies surrounded them, yet they trusted in the God who had saved their forefathers in every peril and mishap, and they had faith that He would not forsake them! Their cries of anguish would surely be heard by God "out of compassion and out of mercy."

Some of the prayers used by the Conversos are full of dignity and beauty. The prayer opening with the words: *En vuestras manos, Señor, encomiendo el alma mia* ("In Thy hands, O Lord, I commit my soul")[42] is full of feeling and moving power. A number of their prayers are the traditional Jewish benedictions recited upon the washing of hands,[43] and the slaughtering of fowl.[44] The prayer beginning: *El uno: el Gran Dios de Israel* is a part of the traditional Passover-song *Ehad mi yodeyah* ("Who knows one?").[45] Similarly the prayer beginning: *Bendito tu Adonay, nuestro Dios, Rey del mundo, que formó el hombre con sabiduría* is a familiar prayer of the Jewish ritual for the morning: "Blessed art Thou, O Lord our God, King of the universe, Who hast formed man in wisdom. . . ."[46]

When they embarked upon a trip they prayed for safe passage by invoking the help of their patron-saint of travel, St. Tobit. As God had directed the path of St. Tobit, so in turn, the saint would protect the traveller asking for his aid.[47] In like manner, when a Converso was in trouble or danger, a prayer was recited importuning God to save the person named in the prayer.[48]

The Conversos usually prayed silently, not daring to emit a sound lest it be their undoing. To avoid suspicion, some ascended the topfloor of their houses and there, secure from the ears of their servants, recited their prayers. The form of praying, we gather from the records, was for the worshipper to stand erect, his feet

---

[42] Appendix VI, Prayer 1. In Appendix VI are to be found all the Converso prayers which I was able to discover in the hundreds of case-records examined.
[43] Appendix VI, Benediction 18a.
[44] Appendix VI, Benedictions 18b, 18c.
[45] Appendix VI, Prayer 10.
[46] Appendix VI, Prayer 2
[47] Appendix VI, Prayer 4. A simpler form is to be found: Appendix VI, Prayer 19e.
[48] Appendix VI, Prayer 15.

together, and face turned heavenward in a pleading gesture for help. On Friday evenings, some of them altered this form and prayed while standing on the staircase. Raphael Valls was accustomed to recite a certain prayer, at the close of which he took three steps backward, reminiscent of the traditional Jewish practice at the close of the *Shemoneh Esreh* prayer (the "Eighteen Benedictions") and the "Mourners' Prayer."[49] Many of them prayed three times daily: in the morning upon waking they would "thank God for the light of the new day which called them to His service,"[50] before their meal at noontime, and again before retiring at night they praised God's might and power, asking pardon for sins committed during the day.

They felt themselves bound together by a common destiny. In traditional Jewish fashion, they held themselves responsible for one another. They knew that a single informer could bring calamity upon them all. They shared their common lot together, encouraging one another in the dark hours of their lives. To make themselves impregnable against their enemies, they developed a number of cryptic expressions which identified them to one another and served as "passwords" among themselves.[51]

They taxed themselves for the maintenance of their own indigent. Although they contributed to the general poor funds of the churches and the community, their group-pride prevented any of their own to solicit help from outside sources. At fixed times, the almoner of the Conversos (a trustworthy person, such as Pedro Onofre Cortes or Raphael Valls) went from house to house asking contributions for their own alms' fund. It was customary to make contributions to the fund, as thank-offerings, during their fast- and feast-days. In this way their piety was translated into concrete good for the benefit of their own needy.[52]

From what has been written above, it is apparent that the Conversos of Majorca remembered and observed at least some of

---

49 AHN *Proc. de Fe,* legajo 1708, 4, fol. 5. Cf Singer's *Authorized Daily Prayer Book,* (London, 1924): "Shemoneh Esreh," p 44ff.; "Mourners' Prayer" ("Kaddish"), p. 77. Cf. also AHN *Rel. de Causas de Fe,* libro 1, 865, fol. 406.

50 Appendix VI, Prayer 7.

51 The initiates spoke among themselves by the use of "expressions peculiar to Jews." When one of them was referred to as "a very good man," it was understood to mean "a good Jew." The term "a good person" carried the connotation of one, not only who observed the law of Moses, but more specifically of one who observed at least one voluntary fast each week By "servientes de Dios" they meant the Jews AHN *Proc. de Fe,* legajos · 1705, 5, fol. 15v; 1709, 3, fols. 61, 85; 1709, 4, fol. 70; 1709, 5, fol 3 AHN *Rel de Causas de Fe* libro 1, 865, fols. 148, 285, 428, 431v, 438, 439, 440; libro 1, 866, fols. 161v, 165.

52 *Ibid.,* libro 1, 865, fols. 276v, 403. The fund was called the "bolsa comun."

the old law of Moses. Narrowed and atrophied as their faith was, and despite the lack of adequate training, nevertheless it retained some of the essentials of Judaism. They upheld monotheism as a challenge to the trinity and the alleged idolatry of Christians. The hope in their ultimate deliverance by a God-appointed Messiah, their attempts at keeping the dietary laws, their observance of the fast- and feast-days, and the recitation of the prayers made of them in fact, they were sure, worshippers of the God of Israel and followers of the law of Moses.

However we might sympathize with the Conversos, even as martyrs to the cause of religious freedom, we must not lose sight of the fact that the inquisition was exercising its duty when it arrested them on charges of relapse into heresy. Moreover, the Conversos' guilt of these charges can scarcely be questioned.

CHAPTER V

DECLINE AND EXTINCTION OF THE MAJORCAN
INQUISITION

Events at the beginning of the eighteenth century made it appear that profound changes would be wrought in the character and efficiency of the inquisition. The Bourbons brought to Spain (1700) a dynasty which would not easily allow its privileges to be impeded by the inquisition. As patrons of arts and letters, they injected into Spanish life an interest and enthusiasm in learning, the like of which was not known since the reign of Ferdinand and Isabella.[1] Charles II, whose throne the Bourbon-king had come to fill, had been, like his predecessors, a protector of the inquisition. But the new king, Philip V (1683-1746), early manifested an unfriendly attitude toward the inquisition when he refused to attend a grand auto de fe prepared in honor of his accession to the throne.[2] There were many who still had reason to fear the inquisition, and this was a happy augury of what might have been a new era.[3] But an incident occurred which changed the course of the history of the eighteenth century, giving the inquisition a new lease upon life.

Beginning in 1707, a group of some twenty Converso families in Madrid had gathered regularly to observe Jewish rites. Over a period of seven years they continued in their heresies, and, in 1714, believing they had attained some permanency, elected a rabbi and sent his name to Leghorn for confirmation.[4] When their synagogue —more precisely a room where the Conversos assembled—was discovered, the inquisition was aroused to new enthusiasm. The first

---

1 They founded the "Biblioteca Nacional," "Real Academia de la Historia," "Academia de las Lenguas," and other learned groups, including universities. Cf. Lea, *Spain*, IV, 387.

2 The Church-historian of Spain, Vicente de la Fuente (quoted by Lea, *Spain*, III, 229), writes· "Felipe V se negó por *primera vez* á concurrir á ellos; mas adelante se le vio asister á uno (1720)." (Italics mine). Although Philip attempted many reforms to correct the abuses of the inquisition (cf. Lea, *Spain* I, 317-36) and reduce the large numbers of unnecessary officials (*Ibid*, II, 202), he followed his predecessors in lauding the inquisition upon his abdication (1724), and commended it to his son Louis as the instrumentality for preserving the purity of the faith. (*Ibid.*, IV, 501).

3 The Wars of the Spanish Succession (1701-14) also had their effect in making this period a very inactive one for the inquisition.

4 Adler, p 96ff.; Lea, *Spain*, III, 229, 308-9. As we have already observed, Leghorn was one of the centers for Converso migration. It was only natural that she became in time "the mother city" to the Conversos attempting to preserve Judaism. *Supra* pp. 77, 96.

important result of the renewed activity was an auto de fe in Madrid, on April 7, 1720, in which five Conversos were relaxed.[5]

This was the signal for a general recrudescence of prosecuting zeal throughout the nation,[6] which also had its effect upon the Majorcan tribunal in making it increasingly watchful over heresies it had so bitterly fought against and had already subdued.

The Majorcan tribunal, however, had already won its decisive victory over the Conversos. That is why, despite stimulation and zeal, it tried only six persons for observing Jewish practices throughout the entire eighteenth century. Indeed, beside three additional persons, these constituted the last victims of the island inquisition until its extinction (July 15, 1834).[7] Four of these Conversos were foreign, and three native Majorcans.

Among the foreign Conversos was Antonio de Mendoza, arrested on July 11, 1712. Mendoza's career was typical of many thousands at this period. Born in Faro (Portugal), and educated as a Catholic, he practiced Judaism surreptitiously during the years he lived with his family, who, at one time or another, were fugitives in Granada, Seville and Valladolid. Finally escaping to Amsterdam, the Mendozas formally re-embraced Judaism, in token of which Antonio, as a boy of thirteen, was circumcised and renamed Moses. But the following year a nostalgia for his old haunts seized the boy and he fled to Spain. He went to live in the port of Santa Maria, abjured his Judaism, and henceforth lived as a Catholic. The wanderlust again took hold of him and he went to Lisbon, then as a soldier to Barcelona, returning again to Lisbon in the capacity of secretary to a Jewish merchant from Algiers. In his employer's service he went to Minorca and finally to Majorca, where he arrived in the company of Raphael Joachin Valls two months before the inquisition imprisoned him. Mendoza and Valls frequently met in Minorca, and they continued their friendship in Majorca. It appears that Valls had maintained his secret adherence to Judaism, despite his oaths to abjure it, and that he had established friendly relations with Mendoza in order that he might be better informed on matters of Jewish practice. When Mendoza was arrested by the inquisition, Valls had good reason to fear what Mendoza might say of him. Accordingly, he fled to Minorca where

---

[5] Roth, pp. 352-3

[6] Lea (*Spain*, IV, 386) estimates that "in sixty-four autos, between 1721 and 1728, there appeared nine-hundred and sixty-two culprits and effigies, of whom one hundred fifty-one were relaxed." Cf. Roth, p. 353. Llorente's figures (*Anales Secretos de la Inquisición Española*, Madrid, n. d., p 211) for the victims during the reign of Philip V are as high as "Quemados Vivos" (burned alive) 1600, "En Estatua" (in effigy) 760, and 9220 condemned to prison

[7] The decree abolishing the inquisition is reproduced in Lea, *Spain*, IV, 545.

he explained his presence as due to the fear of consequences "of a Jew in the inquisition, posing as a Christian." Mendoza remained in the inquisition's prison for almost seven years, when finally, on February 18, 1719, he abjured his Jewish beliefs, and was exiled for six years to Aragon.[8]

On September 1, 1718 an Ibizan privateer, cruising off the Barbary coast, captured a Moorish sloop carrying three young Jews—Jacob Cardozo Nuñez of Bayonne (France), Samuel Nahon, and his cousin, Solomon Nahon, of Tetuan (Morocco)—engaged on a business mission. The three Jews were imprisoned in Ibiza as property of their captors, while arrangements for their ransom were being made with Jewish communities unwilling to have Jews sold as slaves.[9] The man named Cardozo aroused suspicion in the inquisition, which accordingly demanded him as its prisoner: "because of such a renewed Judaizing complicity, it would not be wise to free Cardozo, for his name and background were similar to those who had escaped Spain and Portugal in order to Judaize."[10] On March 6, 1720 Cardozo was transferred from Ibiza to the prison of the inquisition in Majorca. His testimony, confirmed by documents from Leghorn and Bayonne, unmistakably showed his Jewish origin, and clearly indicated his birthplace as Bayonne. At the early age of fifteen his brother took him to Marseilles and thence to Leghorn, where they engaged in business. Upon the death of his brother four years later, he went to Gibraltar to join his other brothers. He left them, but upon his return discovered that they, together with all other Jews, had been banished from Gibraltar by royal edict.[11] He followed them to Tetuan. While journeying to Genoa on business, in company with the Nahons, he was captured and imprisoned in Ibiza. On two separate occasions the Majorcan tribunal sent requests for information about Cardozo to the tribunals of Barcelona, Cordova, Cuenca, Galicia, Granada, Madrid, Saragossa, and Valencia, as well as to Coimbra, Evora, and

---

8 AHN *Proc. de Fe,* legajo 1715, 5, pieza 1, fols 23, 27v-34v; *Ibid.,* pieza 2, fols. 45, 47-51, 73-5, 117v AHN *Rel. de Causas de Fe,* legajo 1716, 3, fol. 38.

9 AHN *Proc de Fe,* legajo 1715, 12, fols. 45-6 The Jews regarded it as a high duty to ransom the captives, (*Bab. Talmud· Baba Bathra,* fol 8), and pirates extracted exorbitant sums because they knew that Jews would pay them. (Cf. Abraham's *Jewish Life in the Middle Ages,* pp 359-63). Samuel and Solomon Nahon were to have been freed upon payment of 1,250 pesos, which they hoped to collect from the Jewish community of Leghorn In January, 1719 one of their captors took them to Leghorn, where they succeeded in escaping. In April the disappointed Ibizan returned empty-handed

10 AHN *Proc. de Fc,* legajo 1715, 12, pieza 3.

11 At the request of King Philip V the Jews were exiled Gibraltar was ceded to England in 1713 by the Treaty of Utrecht, with the understanding that no Jews or Moors would be permitted to live there The Bourbon Philip V had apparently become a good Spaniard! Cf. Lea, *Spain,* III, 312-3

Lisbon, in Portugal, but no incriminating evidence was uncovered against him. Despite this, he remained in prison for fourteen months until his case was finally suspended on May 6, 1721.[12]

Another case of interest to come before the Majorcan tribunal was that of David Daniel, a Jew from Leghorn. He was admitted to the General Hospital in Palma (May 7, 1783), seriously wounded while serving in a regiment of the Walloon Guards. In the hospital he refused to accept the sacrament customarily administered to patients. Through the kindly ministrations of a priest, he was converted to Christianity, and baptized as Carlos Colnix. His wounds healed and he improved rapidly. Upon testifying against "many Jews who illegally lived as traders in the chief cities of Spain," the inquisition claimed Colnix as its prisoner. A special committee was formed to collect and act upon his testimony, and report directly to the inquisitor-general—so much interest had his startling allegations aroused. He was set free to collect additional information about the Majorcan Conversos, whom he had also denounced as practicing Jews. Just as the best results of his investigations seemed to be forthcoming, he fled. When he was apprehended in Saragossa, he made similar charges against Jewish traders. He managed to escape again to Teruel, and finally to Valencia. There he became very ill, and to show his change of heart, asked that he be re-baptized. The special committee of the inquisition soon found that all the testimony of Colnix was a tissue of lies, for it could find no trace of the Jewish traders against whom he had testified. From Valencia he was taken to the inquisition's prison in Madrid, where the poor demented fool doubtless spent his last days.[13]

In addition to these cases, the inquisition tried three native Conversos for observing Jewish practices:[14] Raphael Piña of Mi-

---

[12] AHN *Proc de Fe,* legajo 1715, 12, fols 1-2v, 5-6v, 8-11, 12, 13, 30v-1v, 47, 47v, 50, 51, 53v, 55, 78 Experiences similar to those of Mendoza and Cardozo effectively deterred many Jews from engaging in trade with Spain. Moreover, the restrictions to which ships and their crews were subjected, as part of inquisitorial discipline to keep Spain undefiled from the heresies of the outside world, naturally caused the country to be looked upon with unfriendliness by sailors and traders. The "Visitas de Navios" (ship-inspections) were so organized, and executed by the inquisition officers with such rigor, that ships were discouraged from touching Spain.

[13] Paz "Reclamaciones de los Mallorquines llamados de LA CALLE sobre su condición Social," *RABM,* XVI, 1907, 184-200; for this case pp 196-9 (hereafter: *Reclamaciones*). Of the 4,000 cases tried by the Spanish Inquisition between 1780-1820 only ten concerned foreign Jews discovered in the country without authorization. Roth, p. 353.

[14] Yet Lea (*Spain,* III, 307-8) writes "We hear nothing more of Judaism in Majorca" (after 1691); "during the height of persecution elsewhere, the tribunal celebrated two autos, in which nine penitents appeared—but none of them were Judaizers."(!)

norca, who was reconciled, Raphael Joachin Valls, whose case was finally suspended, and Gabriel Cortes, who was burned in effigy.

In 1718 Raphael Piña voluntarily appealed to the commissioner of the Majorcan Inquisition in Minorca, asking pardon for his sins incurred by forsaking Christianity and observing Judaism. He placed the blame for his heresies upon Raphael Joachin Valls, who had weaned him away from attending mass, finally persuading him to leave Christianity altogether. Valls taught him that Christians were idolaters, since they believed in images of Christ and of saints, made of wood and stone, which were products of men's hands. Christ was neither God nor Messiah. There was only one way to sure salvation: through believing in the law of Moses, which Valls had promised to teach him. A letter describing the entire case, dispatched to the inquisitor in Majorca, remained unanswered because the inquisitor to whom it was addressed had died. After some time had elapsed, the new inquisitor replied to the commissioner, ordering him to proceed with the formal reconciliation of Piña. The penalties for his sins were submitted at the same time: he was to be instructed in the faith, and was ordered to be confined to his own house, beside any other penalties which the commissioner might see fit to impose. All this should be done, the letter cautioned, with the utmost circumspection, to keep it from coming to the attention of the English conquerors of the island.[15]

The case of Raphael Joachin Valls supplies some continuity to our story of the life and activities of those Conversos who escaped death in 1691. Valls had been absolved of heresy as a youth in 1683, and later reconciled in the auto de fe of March 7, 1691, serving a long term in the galleys as penalty for his persistent heresy.[16] Thereafter he returned to his native Majorca and, probably because of his background as well as his own inclinations, it soon became known that he was secretly observing many Jewish practices. If this was true, his early training at the hands of his father (burned alive in 1691), would have prepared him for such a life. His parents' execution by the inquisition inspired in him little devotion to Christianity. Indeed, he was constantly reproached for brooding over their death. As a result of the reaction against Conversos which swept Spain after 1720, he was arrested by the inquisition (October 19, 1722). Many persons denounced him for

---

15 AHN *Proc de Fe*, legajo 1715, 5, pieza 1, fols. 14-18v; *Ibid.*, pieza 2, fols. 15-16, 21v Port Mahon (Minorca) was considered one of the finest harbors in the Mediterranean It was captured by the English in 1708 under General Stanhope, and was finally secured to England under the terms of the Treaty of Utrecht. (The inquisition's commissioner in Minorca at the time was Dr Manuel Martinez).

16 *Supra* p. 86.

clinging to Jewish practices. He was accused of whitewashing his
house in honor of ,the Jewish Sabbath. His neighbor's wife denounced him as early as 1706 for refusing to share with her husband
in the purchase of a hog, ostensibly because of the price, but the
real reason, the woman testified, lay in the Jewish observances
which prevented him from preparing it on the Jewish Sabbath.
Suspicion of circumcising his sons was aroused when Mendoza
revealed that Valls had questioned him about the validity of circumcising with a finger-nail. This suspicion was reinforced when
Valls' three sons had died at very early ages, presumably as a result of his attempts at circumcising them. He was such an ardent
believer in Judaism, it was reported, that he would have followed
Gabriel Cortes (who fled to a foreign country and became an a-
vowed Jew), had it not been for love of his family, whom he refused
to abandon.

His relationships with the English in Minorca, for whom he
acted as commissary, placed Valls under added suspicions as a heretic, because of his dealings with the heretic-conquerors. He argued
that all his transactions with them had been carried out under the
supervision of the English Consul in Majorca, a highly respected
Catholic. His wide travelling also prejudiced his case. Yet application for incriminating information to sixteen tribunals of the
inquisition in Spain and Portugal revealed that no action had ever
been taken against him. He defended himself before the inquisition
as a loyal Catholic. His adherence and faithfulness to Catholicism
could not be questioned, he told the inquisition. Had he not a figure of St. Vincent Ferrer in his little chapel at home, surrounded by
images of many other saints? Apparently his defense was strong
enough to overcome all suspicions of heresy, for his case was suspended (April 28, 1724).[17]

The last case ever to be tried before the Majorcan tribunal for
relapse into Judaism was that of Gabriel Cortes, reconciled in the
auto de fe of March 7, 1691.[18] He was a son of Isabel Cortes, one
of the Conversos executed in the auto de fe of May 1, 1691.[19] As
early as 1704 his brother had denounced him to the inquisition.
Cortes doubtless feared the effect of this denunciation, for soon

[17] AHN *Proc de Fe*, legajo 1715, 5, pieza 1, fols. 1-14, 18-20v, 24-9, 34v-6; *Ibid.*, pieza
2, fols. 16v-17v, 21v, 22, 31, 36v-8, 42-6v, 53-6, 63v, 66-7, 68v, 73-5, 79-82v, 103, 116-
19, 122v, 160-2v. Valls was not put to any torture "because of his sixty-two years of
age, sickness and many wounds and lesions." In going over this trial, it would
appear that the inquisition had just as good a case for heresy as it had had for the
many others it had tried before on the same charges. A greater leniency was obviously then ruling in the decisions of the tribunal.

[18] See p. 87, chapter III, note 96.
[19] See p. 84, chapter III, note 89.

thereafter he disappeared after one of his frequent business trips to Minorca, abandoning his family in Majorca. In 1707 his brother-in-law also denounced him to the tribunal as a fugitive Converso, who had absconded with some thirty-five hundred pesos of his money. It appeared from the evidence gathered by the inquisition that Cortes, aided by a Dutch Jew, had sailed from Mahon (Minorca) to Leghorn. The Jews of Leghorn, it was reported, were gratified that he had finally decided to re-embrace Judaism, expressing the wish that other Majorcan Conversos might have the courage to follow him. In Leghorn he tarried but a short while, going directly to Alexandria, where, with the help of another Jew, he formally returned to Judaism. There he threw off his past life like a cloak, the testimony of his case recited, and married a Jewess. As a dowry he received some four to six-hundred pesos, which he loaned out on interest, desiring only to have enough upon which to live while studying the law of Moses and observing all its precepts. At various times the inquisition received reports of him in Ancona, Italy (where he wore characteristic Jewish garb), and later in Jerusalem and Acre. The evidence of Cortes' relapse into Judaism was strong and undeniable. Three separate demands for his return were made, according to inquisitorial procedure. "Edicts of Citation and Recall" were read both in the Cathedral and in his parish church in Palma. When his continued refusal to present himself for trial was definitely established, he was assigned to the stake for his relapse to Judaism, and his effigy was burned in an auto de fe on September 15, 1720.[20] In the same auto de fe, three other Conversos, charged with maltreating a priest, were condemned to serve in the garrisons and forts of Africa.[21] This was the last auto in which Conversos were condemned.

These marked the last trials and convictions of Conversos by the Majorcan tribunal until it was finally abolished in 1834.

---

20 AHN *Proc. de Fe,* legajo 1707, 13, fols 3-6, 8, 9v, 12, 12v, 22v-36, 43v-4v, 50, 57, 59, 72, 74v *Reclamaciones,* p. 188. *Relacion,* p. 8. *Tratado* (III, cap. 25) dates the auto de fe four years later.

21 They were Joaquin Fuster, Fernando Pico, and Salvador Bonin. *Reclamaciones,* p. 188.

CHAPTER VI

THE CHUETAS: THE DEAD HAND OF THE INQUISITION

Although the Inquisition of Majorca existed with interruptions until 1834, more than a century before its extinction it had passed its last sentence upon a Converso. If this study were an account only of the condemnations of the Conversos by the inquisition, our task would now be completed, and the year 1720 would be the last date recorded. But the fact is that long after the condemnations of individual Conversos had ceased, the Inquisition of Majorca continued to play a part in the history of the Chuetas—the name by which the Conversos and their descendants are today known on the island.

Up to our own day, more than five-hundred years after their conversion to Christianity in 1435, some three-hundred families of Chuetas live in Majorca, comprising an isolated group on the island, still looked upon with suspicion by their neighbors. Many of their antecedents, it is true, had observed the forbidden practices of Judaism, for which they had been duly punished by the inquisition. The penalties and deprivations rising out of heresy fell with equal weight upon the transgressor as well as upon his descendants. In this way, the punishments of the inquisition continued to exert their influence long after the real culprit had paid his penalty. Because of the many condemnations of Conversos in the latter part of the seventeenth century, the stigma of the heretic became at first closely, and finally indelibly, attached to all Chuetas, whether they were condemned by the inquisition or not. The memory of the islanders was strengthened by a device for perpetuating the "infamy of heresy" through the renovation of the old sanbenitos, which the inquisition repeated in 1755.[1] Only this time it ordered, in addition, that the portraits of the condemned be painted in oils, in order to prolong the remembrance of the crimes represented by the sanbenitos. At the same time the inquisition printed a list of the culprits it had punished since 1645.[2] Also, during the same time, the inquisition authorized the reprinting of Padre Garau's book, *La Fee Triunfante*, describing the autos de fe of 1691. By these actions, the

---

[1] *Supra* pp 94, 95

[2] This is the printed list of culprits we have often referred to. *Relacion. Reclamaciones,* p. 196.

122

inquisition, even though it could not impugn the Chuetas' fidelity to Catholicism by preferring formal heresy charges against them, effectively enhanced the ill-will of the islanders against them.[3]

The hatred which the people bore against them as Jews before their conversion in 1435 was doubtless not completely dissipated when the inquisition was established in Majorca. Nevertheless the inquisition must assume a good part of the responsibility for rekindling the hatred, which endures to this day. At times the inquisition acted as the instrumentality of this hatred, rather than as its source, but it cannot be gainsaid that it was an ally of the forces of hatred, because its own chief object was the castigation of the Chuetas. While the inquisition ceased to function after 1834, its influence lived on after its demise. Therefore, a consideration of the plight of the Chuetas of our own day has a place in this work. Running through all the polemic against them has been their condemnation by the inquisition, showing that the hand of an institution dead for more than a hundred years still holds power over them.

The plight of the Chuetas approached its climax with the petition made to King Charles III, on February 12, 1773, in behalf of the then more than four-hundred Chueta families, by their representatives.[4] The petition is eloquent of the disabilities the Chuetas were alleged to have suffered. Although good Catholics, their sons were denied entrance to the higher ranks of the clergy, and their daughters to the religious orders. They were forced to live in a restricted area of the city (of Palma), and the people calumniated them with the names *Hebreos, Judíos, Chuetas.* Guilds, army, navy and public offices were closed to them despite their unflinching loyalty to the king. In short, by the time this petition was written, the Chuetas appeared to have become a proscribed class on the island. Persons in prominent positions vouched for their integrity as good Spanish subjects, and for their faithfulness as members of the Catholic Church. The collector of revenue testified that they paid their

---

3 Lea, *Spain,* II, 313; Roth, p. 96; Taronjí, *Algo Sobre el Estado Religiosa y Social de la Isla de Mallorca,* p. 166ff (hereafter · Taronjí) *Origen de la Inquisición* (fol. 11) devotes its whole notice of the inquisition's activities for 1755 to the permission granted for reprinting Garau's book, stating as the reason for the new edition: "que los individuos de la calle (i e. the Chuetas) compravan á cualquier precio . . . la primera edición que se habia publicado el año 1691, y casi habian logrado ya su total exterminación de aquella obra."

4 "*Maria, Jesús, Josef.*" "Memorial Presentado á Su Magestad (Q D. G) Por Los Individuos Llamados de la Calle de Mallorca . . . " (fol. 1). These representatives were· Bernardo Aguilo, Tomás Aguilo, Domingo Cortes, Tomás Cortes and Francisco Forteza. The more than 400 families constituted about 10,000 persons (according to the petition presented July 18, 1777, fol 1). Antoni Pons (Dels Dies Terribles, 1793-1799," *La Nostra Terra,* Any VI, 1933, 370) estimates the number of Chueta families at that time as 403.

taxes promptly and fully. The secretary of the local marine brought additional proof of their trustworthiness by asserting that of the forty Chuetas who served under him not one had deserted. The bishop of the island commended their religious zeal in a letter written to the head of the king's council considering their petition. He cautioned that unless something was done to mitigate the injustices they suffered in Majorca, they might flee to Minorca, where their abilities and wealth would accrue to the benefit of the heretic-foreigners.[5]

The petition of the Chuetas stirred up a hornet's nest of opposition. The University of Palma answered it by reviving the statutes of *limpieza* (blood that is free from taint of Jewish or Moorish strains), and closed its doors to all Chuetas. This stand reflected the attitude of the municipal council, the ecclesiastical bodies, as well as the gentry of the island.[6] The Chuetas mustered all their forces, and the issue divided the island. Sympathy for the Chuetas' plight took the form of a strongly-worded petition in their defense addressed to the king by an influential old-Christian.[7] In the meantime forces had been unleashed, obviously in-

---

[5] *Reclamaciones*, pp. 189, 190. The bishop's was more than a pious suggestion, for by 1766 there were already enough Jews in Mahon (Minorca's chief-city) to successfully petition the government, through the Board of Jewish Deputies in London, to have their synagogue reopened, despite the ruling of the *Jurat* of Minorca who termed its closure to be in consonance with the terms of the Treaty of Utrecht Cf. Emanuel, *A Century and a Half of Jewish History*, p. 6.

[6] "*Jesús, Maria y Jose.*" "Papel en Derecho Respuesta al Manifiesta que entregaron á las Señores del Consejo los Diputados de los Individuos, llamados de la Calle, que habitan en la Isla de Mallorca, en satisfacción de lo que respectivamente su opuso por lo Ciudad, Cabildo Eclesiastico, y Universidad de la Ciudad de ,Palma, Capital de aquella Isla. A Fin de que no se conceda á los Descendientes de Judios la igualidad que solicitan, con los hombres buenos del Estado general del Reyno de Mallorca, y se observen como hasta aqui los respectivos Estatutos de Limpieza de aquella Isla, y la costumbre immemorial de excluirlos de todas las Dignidades, Oficios Publicos, y Entrada en los Cuerpos y Gremios de Mallorca." Those opposing the Chuetas deny that they have been forced to live in the isolated *Calle;* they do so voluntarily for they own large houses outside it. It was the Chuetas who had kept themselves aloof. Up to the time of their petition, none of them went to the general hospital, but out of their "bolsa comun" (community fund collected among themselves, see *supra* p 113) they provided for physicians and medicines. By now all the Majorcans had looked upon them as a group apart, because of their own faults! They refused to work in the fields, for they disdained making a living with their hands. (fols 3, 5) They called *themselves* Chuetas "Este Apodo (Chuetas) ellos mismos se lo aplicán voluntariamente . . ." (fol. 3v). The Chuetas were still suspected of heresies by the people. How could they believe they were loyal Christians when they had so many times been arrested by the inquisition for relapsing into Jewish practices? (fol 29ff.) The fundamental basis of their opposition, however, the writers placed upon the material in Padre Garau's book. (fol 7). Yet Antonio Fernandez de Córdoba, prosecuting officer (fiscal) in the Royal Courts of Majorca during this period, found no fault in the Chuetas, to whom he was never friendly. Cf. his *Inventario de las Noticias Instrumentales del Reyno de Mallorca*, AH, Est. 21, gr 5a, no 88. See also Michel, *Histoire des Races Maudites*, II, 35.

[7] "Manifiesto entregado a los Señores del Real y Supremo Consejo, en respuesta a que quanto por la ciudad, Cabildo Eclesiastico, y Universidad de la Ciudad de Palma, Capital de Reino de Mallorca se ha opuesto á dicho Memorial Sobre que

tended to stir up resentment against the Chuetas in an effort to defeat their demands. The *Tratado del Origen de las Sinagogas y Judíos de esta Isla de Mallorca,*[8] and the *Anales Judaicos de Mallorca,*[9] both pieces of patently anti-Chueta literature, strategically made their appearance at this time. Their purpose was clear: to recapitulate the ugly legends about the Chuetas, before and after their conversion, to point to their repeated arrests by the inquisition, in order to reawaken hatreds against them so that they be kept from achieving equality.

When no response had come to the petitions of the Chuetas and their friends by 1781,[10] a plan of wholesale expatriation from Majorca was seriously considered by the Chuetas themselves.[11] The islanders, anticipating a victory, also entertained a plan for exiling the Chuetas to the rocky and barren island of Cabrera, and thus definitively ridding themselves of the troublesome people.[12]

The jubilation was short-lived, for the following year the king acquiesced in the Chuetas' requests. He issued three distinct decrees, dated December 10, 1782, October 9, 1785, and April 13, 1788, which sincerely attempted to give the Chuetas the equality and justice they asked for.[13] The first decree gave them freedom to live in any part of Palma and the islands. To make this effective, every vestige of gate or door leading to "the street" (*la calle*: the district where they had been forced to live), was ordered to be destroyed, so that henceforth they should not be a class apart among

---

No obstante Su Estirpe Hebrea, se les trate en todo como á los demas Vasallos Hombres-buenos del estado General, y por ser Christianos Católicos como ellos." (8 fols) The author was Don José Lináres Montefrío. Taronjí, p. 308.

8 The anti-Chueta tract *Tratado* was written as a reply to the petition The date appearing at its close is significantly enough October 31, 1773. No time was lost to present the other point of view in order to move those in power to decide against granting the Chuetas' petition. Although the *Tratado* was never printed, a number of copies in manuscript found their way into the hands of those persons who might profit by it ! One of these was retained in the Villalonga family, to which the author was kindly given access.

9 In the first paragraph of this work are the words "hecho en este de 1775." The place and date of publication on its title page (Burdeos, 1847) is an obvious falsification

10 Although it appears that the king had already come to a favorable decision by 1779. Cf. Taronjí, p. 293

11 *Reclamaciones,* p 192.

12 Cabrera is one of the smaller islands of the Balearic group. It is almost uninhabitable. The inference of such a proposition is clear—to have the Chuetas starve on the bleak island ! The Majorcans apparently quickly forgot the benefits the Chuetas had brought to the island: in 1750 they supplied the poor with tools and implements, again in 1766 they assisted liberally in rebuilding the roads of the island. *Reclamaciones,* p 185.

13 *Reales Cedulas de D. Carlos III,* Libro XII, Ley VI, Titulo I, cf Taronjí, pp. 287-97, Lardizabal y Uribe, *Apología por los Agótes de Navarra, y los Chuetas de Mallorca,* (hereafter · Lardizibal) ; Soler, *Un Milagro y Una Mentira · Vindicación de los Mallorquines Christianos de Estirpe Hebrea,* (hereafter · Soler) pp. 107-9.

the inhabitants of the island. Penalties of imprisonment awaited those who mistreated them and insulted them by calling them Jews, Hebrews, or Chuetas. The second decree gave them the privilege of serving in the army, navy, and in every service of the state. The final decree qualified them to enter all crafts, trades, and all branches of agriculture, brooking no impediment to their progress.[14] The king placed the Chuetas under his royal protection, and demanded that his will, as expressed in the decrees, be executed.

Decrees, however, could not eradicate prejudices and hatreds of long-standing. The royal decrees were wantonly disregarded soon after they were issued, perhaps because no one would enforce them. Miguel de Lardizibal, in his book published as early as 1786 (after two of the decrees had been announced), pleaded with the Majorcans to free the Chuetas from the shackles of old prejudices which continued to make of them "the most unhappy people in all of Spain."[15] This was the year (1786), also, from which another writer dated "the moral revolution for cultivated men", yet the Chuetas were still suffering from persecution which had been outlawed by the king![16]

Napoleon's campaign in Spain temporarily brought the Chuetas some relief. Joseph Bonaparte, immediately after he was placed upon the Spanish throne, formally abolished the inquisition (1808).[17] During the ensuing war with France, the Chuetas were allowed to join the army. (What laws and decrees were not able to effect, war did, temporarily!) But upon the slightest pretext, the

---

[14] The title page of the first decree reads· "Real Cedula de S. M. y Señores del Consejo Por lo Qual Se Mando que á los Individuos del Barrio, llamado de la Calle de la Ciudad de Palma, en el Reyno de Mallorca, no solo no se les impida habitar en qualquiera otro sitio de la Ciudad ó Isla, sino que se les favorezca y conceda toda protección, para que así lo executen derribandose qualquier arco, puerta, ú otro señal que los haya distinguido de lo restante del pueblo . . Que se prohiba insultar y maltratar á dichos individuos, ni llamarlos un voces odiosas y de, menosprecio, y mucho menos, Judíos, ó Hebreos, y Chuetas. . ." The second decree proclaims them "aptos al servicio de mar y tierra en el Exército, y Armada Real, y para otro qualquier servicio del estado." The last decree makes the Chuetas "idóneos para exercer las artes, oficios y labranza, del mismo modo que á los demas vasallos del estado. . ." Cf. Taronjí, pp. 293, 4, 6

[15] Lardizibal, p. 1ff.

[16] Soler, p. 7; Llebrés, *Memoria instructiva sobre el estado actual de la isla de Mallorca*, Michel, *Histoire des Races Maudites*, II, 39-41, Grasset de St. Sauveur, *Voyage, dans les îles Baleares*, pp. 101-4· "I shall never forget one day, when I was walking in the cloister of the Dominicans, and looking with concern on these paintings (of the Sanbenitos and the pictures of the Inquisition's victims), a monk approached me and made me observe several among them distinguished by crossed bones; these said he are the portraits of those whose ashes were dug up and cast to the winds My blood chilled, and I turned from him with horror My heart sickened at the scene." The *Relacion,* printed in 1755, was still widespread enough for Grasset to buy a copy of it in Majorca as late as the years 1801-05, when he travelled through the islands.

[17] Lea, *Spain,* II, 445.

hatred flared up again. A mutiny of troops, rebelling against being transferred to the mainland, spent its force by sacking the *Chueteria*, where the Chuetas dwelled, on February 22, 1809.

The Cádiz Constitution, confirming Bonaparte's action in a-bolishing the inquisition (1813), engendered an enthusiasm in Majorca which bid fair to wipe out all the old prejudices. To celebrate their newly-acquired freedom, one of the Chuetas tendered a banquet to the inhabitants of Palma, in the city's largest square, which a contemporary poet commemorated in verse.[18] The inquisition was suppressed by the new Constitution, but only for seventeen months, for it returned with the restoration of King Ferdinand VII. The sanbenitos, which had mysteriously disappeared from the Dominican Church in 1812, were just as mysteriously replaced in 1814. The pillar, erected by the inquisition in 1679 to mark the spot of the secret synagogue, was also ordered to be restored.[19]

The constitutional revolution of 1820 again abolished the inquisition.[20] Once more the Chuetas were permitted to enroll in the army. This appeared to be a compensation for all the misfortunes of the earlier revolutions. The Dominican Church and the Palace of the Inquisition both promptly fell to the fury which a small band of liberals were able to instil in the islanders. The sanbenitos in the Dominican Church were collected and burned in the convent's gardens. This incident was accounted the triumph of the revolution on the island.[21] By November 6, 1823, however, the reaction

---

18 Taronjí, p. 255ff. The host, Valentí, had 3871 guests at the banquet, which the poet Guillermo Roca described

19 One of the Conversos, desiring to destroy the remembrance of that event, bought the column and erased the inscription But he was obliged to restore it in 1814 *Anales Judaicos de Mallorca*, IV, cap. 32

20 The entry for 1820 in the *Apuntes* (fol 16) is as follows· "El Rey N. S. a consecuencia de haber jurado en 7 de Marzo de 1820 el código Constitucional, mandó entre otras cosas la abolición de la Inquisición." En Mallorca fué extinguida el dia 16 de los mismos para cuyo objeto paso·al Tribunal el Ilmo. Sr. Obispo Don Pedro Gonzalez Vallejo á intimar la orden a los SS. Inquisidores . . . Immediamente se dió libertad a todos los presos que allí estaban encarcelados (tal vez por supuestos delitos) y a las cuatro de la tarde se juntó una infinidad de gente del pueblo mallorquin, enfurecido del mal proceder de los extinguidos, fueron al Tribbunal y á las cinco habian ya hecho un entero saqueo del Secreto, destrucción y quema de todo cuanto en el habia Por la mañana del siguiente dia apareció á manero de pasquin en el umbral del portal principal del oficio la siguiente

> *Cuartilla*
> Esta casa bien mirada,
> Al infierno ha parecido
> Hera buena la entrada
> Y muy mala la salida."

Cf. also the references to this event in *Hist. Gen.*, II, 651.

21 The unpublished Memoirs of the late Francisco Villalonga y Fabregues (which he put into my hands before his death late in 1933) reads (p. 4) . "It was a war unto

had again set in, the Chuetas were disarmed, and their homes were thoroughly sacked. The battle cry which hung upon the lips of the fickle populace was: *"Viva la Religión, Viva el Rey, Viva la Inquisición."* The Chuetas were villified as the authors of "the accursed Constitution," for which impertinence they suffered through the loss of life and property![22]

The death of Ferdinand VII, and the revival of constitutionalism in Queen Christina's reign, brought some renewed hope to the Chuetas. The following year, by the decree of July 15, 1834, the inquisition was finally declared extinct. The Chuetas were thereupon allowed once more to enter the army and navy, and public offices were soon opened to them, so that as early as the 1830's two eminent Chuetas served on the City Council of Palma. Some latent ill-feeling of the populace broke out against them when, in 1856, a suit was brought to establish their rights to membership in the exclusive club "Circulo Balear." They vindicated their rights, but only at the expense of much hurtful recrimination.[23]

Again, at this period, when it appeared they were gaining the privileges they had long fought for, portions of Padre Garau's *La Fee Triunfante* were reprinted in a book entitled *La Sinagoga Balear*. This book included the names of those whom the inquisition had condemned almost two centuries before. The author of this work sought to establish that the descendants of those condemned by the inquisition still secretly adhered to Judaism, thus making the Chuetas unfit to share in the dignities and preferments of a Catholic country.[24] The intended victims of the book bought up all the copies that could be found, and destroyed them.[25]

The Chuetas found a champion in the Valencian, Tomás Bertran Soler, who promptly replied to the charges in his book, "A Miracle and a Lie: A Vindication of the Majorcan-Christians of the Hebrew Race" (*Un Milagro y Una Mentira: Vindicación de los*

---

death my grandfather vowed against the old régime when he was exiled from Majorca during the period of the restoration! Through his influence—curiously enough he was a member of an old family which supplied many officials to the inquisition—the Dominican Monastery and the Inquisition's Palace were destroyed."

[22] Oliver, *Mallorca durante la Primera Revolución*, pp. 608-11, 646. By 1825 an order restoring the property of the inquisition was put into effect. *Apuntes,* fol. 19.

[23] Taronjí, p. 259.

[24] The author was Juan de la Puerta Vizcaino. The book contains descriptions of the autos de fe in which the Conversos suffered, and a reprint of the *Relacion.* It gives prominence to the reply of the anti-Chuetas to the Chuetas' petition (cf. *supra* p 124, note 6), but neglects the Royal Decrees which officially gave them equality with other Majorcans.

[25] Mariano Aguiló, the Director of the Library of the University of Barcelona (and

Mallorquines Christianos de Estirpe Hebrea). This work was written in a remarkably modern spirit, embracing sound scholarship with the best traditions of nineteenth-century liberalism. One by one Soler dismissed the charges levelled against the Chuetas as false and groundless. He declared that ignorance and fanaticism alone had brought this tragedy upon Majorca. He wanted the Majorcans to realize that to be the descendants of Jews should be a source of honor and pride, rather than a shame and disgrace. He argued that the major portion of the early Christian Church, including the Apostles, were Jews. Jews were noblemen and treasurers in the government of Spain until the time of Ferdinand and Isabella. The Jews, in truth, had the purest blood of any people. Jewish blood flowed in the veins of the most distinguished Spanish families.[26] Why, then, this eternal prejudice against a people who had long forgotten their Jewish origins, and who had remained faithful to the Church? Why persecute all of them because of those whom the inquisition had long before punished for their heresies? And why persecute the descendants of those heretics, who are now so demonstrably faithful to the Church? Soler's impassioned appeal for justice and tolerance for the Chuetas scarcely made an impression upon the islanders.[27]

Prejudice against the Chuetas did not abate with the passing of the years, despite the eloquent pleas made in their behalf. Twenty years after Soler's appeal, in 1877, José Taronjí, a priest of the proscribed class, unable to restrain his indignation any longer, wrote a book which revealed that little progress had been made by his people in winning their rights. Socially, they were still ostracized. The old-Christians would sanction no marriages with their children, and priests sometimes refused to officiate at such "mixed-marriages." They were often refused entry to the guilds. Taronjí placed the blame at the door of the clergy who, obstinately and resolutely refusing to recognize the Chuetas as equals, were continually encouraging whatever prejudice still existed against them. Padre Taronjí's book stirred up great interest in the "outcasts of Majorca," and the liberal press of Spain joined leading scholars in declaring

---

a Chueta himself) declared that the entire work was a plot to extort money from the Chuetas. Cf. Kayserling, "Notes sur l'histoire des Juifs de Majorque," *REJ*, XLIV, 1902, 300.

26 Cf. Mendoza y Bovadilla, *El Tizon de la Nobleza.*

27 Soler, pp. 19, 22, 29, 31, 43, 44, 50, 65-8, 93, 94, 102, 107-10, 113-16, 126. A short time later (June 10, 1859) an interview with a Chueta appeared in the *Jewish Chronicle*, London, XVI, 234, indicating that prejudice still obtained against his people on the island.

that the Chuetas should long ago have been granted the genuine freedom and equality they deserved.[28]

With the birth of the new Spanish Republic (1931), it would appear that such out-moded prejudice would have vanished like smoke. But not so in Majorca. The old tracts have been reprinted, intending to incite the people against the Chuetas, as an antidote against whatever rights the Republic might confer upon them. A new edition of Padre Garau's book has been published (1931). Included among the documents in its appendix is the old list of the inquisition's culprits, originally issued in 1755.[29] Republican Spain, apparently, has not yet succeeded in obliterating an ancient prejudice held against a group of people persecuted on account of their Jewish antecedents.[30]

Some three-hundred Chueta families still live, for the most part in the *Chueteria,* in Palma, carrying on the trades of silversmith, goldsmith, and petty merchant and shop-keeper, which have come as part of their legacy from their forebears. Some have risen to positions of leadership in banking, business, and in the professions.[31] With the legacy of their forebears has come also the exclusion which, with few exceptions, characterizes their life even today. They are subjected to villification, and the contemptuous names,

---

[28] Taronjí, p. 309ff. Among the leading scholars who advocated freedom for the oppressed Chuetas were José Maria Quadrado, the distinguished historian, Antonio Maria Salom, José Maria Settier, Joaquin Fiol and others. A few years before the publication of Taronjí's book there appeared a poem by Francisco Pelayo Briz, in *Calendari Catalá del any 1870,* Barcelona, which, with great moving power, immortalized the victims of the autos de fe of 1691 as martyrs. The reaction of the Spanish press is preserved in *Juicio de la Prensa Española* . . . etc.

[29] I. e. the *Relacion.* In the same year (1931) significantly enough, Quadrado's interesting study on the ghetto of Majorca in 1391 ("La Juderia de la Capital de Mallorca en 1391") was also reprinted. It was circulating widely in Palma in 1932. Quadrado's work appeared originally in *BAH* (IX, 1886) and reprinted the following year (April 30, 1887) in *Museo Balear de Historia, Literatura, Ciencias y Artes,* IV, no. 8. It also appeared in *REJ* (XIV, 1887, 259-61) in Isidore Loeb's article: "Notes sur l'Histoire des Juifs en Espagne."

[30] The subject of the Chuetas has been frequently discussed in the last decades. In 1909, Miguel Santos Oliver, an important Majorcan author, wrote of the continued exclusion of the Chuetas in his *Hojas del Sábado,* p. 242. In 1916 no less a novelist than Vicente Blasco-Ibáñez, in his book *Los Muertos Mandan,* portrayed, with great sympathy and understanding, the prejudices and difficulties which the Chuetas suffered. Mention should also be made of Sylvette de Lamar's book *Jews with the Cross* (London, 1932), although it has no merit either as an historical or literary production; and the novel *Sea Change* by Eleanor Mercein Kelly (New York, 1931), in which one of the chief characters is a Chueta. A small treatment of them appears in Lewis Browne's *How Odd of God* (New York, 1934), pp. 57-60. These illustrate the interest manifested in the Chueta problem in our own day. The reader is also referred to Azriel Karlbach's report (in the *Jewish Daily Forward,* Section II, October 9, 1932) of his participation in the Day of Atonement Services of the Chuetas in 1930!

[31] Some are members of the City Council, others are in banking, engineering and in other professions.

Judío and Chueta, are occasionally flung at them in the streets. Only in the last decades have a few marriages taken place between old-Christian and Chueta families. For the most part the Chuetas intermarry among themselves, their offspring revealing, after so many generations of inbreeding, the outstanding Semitic characteristics, almost to a point of caricature. Yet they are faithful Catholics, quite ignorant of the Judaism for which they are made to suffer. Their women may be identified on the streets by the enormous crosses they wear. They give liberally to the support of the Church. In their poorest homes are to be found highly-decorated altars, adorned with pictures and images of the Saviour and the saints.

The Chuetas constitute one of the tragedies of the modern world, living among an island-people who seem unable to rid themselves of their provincial and fanatical prejudices, which the activities of the inquisition have played no small part to perpetuate. Up to our day the Chuetas remain a pariah-folk in the Mediterranean region, isolated in a Catholic land, among peoples whose faith they share, and whose life they have enriched by poets and writers.[32] This anomalous situation is in large part a relic of the Spanish zeal for unity of the faith, inspiring the establishment of the Spanish Inquisition, and which, beginning in the fifteenth century, has not altogether spent its force in our times, a century after its extinction.

---

32 Bover, *Biblioteca de Escritores Baleares,* where the Chuetas are represented by the names of Aguiló, Cortes, Forteza, Valenti, Valls, etc. I, 3-6, 309-12, 561-2; II, 431, 473, 474, 487.

APPENDICES

APPENDICES

INQUISITORS OF THE MAJORCAN TRIBUNAL

A. *For the Combined Tribunal of the Balearic Islands, Cerdagne and Roussillon*

DATE	NAME	SOURCE OF INFORMATION
1) 1332-1343	Ramon Durfort	Lea, *Middle Ages*, II, 177
2) 1357-1394	Jaime Domingo[1]	*Hist. Gen.*, III, 361
3) Appointed 1394	Pedro Rippe	*Ibid*, II, 652; III, 361; Binimelis, *Hist. de Mall.*, V, 394
4) Appointed 1404	Pedro Tur	*Ibid*, V, 394; *Hist. Gen.*, II, 652; III, 361
5) Appointed 1413	Bernardo Pages[2]	Binimelis, V, 394; *Hist. Gen.*, II, 652; III, 361

B. *For the Independent Tribunal of the Balearic Islands*

6) Appointed 1413	Guillermo Sagarra	*Hist. Gen.*, II, 652; III, 362; Lea, *Middle Ages*, 177
7) 1419 ?	Julian Talládas	*Hist. Gen.*, II, 652
8) 1420-1436	Antonio Murta	Binimelis, V, 394; Cronicon, 156; *Hist Gen.*, II, 653; III, 362
9) 1436-1437?	Bernardo Vicens[3]	*Hist. Gen.*, II, 653
10) 1437-1460?	Francisco Miró	*Ibid;* Binimelis V, 394
11) 1460-1477	Juan Ginard	Apuntes[4], fol. 46; *Hist. Gen.*, II, 653; III, 362
12) 1477-1484	Nicolas Merola	Apuntes, fol. 46; *Hist. Gen.*, II, 653; III, 362
13) 1484-1488	Rafael Garcías	*Ibid*, II, 653

C. *For the New Tribunal Established by Ferdinand and Isabella*

14) 1488-1489	Pedro Perez de Munebrega	*Hist. Gen.*, II, 653; III, 363; Lea, *Spain*, I, 267
15) 1488-1489	Sancho Martin	
16) 1489-1490	Juan Ramon	
17) 1490-1491	Juan de Astorga	*Hist. Gen.*, II, 653; III, 363
18) 1491-1493	Gomez de Cienfuegos	*Ibid*
19) 1493-1495	Pedro Gual	*Ibid*
20) 1495-1500	Nuño de Villalobos	*Ibid*

[1] Domingo Jaume Cf. *Hist. Gen.*, II, 652.

[2] Pedro Pages. Cf. *Hist. Gen.*, II, 652.

[3] Others say that Benet (Bernardo) Vicens succeeded, not preceded, Antonio Murta. *Hist. Gen.*, III, 362.

[4] *Apuntes para la historia General del Santo Oficio de Mallorca.*

21)	1500-1503	Francisco de Oro-pesa	*Ibid,* Cronicon, 219
22)	1503	Guillermo Casél-las[5]	*Hist. Gcn.,* II, 653-5 ; III, 363 L
23)	1503-1506	Juan de Loaysa	*Hist Gen.,* II, 655 ; III, 364
24)	1506-1512	Juan de Anguera	*Ibid*
25)	1512-1516	Pedro Vicente Al-emany	*Hist Gen.,* II, 655
26)	1516-1520	Juan Navardu	*Ibid,* III, 364
27)	1521-1522	Pedro Pont	Apuntes, fol. lv ; Binimelis, V, 84
28)	1522 ?[6]-1529	Arnaldo Alberti y Company	Binimelis, IV, 396 ; *Hist. Gen.,* II, 655 ; III, 364
29)	1529-1534	Bartolomé Sebas-tian	*Ibid,* Binimelis, IV, 396
30)	1534-1538	Juan Navardu	*Hist. Gen.,* II, 655 ; III, 364
31)	1538-1541	Juan Crespi	*Hist. Gen.,* III, 364
32)	1541-1565	Nicolas Montañ-ans y Berard	Binimelis, V, 396 ; *Hist. Gen.,* II, 655 ; III, 364
33)	1565	Miguel Gual	*Ibid*
34)	1566[7]-1569	Diego de Arnedo	*Hist. Gen.,* III, 364
35)	1569-1578	Andres Santos de Herrera	*Hist. Gen.,* II, 655
36)	1578-1580	Felix Evia de Ovieda	Apuntes, fol. 2v ; Binimelis, V, 396 ; *Hist. Gen,* II, 655-6 ; III, 364 ; AHN *Rel. de Caus. de Fe,* libro 1, 862, fol. 345
37)	1580[8]-1594	Juan Salvador Abrines	Binimelis, IV, 396 ; *Hist. Gen.,* II, 656 ; III, 364
38)	1594	Antonio Reus	*Hist. Gen.,* II, 656
39)	1595-1605	Francisco de Es-quivel	*Ibid,* III, 364 ; Binimelis, IV, 397
40)	1605-1611	Juan Gutierrez Flores	*Hist. Gen.,* II, 656 ; III, 364
41)	1611-1612	Antonio Creus	*Ibid*
42)	1612-1616	Isidro de Santos Vicente	*Ibid,* Apuntes, fol. 3 ; Binimelis, IV, 397
43)	1616-1620	Juan de Godoy	*Hist. Gen.,* II, 656 ; III, 364
44)	1620-1623	Bartolomé Piza	*Hist. Gen.,* II, 656
45)	1623-1625	Pedro Diez de Ci-enfuegos	*Hist. Gen.,* III, 364
46)	1625-1631	Andres Bravo	*Ibid*
47)	1631-1637	Blaz Alejandro de la Zaeta	*Ibid;* Apuntes, fol. 3v
48)	1637	Pedro Febrer	*Hist. Gen.,* II, 656-7 ; III, 364

---

[5] Cronicon (p. 222) places his régime in 1509.

[6] *Hist. Gen.* (III, 364) places his régime as beginning in 1520, and again (II, 655) from 1526

[7] *Hist. Gen.* (II, 655) places his régime in 1565

[8] Abrines served from 1580 to 1593 as inquisitor pro tem in the absence of Evia de Ovieda, and was not appointed inquisitor until 1593 He died the following year. *Hist. Gen.,* II, 656.

49) 1637-1643	Francisco de Gregorio	AHN *Rel. de Caus. de Fe*, libro 1, 862, fol. 345; *Hist. Gen*, II, 657; III, 364
50) 1643⁹-1648	Miguel Lopez de Vitoria Eguinoa	*Hist. Gen.*, II, 657
51)[10] 1665	Francisco de Sarabia y Ojeda	*Ibid*
52) 1666-1668	Hyeronimo de Escobar	AHN *Rel. de Caus. de Fe*, libro 1, 864, fol. 120
53) 1668-1673	Baltazar Miguel del Prado	AHN *Proc. de Fe*, legajo 1708, 2, fol. 9
54) 1673-1680	Francisco Rodriguez de Cossio Barreda[11]	*Ibid*
55) 1677-1682	Juan Bautista Desbach	AHN *Proc. de Fe*, legajo 1709, 4, fol. 4
56) 1680-1682	Francisco Baca de Lederma	AHN *Rel. de Caus. de Fe*, libro 1, 864, fols. 210, 240
57) 1682-1684	Nicolas Rodriguez Fermossino	AHN *Proc. de Fe*, legajos: 1708, 4, fol. 4; 1709, 10, fol. 6; AHN *Rel. de Caus. de Fe*, libro 1, 864, fols. 124, 302
58) 1684-1693	Andres Fernandez de Avila y Salcedo	*Hist. Gen.*, II, 657
59) 1687-1694	Joseph Hualte	AHN *Proc. de Fe*, legajo 1708, 4, fols. 36, 84
60) 1688-1692	Pedro Guerrero de Bolaños	AHN *Proc. de Fc*, legajos: 1705, 5, fol. 20; 1708, 4, fol. 42; 1710, 1, fol. 1
61) 1693-1699	Pablo Marina y Hugalde	*Hist. Gen.*, II, 657
62) 1699-1703	Geronimo Ibañez y Zarate	Apuntes, fol. 8
63) 1700-1720	Jorge Truyole y Dameto	AHN *Proc. de Fe*, legajo 1715, 5, fols. 35v, 79v; *Hist. Gen.*, II, 657
64) 1704-1720	Juan de Tarrancon y Aledo	AHN *Proc. de Fe*, legajos: 1707, 13, fol. 3; 1715, 5, fol. 14
65) 1721-1731	Matias Escalso y Acedo	AHN *Proc. de Fe*, legajo 1715, 5, fol. 24v; Apuntes, fol. 10; *Hist. Gen.*, II, 657
66) 1727-1739	Aurelio Esterripa Tranajáuregui	Apuntes, fol. 10; *Hist. Gen.*, II, 657

9 Variously reported that he was appointed to his post in 1648 (*Hist. Gen.*, III, 364).

10 This writer has not been able to discover the names of the inquisitor or inquisitors holding office between 1648 and 1665 The *Hist. Gen.* (II, 657) places Pedro Guerrero de Bolaños and Baltazar Miguel del Prado as the inquisitors during this time. Our records, which we follow unless there is overwhelming evidence pointing to other conclusions, place Pedro Guerrero de Bolaños between 1687 and 1692, and Baltazar Miguel de Prado between 1668 and 1673.

11 This inquisitor was removed from office in 1680. He is the only one on record against whom such proceedings were taken.

67) 1739-1746	Antonio Pelegrin Venero	Apuntes, fol. 11
68) 1746-1747	Manuel de Orneta	Apuntes, fol. 11; *Hist. Gen.,* II, 657
69) 1747-1754	Diego Perez de Haro	Apuntes, fol. 11
70) 1754-1761	Juan Andres Alvarez y Muns	*Hist. Gen.,* II, 657
71) 1759-1763	Pedro Antonio Fernandez de Arcaya	*Origen de la Inq.,*[12] fol. 13
72) 1759-1763	Joseph Rodriguez de Caceres	*Ibid*
73) 1763-1787	José Albert y Gil	*Hist. Gen.,* II, 657
74) 1787-1790	José Mata Lináres	*Ibid*
75) 1790-1806	Manuel Fuentes y Oñate	*Hist. Gen,* II, 658
76) 1806-1813	Juan Fernandez Legaria	Apuntes, fol. 14; *Hist. Gen.,* II, 658
77) 1806-1813	Márcos Fernandez Alonso	*Ibid*
78) 1814-1817	Márcos Ignacio Rosselló	*Ibid*
79) 1819-1820	Pedro Larroy y Lasala	Apuntes, fol. 16; *Hist. Gen.,* II, 658
80) 1819-1820	Dámaso Bueno	*Ibid*
81) 1819-1820	Mariano Madramany y Calatayud	*Ibid*
82) 1830	Francisco Antonio Andraca	Lea, *Spain,* IV, 459

---

[12] *Origen de la Inquisición,* Cuerpo de Manuscritos, BN

RECONCILIATIONS AND RELAXATIONS IN THE INQUISITION OF MAJORCA (From Its Foundation To 1691)

A. *Reconciliations Through the Edicts of Grace*

(Memoria de los Reconciliados por el Santo Oficio de la Inquisición de Mallorca por los Edictos de Gracia, desde su fundacion en este Reyno. AHN *Relaciones de Causas de Fe*, libro 1, 866, fols. 1-48)

	I Rec. por 1ero Edicto de Gracia, 18 de Agosto 1488	II y en el 2do Edicto de Gracia, 1 de Julio, 1491
	,,	
1 Amada, muger de Gabriel Porsell[1]	,,	,,
2 Antonia Benvenguda, muger de Bonanat Tagamanent	,,	,,
3 Antonia, muger de Juan Arnau	,,	,,
4 Aldonza[2], muger de Pablo Roger	,,	,,
5 Angelina, muger de Geronimo Vila	,,	,,
6 Angelina, muger de Juan Morro	,,	,,
7 Antonio Cortes	,,	
8 Aneta, muger de Francisco Garrer	,,	
9 Aldonza, muger de Juan Cortes	,,	
10 Aldonza, muger de Francisco Luqui	,,	,,
11 Angelina, muger de Juan Serra	,,	,,
12 Aldonza, muger de Pedro Pellicer	,,	,,
13 Antonia Valeriola	,,	,,
14 Angelina, muger de Galceran de Quart	,,	
15 Angelina, muger de Raphael Luqui	,,	
16 Aldonza, muger de Daniel Valeriola	,,	,,
17 Aldonza, muger de Jayme Aguilo	,,	,,
18 Aldonza, muger de Bonanat Arnau	,,	,,
19 Bernardo Dolcet	,,	,,
20 Bernardo Piera	,,	,,
21 Bernardo Redondo	,,	,,
22 Balthasar Boga	,,	,,
23 Blanca, muger de Bartolome Mulet	,,	,,
24 Bonanada, muger de Daniel Savanals	,,	,,
25 Bartolomea Bonomada, muger de Gaspar Plegamans	,,	
26 Blanquina, muger de Francisco Bennaser	,,	,,
27 Blanquina, muger de Galceran Berarde	,,	
28 Beatriz, muger de Gabriel Mulet	,,	,,
29 Beneta, muger de Raphael Cortes	,,	,,
30 Blanquina, muger de Juan Amoros	,,	
31 Bartholome Soldevila	,,	
32 Benguda, muger de Gabriel Manuel Arbona		

---

1 All reconciliations were of Conversos, unless otherwise stated.

2 The alphabetizing and spelling may be faulty in places. These faults occur in the original records, from which these lists are faithfully rendered.

	I	II
33 Blanquina Vila, viuda de Jayme Vila	,,	,,
34 Blanquina Graciosa, muger de Pablo Cortes	,,	
35 Bartholomea, muger de Simon Garriga	,,	,,
36 Benguda, muger de Berenguer Vila	,,	,,
37 Blanca, muger de Juan Burgos	,,	,,
38 Beneta, muger de Galceran Moya	,,	
39 Beatriz, muger de Thomas Moya	,,	,,
40 Benguda, muger de Raphael Savanals	,,	,,
41 Benguda, muger de Gabriel Torner	,,	,,
42 Benguda, muger de Pablo Juan	,,	,,
43 Bernardo Boga	,,	,,
44 Benguda, muger de Pedro Galiana	,,	
45 Bonanada, muger de Gabriel Pelegri	,,	
46 Beatriz, muger de Miguel Garcia	,,	,,
47 Berenguer Arnau	,,	
48 Beatriz, muger de Galceran Raphal	,,	,,
49 Blanquina, muger de Gabriel Morro	,,	,,
50 Beneta, muger de Bonanat Bennaser	,,	,,
51 Blanquina, muger de Pedro Torner	,,	,,
52 Clara, muger de Maestro Juan Roger	,,	,,
53 Coloma, muger de Pedro Burgos	,,	,,
54 Clara, muger de Raphael Marti	,,	,,
55 Clara, muger de Raphael Aguilo	,,	,,
56 Coloma, muger de Matheo Burgos	,,	,,
57 Coloma, muger de Pedro Aguilo	,,	,,
58 Coloma, muger de Berenguer Arnau	,,	,,
59 Catalina, muger de Francisco San Marti	,,	,,
60 Clara, muger de Juan Berart	,,	,,
61 Clara, muger de Pablo Fuster	,,	,,
62 Coloma, muger de Salvador Perera	,,	,,
63 Catalina Tarongi, muger de Maestro Pedro Viñes	,,	
64 Coloma, muger de Pedro Boga	,,	
65 Clara, muger de Jayme Marti	,,	,,
66 Coloma, muger de Raphael Valeriola	,,	,,
67 Clara, muger de Jayme Serra	,,	
68 Catalina, muger de Pedro Daniel Marti	,,	
69 Clara, muger de Jayme Valeriola	,,	,,
70 Coloma, muger de Francisco Valeriola	,,	,,
71 Clara Revella, muger de Fernando Cessa Fuster	,,	,,
72 Coloma, muger de Juan Oliver	,,	,,
73 Clara, muger de Francisco Cessa	,,	
74 Dolça, muger de Juan Gostins	,,	,,
75 Daniel Silvestre	,,	,,
76 Dolça, muger de Daniel Silvestre	,,	,,
77 Daniel Vidal	,,	
78 Daniel Timbers	,,	,,
79 Daniel Forteza	,,	,,
80 Daniel Siger	,,	
81 Daniel Berart	,,	,,
82 Dolça, muger de Juan Morro	,,	,,
83 Diego Diez	,,	,,
84 Daniel Bellocs	,,	,,

	I	II
85 Dolça, muger de Canet de Tinen	,,	
86 Daniel Valeriola	,,	,,
87 Daniel Sabanals	,,	,,
88 Daniel Cortes	,,	,,
89 Eleonor, muger de Gil Navarro	,,	,,
90 Eleonor, muger de Miguel Sabanals	,,	,,
91 Eleonor, muger de Daniel Umbert	,,	,,
92 Eulalia, muger de Pablo Canet	,,	,,
93 Eleonor Savadora, muger de Pablo Despla	,,	,,
94 Esclamonda, muger de Pedro Junet	,,	,,
95 Esperanca, muger de Bartholome Soldevila	,,	,,
96 Eleonor, muger de Juanot Fonat	,,	,,
97 Eulalia, muger de Pablo Forteza	,,	,,
98 Eleonor, muger de Juanot Castello	,,	
99 Eldonza, muger de Pedro Mulet	,,	,,
100 Eleonor, muger de Juanot Cortes	,,	
101 Eleonor, muger de Balthasar Socorrat	,,	,,
102 Eleonor, muger de Antonio Bonnin	,,	
103 Eleonor, muger de Gabriel Berart	,,	,,
104 Eleonor, muger de Pedro Colom	,,	,,
105 Eulalia, muger de Gaspar Moya	,,	,,
106 Eleonor, muger de Vidal Arnau	,,	,,
107 Eleonor, muger de Manuel Gatzar	,,	,,
108 Eleonor, muger de Juan Miro	,,	
109 Francisco Puhol	,,	
110 Francisco Sans	,,	,,
111 Floreta Garces, muger de Juan Cauto	,,	,,
112 Francisca, muger de Daniel Berarde	,,	,,
113 Francisca, muger de Melchor Bages	,,	,,
114 Francisco Merio	,,	,,
115 Francisca, muger de Daniel Silvestre	,,	,,
116 Francisca, muger de Pablo Marti	,,	
117 Francisca, muger de Gabriel Bonet	,,	,,
118 Francisco Loqui	,,	,,
119 Francisca, muger de Francisco Sans	,,	,,
120 Floreta, muger de Francisco Arnau	,,	,,
121 Francisca, muger de Raphael Berart	,,	,,
122 Francisco Vidal	,,	,,
123 Fernando Cessa	,,	,,
124 Francisca, muger de Pedro Malferit	,,	
125 Floreta, muger de Francisco Rosell	,,	,,
126 Ferrer de Quart	,,	,,
127 Francisco Vallsequa	,,	,,
128 Francisco Bennaser	,,	
129 Francisca, muger de Pablo Torner	,,	,,
130 Francisco Sant Marty	,,	,,
131 Gabriel Cabrera	,,	
132 Graciosa, muger de Raphael Canet	,,	
133 Graciosa, muger de Juan Bonnin	,,	,,
134 Graciosa, muger de Balthasar Boga	,,	
135 Graciosa, muger de Raphael Vila	,,	,,
136 Gabriel Cauto		

		I	II
137	Gostanca, muger de Gaspar Silvestre	,,	,,
138	Gostanca, muger de Salvador Bonet	,,	,,
139	Gabriel Morro	,,	,,
140	Graciosa, muger de Gilabert Torrella	,,	
141	Graciosa, muger de Juan Moya	,,	
142	Gil Navarro	,,	
143	Graciosa Cardona, muger de Dionis Rosell	,,	,,
144	Gaspar Moya	,,	,,
145	Gabriel Porsell	,,	
146	Graciosa Miguela, muger de Pablo Domingo	,,	,,
147	Graciosa, muger de Juan de Segovia	,,	,,
148	Graciosa, muger de Bonanat Morro	,,	,,
149	Graciosa Aldomara	,,	,,
150	Graciosa, muger de Juan Morro	,,	,,
151	Graciosa, muger de Pedro Galiana	,,	,,
152	Graciosa, muger de Jayme Morro	,,	,,
153	Graciosa, muger de Juan Plegamans	,,	,,
154	Graciosa, muger de Diego Diez	,,	,,
155	Galceran de Quart	,,	
156	Graciosa, muger de Luis Lorens	,,	,,
157	Graciosa, muger de Jayme Arnau	,,	,,
158	Galceran Brondo	,,	,,
159	Gabriel Plegamans	,,	
160	Galceran Valeriola	,,	
161	Gaspar Silvestre	,,	,,
162	Gabriel Ripoll	,,	,,
163	Graciosa, muger de Gaspar Tudela	,,	,,
164	Gabriel Serra	,,	
165	Gabriel Mulet	,,	,,
166	Galceran Moya	,,	,,
167	Graciosa, muger de Maestre Garriga	,,	
168	Gabriel Tarongi	,,	,,
169	Galceran Bonnin	,,	,,
170	Joaneta, muger de Bernardo Dolcet	,,	
171	Isabel, muger de Raphael Baro	,,	,,
172	Isabel, muger de Pedro Torres	,,	,,
173	Juaneta, muger de Francisco Cessa	,,	
174	Juaneta, muger de Miguel Dameto	,,	
175	Juaneta, muger de Pedro Soldevila	,,	,,
176	Juaneta, muger de Andreu Aris	,,	
177	Juana, muger de Daniel Loscos	,,	
178	Juaneta, muger de Gabriel Miro	,,	
179	Juana, muger de Pablo Tarongi	,,	,,
180	Juana, muger de Daniel Cessa	,,	
181	Isabel, muger de Gabriel Cortes	,,	,,
182	Juana, muger de Raphael Espinach	,,	,,
183	Juana, muger de Raphael Morro	,,	,,
184	Juana, muger de Antonio Cortes	,,	,,
185	Juana, muger de Juan Biabrera	,,	,,
186	Isabel, muger de Juan San Marty	,,	,,
187	Juana, muger de Pablo Muntañer	,,	
188	Juana, muger de Thomas Valeriola	,,	

	I	II
189 Juan Olivar	”	
190 Juana, muger de Juan Serra	”	
191 Isabel, muger de Daniel Gilabert	”	”
192 Juana, muger de Pedro Cauti	”	
193 Juaneta, muger de Bernardo Boga	”	”
194 Juana, muger de Daniel Ariz	”	
195 Juan Marti	”	
196 Isabel, muger de Juan Torres	”	”
197 Isabel, muger de Francisco Morro	”	”
198 Isabel, muger de Salvador Giner	”	”
199 Jayme Viabreba	”	
200 Juan Moya	”	”
201 Isabel, muger de Perote Rodriguez	”	”
202 Jayme Rement	”	
203 Juana Mayor, muger de Pedro Locatella	”	
204 Juaneta, muger de Nicolas Vila	”	”
205 Jayme Morro	”	
206 Juana, muger de Pablo Naber	”	”
207 Isabel, muger de Luis Giger	”	
208 Jayme Arnau	”	”
209 Juaneta, muger de Salvador Brull	”	”
210 Juana, muger de Daniel Cortes	”	”
211 Juan Burgos	”	”
212 Juana, muger de Oliver	”	
213 Isabel, muger de Lazaro	”	
214 Juan Salvat	”	
215 Jayme Valeriola	”	”
216 Isabel, muger de Ferrer de Quart	”	”
217 Juan Forteza	”	”
218 Jayme Arnau	”	”
219 Isabel, muger de Juan Salvat	”	”
220 Juan Valeriola	”	”
221 Juaneta Valeriola, muger de Juan Valeriola	”	
222 Juaneta, muger de Bernardo Redondo	”	
223 Isabel, muger de Leonardo Zaportellas	”	
224 Isabel, muger de Pablo Berarde	”	”
225 Jayme Farrega	”	”
226 Juan Sabanals, hijo de Raphael Sabanals	”	”
227 Juan Miro	”	
228 Isabel, muger de Gabriel Tarongi	”	”
229 Juan Costello	”	”
230 Isabel, muger de Juan Ciutar	”	
231 Jayme Remesa	”	”
232 Juan Morro	”	”
233 Juan Funcar	”	”
234 Isabel, muger de Pedro Perez	”	
235 Jayme San Marty	”	”
236 Jayme Funcar	”	
237 Juana, muger de Pedro Cauto	”	”
238 Juan Desgrau	”	
239 Jayme Perez	”	
240 Juan Morro	”	

	I	II
241 Luisa, muger de Bartholome Suñer	,,	,,
242 Leonardo Zaportella	,,	
243 Lorenco de Luna	,,	,,
244 Lorenca, muger de Gabriel Morro	,,	
245 Lorenca, muger de Daniel Giger	,,	,,
246 Luis Giger	,,	
247 Lorenca, muger de Pablo Tarrega	,,	
248 Lorenca Masipa, viuda	,,	,,
249 Marthena, muger de Pablo Sitges	,,	,,
250 Margarita, muger de Jayme Roger	,,	
251 Miguel Dameto	,,	,,
252 Maria, muger de Vidal Provensal	,,	,,
253 Magdalena, muger de Sebastian Compañy	,,	,,
254 Maria, muger del Maestro Alesandro Adret	,,	
255 Manuel Arnau	,,	,,
256 Maria, muger de Pablo Quart	,,	,,
257 Magdalena, muger de Plegamans	,,	
258 Matheo de Burgos	,,	,,
259 Magdalena, muger de Juan Poloni	,,	
260 Margarita, muger de Juan Zaflor	,,	,,
261 Margarita, muger de Raphael Vallsequa	,,	,,
262 Magdalena, muger de Raphael Vidal	,,	,,
263 Mariana Bonenada, muger de Juan Frigola	,,	,,
264 Miguel Morro	,,	,,
265 Nicolas Cortes	,,	,,
266 Nicolas Vila	,,	,,
267 Pablo Pellicer	,,	,,
268 Pablo Roger	,,	,,
269 Pareta, muger de Pablo Coll	,,	,,
270 Pablo Fuster	,,	
271 Pedro Aguilo	,,	,,
272 Pareta, muger de Juan Morro	,,	,,
273 Pablo Muntañer	,,	,,
274 Pedro Soldevilla	,,	,,
275 Pedro Bonet	,,	,,
276 Perot Rodriguez	,,	,,
277 Pedro Berarde	,,	,,
278 Pedro Cauti	,,	,,
279 Pedro Mulet	,,	,,
280 Policena, muger de Gabriel Vidal	,,	
281 Pablo Suan	,,	,,
282 Pareta Laflor	,,	,,
283 Pareta, muger de Thomas Gener	,,	,,
284 Pablo Sitges	,,	,,
285 Peret Vilanova	,,	,,
286 Pedro Suñer	,,	,,
287 Pereta, muger de Gabriel Cortes	,,	
288 Pablo Tarongi	,,	,,
289 Pereta, muger de Juan Funcar	,,	,,
290 Pereta, muger de Lorenco Cauto	,,	
291 Pablo de Quart	,,	,,
292 Pereta, muger de Pons Valeriola	,,	,,

	I	II
	,,	,,
293 Pablo Forteza	,,	
294 Pons Valeriola	,,	
295 Pablo Sercos	,,	,,
296 Pedro Cauti	,,	,,
297 Pereta, muger de Gabriel Sessa	,,	,,
298 Raphael Morro	,,	,,
299 Raphael Cortes	,,	,,
300 Raphael Berarde	,,	,,
301 Raphael Olivar	,,	,,
302 Raphael Pelegri	,,	,,
303 Raphael Torrella	,,	,,
304 Raphael Baro	,,	,,
305 Selamonda, muger de Juan Beltran	,,	,,
306 Speranca, muger de Pedro Sala	,,	
307 Speranca, muger de Juan Rementa	,,	,,
308 Speranca, muger de Bernardo Riera	,,	,,
309 Simon Arnau	,,	,,
310 Salvador Giner	,,	,,
311 Selamonda, muger de Bernardo Canet	,,	
312 Serena Bonanada, muger de Pedro Cortes	,,	,,
313 Simona, muger de Jayme Oliver	,,	
314 Salavat Savanals	,,	,,
315 Simona, muger de Daniel Vidal	,,	,,
316 Speranca, muger de Pedro Valdaura	,,	,,
317 Selamonda, muger de Galceran Salvador	,,	
318 Simona Zaportella	,,	,,
319 Speranca, muger de Bonanat Fuster	,,	,,
320 Selamonda, muger de Jayme Tarrega	,,	,,
321 Salvat Bonet	,,	,,
322 Thomas Valeriola	,,	
323 Thomas Bonnin	,,	,,
324 Thomas Moya	,,	,,
325 Thomas Gener	,,	,,
326 Vidal Provensal	,,	,,
327 Violante, muger de Pedro Bonet	,,	
328 Violante, muger de Gabriel Lozano	,,	,,
329 Ursula, muger de Bartolome Coll	,,	,,
330 Violante, muger de Jayme Vila	,,	,,
331 Vidal Arnau	,,	,,
332 Violante, muger de Peret de Vilanova	,,	,,
333 Violante, muger de Juan Savanals	,,	,,
334 Ursula, muger de Pablo Corredor	,,	,,
335 Violante, muger de Pedro Salvador	,,	
336 Violante, muger de Daniel Cabrit	,,	,,
337 Violante, muger de Juan Massana	,,	,,
338 Antonia, muger de Ferrer Prats	en 1er Edicto de Gracia, 26 de Março, de 1490	
339 Antonia, muger de Juan de Quart	,,	,,
340 Aldonza, muger de Gabriel Torrella	,,	,,
341 Antonia, muger de Pedro Jordi	,,	,,

		I	II
342	Antonio Boga	,,	,,
343	Agnes, muger de Juan Lletor	,,	,,
344	Beatriz, doncella, hixa de Pablo Roger	,,	,,
345	Brianda, esclava de Jayme Roger, AM³	,,	,,
346	Beatriz, muger de Fonat Quintanal	,,	,,
347	Berenguer Vila, alias Vivet	,,	,,
348	Bonanat Cortes	,,	,,
349	Blanca, doncella, hixa de Raphael Berard	,,	
350	Blanquina, doncella, hixa de Balthazar Socorrats	,,	
351	Blanquina, muger de Daniel Berard	,,	
352	Benguda, muger de Pablo Bonnin	,,	,,
353	Benguda, muger de Francisco Puhol	,,	,,
354	Benguda, doncella, hixa de Daniel Cortes	,,	
355	Bartholome Fuster	,,	,,
356	Beatriz, doncella, hixa de Bartolome Coll	,,	'
357	Benguda, muger de Galceran Cauti	,,	
358	Coloma, doncella, hixa de Pablo Roger	,,	,,
359	Clara, muger de Francisco Barcelo	,, `	,,
360	Clara, muger de Antonio Boga	,,	,,
361	Clara, muger de Matheu Morro	,,	,,
362	Coloma, muger de Bartolome Gostins	,,	
363	Clara Cardona, muger de Gabriel Desgrau	,,	
364	Clara, muger de Antonio Artes	,,	,,
365	Daniel Pau	,,	,,
366	Dalman Cassella	,,	,,
367	Dolça, muger de Juan Gostins	,,	
368	Eleonor, muger de Pablo Moya	,,	
369	Eulalia, doncella, hixa de Gabriel Benatenell	,,	'
370	Eufrasina, muger de Marty San Marty	,,	
371	Eleonor, muger de Bartholome Fuster	,,	
372	Eulalia, muger de Dalman	,,	
373	Eleonor, doncella, hixa de Gabriel Vidal	,,	
374	Francisco Desgrau	,,	
375	Francisca, muger de Juan Zaportella	,,	,,
376	Francisco Valeriola	,,	
377	Floreta, muger de Nicolas Torres	,,	,,
378	Francisca Coll, doncella	,,	
379	Francisca, muger de Gabriel Barcelo	,,	
380	Francisco Jayme	,,	
381	Francisco Terongi	,,	,,
382	Francisco Arnau, (yerno de Castello)	,,	
383	Graciosa, muger de Gabriel Torres	,,	,,
384	Gaspar Lozano	,,	
385	Gaspar Desgrau	,,	
386	Geronimo Vila	,,	,,
387	Graciosa, muger de Francisco	,,	,,
388	Graciosa, doncella, hixa de Leonor Socorrats	,,	,,
389	Graciosa, muger de Miguel Piña	,,	,,
390	Gabriel Arnau	,,	
391	Gabriela Bendona	,,	,,

³ AM=Apostata Mohametano

#	Name	I	II
392	Graciosa Galiana, muger de Ferrer Galiana	,,	
393	Juan Arnau	,,	
394	Juana, muger de Juan Valeriola	,,	,,
395	Isabel, muger de Leonardo Suñer	,,	,,
396	Juan Suñer	,,	
397	Juana, muger de Pablo Valeriola	,,	,,
398	Juan de Quart	,,	,,
399	Jayme Funcar Cobell	,,	
400	Isabel, doncella, hixa de Bonanat Mulet	,,	
401	Isabel Boga, Madre de Bernardo Boga	,,	,,
402	Lazaro Pellicer	,,	,,
403	Lenoardo Suñer	,,	,,
404	Melchor Bages	,,	,,
405	Margarita, muger de Gabriel Valls	,,	
406	Maestro Rodrigo	,,	
407	Margarita, doncella, hixa de Raphael Savanals	,,	
408	Margarita, doncella, hixa de Juan Salvat	,,	
409	Michaela, muger de Gabriel Berard	,,	,,
410	Pedro Arnau	,,	
411	Pablo Benet, hixo de Pedro Benet	,,	,,
412	Pablo Valeriola	,,	,,
413	Pedro Ferrando	,,	
414	Ramon Frigola	,,	,,
415	Raphael Vila	,,	
416	Raphael Segui	,,	,,
417	Raphael Aguilo	,,	
418	Selamonda, doncella, hixa de Audres Arnau	,,	
419	Speranca, doncella, hixa de Pedro Pallas	,,	,,
420	Tecla, doncella, hixa de Pedro Pallas	,,	
421	Violante, doncella, hixa de Balthazar Socarrats	,,	
422	Violante, doncella, hixa de Daniel Cortes	,,	
423	Violante, muger de Raphael Vila	,,	,,
424	Violante, muger de Francisco Arnau		,,
425	Aldonza, muger de Francisco Fiol		,,
426	Antonia, muger de Francisco Sequi		,,
427	Aldonza, muger de Pedro Mulet		,,
428	Antonio Bonnin		,,
429	Anita, muger de Pablo Cabrera		,,
430	Anita, muger de Arnau Garret		,,
431	Bonanada Serenet		,,
432	Blanquina, muger de Pablo Torner		,,
433	Blanquina, muger de Pedro Galiana		,,
434	Benguda, muger de Glaceran Sani		,,
435	Catalina, muger de Manuel Gostins		,,
436	Clara, muger de Gabriel Unis		,,
437	Clara Marquona		,,
438	Coloma, muger de Daniel Bombarda		,,
439	Catalina, muger de Pedro Vives		,,
440	Coloma, muger de Raphael Boga		,,
441	Clara, muger de Pedro Bager		,,
442	Catalina, muger de Daniel Masip		,,
443	Dolça Caneta		,,

444 Elisenda, muger de Pedro Lops
445 Eulalia Marcona, muger de Dalman Cortilla
446 Eufrasina, muger de Pablo Torner
447 Francisco Sanç
448 Francisca, muger de Francisco Revell
449 Floreta, muger de Gabriel Cortes
450 Graciosa, muger de Pedro Arnau
451 Juan de Segobia
452 Juana, muger de Bernardo Reds
453 Juana, muger de Pablo Munyoz
454 Juana Ripola, muger de Gabriel Ripol
455 Isabel, muger de Gabriel Sitges
456 Isabel, muger de Lazaro Pellisser
457 Isabel de Perets
458 Leonor, muger de Salvador Funcar
459 Luis Lorens
460 Margarita, muger de Gabriel Plegamans
461 Margarita, muger de Salvat Savanals

II
"
"
"
"
"
"
"
"
"
"
"
"
"
"
"
"
"

y en 2do Edic-
to de Gracia,
en 30 de dicho
mes de Julio

462 Nicolas Gener
463 Nicolas Torres
464 Pedro Lops
465 Pablo Cabrera
466 Violante, muger de Andres Arnau
467 Violante, muger de Simon Bennaser
468 Violante, muger de Manuel Arnau
469 Violante, muger de Pablo Muntañer
470 Violante, muger de Miguel Dameto
471 Violante, muger de Juan Serra
472 Violante, muger de Thomas Valeriola
473 Venguda, muger de Gabriel Genetar
474 Violante, muger de Gabriel Miro
475 Violante, muger de Juan Forteza

"
"
"
"
"
"
"
"
"
"
"
"
"
"

en 30 de Julio
de 1491

476 Aneta, doncella, hixa de Juan Muntañer
477 Aldonza, doncella, hixa de Juan Olibar
478 Aldonza Nabesa
479 Antonina Simona
480 Antonina, muger de Nicolas Gener
481 Bonanada, muger de Bonanat Berard
482 Beatriz, muger de Gaspar Rebassa
483 Blanca, muger de Daniel Pau
484 Brianda, muger de Raphael Revell
485 Beatriz, muger de Bartholome Gari
486 Benguda, muger de Juan Montarago
487 Bonanada, muger de Luis Corella
488 Beneta, muger de Raphael Umbert
489 Blanca Pons
490 Catalina, muger de Miguel Blaned
491 Coloma, muger de Juan Berlanguez

"
"
"
"
"
"
"
"
"
"
"
"
"
"
"
"

492 Coloma Vida, doncella
493 Clara Cotamallero, muger de Pedro Juan Finder
494 Clara, muger de Raphael Olibar
495 Clara, muger de Galceran Seros
496 Clara, muger de Pedro Sala
497 Dolça, muger de Jayme Segura
498 Daniel Silvestre·
499 Daniel Tagamanent
500 Daniel Pau
501 Eulalia, muger de Pedro Rebassa
502 Eulalia, muger de Pedro Puhol
503 Eufrasina, muger de Pedro Valeriola
504 Esclamunda, muger de Pedro Canet
505 Esclamunda, muger de Galceran Corella
506 Francisca, muger de Salvador Costello
507 Francisco Fiol
508 Francisca, muger de Gonzalvo
509 Francisco Garret
510 Graciosa, muger de Galceran Moya
511 Gabriel Sani
512 Galceran Fortesa
513 Gabriel Genestar
514 Gabriel Torrella
515 Gabriel Morro

516 Gabriel Torres
517 Graciosa, muger de Antonio Letor
518 Juan Zaportella
519 Juan Colom
520 Juanot Navarro
521 Jayme Segura
522 Juan Torres
523 Jayme Torres
524 Juana, doncella, hixa de Juan Letor
525 Juan Colom
526 Juan Etates
527 Juan Bonnin
528 Jayme Cabrera
529 Jayme Vila
530 Juan Covreador
531 Juan Serra
532 Isabel, doncella, hixa de Juan Muntañer (esposa de Tho. Rebassa)
533 Isabel, muger de Daniel Tagamanent
534 Isabel, muger de Simon Cauti
535 Leonor, doncella, hixa de Pablo Roger
536 Leonor, muger de Miguel Oliber
537 Leonor, muger de Jayme Vila
538 Leonor, muger de Jayme Mercat
539 Leonor, muger de Gabriel Nageri

II
"
"
"
"
"
"
"
"
"
"
"
"
"
"
"
"
"
"
"
"
"
"
"
"

2do Edicto de
Gracia, en 30
de Julio de
1491
"
"
"
"
"
"
"
"
"
"
"
"
"
"
"
"

"
"
"
"
"
"
"

		II
540	Luna, muger de Pablo Rebassa	,,
541	Margarita, muger de Raphael Pico	,,
542	Pedro Sala	,,
543	Pablo Coll	,,
544	Pedro Genestar	,,
545	Pablo Torner	,,
546	Pablo Bonnin	,,
547	Pedro Canet	,,
548	Pablo Rebassa	,,
549	Pereta, muger de Juan Torres	,,
550	Raphael Revell	,,
551	Raphael Olibar	,,
552	Raphael Umbert	,,
553	Salvador Castello	,,
554	Salvat Savanals	,,
555	Violante Boga, hixa de Pedro Boga	,,
556	Violante Mortaya	,,
557	Violante Boga, hixa de Jaime Pico	,,
558	Violante, muger de Luis Berart	,,
559	Violante, muger de Francisco Arnau	,,

en 2do Edicto
de Gracia, en
13 de Octubre
de 1492

560 Juan Frigola   ,,

B: *Reconciliations Through Regular Trial-Procedure*

(Memoria de los Reconciliados por el Santo Oficio de la Inquisición del Reyno de Mallorca, desde su fundacion, sacada por el libro, donde estan registrados, y de sus processos. AHN *Relaciones de Causas de Fe,* libro 1, 866, fols. 52-91v)

1	Antonia, muger de Nicolas Gener[4]	19 de Diziembre, 1478
2	Catalina, muger de Lorenço Gener	,,
3	Lorenço Gener	,,
4	Nicolas Gener	,,
5	Leonor, muger de Juan Navarro	4 de Abril, 1497
6	Raphael Tagamanent	17 de Enero, 1482
7	Miguel Zuñer	26 de Noviembre, 1485
8	Clara, muger de Pedro Juan	,,
9	Leonor Funcar	16 de Diziembre, 1486
10	Aldonza, muger de Francisco Fiol	17 de Março, 1487
11	Pedro Bager	13 de Março, 1487
12	Aldonza, muger de Juan Muntañer	21 de Mayo, 1487
13	Clara, muger de Pedro Bager	26 de Mayo, 1487
14	Dolça, muger de Miguel Muntarago	17 de Março, 1487
15	Dolça Sitges	,,
16	Juan Muntañer	17 de Mayo, 1487
17	Pablo Cabrera	26 de Mayo, 1487
18	Francisca, muger de Raphael Vanrel	13 de Agosto, 1488
19	Raphael Berard	,,

---

[4] All the reconciliations were of Conversos, unless otherwise stated.

20	Daniel Sabanals	16 de Agosto, 1488
21	Esclamonda, muger de Juan Beltran	,,
22	Aldonza, muger de Raphael Tudela	4 de Abril, 1489
23	Aldonza, muger de Andres Bonnin	,,
24	Beatriz, muger de Jayme Piña	,,
25	Catalina, muger de Simon Arnau	,,
26	Isabel, muger de Jayme Bonnin .	,,
27	Blanca, muger de Juan Moya	11 de Noviembre, 1489
28	Francisco Arnau	,,
29	Gaspar Nadal	,,
30	Griselda, muger de Gabriel Revel	,,
31	Pedro Boga	,,
32	Clara, muger de Francisco Desgrau	8 de Febrero, 1490
33	Dolça, muger de Andres Bonnin	,,
34	Guillem Unis	,,
35	Galceran Salvi	,,
36	Juan Moya	,,
37	Raphael Tudela	,,
38	Violante, muger de Poncio Berard	23 de Março, 1490
39	Beatriz, hixa de Pablo Cortes	,,
40	Pereta, muger de Lorenco Cauto	11 de Mayo, 1490
41	Aneta, muger de Pablo Cabrera	,,
42	Francisca, muger de Francisco Revel	15 de Mayo, 1490
43	Francisco Barcelo	,,
44	Juan Gostins	,,
45	Leonor, muger de Jofre Rebassa	,,
46	Pereta, viuda de Leonardo Rebassa	,,
47	Pereta, muger de Francisco Brull	,,
48	Violante, viuda de Francisco Bonnin	,,
49	Brigida, esposa de Perot Pardo	10 de Julio, 1490
50	Eufrasia, esposa de Alonso Pardo	,,
51	Angelina, esposa de Phelipe Polit	25 de Agosto, 1490
52	Flor, esposa de Sepastian Truyal	26 de Agosto, 1490
53	Beatriz Forteza, esposa 1ª de Juan Palon, 2ª de Mathias Forteza	4 de Setiembre, 1490
54	Pedro Jordi	,,
55	Galceran de Quart	,,
56	Leonor, esposa de Francis Jayme	,,
57	Leonor Sania, esposa de Manuel Camyelles	,,
58	Miguel Jorda, ingles, *por hereje luterano*	,,
59	Violante, muger de Raphael Vidal	,,
60	Juana, muger de Luis Cavilleres	14 de Setiembre, 1490
61	Jofre Rebassa	,,
62	Leonor Fullosa, viuda de Juan Casses	,,
63	Pereta, muger de Pablo Porsell	21 de Diziembre, 1490
64	Blanca, muger de Juan Muntañer	,,
65	Antonia, muger de Juan Porsell	,,
66	Aldonza, muger de Jayme Cortes	,,
67	Antonio Sessa	,,
68	Bonanada, muger de Raphael Pelegri	,,
69	Benvenguda, muger de Manuel Arbona	,,

70	Blanca, muger de Francisco Bennasar	**21 de Diziembre, 1490**
71	Clara, muger de Jayme Serra	,,
72	Daniel Vidal	.,
73	Dolça, muger de Miguel Montarego	,,
74	Graciosa, muger de Juan Bonnin	..
75	Gabriel Vidal	,,
76	Gaspar Lozano	,,
77	Graciosa, viuda de Ferrario Galiano	,,
78	Juan Piña	,,
79	Juana, muger de Olibar de Conguan	,,
80	Juana, muger de Bernard Dolcet	,,
81	Leonardo Zaportella	,,
82	Luis Giger	,,
83	Margarita, muger de Juan Colom	.,
84	Pablo Porsell	,,
85	Policena, muger de Gabriel Vidal	,,
86	Violante, muger de Antonio Serra	,,
87	Violante, muger de Gabriel Lazarro	,,
88	Isabel, muger de Luis Giger	,,
89	Isabel, muger de Leonardo Zaportella	,,
90	Catalina, esclava de Guillermo Vives, AM[5]	20 de Setiembre, 1492
91	Catalina, muger de Laureto Gener	14 de Octubre, 1492
92	Luis Rebassa	,,
93	Maria, muger de Marco Masipe	,,
94	Diego Aguilon	11 de Mayo, 1493
95	Juan Alessandre Adret	,,
96	Pereta, muger de Lorenço Cauto	18 de Mayo, 1493
97	Fernando (natural de Castilla)	21 de Março, 1494
98	Violante, muger de Bartholome Bennasar	,,
99	Anton Moragues, *por herexe luterano*	9 de Enero, 1495
100	Juan Pellicer	9 de Mayo, 1495
101	Nicolau Giger	,,
102	Nicolas Pellicer	,,
103	Vicente Pañellas	24 de Setiembre, 1495
104	Daniel Morro	,,
105	Daniel Piña	17 de Julio, 1496
106	Antonio Forteza	17 de Abril, 1497
107	Pedro de la Mota, AM	25 de Junio, 1497
108	Leonor, muger de Paulo Bonnin	7 de Octubre, 1498
109	Isabel Mesguida, muger de Bartolome Miguel, AM	17 de Março, 1499
110	Clara, hixa de Antonio Serra	13 de Abril, 1502
111	Beatriz, muger de Luis Hernandez, portugues	23 de Abril, 1502
112	Jayme Rosiñol	,,
113	Luis Hernandez, portugues	,,
114	Frey Nicolau de Puigdorfila, Caballero del orden de San Juan, *por invocación de demonio*	17 de Mayo, 1502
115	Bonanat Bennaser	5 de Junio, 1503

---

[5] Apostata Mohametano.

116	Coloma, muger de Pablo Lloscos	5 de Junio, 1503
117	Juan, hixo de Pablo Lloscos	"
118	Felipe Albanell	"
119	Raphael, hixo de Pablo Lloscos	25 de Noviembre, 1503
120	Juanot Burgos	"
121	Pablo, hixo de Juan Sierra	"
122	Raphaela, muger de Jayme Lops	
123	Clara, muger de Juanot Togores	14 de Enero, 1504
124	Bernardo de Puigdorfila, *por diversas herexias*	28 de Junio, 1504
125	Bonanat Berarde	1 de Setiembre, 1504
126	Clara Cerdona, muger de Gabriel Desgrau	4 de Março, 1506
127	Andres Arnau	10 de Setiembre, 1507
128	Coloma, muger de Andres Arnau	10 de Diziembre, 1507
129	Leonor, muger de Jayme Silvestre	"
130	Juana, escalva de Jayme Mercer, AM	26 de Março, 1508
131	Catalina, esclava de Martin Arnau Garcia, AM	"
132	Speranca, hija de Juanot Amoros	8 de Mayo, 1508
133	Bonanada, muger de Luis Urella	28 de Junio, 1508
134	Andrena Tonis, *por Receptadora de Judios*	10 de Junio, 1508
135	Juan Frigola	"
136	Isabel, muger de Jayme de San Marti, *por fautora y Receptadora de Judios*	"
137	Benvenguda, muger de Manuel Arbona	6 de Agosto, 1508
138	Clara, muger de Diego Serra	"
139	Graciosa, muger de Juan Bonnin	"
140	Jayme San Marti, *por Judio y fautor de herejes*	"
141	Margarita, muger de Juan Colom	"
142	Juan Colom	13 de Agosto, 1508
143	Antonia Coll	30 de Noviembre, 1508
144	Eulalia, hixa de Gabriel Genetar	"
145	Francisca, muger de Gaspar Baroni	"
146	Juan Zaportella	"
147	Francisco San Marti	8 de Febrero, 1509
148	Eufrasina, muger de Pedro Claramunt	8 de Mayo, 1509
149	Antonia, muger de Ferrer Prats	23 de Junio, 1509
150	Coloma, muger de Raphael Boga	28 de Junio, 1509
151	Francisco Desgrau	"
152	Graciosa, muger de Miguel Piña	"
153	Galceran Galiana	"
154	Pedro Pellizer	"
155	Salvat Goscons	"
156	Pareta Caorona	"
157	Gil Navarro	16 de Setiembre, 1509
158	Magdalena, muger de Sebastian Compañy	7 de Octubre, 1509
159	Jayme Lops	26 de Octubre, 1509
160	Coloma, muger de Matheo Burgos	16 de Diziembre, 1509
161	Juana Corteza, muger de Gabriel Dolcet	"
162	Juan Castello	15 de Julio, 1511

163 Leonor, muger de Juan Castello	15 de Julio, 1511
164 Violante, muger de Juan Covredor, hixa de Juan Castello	,,
165 Beatriz, muger de Daniel Arnau	3 de Setiembre, 1511
166 Nicolas Jiger	,,
167 Gabriel Sabi	4 de Julio, 1512
168 Guillem Sabi	,,
169 no esta el # 169	
170 Isabel Costanza	15 de Julio, 1513
171 Dalman Cartella	18 de Octubre, 1513
172 Gabriel Serra	
173 Mariana Bonanada, muger de Juan Frigola	6 de Noviembre, 1513
174 Beatriz, muger de Juan Piña	28 de Mayo, 1514
175 Damiata, muger de Daniel Piña	,,
176 Graciosa, doncella, hixa de Gabriel Piris	,,
177 Lorença, muger de Juan Bonet	,,
178 Pereta, muger de Francisco Bonnin	,,
179 Margarita, muger de Juan Mieres, *por diversas herexias*	8 de Octubre, 1514
180 Margarita, muger de Pablo Rebassa	,,
181 Sebastian Llodia, *por diversas herexias*	,,
182 Matheo Burgos	14 de Mayo, 1516
183 Aldonza, muger de Jayme Veni	,,
184 Catalina, muger de Francisco Pau	4 de Abril, 1517
185 Francisca Boga, muger de Christobal Pasqual	,,
186 Gabriel Morro	,,
187 Graciosa, muger de Pedro Aldomar	,,
188 Pereta, muger de Manuel Coll	,,
189 Violante, muger de Juan Borbolla	,,
190 Isabel Bennaser, muger de Thomas Valeriola	,,
191 Aneta, muger de Juan Boget	1 de Agosto, 1517
192 Aneta, muger de Maestro Ferrando	,,
193 Francisca, muger de Francisco Badia	,,
194 Graciosa, muger de Jayme Morro	,,
195 Juan Berlangues	,,
196 Coloma, muger de Jayme Bages	,,
197 Jayme Braga	,,
198 Juana, muger de Bernardo Dulcet	20 de Março, 1518
199 Vidal Arnau Cabrit	,,
200 Bartholome Fuster	,,
201 Juan, esclavo de Juan Nicolau, AM	,,
202 Leonor Berarda, muger en 1as nupcias de Jayme Sierra, y en 2as de Cristoval Bosch	,,
203 Leonor, muger de Bartholome Fuster	,,
204 Isabel, muger de Luis de Sevilla	,,
205 Aldonza, muger de Hyeronimo Nabes	15 de Abril, 1519
206 Antonia, muger en 1as nupcias de Pablo Porsel, y en 2as de Pablo Terongi	,,
207 Antonio Piña	,,

208	Grisalda, muger de Gabriel Revell	15 de Abril, 1519
209	Juan Bonnin	,,
210	Leonor, muger de Jofre Rebassa	,,
211	Pereta, muger de Pablo Coll	,,
212	Isabel, muger de Juan Torres	,,
213	Isabel, muger de Juan Lunes	9 de Agosto, 1521
214	Antonio, muger de Nicolas Pellicer	,,
215	Clara, muger de Jayme Marti	,,
216	Francisco Arnau	,,
217	Gabriel Arnau	,,
218	Juan de Quart	,,
219	Margarita, muger de Raphael Pico	,,
220	Margarita, muger de Gabriel Morro	,,
221	Juana, muger de Gabriel Sastre	22 de Setiembre, 1521
222	Juana Garzes, hixa de Juan Cauto y Floreta Garzes	13 de Noviembre, 1521
223	Graciosa, muger de Francisco Bonnin	7 de Julio, 1522
224	Magdalena, muger de Juan Oliber, AM	,,
225	Paulo Bonnin	20 de Julio, 1522
226	Juan Óliber, AM	,,
227	Bernardo Boga	
228	Francisco Aguilo	24 de Setiembre, 1522
229	Gabriel Roger	,,
230	Jayme, hixo de Bartholome Aguilo	,
231	Policena Burgos, muger de Francisco Bennaser	,,
232	Violante Aguilona, muger de Jayme Forteza	,,
233	Aldonza, muger de Juan Sureda	4 de Setiembre, 1523
234	Bartholome Aguilo	,,
235	Graciosa, muger de Jayme Sureda	4 de Diziembre, 1523
236	Juan Sureda	,,
237	Luis, hixo de Bartholome Aguilo	,,
238	Leonor, hixa de Jayme Lop, muger de Leonardo Zaportella	1 de Noviembre, 1524
239	Clara Tornesa, muger de Daniel Lop	24 de Diziembre, 1525
240	Gabriel Roger	,,
241	Andreu Arnau, hixo de Andrenet	20 de Mayo, 1530
242	Andres Arnau	15 de Julio, 1530
243	Miguel, esclavo de Francisco Rosell, AM	,,
244	Pablo Lloscos	,,
245	Pereta Rebassa, muger de Pablo Lloscos	,,
246	Nicolas de Maestro Juan, AM	18 de Diziembre, 1530
247	Francisco Bennaser	10 de Março, 1531
248	Juan Moya, esclavo de Juan Moya, AM	,,
249	Juana Fustera, muger de Francisco Bennaser	,,
250	Francisco de Sadona, AM	,,
251	Juana, muger de Pedro Belver, *por herexe luterano*	,,
252	Miguel Piña	,,

253	Miguel Cuberter, *por tratos con el demonio*	10 de Março, 1531
254	Raphael Boga	,,
255	Juana, esclava de Fernando Porras, AM	7 de Diziembre, 1534
256	Juan Baptista Grande, *por herexe luterano*	10 de Junio, 1535
257	Antonio de Rueda, AM	29 de Agosto, 1535
258	Juan (natural de Pasache), AM	,,
259	Juan Valencia, AM	19 de Setiembre, 1535
260	Maria Muñoza, AM	23 de Diziembre, 1535
261	Balthasar Bonnin	10 de Julio, 1536
262	Bartholome, esclavo de Francisco Anglanda, AM	,,
263	Juan Espeyti, frayle geronimo del Convento de Sn. Bartholome, *por moro y judio*	,,
264	Pablo Bonnin	,,
265	Juan Llorens, AM	29 de Julio, 1537
266	Bartholome Reyes, AM	15 de Noviembre, 1541
267	Berenguer Pons, *por diversas herexias*	21 de Diziembre, 1541
268	Beatriz, hixa de Juanot Colom, muger de Juan Lopis	17 de Junio, 1542
269	Juan Lopis	,,
270	Juan de Salerno, AM	,,
271	Juan (natural de Mico), AM	,,
272	Phelip de Tavera, AM	5 de Noviembre, 1542
273	Pablo Thomas, AM	,,
274	Jayme Rosell, AM	,,
275	Juan Morales, AM	24 de Junio, 1544
276	Bartholome Aguilon	4 de Diziembre, 1544
277	Martin Perez, *por herexe luterano*	12 de Março, 1548
278	Pedro Acorita, AM	6 de Agosto, 1546
279	Miguel Moriscador, esclavo de Juanot Rosiñol, AM	5 de Octubre, 1546
280	Juan, esclavo del Sacristan Montañans, AM	8 de Octubre, 1547
281	Andres, AM	17 de Noviembre, 1547
282	Juan, esclavo de Jayme Moragas, AM	8 de Março, 1548
283	Juan Sureda, esclavo de Juan Sureda, AM	,,
284	Antonio Marzal, *por herexe luterano*	21 de Febrero, 1552
285	Raphael Basset, *por herexe luterano*	4 de Diziembre, 1552
286	Roberto Cansangui, AM	,,
287	Pedro Pablo Griego, hixo de Pedro Martin, AM	23 de Setiembre, 1562
288	Jacobo de Bega, *por herexe luterano*	30 de Noviembre, 1563
289	Juan de Moncaya, *por herexe luterano*	20 de Junio, 1567
290	Thomas Baptista, *por herexe luterano*	,,
291	Ferrer Pons, *por herexe luterano*	5 de Julio, 1567
292	Juan Rexai, *por diversas heregias*	5 de Octubre, 1567
293	Miguel Forner, AM	,,
294	Juan Esteban, AM	7 de Octubre, 1567
295	Nicolas Aleroc, AM	6 de Noviembre, 1575
296	Pedro Vegi, AM	,,

297	Juan de Maura, AM	17 de Junio, 1579
298	Alonso de Benavides, esclavo de Leonart, AM	6 de Setiembre, 1579
299	Miguel Granadinos, esclavo de Christobal Garriga, AM	,,
300	Maria Diez, viuda de Fernando Gonzales	,,
301	Alvaro Vorger, AM	4 de Junio, 1581
302	Diego Xaxua, esclavo de M. Rusiñol, AM	,,
303	Gaspar Ruiz, esclavo de Jayme Lloscos, AM	,,
304	Luis de Vergara, esclavo de Baylio Veri, AM	,,
305	Maria Soler, AM	16 de Febrero, 1582
306	Andres Doms, *por herexe luterano*	7 de Febrero, 1583
307	Roberto Fauler, *por herexe luterano*	,,
308	Maria Faxar, esclava de Francisco del Aguila, AM	,,
309	Juan Bacos, *por herexe luterano*	,,
310	Miguel Pandur, AM	16 de Junio, 1585
311	Juan Navarro, AM	,,
312	Juan Ruiz, esclavo de Juan Nicolau, AM	3 de Noviembre, 1586
313	Drusiana Berardi, AM	22 de Agosto, 1587
314	Beatriz Sureda, AM	20 de Setiembre, 1587
315	Ricardo Ricardi, *por herexe luterano*	28 de Agosto, 1588
316	Pedro Berard, *por herexe luterano*	18 de Octubre, 1589
317	Guillem Castelnon, *por herexe luterano*	,,
318	Miguel Phelin, AM	4 de Octubre, 1592
319	Hyeronimo Francisco, AM	16 de Mayo, 1595
320	Juan Caynet, AM	29 de Setiembre, 1595
321	Gonzalo Monjarique, AM	,,
322	Hyeronimo Feldepelo, AM	26 de Noviembre, 1595
323	Bartholome Vançal, AM	20 de Enero, 1596
324	Pedro Juan, esclavo de Francisco Garcia, AM	21 de Diziembre, 1598
325	Juan Planellas, AM	21 de Setiembre, 1600
326	Juan Serra, AM	,,
327	Daniel Clemente, *por herexe luterano*	13 de Mayo, 1601
328	Henrique Diquez, *por herexe luterano*	,,
329	Francisco Aen, *por herexe luterano*	,,
330	Ricardo Dors, *por herexe luterano*	21 de Diziembre, 1601
331	Jacobo Estephano, *por herexe luterano*	17 de Abril, 1603
332	Gabino de Santayna, AM	,,
333	Marquessa Dezcano, AM	,,
334	Honorato Anoto, AM	23 de Março, 1605
335	Roberto della Pulla, *por herexe luterano*	13 de Abril, 1607
336	Yacoma Ge. *por herexe calvanismo*	28 de Octubre, 1610
337	Henrique (flamenco), AM	17 de Mayo, 1613
338	Miguel Lobet, AM	13 de Agosto, 1613
339	Alonso de Montemayor, AM	18 de Agosto, 1613
340	Alonso de Mena, AM	,,
341	Alonso de Molina, AM	,,

342 Alonso de Valdivia, AM   18 de Agosto, 1613
343 Benito de Valladolid, AM   ,,
344 Diego Bizcania, AM   ,,
345 Diego Fernandez, AM   ,,
346 Francisco Fernandez, AM   ,,
347 Gaspar Faxardo, AM   ,,
348 Gaspar Fernandez, AM   ,,
349 Gabriel Garcia, AM   ,,
350 Gabriel de Mata, AM   ,,
351 Gabriel Phelipe de Santiago, AM   ,,
352 Hyeronimo Turninani Gibar, AM   ,,
353 Hyeronimo Gibar, AM   ,,
354 Hyeronimo Perez de Guzman, AM   ,,
355 Hernando Flores, AM   ,,
356 Juan Gutierrez, AM   ,,
357 Joseph Carnicer, AM   ,,
358 Juan Cozar, AM   ,,
359 Luis Diez, AM   ,,
360 Luis del Campo, AM   ,,
361 Luis de Molina, AM   ,,
362 Miguel Algage, AM   ,,
363 Pedro Ferrer, AM   ,,
364 Dodrigo Socias, AM   ,,
365 Christobal Bogant, *por herexe luterano*   29 de Noviembre, 1613
366 Juan Garcia, AM   24 de Febrero, 1614
367 Juan Ruso, AM   ,,
368 Maria Ubelta Sureda, AM   28 de Febrero, 1614
369 Domingo Aldete, AM   22 de Junio, 1614
370 Juan Garcia, AM   ,,
371 Christobal Labrador, A M   15 de Febrero, 1615
372 Phelipe Pedro, AM   ,,
373 Guillermo Carlar, AM
374 Diego Salvador, AM   9 de Março, 1625
375 Maria, esclava, AM   27 de Julio, 1625
376 Pedro Campano, AM   7 de Julio, 1626
377 Juan, AM   21 de Setiembre, 1626
378 Esteban, AM   17 de Mayo, 1633
379 Juan Martin, AM   ,,
380 Domingo Jacometo, AM   17 de Octubre, 1634
381 Habraham Clemente, AM *y luterano*   29 de Octubre, 1634
382 Juan Baptista de Polonia, AM   14 de Febrero, 1635
383 Armen Drich, *por herexe luterano*   2 de Abril, 1645
384 Cornelio Janza, *por herexe luterano*   ,,
385 Thobias Gerardo, *por herexe luterano*   ,,
386 Umbert Guislindh, *por herexe luterano*   ,,
387 Antonio Berdeguer, AM   23 de Março, 1673
388 Juan Marti, AM   ,,
389 Antonio Plauto, AM   12 de Mayo, 1673
390 Antonio Joseph Ferregut, AM   ,,
391 Francisco Ramon, AM   ,,
392 Pedro Juan Fontañils, AM   ,,

393	Barbara Maria, AM·	13 de Enero, 1675
394	Francisco de Saravia, AM	,,
395	Juan Baptista, AM	,,
396	Jayme Juañ, AM	,,
397	Juana Borras y Ferranda, AM *y por sortilega, embustera, invocar al diablo, etc., etc.*	,,
398	Raphael Piña	16 de Abril, 1679
399	Isabel Marti y Forteza, viuda Raphael Valentin Forteza	,,
400	Isabel Marti, muger de Juan Baptista Marti, alias Berdet	,,
401	Isabel Cortez y Forteza, hixa de Joseph Cortez y Maria Forteza	,,
402	Isabel Marti, muger de Pedro Balthasar Marti, alias el Hereu	,,
403	Isabel Bonnin, muger de Raphael Valls	,,
404	Isabel Marti, muger de Agustin Antonio Cortes	,,
405	Isabel Forteza, viuda de Juanot Marti	,,
406	Isabel Marti, hixa de Raphael Marti, menor, y de Catalina Pomar	,,
407	Francisco Marti, soltero, hixo de Francisco Marti, alias Berdet	,,
408	Gabriel Joseph de Joseph, alias el Consul	,,
409	Gabriel Cortes de Francisco, alias el Pota	,,
410	Francisco Bonnin de Francisco	,,
411	Isabel Cortes, muger de Miguel Cortes de Francisco, alias Calenos	,,
412	Catalina Aguilo, muger de Juan Antonio Cortes de Joseph	,,
413	Magdalena Piña, muger de Francisco Bonnin de Francisco	,,
414	Beatriz Forteza, muger de Miguel Cortes de Joseph	,,
415	Francisco Tarongi de Raphael	,,
416	Maria Forteza, viuda de Joseph Cortes	,,
417	Margarita Marti y Sureda, hixa de Antonio Marti, alias Porro	,,
418	Margarita Aguilo, muger de Raphael Balthasar Marti, alias Falet	,,
419	Margarita Marti, muger de Pedro Onofre Cortes de Guillermo, alias Moxina	,,
420	Bartholome Balthasar Marti, alias el mal ric	,,
421	Francisca Pomar, muger de Joseph Bonnin	,,
422	Ana Cortes, muger de Joanot Sureda	,,
423	Bartholome Forteza, alias Menyus	,,
424	Joanot Forteza	,,
425	Leonor Piña, muger de Pedro Juan Bonnin	
426	Leonor Marti, viuda de Raphael Geronimo Cortes	,,

427 Margarita Marti, doncella, hixa de Raphael Marti, alias del Arpa, y Catalina Pomar   16 de Abril, 1679
428 Juan Antonio Cortes de Joseph   "
429 Pedro Onofre Cortes de Guillermo, alias Moxina   "
430 Juana Bentura Tarongi, muger de Miguel Melchor Cortes   "
431 Agustin Antonio Cortes   "
432 Antonio Ramon Marti, alias Porro   "
433 Raphael Joseph Tarongi, alias Felos   "
434 Raphael Cortes de Alphonso, alias Cabeza-loca   "
435 Raphael Balthasar Marti, alias Falet   "
436 Quiteria Marti, muger de Bernardo Aguilo, alias Zorra   "
437 Teresa Cortes, muger de Onofre Aguilo de Pedro   "
438 Miguel Tarongi, alias de la Bolta   "
439 Margarita Sureda, muger de Antonio Ramon Marti, alias Porro   "
440 Miguel Cortes de Joseph   "
441 Raphael Valls   "
442 Miguel Marti, alias del Arpa   "
443 Margarita Marti, muger de Miguel Tarongi, alias de la Bolta   "
444 Miguel Pomar   "
445 Raphael Forteza de Baptista, alias el rey   "
446 Juan Baptista Marti, alias Berdet   "
447 Balthasar Joachim Marti, alias el Hereu   "
448 Ana Marti, doncella, hixa de Raphael Marti, alias del Arpa, y Catalina Pomar   23 de Abril, 1679
449 Agustin Cortes de Alphonso, hixo de Raphael Alphonso Cortes, y Clara Moya   "
450 Agustin Alphonso Cortes   "
451 Agustin Cortes, mayor   "
452 Agustin Cortes de Gabriel   "
453 Agustin Salvador Cortes   "
454 Francisco Forteza de Valenti   "
455 Francisca Tarongi, muger de Bartholome Aguilo   "
456 Gabriel Melchor Marti, alias Barbassa   "
457 Bartholome Cortes de Gabriel, hixo de Gabriel Cortes de Augustin   "
458 Ana Pomar, muger de Raphael Valls, mayor   "
459 Francisca Aguilo, muger de Francisco Tarongi de Raphael   "
460 Margarita Bonnin, muger de Raphael Piña   "
461 Mariana Florentina Forteza, muger de Onofre Cortes de Melchor, alias Don Juan   "

462	Margarita Ana Piña, doncella, hixa de Gabriel Piña, alias Cap de Olleta	23 de Abril, 1679
463	Raphael Marti, menor, alias del Arpa	"
464	Raphael Joseph Marti, alias Barbassa	"
465	Agustin Cortes de Jayme, alias Gambeta	"
466	Raphael Cortes, hixo de Jayme Cortes de Agustin	"
467	Raphael Jayme Cortes, hixo de Agustin Antonio Cortes	"
468	Francisca Tarongi, muger de Raphael Joseph Tarongi, alias Felos	"
469	Magdalena Forteza, muger de Gabriel Piña, alias Cap de Olleta	"
470	Isabel Cortes, muger de Miguel Alexos Cortes	"
471	Isabel Fuster, muger de Miguel Pomar	"
472	Juana Cortes, muger de Bartolome Forteza, alias Menyus	"
473	Francisco Joseph Tarongi, hixo de Raphael Joseph Tarongi, alias Felos	"
474	Francisca Tarongi, muger de Raphael Cortes de Alfonso, alias Cabeza-loca	"
475	Catalina Forteza, muger de Bartholome Balthasar Marti, alias el mal ric	"
476	Catalina Aguilo, muger de Miguel Marti, alias del Arpa	"
477	Catalina Pomar, viuda de Raphael Marti, menor	"
478	Miguel Cortes de Francisco, alias Calenos	"
479	Quiteria Cortes, viuda de Bartholome Christoval Forteza, alias el mayor	"
480	Geronimo Cortes, soltero, hixo de Gabriel Cortes de Agustin, alias Capalt	"
481	Gabriel Cortes de Agustin, alias Capalt	"
482	Mariana Cortes, viuda de Pedro Juan Aguilo	"
483	Isabel Pomar, viuda de Benito Pomar	"
484	Isabel Aguilo, muger de Miguel Andres Cortes, alias Frai Borrat	"
485	Isabel Cortes, muger de Miguel Angel Cortes	"
486	Isabel Pomar, muger de Raphael Marti, menor, alias del Arpa	"
487	Gabriel Carlos Cortes, hixo de Raphael Geronimo Cortes	"
488	Francisco Forteza, muger de Miguel Geronimo Tarongi	"
489	Miguel Andres Cortes, alias Frai Borrat	"
490	Miguel Angel Cortes	"
491	Miguel Melchor Cortes	"

492 Miguel Piña — 23 de Abril, 1679
493 Juan Baptista Piña — "
494 Onofre Cortes de Melchor, alias Don Juan — "
495 Magdalena Aguilo, muger de Juanot Forteza — "
496 Miguel Geronimo Tarongi — "
497 Mariana Cortes, muger de Agustin Cortes
de Gabriel — "
498 Leonor, muger de Miguel Piña — "
499 Gabriel Piña, alias Cap de Olleta — "
500 Catalina Bonnin, muger de Raphael Agustin Pomar, alias Xotento — 30 de Abril, 1679
501 Bartholome Tarongi, alias el Conde — "
502 Agustin Cortes de Raphael, alias Brugea — "
503 Ana Marti, muger de Agustin Salvador
Cortes — "
504 Francisca Cortes, viuda de Raphael Diego
Forteza, alias el Pages — "
505 Raphael Bentura Cortes, alias Bossa — "
506 Francisca Fuster, muger de Juan Pomar
de Benito — "
507 Juana Ana, doncella, hixa de Gabriel
Piña, alias Cap de Olleta — "
508 Francisca Cortes, muger de Onofre Aguilo
de Onofre — "
509 Catalina Valls, muger de Joseph Francisco
Forteza — "
510 Geronima Pomar, muger de Raphael Nadal Pomar de Benito — "
511 Francisca Forteza, viuda de Esteban Galiana — "
512 Agustin Joseph Cortes, hixo de Raphael
Joseph Cortes, alias Moyanet — "
513 Agustin Joachim Cortes, alias Vila — "
514 Beatriz Cortes, doncella, hixa de Agustin
Cortes, mayor — "
515 Isabel Marti, muger de Bartholome Tarongi, alias el Conde — "
516 Isabel Valls, viuda de Juan Baptista Forteza — "
517 Francisco Forteza de Joseph — "
518 Francisca Marti, viuda de Geronimo Diego Cortes — "
519 Leonor Marti, muger de Gabriel Juan
Forteza, alias el Pabordo — "
520 Isabel Moya, viuda de Raphael Bentura
Cortes — "
521 Isabel Cortes, viuda de Raphael Joseph
Cortes, alias Moyanet — "
522 Isabel Cortes, muger de Pedro Juan Aguilo
de Pedro — "

523 Gabriel Nicolas Marti, hixo de Miguel Ramon Marti   30 de Abril, 1679
524 Gabriel Thomas Cortes, alias Vila   "
525 Juana Ana Marti, muger de Raphael Nicolas Forteza   "
526 Joseph Francisco Forteza   "
527 Juan Pomar de Benito   "
528 Juanot Nicolas Marti, hixo de Miguel Ramon Marti   "
529 Juan Baptista Forteza, hixo de Juan Baptista Forteza   "
530 Joseph Marti de Francisco, alias Embuy   "
531 Jayme Cortes de Agustin   "
532 Juana Miro, muger de Juan Pomar de Jayme   "
533 Mariana Forteza y Valls, doncella, hixa de Juan Baptista   "
534 Miguel Geronimo Aguilo, hixo de Pedro Juan Aguilo de Pedro   "
535 Isabel Marti, muger de Jayme Cortes de Agustin   "
536 Raphael Nicolas Forteza   "
537 Raphael Bonnin, soltero, hixo de Joseph Bonnin   "
538 Raphael Joseph Cortes de Agustin, alias Filoa   "
539 Raphael Agustin Pomar, alias Xotento   "
540 Raphael Nadal Pomar de Benito   "
541 Pedro Juan Bernardo de Forteza, hixo de Raphael Diego de Forteza, alias el Pages   "
542 Pedro Juan Tarongi, hixo de Bartholome Tarongi, alias el Conde   "
543 Pedro Juan Aguilo de Pedro   "
544 Pedro Miguel Pomar   "
545 Onofre Cortes, soltero, hixo de Agustin Cortes, mayor   "
546 Onofre Aguilo de Onofre   "
547 Pedro Juan Aguilo, soltero, hixo de Pedro Juan Aguilo de Pedro   "
548 Mariana Cortes y Moya, muger de Agustin Cortes, mayor   "
549 Margarita Cortes, muger de Agustin Cortes de Jayme, alias Gambeta   "
550 Margarita Tarongi, doncella, hixa de Bartholome Tarongi, alias el Conde   "
551 Leonor Cortes, muger de Joseph Marti de Francisco, alias Embuy   "
552 Leonor Cortes, muger de Gabriel Melchor Marti, alias Barbassa   "
553 Margarita Marti, muger de Francisco Forteza de Joseph   "

554 Isabel Pomar, viuda de Francisco Bonnin   30 de Abril, 1679
555 Leonor Valls, muger de Juan Pico   "
556 Isabel Cortes, muger de Agustin Joachim
     Cortes, alias Vila   "
557 Isabel Tarongi, muger de Agustin Cortes
     de Raphael, alias Brugea   "
558 Isabel Cortes, muger de Raphael Joseph
     Marti, alias Barbassa   "
559 Violante Marti, viuda de Onofre Cortes   "
560 Miguel Geronimo Marti, soltero, hixo de
     Raphael Joseph Marti   3 de Mayo, 1679
561 Margarita Tarongi, doncella, hixa Raph-
     ael Joseph Tarongi, alias Felos   "
562 Miguel Gaspar Forteza, hixo de Raphael
     Forteza de Baptista, alias el rey   "
563 Raphael Cortes de Gabriel   "
564 Leonor Cortes, muger de Agustin Alfonso
     Cortes   "
565 Violante Forteza, muger de Raphael Jo-
     seph Cortes de Agustin, alias Filoa   "
566 Raphael Christoval Forteza, hixo de Bar-
     tholome Forteza, alias Menyus   "
567 Raphael Bentura Marti, hixo de Barthol-
     ome Balthasar Marti, alias el mal ric   "
568 Raphael Bentura Cortes, hixo de Raphael
     Joseph Cortes, alias Moyanet   "
569 Leonor Pomar, muger de Raphael Joseph
     Valls   "
570 Leonor Cortes, viuda de Raphael Cortes,
     alias Brugea   "
571 Mariana Valls, viuda de Benito Forteza   "
572 Miguel Valls (vecino de Campos),
     hixo de Raphael Valls, mayor   "
573 Jacinta Cortes, hixa de Juan Antonio Cor-
     tes de Joseph   "
574 Juana Cortes, muger de Gabriel Cortes de
     Francisco, alias Pota   "
575 Juana Pomar, muger de Raphael Bonnin   "
576 Leonor Galiana, muger de Francisco Piña   "
577 Jayme Pomar   "
578 Joseph Andres Cortes, hixo de Juan An-
     tonio Cortes de Joseph   "
579 Juana Ana, doncella, hixa de Raphael
     Piña de Juan   "
580 Joseph Aguilo, hixo de Onofre Aguilo de
     Pedro   "
581 Jacinta Cortes, doncella, hixa de Geronimo
     Diego Cortes   "
582 Francisca, doncella, hixa de Miguel Cortes   "
583 Francisco Bonnin de Joseph   "

584 Guillermo Cortes, hixo de Pedro Onofre
     Cortes de Guillermo   3 de Mayo, 1679
585 Guillermo Thomas Tarongi, hixo de Raph-
     ael Joseph Tarongi, alias Felos   ”
586 Juan Pomar de Jayme   ”
587 Margarita Marti, viuda de Miguel Cortes
     de Raphael   ”
588 Mariana Bonnin, muger de Joachim For-
     teza   ”
589 Margarita Aguilo, muger de Jayme Miguel
     Valls   ”
590 Margarita Lluch Cortes, muger de Raph-
     ael Crespin Cortes, alias Vila   ”
591 Raphael Joseph Valls   ”
592 Raphael Piña de Juan   ”
593 Melchor Aguilo, hixo de Onofre Aguilo
    · de Pedro   ”
594 Melchor Joseph Marti, hixo de Raphael
     Joseph Marti, alias Barbassa   ”
595 Melchor Joseph Forteza, hixo de Barthol-
     ome Forteza, alias Menyus   ”
596 Ana Aguilo, muger de Raphael Cortes de
     Gabriel   ”
597 Ana Cortes, muger de Gabriel Joseph
     Cortes, alias de Consul   ‘
598 Catalina Tarongi, muger de Guillermo Ta-
     rongi, alias Morro Fes   ”
599 Clara Moya, viuda de Raphael Alfonso
     Cortes   ”
600 Bartholome Cortes de Alfonso
601 Bernardo Aguilo, soltero, hixo de Ber-
     nardo Aguilo, alias Zorra   ”
602 Bernardo Joachim Aguilo   ”
603 Francisca Pomar, viuda de Miguel Ramon
     Marti   ”
604 Francisca Marti, muger de Francisco
     Marti, alias Berdet   ”
605 Francisca Forteza, muger de Balthaser
     Joachim Marti, alias el Hereu   ”
606 Catalina Fuster, viuda de Balthasar For-
     teza de Valenti   ”
607 Catalina Tarongi, viuda de Raphael Ra-
     mon Marti   ”
608 Juan Piña, hixo de Raphael Piña de Juan
609 Leonor Valeriola, muger de Raphael Piña
     de Juan   28 de Mayo, ·1679
610 Margarita Piña, doncella, hixa de Raphael
     Piña de Juan   ”
611 Leonor Valls, doncella, hixa de Raphael
     Joseph Valls   ”

612 Isabel Aguilo, doncella, hixa de Onofre
   Aguilo de Onofre   28 de Mayo, 1679
613 Mariana, doncella, hixa de Benito Pomar   ,,
614 Joseph Bonnin   ,,
615 Raphael Crespin Cortes, alias Vila, (en
   el auto general que se celebró en Madrid)   30 de Junio, 1680
616 Gaspar Puch, AM   18 de Setiembre, 1682
617 Francisco de Betino Retorini, AM   24 de Febrero, 1685
618 Juan Baptista, AM   11 de Enero, 1688
619 Pedro Trullat, *por herege Hugonote*   1 de Mayo, 1688
620 Francisco Vicente Tarongi, hixo de Guil-
   lermo Tarongi, alias Morro Fes   18 de Mayo, 1689
621 Juan Arbona, AM   26 de Abril, 1689
622 Bartholome Martinez de Castro, AM   24 de Mayo, 1690
623 Christoval Rodriguez, AM   ,,
624 Juan Joseph Cayetano, AM   ,,
625 Jier Blee, AM   ,,
626 Pedro Juan Jober, AM   ,,
627 Miguel Martos, AM   ,,
628 Raphael Geronimo Cortes, hixo de Agus-
   tin Cortes de Raphael, alias Brugea   ,,
629 Francisca Cortes, hixa de Agustin Cortes
   de Raphael   7 de Março, 1691
630 Francisco Valls, hixo de Raphael Valls   ,,
631 Beatriz Cortes, muger de Pedro Juan Ta-
   rongi, alias el Conde   ,,
632 Gabriel Cortes, hixo de Raphael Joseph
   Cortes, alias Moyanet   ,,
633 Geronima Pomar, muger de Pedro Juan
   Miro   ,,
634 Joanot, hixo de Pedro Onofre Cortes de
   Guillermo, alias Moxina   ,,
635 Juan Antonio Pomar   ,,
636 Juana Miro, 2ª muger de Pedro Onofre
   Cortes de Guillermo   ,,
637 Juana, viuda de Jayme Vila, *por diferentes
   supersticiones, etc.*   ,,
638 Leonor Cortes, doncella, hixa de Raphael
   Joseph Cortes, alias Moyanet   ,,
639 Leonor Cortes, doncella, hixa Agustin Cor-
   tes, mayor   ,,
640 Miguel Crespin Tarongi   ,,
641 Miguel, hixo de Raphael Valls   ,,
642 Onofre Joseph, hixo de Raphael Joseph
   Cortes, alias Moyanet   ,,
643 Raphael Joachim Valls   ,,
644 Miguel Piña, hixo de Miguel, (difunto)   2 de Julio, 1691
645 Mariana Miro, (difunta), muger que fue
   de Raphael Bentura Cortes, alias Bossa   ,,
646 Leonor Valls, viuda de Gregorio Forteza,
   (difunta)   ,,

C: *Relaxations*

(Memoria de los Relaxados por el Santo oficio de la Inquisición de Mallorca, desde su fundacion y sacada por el libro, donde estan registrados, aviendose recondocido sus processos. AHN *Relaciones de Causas de Fe,* libro 1, 866, fols. 92-119v)

1	Antonio Vidal, soltero, hixo de Juan Vidal, *fugitivo*[6]	E[7]	21 de Mayo, 1489
2	Angelina Vinet, muger de Luis Vives, *fugitivo*	E	11 de Julio, 1489
3	Francisca, muger de Luis Miro, *fugitivo*	E	,,
4	Francisca, muger de Guillem Ramon Sagarriga, *fugitivo*	E	,,
5	Gabriel Llop	P[8]	,,
6	Luis Miro, *fugitivo*	E	,,
7	Luis Vives, *fugitivo*	E	,,
8	Luis Martinez, *fugitivo*	E	,,
9	Leonart Vidal	E	,,
10	Leonart Torrela, *fugitivo*	E	,,
11	Luis Soler, *fugitivo*	E	,,
12	Pareta Gual, muger en 1ᵃˢ nupcias del honorable Martin Gual, y en 2ᵈᵃˢ del honorable Martin Varions	P	,,
13	Pedro Pau, *fugitivo*	E	,,
14	Pedro Palles, *fugitivo*	E	,,
15	Padro Nabes, *fugitivo*	E	,,
16	Ramon Vidal, *fugitivo*	E	,,
17	Violante, muger de Luis Soler, *fugitivo*	E	,,
18	Isabel, muger Pedro Pau, *fugitivo*	E	
19	Graciosa, muger de Guillermo Vives, *fugitivo*	E	y exhumados sus huesos, 11 de Julio, 1489
20	Lorenço Giner, *fugitivo*	E	13 de Agosto, 1489
21	Leonor, muger de Pedro Palles, *fugitivo*	E	,,
22	Francisca, muger de Luis Coll, *fugitivo*	E	24 de Octubre, 1489
23	Jayme Castellar, *fugitivo*	E	,,
24	Juan Cunnilleres, *fugitivo*	E	,,
25	Jayme Soldevilla, *fugitivo*	E	,,
26	Juana, muger de Jayme Soldevilla, Vidal, *fugitivo*	E	,,
27	Jayme Leo, *fugitivo*	E	,,
28	Juan Plegamans, *fugitivo*	E	,,
29	Leonor, viuda de Jayme Serra	P	,,
30	Luis Coll, *fugitivo*	E	,,
31	Maria Sanchez, muger de Juan *fugitivo*	E	,,

---

[6] All the relaxations were of Conversos, unless otherwise stated

[7] E= Relaxado en Estatua (Relaxed in effigy).

[8] P= Relaxado en Persona (Relaxed in person).

32	Isabel, muger de Daniel Pardo, *fugitivo*	E	24 de Octubre, 1489
33	Dolça, muger de Lorenço Vendrell, *fugitivo*	E	,,
34	Francisco Ravell, *fugitivo*	E	28 de Octubre, 1489
35	Aldonza, muger de Matheo Funcar, *fugitivo*	E	,,
			(y despues en Persona en 31 de Mayo, 1490)
36	Bonanat Tagamanent, *fugitivo*	E	28 de Octubre, 1488
37	Cilia, muger de Pedro Arbona, *fugitivo*	E	,,
38	Catalina Cabreda, muger de Simeon Arnau	P	,,
39	Gabriel Ravell, *fugitivo*	E	,,
40	Manuel Narbona, *fugitivo*	E	,,
41	Matheo Funcar	E	,,
42	Manuel de Thomas Pardo, *fugitivo*	E	,,
43	Pedro Arbona, *fugitivo*	E	,,
44	Pereta, muger de Raphael Carbonell	E	,,
45	Pau Baldaura	E	,,
46	Pau Marty, *fugitivo*	E	,,
47	Pedro Salvador, *fugitivo*	E	,,
48	Pedro Colom, *fugitivo*	E	,,
49	Raphael Tagamanent, *fugitivo*	E	,,
50	Raphael Valeriola	E	,,
51	Violante, muger de Manuel Thomas Pardo, *fugitivo*	E	,,
52	Antonio Sevilla	P	21 de Mayo, 1490
53	Aldonza, muger de Gaspar Brondo	P	,,
54	Coloma, muger de Antonio Sevilla	P	,,
55	Gaspar Brondo	P	,,
56	Juan Lopez	P	,,
57	Leonor, muger de Juan Lopez	P	,,
58	Leonor, muger de Pedro Miro	P	,,
59	Maria, muger de Francisca Esparça	P	,,
60	Pedro Miro	P	,,
61	Esclamonda, muger de Leonardo Torrella	P	,,
62	Violante, muger de Bartholome Bennasser	P	,,
63	Violante, muger de Francisco Subirats	P	,,
64	Isabel, muger de Galceran Valeriola	P	,,
65	Madona Ester, muger de Tagamanent	P	,,
66	Galceran Loqui	P	1 de Agosto, 1490
67	Eufrasia, muger de Martin San Martin	E	4 de Setiembre, 1490
68	Francisca, muger de Gabriel Bonet	P	,,
69	Gabriel Porsell	P	,,
70	Gabriel Plegamans	E	,,
71	Graciosa, muger de Raphael Vila	E	,,
72	Juan Porsell	E	,,
73	Jayme Oliber	E	,,
74	Maestro Miguel Oliber	E	,,

75	Pablo Fuster	E	4 de Setiembre, 1490
76	Amada, muger de Gabriel Porsell	E	,,
77	Andreu Bonnin	E	,,
78	Angelina Lagortera, viuda	E	,,
79	Blanca, muger de Pablo Torres	P	,,
80	Gabriel Nagarri	E	,,
81	Gabriel Bonet	E	,,
82	Jayme Segura	E	,,
83	Jayme Cortes	E	,,
84	Juaneta, muger de Juan Dessi	E	,,
85	Jaymeta, muger de Pedro Montarrago	E	,,
86	Martin de San Marti	E	
87	Catalina, muger de Franci Coll	E	11 de Mayo, 1493
88	Arnau Domenech	E	,,
89	Aldonza, muger de Pablo Bonnin	E	,,
90	Aldonza, muger de Arnau Domenech	E	,,
91	Aldonza, hixa de Luis Soler	E	,,
92	Aldonza, Neboda de Pedro Palles	E	,,
93	Beatriz, muger de Pedro Sevia	E	,,
94	Beatriz, muger de Luis Martinez	E	,,
95	Beatriz, muger de Manuel Rodes	E	,,
96	Blanca, muger de Pedro	E	,,
97	Clara, muger de Juanot Dariz	E	,,
98	Catalina, muger de Franci Pau	P	,,
99	Catalina, muger de Juan Arenos	E	,,
100	Domingo de Santa Cruz	E	,,
101	Damiata, muger de Pedro Ferrando	E	,,
102	Daniel Tagamanent	E	,,
103	Daniel Socorrats	E	,,
104	Eulalia Viussa, viuda	E	,,
105	Franci Pau	P	,,
106	Galceran Raphael	E	,,
107	Gelebert Lozano	E	,,
108	Galceran Valeriola	E	,,
109	Geronimo Nabes	E	,,
110	Joanot Dariz	E	,,
111	Juan Fonat	P	,,
112	Jayme Cunnilleres	E	,,
113	Juan Roger	E	,,
114	Juan Arnau	E	,,
115	Juan Alexandre Adret	E	,,
116	Juan Vidal	E	,,
117	Juan Lletos	E	,,
118	Juan Arenos	E	,,
119	Juan Pi	E	,,
120	Leonor, muger de Jayme Sabater	E	,,
121	Loquina, muger de Arenos	E	,,
122	Leonor, Neboda de Pedro Palles	E	,,
123	Marquesina, hermana de Doña Pareta	E	,,
124	Pedro Sener	E	,,
125	Pedro Sala	E	,,

126	Pedro Puhol	E	11 de Mayo, 1493
127	Pablo Arnau	E	,,
128	Pedro Llevia	E	,,
129	Pedro Velvivre	P	,,
130	Pedro Galiana	E	,,
131	Pedro Cintero	E	,,
132	Salvat Roger	E	,,
133	Salvat Vivis	E	,,
134	Salvat Savanals	E	,,
135	Violante, muger de Raphael Taga-manent	E	,,
136	Violante, muger de Luis Torrella	E	,,
137	Clara, muger de Daniel Valeriola	E	,,
138	Andres Arnau	E	6 de Agosto, 1495
139	Aldonza, muger de Pablo Valeriola	E	,,
140	Berenguer Arnau	E	,,
141	Blanca, muger de Juan Frigola	E	,,
142	Bartholome Mulet	E	,,
143	Blanca, muger de Juan Provensal Sala	E	,,
144	Beatribz, muger de Maestro Alexandre Adret	E	,,
145	Daniel Valeriola	E	,,
146	Francisco Valeriola	E	,,
147	Graciosa, muger de Francisco Valeriola	E	,,
148	Juan Frigola	E	,,
149	Jayme Roger	E	,,
150	Juan Arnau	E	,,
151	Juan Provensal	E	,,
152	Jayme Arnau	E	,,
153	Luis Berarte	E	,,
154	Manuel Rodes	E	,,
155	Pablo Valeriola	E	,,
156	Pedro Pardo	E	,,
157	Dolça, muger de Raphael Tudela	E	,,
158	Antonia, muger de Matheo Giger	E	1 de Agosto, 1496
159	Matheo Giger	E	,,
160	Aneta, muger de Francis Fiol	E	,,
161	Antonio Brull	E	,,
162	Anita, muger de Bernardo Bonhorn	E	,,
163	Arnau Garret	E	,,
164	Antonio, muger de Pedro Torrella	E	,,
165	Andreu Juan	E	,,
166	Antonio Artes	E	,,
167	Bernardo Cauti	E	,,
168	Bernardo Bonhorn	E	,,
169	Bonanat Arnau	E	,,
170	Beneta, muger de Gabriel Soldevilla	E	,,
171	Blanca, muger de Andreu Juan Suan	E	,,
172	Gabriel Carbonell	E	,,
173	Gabriel Arnau	E	,,
174	Gabriel Miro	E	,,

175	Bonanat Dameto	E	1 de Agosto, 1496
176	Blanca, madre de Luis Berarde	E	,,
177	Gabriel Soldevilla	E	,,
178	Juan ó Pedro Galiana	E	,,
179	Bonanat Morro	E	,,
180	Floreta, muger de Galceran Miro	E	,,
181	Francisco Arnau	E	,,
182	Daniel Vida	E	,,
183	Dolça, muger de Galceran Brondo	E	,,
184	Coloma, muger de Jayme Cabrera	E	,,
185	Jayme Cabrera	E	,,
186	Juaneta, muger de Bonanat Dameto	E	,,
187	Coloma, muger de Gabriel Cauto	E	,,
188	Coloma, muger de Pablo Forteza	E	,,
189	Clara, muger de Pedro Morro	E	,,
190	Clara, muger de Raphael Aguilon	E	,,
191	Daniel Silvestre	E	,,
192	Dolça, muger de Luis Mulet	E	
193	Agata, muger de Pedro Morro	E	14 de Junio, 1497
194	Berenguer Arnau	E	y exhumados sus huesos, 14 de Junio, 1497
195	Bartholome Terradas	E	,,
196	Coloma, muger de Jayme Dameto	E	,,
197	Catalina, muger de Lorenço Dameto	E	,,
198	Galceran Moya	E	,,
199	Graciosa, muger de Gabriel Belloch	E	,,
200	Graciosa, muger de Daniel Forteza	E	,,
201	Gabriel Tritañy	E	,,
202	Graciosa, muger de Gabriel Tritañy	E	,,
203	Gabriel Berart	E	,,
204	Godoy, muger de Ferrer Miro	E	,,
205	Gabriel Cessa	E	,,
206	Graciosa, muger de Juan Toledano	E	,,
207	Gabriel Vicens	E	,,
208	Graciosa, muger de Juan Desgrau	E	,,
209	Galceran Rebassa	E	,,
210	Juana, muger de Raphael Morro	E	,,
211	Jayme Roger	E	,,
212	Jayme Vida	E	,,
213	Juan Silvestre	E	,,
214	Juan Morro	E	,,
215	Juaneta, muger de Miguel Morro	E	,,
216	Juana, muger de Simon Cauto	E	,,
217	Juan Ravell	E	,,
218	Jofre Valeriola	E	,,
219	Juan Berarde	E	,,
220	Juan Desgrau	E	,,
221	Jayme Dameto	E	,,
222	Luis Valeriola	E	,,
223	Luis Torrella	E	,,

224	Luis Pardo	E	14 de Junio, 1497
225	Luis Mulet	E	,,
226	Lorenço Dameto	E	,,
227	Leonor, muger de Gabriel	E	,,
228	Leonor, muger de Ponce Berart	E	,,
229	Margarita, muger de Galceran Quart	E	,,
230	Margarita, muger de Pedro Aguilo	E	,,
231	Martina, muger de Pablo Nadal	E	,,
232	Pablo Tarrega	E	,,
233	Pablo Forteza	E	,,
234	Pedro Morro	E	,,
235	Pablo Berarde	E	,,
236	Ponce Berarde	E	,,
237	Pablo Nadal	E	,,
238	Pablo Cessa	E	,,
239	Pedro Burgos	E	,,
240	Pedro Corredor	E	,,
241	Raphaela, muger de Juan Serra	E	,,
242	Raphaela, muger de Daniel Forteza	E	,,
243	Raphael Savanals	E	,,
244	Raphael Berard	E	,,
245	Simon Cauto	E	,,
246	Simon Bennaser	E	,,
247	Thomas Gual	E	,,
248	Ursula, muger de Luis Pardo	E	,,
249	Ursula, muger de Jayme Valeriola	E	,,
250	Violante, muger de Arnau Callar	E	,,
251	Benguda, muger de Juan Moya	E	,,
252	Violante, muger de Jayme Sabater	E	,,
253	Pedro de Sevilla ó Alcaraz	E	16 de Agosto, 1497
254	Juana, muger de Gabriel Cessa	E	,,
255	Leonor Sania	E	,,
256	Antonia Prats, relapsa *por invocar demonios*	P	30 de Enero, 1499
257	Beatriz Villanova	P	,,
258	Daniel Xiger, *fugitivo*	E	11 de Julio, 1499
259	Angelina, muger de Juan Morro	P	21 de Diziembre, 1501
260	Coloma Piña, viuda de Joanot Alvero	P	,,
261	Coloma, muger de Berenguer Arnau	P	,,
262	Fransoya, muger de Pablo Martin	P	,,
263	Esclamonda, muger de Jayme Rosiñol	P	,,
264	Isabel, muger de Bernardo Lunes	P	,,
265	Pareta, muger de Thomas Gener	P	,,
266	Antonia, muger de Galceran Rebassa	E	23 de Abril, 1502
267	Andreu, hixo de Jayme Andreu	E	,,
268	Aneta, muger de Juan Forteza	P	,,
269	Antonia, muger de Pablo de Quart	P	,,
270	Aneta, muger de Gabriel Muntañer	E	,,
271	Antonia, muger de Jayme Funcar	E	,,
272	Aldonza, muger de Pau Berart	P	,,
273	Antonio Boga	E	,,

274	Bartholome Umbert	E	23 de Abril, 1502
275	Catalina, muger de Bartholome Umbert	E	,,
276	Dolça, muger de Pedro Mulet	E	,,
277	Gabriel Muntañer	E	,,
278	Gilaberto, hixo de Thomas Valeriola	E	,,
279	Graciosa, hixa de Anton Castellano	E	,,
280	Juan, hixo de Pedro Mulet	E	,,
281	Juana, muger de Juan Mulet, hixa de Bartholome Mulet	P	,,
282	Manuel, hixo de Bartholome Coll	E	,,
283	Pablo Bennaser	E	,,
284	Pinoy Sabater	E	,,
285	Pablo Garro	E	,,
286	Raphael Martin	E	,,
287	Salvat Roger, hixo de Pablo	E	,,
288	Juan Piña	E	,,
289	Brianda, muger de Raphael Ravell	P	7 de Abril, 1503
290	Jayme Cabrera	P	,,
291	Leonor, soltera, hixa de Pedro Cauti	P	,,
292	Pedro Cauti	P	,,
293	Pedro Mulet	P	,,
294	Pablo Lloscos	P	,,
295	Violante, muger de Pedro Cauti	P	,,
296	Blanca, muger de Juan Burgos	P	25 de Noviembre, 1503
297	Catalina, muger de Lorenço Gener	E	,,
298	Daniel Berarde	E	,,
299	Francisco Goscons	E	,,
300	Franci Valeriola	E	,,
301	Francina, muger de Daniel Berarde	E	,,
302	Gabriel Mulet	E	,,
303	Juan Serra	E	,,
304	Leonor, hixa de Juan Serra, muger de Juan Fonat	P	,,
305	Vidal Provensal	E	,,
306	Violante, muger de Juan Serra	P	,,
307	Isabel, muger de Juan Bonnin	P	,,
308	Juana, muger de Daniel Cortes	E	22 de Junio, 1504
309	Juana, muger de Juan Munios	P	,,
310	Juan de Lunes	P	
311	Clara, muger de Francisco Barcelo	P	24 de Enero, 1505
312	Isabel, muger de Gabriel Cortes	P	24 de Febrero, 1505
313	Beatriz, muger de Bonanat Berarde	P	,,
314	Costanzá, muger de Juan de Lunes	P	
315	Aneta, muger de Pablo Cabrera	P	6 de Setiembre, 1505
316	Blanquina Vila	P	,,
317	Esperança, doncella, hixa de Lagortera	P	,,
318	Juana, muger de Olibares de Conga	P	
319	Aldonza, muger de Raphael Vila	P	4 de Março, 1506
320	Pablo Cabrera	P	,,
321	Francisca Coll, muger de Gonzalo Ruis	P	22 de Junio, 1506

322	Clara, muger de Raphael Aguilon	P	20 de Setiembre, 1507
323	Raphael Aguilon	P	,,
324	Antonina Coll	E	20 de Julio, 1508
325	Blanquina, muger de Juanot Amores	P	,,
326	Clara, viuda de Franci Moro	E	,,
327	Clara, viuda de Pedro Sala	E	,,
328	Catalina, muger de Caramoni	E	,,
329	Dolça, muger de Franci de Grau	E	,,
330	Eulalia, muger de Gabriel Vila	E	,,
331	Elisenda, muger de Pedro Llop	E	,,
332	Floreta, muger de Galceran Bonnin	E	,,
333	Franci Morro	P	,,
334	Juan Amoros	P	,,
335	Leonor, muger de Miguel Oliber	P	,,
336	Pedro Llop	P	,,
337	Raphael Ravel	P	,,
338	Raphaela, muger de Jayme Llops	P	,,
339	Alfonso Sintero, *fugitivo*	E	28 de Junio, 1509
340	La muger del dicho Sintero que no se dice su nombre, *fugitivo*	E	,,
341	Benguda, muger de Gabriel Genetar	E	,,
342	Beatriz Castellar, hixa de Jayme Castellar	E	,,
343	Coloma Valeriola, muger de Raphael Valeriola	E	,,
344	Dolca, muger de Jorge Coll	E	,,
345	Leonardo, hixo de Pedro Benet	E	,,
346	Leonor, hixa de Jayme Castellar	E	,,
347	Salvador, hixo de Jayme Castellar	P	,,
348	Violante, muger de Gabriel Arnau	E	,,
349	Violante, muger de Jayme Fornes	E	,,
350	Violante, hixa de Jayme Castellar	E	,,
351	Dolça, muger de Pedro Pellicer	P	,,
352	Violante, muger de Daniel Lloscos	E	,,
353	Francisco Fiol	E	23 de Julio, 1509
354	Floreta, muger de Balthasar Boga	E	,,
355	Floreta, muger de Jayme Forteza	E	,,
356	Jayme Biabrera	E	,,
357	Jayme Fornes	E	,,
358	Lorença, muger de Pau Tarrega	E	,,
359	Manuel Goscons	E	,,
360	Jorge Coll	E	,,
361	Blanca, muger de Franci Bennaser	E	28 de Setiembre, 1509
362	Leonor, muger de Gil Navarro	E	,,
363	Bartholome, hixo de Jayme Castellar, *fugitivo*	E	,,
364	Dolça, muger de Pedro Phelipe	E	,,
365	Daniel Llop	P	,,
366	Gil Navarro	P	,,
367	Jayme San Martin	P	,,

368 Eufrasina, muger de Pedro Claramunt	P	12 de Octubre, 1510
369 Isabel, muger de Leonardo Zaportella	E	15 de Abril, 1511
370 Isabel, muger de Lazaro Pellizer	E	,,
371 Coloma, muger de Bonanat Fuster	E	,,
372 Clara, muger de Raphael Olibar	E	,,
373 Clara, muger de Manuel Rodes	E	,,
374 Clara, muger de Jayme Rodes	E	,,
375 Clara, muger de Nicolas Cortes	E	,,
376 Coloma, muger de Bartholome Boscons	E	,,
377 Coloma Lunes	E	,,
378 Catalina, muger de Francisco San Martin	E	,,
379 Antonia, muger de Julian Roig	E	,,
380 Arnau Callar	E	15 de Julio, 1511
381 Aldonza, muger de Juan Zagrau	E	,,
382 Blanca, muger de Ferrer Puhol	E	,,
383 Beneta, muger de Galceran Moya	E	,,
384 Bonanat Fuster	E	,,
385 Beatriz, hixa de Gil Navarro	E	,,
386 Blanquina, hixa de Galceran Unis	E	,,
387 Brianda, hixa de Bartholome Miro	E	,,
388 Benvenguda, muger de Nicolas Portell	E	,,
389 Coloma, muger de Bonanat Taga-manent	E	,,
390 Castellana, muger de Pedro Boga	E	,,
391 Diana, muger de Dalmacio Cartella	E	,,
392 Dolça, muger de Vidal Escales	E	,,
393 Dolça, muger de Jayme Zagrau	E	,,
394 Eufrasia, muger de Simon Castellon	E	,,
395 Esperança, muger de Pablo Bennasser	E	,,
396 Esclamonda, muger de Raphael Fuster	E	,,
397 Eulalia, muger de Melchor Garau	E	,,
398 Francisco Thomas	E	,,
399 Ferrer Prats, yerno de Leonardo Zaportella	E	,,
400 Francesch Velvivre	E	,,
401 Gabriel Desgrau	E	,,
402 Galceran, soltero, hixo de Leonardo Zaportella	E	,,
403 Graciosa, muger de Francesch San Marty, mayor	E	,,
404 Graciosa, muger de Jayme Arnau	E	,,
405 Gabriel Cortes	E	,,
406 Graciosa, muger de Juan Piña	E	,,
407 Graciosa, muger de Ramon Vages	E	,,
408 Juan Bonet	E	,,
409 Julian Roig	E	,,
410 Juan, hixo de Lazaro Pellizer	E	,,
411 Juana, hixa de Lazaro Pellizer	E	,,
412 Juana, muger en 1as nupcias de Jayme Valenzia y en 2das de Pedro Diaz	E	,,

413	Juana, muger de Matheu Sufrin	E	15 de Julio, 1511
414	Juan Forteza	E	,,
415	Leonor, muger de Francisco Vidal	E	,,
416	Leonardo Zaportella	E	,,
417	Lazaro Pellizer	E	,,
418	Lorença, muger de Gabriel Morro	E	,,
419	Leonor, muger de Juan Silvestre	E	,,
420	Luis Cavaller	E	,,
421	Miguel Piña	E	,,
422	Miguel Morro	E	,,
423	Raphael Fuster	E	,,
424	Benguda, muger de Juan Fuster	E	,,
425	Ursula, suegra de Balthasar Socorrat	E	,,
426	Violante, muger de Pablo Bonnin	E	,,
427	Unisa, hixa de Galceran Unis	E	,,
428	Pablo Llegortera	E	,,
429	Pablo Morro	E	,,
430	Pereta, muger de Thomas Valeriola	E	,,
431	Pedro Carmoni	E	,,
432	Pedro Segura	E	23 de Octubre, 1511
433	Manuel, hixo de Galceran Unis	E	,,
434	Pedro Giger	E	6 de Noviembre, 1511
435	Aneta, muger de Gabriel Cabrera	E	23 de Octubre, 1512
436	Benvenguda, muger de Galceran Sani	E	,,
437	Floreta, muger de Gabriel Cortes	E	,,
438	Guillem Tarongi	E	,,
439	Galceran Sani	E	,,
440	Leonor, muger en 1ᵃˢ nupcias de Alonso Gallego, y an 2ᵃˢ de Gaspar Redondo	E	,,
441	Maria, muger de Raphael Rameta	E	,,
442	Nadal Sessa	E	,,
443	Antonio Canet, *fugitivo*	E	18 de Octubre, 1513
444	Clara, muger de Pedro Marco, *fugitivo*	E	,,
445	Clara, muger de Juan Pi, *fugitivo*	E	,,
446	Esperança, muger de Tonet, hermana de Melchor Socorrats	E	,,
447	Esperança, hixa de Francisco Arnau	E	,,
448	Franci, hixo de Leonardo Torrella	E	,,
449	Leonor, hixa de Madona Salmons	E	,,
450	Marco, hixo de Madona Salmons	E	,,
451	Pareta, muger de Manuel Coll	E	,,
452	Peret, hixo de Leonardo Torrella, *fugitivo*	E	,,
453	Raphael Carbonell	E	,,
454	Isabel, muger de Luis Diaz	E	,,
455	Andres Tur, *por Moro fugitivo*, AM	E	31 de Março, 1514
456	Blanca, muger de Pere Corredor	E	14 de Junio, 1514
457	Esperança, muger de Nicolas Rementa	E	,,
458	Graciosa, muger de Pedro Sala	E	,,
459	Graciosa, muger de Juan Cunieres	E	,,

460	Aldonza, muger en 1ᵃˢ nupcias de Gabriel Piris, y en 2ᵃˢ de Pablo Piña	E	14 de Março, 1516
461	Bonanat Berarde	E	,,
462	Daniel Arnau	E	,,
463	Franci, hixo de Pedro Pau	E	,,
464	Leonor, hixa de Luis Salmons	E	,,
465	Maria, hixa de Luis Salmons	E	,,
466	Violante, hixa de Luis Salmons	E	,,
467	Violante, muger de Juan Savanals	E	,,
468	Isabel, muger de Luis Salmons	E	
469	Angelina, muger de Gabriel Torres	E	4 de Abril, 1517
470	Angelina, muger de Marco	E	,,
471	Bartholome Coll	E	,,
472	Beatriz, muger de Pedro Valeriola	E	,,
473	Beatriz, muger de Juan Piña	E	,,
474	Coloma, muger de Gabriel Naxeri, mayor	E	,,
475	Coloma, muger de Juan Berlanguez	E	,,
476	Pablo Bonnin	E	,,
477	Francisco Bennaser	E	,,
478	Julian Colom	E	,,
479	Francisca, muger de Juan Duran	E	,,
480	Leonor, muger de Ponce Berarde	E	,,
481	Ursula, muger de Bartholome Coll	E	,,
482	Violante, muger de Nicolas Piña	E	
483	Juan Goscons	P	1 de Agosto, 1517
484	Eulalia, 1ᵃ muger de Pedro Genestar	E	20 de Mayo, 1518
485	Miguel Garcia	E	,,
486	Antonia, muger de Pedro Jordi	E	,,
487	Graciosa, muger de Anton Fullos	E	,,
488	Marthena, muger de Juan Burgos	E	,,
489	Raphael Pelegri	E	,,
490	Violante, muger de Daniel Cabrit	E	,,
491	Beatriz, muger de Miguel Garcia	E	
492	Nicolas Boti, *por herege blasfemo, relapso negativo*	P	10 de Julio, 1518
493	Aldonza, muger de Juan Gascons	E	9 de Agosto, 1521
494	Bonanada, muger de Daniel Savanals	E	,,
495	Bernardo Garriga	E	,,
496	Daniel Cabrit	E	,,
497	Daniel Morro	E	,,
498	Esperança, muger de Gaspar Tudela	E	,,
499	Floreta Gatzes, muger de Juan Cauto	P	,,
500	Franci Bonnin	E	,,
501	Gonzalvo Ruis	E	,,
502	Graciosa, muger de Juan Plegamans	E	,,
503	Gaspar Tudela	E	,,
504	Graciosa, muger de Gabriel Torres	E	,,
505	Gabriel Galiana	E	,,
506	Juana, muger en 2ᵃˢ nupcias de Cerda	E	,,
507	Manuel Morro	E	,,

508	Pedro Arnau	E	9 de Agosto, 1521
509	Praxedis, muger de Maestro Juan Toledo	E	„
510	Raphael Plegamans	E	„
511	Violante, muger de Pedro Salvador	E	„
512	Isabel, muger de Francisco de Soler	E	„
513	Isabel, hixa de Daniel Pardo	E	„
514	Aldonza, muger de Jayme Aguilo	E	21 de Setiembre, 1522
515	Aldonza Fuster	E	„
516	Coloma, muger de Pedro Burgos	E	24 de Setiembre, 1522
517	Coloma, muger de Bartholome Aguilon	E	„
518	Jayme Aguilo	E	„
519	Jayme Llops	E	„
520	Leonor, muger de Miguel Torres	E	„
521	Isabel, muger de Gabriel Roger	E	„
522	Gondisalvi, Pintor, natural de Montalegro, en Castilla, *por herege luterano, negativo*	P	4 de Diziembre, 1523
523	Francisca, muger de Antonio Piña	E	15 de Julio, 1530
524	Juan Muntañer	E	„
525	Juana, muger de Raphael Morro	E	„
526	Juana Corteza, muger de Gabriel Dolcet	E	„
527	Violante, muger de Bartholome Bennaser	E	„
528	Antonia, muger de Bartholome Forteza	E	„
529	Francisca, muger de Juan Zaportella	E	10 de Março, 1531
530	Juan Zaportella	E	„
531	Juan Valeriola	E	„
532	Juana, muger de Juan Valeriola	E	„
533	Leonor, muger de Joanot Lloscos	E	„
534	Isabel, hixa de Juan Zaportella, muger de Gabriel Vidal	E	„
535	Daniel Piña	P	16 de Setiembre, 1531
536	Juana, viuda Pedro Valleter	E	4 de Octubre, 1534
537	Isabel Costanza, *por judia y sortilega, hechizera relapsa*	P	4 de Diziembre, 1534
538	Antonio Cladera, AM	P	10 de Julio, 1535
539	Antonio Ginarde, AM	E	„
540	Antonio Vilar, AM	E	„
541	Bartholome Natar, AM	E	„
542	Geronimo Albarado, AM	P	„
543	Juana, hixa de Sebastina Lledo, AM	E	„
544	Margarita, hixa de Bartholome Perera	E	„
545	Martin Noguera, AM	E	„
546	Paula, hixa de Bartholome Perera	E	„
547	Berenguer Salom	E	10 de Julio, 1536
548	Juan Frances, AM	E	„
549	Leonart Zaportella	E	„
550	Jayme Torrella, AM	P	4 de Junio, 1581

551	Joseph Gener, AM	E	26 de Noviembre, 1584
552	Francisco Perez, AM	P	6 de Abril, 1620
553	Francisco Berdera, AM	E	2 de Abril, 1645,
554	Gregorio Truyol, AM	E	"
555	Juan Anhelout, *fugitivo, por herege luterano*	E	2 de Abril, **1645**
556	Miguel Coll, AM	E	"
557	Alonso de Jacob Lopez, hixo de Habraham Lopez	E	13 de Enero, 1675
558	Lazaro Rodriguez, *fugitivo*	E	"
559	Beatrib Lopez, muger de Lazaro Rodriguez, *fugitivo*	E	"
560	Gaspar Rodriguez, *fugitivo*	E	"
561	Isabel Mendez, *fugitivo*	E	"
562	Antonio Maldonado, *fugitivo*	E	"
563	Doña Beatriz Pereira, muger de Antonio Maldonado, *fugitivo*	E	"
564	Francisca Cortes, muger de Onofre Aguilo de Onofre	P	1 de Mayo, 1691
565	Catalina Pomar, viuda de Raphael Marti, menor, alias del Arpa	P	"
566	Isabel Cortez, viuda de Raphael Joseph Cortes, alias Moyanet	P	"
567	Catalina Bonnin, muger de Raphael Agustin Pomar, alias Xotento	P	"
568	Mariana Cortes y Moya, viuda de Agustin Cortes, mayor	P	"
569	Teresa Cortes, viuda de Onofre Aguilo de Pedro	P	"
570	Raphael Joseph Cortes de Agustin, alias Filoa	P	"
571	Ana Marti, viuda de Agustin Salvador Cortes	P	"
572	Raphael Crespin Cortes, alias Vila	P	"
573	Onofre Cortes de Agustin, soltero, hixo de Agustin Cortes, mayor	P	"
574	Maria Forteza, viuda de Joseph Cortes	P	"
575	Isabel Cortes, muger de Miguel Alexos Cortes	P	"
576	Miguel Valls, soltero, hixo de Raphael Valls de Campos y Ana Pomar	P	"
577	Isabel Bonnin, muger de Raphael Valls, mayor	P	"
578	Francisca Forteza, viuda de Miguel Geronimo Tarongi	P	"
579	Pedro Onofre Cortes de Guillermo, alias Moxina	P	"
580	Raphael Agustin Pomar, alias Xotento	P	"
581	Melchor Joseph Forteza, alias Menyus	P	"
582	Francisca Cortes, muger de Gabriel Cortes de Agustin, alias Capalt	P	"

583 Violante Marti, viuda de Onofre
     Cortes   P   1 de Mayo, 1691
584 Isabel Marti, muger de Juan Bap-
     tista Marti, alias Berdet   P   ,,
585 Miguel Marti, alias del Arpa   P   6 de Mayo, 1691
586 Raphael Bentura Cortes, soltero,
     hixo de Raphael Joseph Cortes, alias
     Moyanet   P   ,,
587 Joseph Aguilo, soltero, hixo de Onofre
     Aguilo de Pedro y de Teresa Cortes   P   ,,
588 Isabel Pomar, viuda de Francisco
     Bonnin   P   ,,
589 Isabel Tarongi, muger de Agustin
     Cortes de Raphael, alias Brugea   P   ,,
590 Isabel Marti, muger de Bartholome
     Tarongi, alias el Conde   P   ,,
591 Juana Cortes, viuda de Bartholome
     Forteza, alias Menyus   P   ,,
592 Margarita Tarongi, doncella, hixa de
     Raphael Joseph Tarongi, alias Felos   P   ,,
593 Beatriz Cortes, muger de Melchor
     Joseph Forteza, alias Menyus   P   ,,
594 Violante Forteza, muger de Raphael
     Joseph Cortes de Agustin, alias Filoa   P   ,,
595 Catalina, muger de Guillermo Tarongi,
     alias Morro Fes,   P   *y quemado vivo*
                                                        6 de Mayo, 1691

596 Raphael Benito Tarongi, soltero, hixo
     de Raphael Joseph Tarongi, alias Felos P   *y quemado vivo*
                                                        6 de Mayo, 1691
597 Raphael Valls, mayor   P   *y quemado vivo*
                                                        6 de Mayo, 1691
598 Isabel Aguilo, muger de Pedro
     Juan Aguilo de Pedro Juan   P   ,,
599 Leonor Cortes, muger de Joseph
     Marti de Francisco alias Bruy, difunta E   con sus huesos
                                                        6 de Mayo, 1691

600 Leonor Marti, viuda de Raphael
     Geronimo Cortes, difunta   E   con sus huesos
                                                        6 de Mayo, 1691
601 Agustin Cortes, mayor, difunto   E   con sus huesos
                                                        6 de Mayo, 1691
602 Margarita Marti, viuda de Miguel Ta-
     rongi, alias de la Bolta, difunta   E   ,,
603 Francisco Joseph Tarongi, hixo de
     Raphael Joseph Tarongi, alias Felos   E   ,,
604 Guillermo Thomas Tarongi, hixo de
     Raphael Joseph Tarongi, alias Felos   E   ,,
605 Agustin Cortes de Alfonso, alias
     Formatje, *fugitivo*   E   ,,

606	Francisca Marti, viuda de Francisco Marti, alias Berdert	P	2 de Julio, 1691
607	Magdalena Forteza, viuda de Gabriel Piña, alias Cap de Olleta	P	,,
608	Miguel Forteza, soltero, hixo de Raphael Forteza de Gaspar, alias Butzeta, *fugitivo*	E	,,

APPENDIX III

TABULATED RECORD OF RECONCILIATIONS AND RELAXATIONS IN THE INQUISITION OF MAJORCA, 1488-1771

(Exclusive of reconciliations through the Edicts of Grace[1])

YEARS	RECONCILED		RELAXED	
	CONVERSOS	OTHERS	CONVERSOS	OTHERS
1488-1499	89	3	258 (incl. 28 in person)	1
1500-1509	47	5	106 (incl 46 in person)	0
1510-1519	49	2	120 (incl. 5 in person)	2
1520-1529	25	2	29 (incl. 1 in person)	1
1530-1539	10	15	17 (incl. 2 in person)	11
1540-1549	1	17	0	0
1550-1559	0	3	0	0
1560-1569	0	8	0	0
1570-1579	2	27	0	0
1580-1589	0	17	0	2
1590-1599	0	7	0	0
1600-1609	0	9	0	0
1610-1619	0.	38	0	0
1620-1629	0	4	0	1
1630-1639	0	5	0	0
1640-1649	0	4	0	4
1650-1659	0	0	0	0
1660-1669	0	0	0	0
1670-1679	217	11	7 (incl. 1 person burned alive)	0
1680-1689	1	5	0	0
1690-1699	18	21	56 (incl. 37 in person, of whom 3 were burned alive)	0
1700-1709	0	0	0	0
1710-1719	0	0	0	0
1720-1729	1	1	1	0
1730-1739	0	0	0	0

[1] For figures of reconciliations through the Edicts of Grace, see *supra.*, p. 47ff Cf. also Appendix II

YEARS	RECONCILED		RELAXED	
	CONVERSOS	OTHERS	CONVERSOS	OTHERS
1740-1749	0	0	0	0
1750-1759	0	0	0	0
1760-1769	0	0	0	0
1770-1771[2]	0	0	0	0
Totals[3]	460	204	594	22

(incl. 120 in person, of
whom 4 were burned alive)

[2] Our records go only as far as 1771. The inquisition doubtless enjoyed some activity after this date, but the records for those years have not yet been located, if indeed there are any extant. The records we do possess show that the tribunal's business diminished rapidly with the passing of the years, and may have altogether ceased by 1771.

[3] Cf. with Lea's figures (*Spain,* IV, 524) which are far greater than mine (and Lea's are far less than those of Llorente, *Ibid*), even when the several hundred cases suspended are taken into consideration

APPENDIX IV

THE INDICTMENT OF THE CONVERSOS

(From AHN, *Processos de Fe,* legajo 1709, 1, pieza 3)

Inquisición de Mallorca del año dc 1674. Copia de las testificaciones recevidas contra los descendientes de judios que estan en la calle del Sayell. Y en especial contra Agustin Cortes y otros de dicha Calle. Por observancias Judaicas. Remitense a los SS. del Consejo en cumplimiento de lo que mandan por carta de trece de Julio de 1672.

El Dr. Fontamar, Promotor y Abagado fiscal de este Santo Oficio ante Vuestra Alteza paresco y como mejor aya lugar de derecho digo ademas de que Lorença Galiana Forteza Sureda, mujer de Pomar, Antonio Martin, Bartholome Martin, Gabriel Burgos, Guillermo Martin, Raphael Martin, Cathalina Pomar, Antonio Fuster, Gabriel Burgos, Onofre Aguilo, Francisco Bonin, Agustin Cortes, Beatriz Cortes, Raphael y Benito Pomares, todos de la Nación Hebrea y los demás en comun que viven en esta presente Ciudad de Mallorca, se hallan notados y testificados en los libros y testificadores de esta Inquisición de aver hecho, dicho y cometido y observado ceremonias tocantes al Judaismo á venido tambien a mi noticia como todos los demás de la dicha Nación siguen, tienen y guardan la muerta y caduca ley de Moysen, y que de ello á avido y ay muchos y muy graves escandalos entre los fieles y cathólicos christianos y an resultado otros muchos inconvenientes, crimines y delitos en ofensa de Dios Nuestro Señor; daño y menosprecio de Nuestra Santa fée Catholica y ley evangelica segun y conforme resulta y parece por los dichos testificadores y libros y por los capitulos siguientes:

1: Haviendose convertido los de la Nación hebrea habitantes en esta dicha Ciudad de Mallorca, vivieron todos juntos a lo ultimo de ella en unos barrios que se llaman la Calatrava y en ellos se fundo una Iglesia que se diçe Santa Fé para ser instruidos en ella y despues porque crucificaron a un muchacho y porque davan pocas muestras de fidelidad fueron quitados de alli y puestos en medio y en lo mas seguro dc la dicha Ciudad que son las dos calles del Sayell y de la Bolseria a donde al presente estan, y aviendose mezclado algunos de ellos en aquel tiempo con personas de los verdaderos catholicos aora les tienen tan grande odio y hacen tanto menosprecio que en todas las ocasiones de riñas les dicen *calatravas* por muy gran injuria.

2: Que ne admiten en sus conversaciones ni juntas a los que son por todas partes de su mismo Nación y en llegando alguna otra persona de los demás naturales de este Reyno cesan los de la nación de hablar con el argullo y alegria que acostumbran entre ellos y convenzan a tratar de otras diferentes materias, y a los que de ellos se mezclan con christianos en caso de matrimonio lo tienen por muy grande afrenta y los dicen los demás que son de la Nación, que son mal mezclados y los tienen a mucha baxesa por el odio tan grande que tienen a los christianos y menosprecio que hacen de ellos.

3: Que observan en ponerse nombres de Santos del Testamento viejo y que no ayan pasado martirios y estiman mucho ser procedidos por todas partes de la dicha Nación y que les tengan por tales y les lamen Judios.

184

4: Que entre si tienen señalados las tribus de que cada uno de ellos son descendientes, haciendo diferencia de tribu a tribu de modo que quando se mezclan los de algun tribu con los de otro tribu que no sea tenido por tan bueno les dicen los de aquel que an degenerado pues se an puesto y mezclado con tribu inferior.

5: Que no tienen en sus casas pinturas de Nuestro Señor Jesu Christo ni de su Bendita Madre la Virgen Maria Nuestra Señora ni otras de Santos del Testamento nuevo y tienen muchas del viejo como son: de Moysen, Josue, Aron, Abraham, Elias, Joseph, y de otros muchos Patriarcas y profetas sin que se hallen estas pinturas sino es entre los de dicha Nación y de ordinario llaman a los que son catholicos *cananeos,* haciendo gran menosprecio dellos diciendoles tambien *canalla* y que an nacido para trabajar y ellos para regalarse.

6: Que assi mismo usan y observan entre si particular y extraño modo de juramento y maldiciones muy diferentes de lo que se acostumbran por los demás naturales de este Reyno, de modo que de oirselo se escandalizan muchos.

7: Que aborrecen tanto a los christianos que por no se mezclar con ellos han solicitar a personas estrangeras ofreciéndoles gran suma de dineros en casos en que no an tenido ocasion afectuar matrimonios entre ellos mismos porque se cassasen y siguiesen las ceremonias y ley de su dicha Nación y siendo muy miserables de ordinario acostumbran pasar grandes cantidades en dispensas para casarse con los parientes que son mas próximos diciendo que asi se abiene mejor su sangre ó, resucita la una a la otra, y en esta conformidad se acostumbran a casar primos hermanos con primas hermanas y se prometen desde muy pequeños.

8: Que para tratar y afectuar todos los contratos matrimoniales se acostumbraron juntar los parientes de ambas partes en huertos, claustros ó en cementerios de Iglesia y conventos a ciertas horas que para solo este efecto tenian señaladas y guardan dichas ceremonias particulares, y entre ellos es que aviendo resuelto los dichos contratos hacen ciertas sortijas ó anillos abentajados de oro y se lo entregan a las mujeres con quines se an afectuado en señal y firmeza de los dichos contratos, todo en guarda y observancia de la ley de Moysen segun se deve presumir de tales personas y mas no se acostumbrando tal entre los demás naturales del Reyno.

9: Que todos los de dicha Nación ó la mayor parte de ellos se ocupan en oficios de peso ó medida como son de mercaderes, plateros, velluteros y entre otros de este género para poder mejor engañar a los verdaderos catholicos.

10: Que asi mesmo para mejor injuriar mas a la ley evangélica conforme se deve presumir acostumbran hacer muy grandes diligencias para obtener Rectorias y Beneficios eclesiasticos como tengan obligación de administrar sacramentos y los sacerdotes que hay de dicha Nación se ofrecen voluntariamente a los Rectores y Curas mostrando particulares deseos mas que otros que se admitiesen por sus manos aunque sea sin limosna alguna siendo assi que estan mas poco devotos y que no les guarda si se les assientan las cosas de la Iglesia.

11: Que en ocasiones que celebran algunas buenas nuevas, andado algunos dellos muestras de hacer sacrificios de muchachos y de otros animales como son corderos.

12: Que tienen tambien ciertas varas derechas levantadas puestas en unos agujeros de las mesas que estan en las entradas de sus puertas, y casas y tiendas y a los que acuden a comprár de ellas les dicen y mandan que guarden muy gran respeto a las dichas varas y que la primera reverencia y cortesia se deve a ellas.

13: Que assi mismo tienen gobierno distinto y separado del que se tiene por los demás naturales de este reyno de modo que aunque se ofresian riñas y haya heridos y muerte entre los de dicha Nación los ocultan de la justicia y lo acomodan y componen todo a su modo sin que para ello intervenga persona que no sea de la Nación y las que para este efecto tienen señaladas y nombradas.

14: Que para ayudarse los unos a los otros quales quieras necesidades van dos personas de la dicha Nación pidiendo limosna para un hermano y esto lo executan dos personas por ellos nombradas en día de fiesta y en otros de entre semana que no lo son, sin estenderse ni salir fuera de sus mismas calles.

15: Que señaladamente acostumbran en todos los dias de sábado a la nochecer hacer como hacen una cerca dos personas que para ello estan destinadas y contribuyen todos los de la dicha Nación muy largamente de manera que recojen en los sabados de un año muy gran suma de dinero contribuiendo hasta los mas pobres y todos conformes las haciendas que tienen usando para esto de unas mesmas palabras y acciónes conque se entienden para contribuir tan largamente y todo este dinero que juntan lo remiten a la Sinagoga que los de dicha Nación tienen en Roma, adonde reside de continuo una persona porquanto de los que estan en este dicho reyno y es cierto que cierto sera para que alli entrega la parte que a estos les toca del tributo que se a entendido hacen generalmente todos los demás que la dicha Nación estan dilatados en los reynos de España y en otras partes porque se les permita tener en Roma la dicha Sinagoga y sobre todo los que ay en este reyno son mas largos y puntuales que todos los demás de otras provincias.

16: Que en dicha Ciudad tienen puesto destinado dentro de las calles sobredichas donde viven todos y en el se congregan algunas noches y hacen sus juntas a oras extraordinarias demostrando en las tales tener mucho argullo y contento hablándose los unos a los otros desde las ventanas de sus casas y todo lo executan con mucha cautela tanto que no se fian de los de su misma Nación hasta que son ya cassados y por esto despues que los an casado les preguntan algunas personas si les an comunicado los de su Nación el secreto.

17: Que no solo no comen tocino pero ni las viandas que se ayan guisado con el y esto observan con tanto extremo que dexan de comer carnero en los dias que se matan los tocinos porque se matan en la misma carniceria y se cortan en las mismas tablas, y por mayor disimulación compran algunos tocinos y despues toman a vender todo lo gordo de ellos y de lo mas magro hacen algunas sobreasadas poniendo en ellas mucha carne de Baca y de carnero y tanta pimienta que apenas se conoce si tienen algo de tocino y por mas gran (?) se alaban que comen de ellas y procuran que se les vean comer los Catholicos y quando comen otras cosas las esconder dellos y aviendo men[r] manteca de puerco entre año para alguna medicina la buscan porque ellos nunca la tienen y hallando la entre los Catholicos lo tienen á gran maravilla.

18: Que tanpoco comen pescado de escata ni de animales de pelo agudo como crastados, cabritos, ni conejos y si por caso les presenten algunos los tornan á vender y si son convidados de los Catholicos se escusan y no quieren comer de los tales pescados ni carnes de dichos animales y mucho menos de los cabritos siendo en esta tierra muy relagados y abentejados.

19: Que no siendo tan buenos los corderos hacen muy gran estimación de ellos y los buscan con gran cuydado y diligencia y no reparan en pagar qualquier precio por ellos y mas en ciertos tiempos de entre año que celebran fiestas particulares y siendo mucho mejores los cabritos y muy mas estimados en todo el Reyno los de la Nación los aborrecen tanto que si algunos labradores aciertan á passar por las dichas calles y les preguntan si quieren comprar cabritos los de la nación se encolerizan y les dicen que se vayan y que les quiten de alli aquellos diabol(t)es diciendo lo por los cabritos.

20: Que tanpoco de comen de aves que ellos no ayan muerto y si les presentan algunas las venden y tornan á comprar otras vivas que degueltan a su modo y con ciertas ceremonias.

21: Que por ningun modo comen carne que tenga sevo ni gozo era(?) quitando se la del todo a la carne que la tiene y acostumbran comer siempre de la carne mas magra como es de piernas y esta de ciertas partes señaladas dellos y son muy aficionados á comer de los animales que se acostumbravan sacrificar en la ley vieja y assi gastan dellos y estan muy contentos quandose matan Bueyes y mas si tienen cierta señal avisandose los unos a los otros paraque acudan y siendo carne muy peor que la de los castrados y mas cara y no comiendo de la de estos compran de aquella a toda prissa.

22: Que amasan el pan muy diferente de lo que se acostumbran entre los demás naturales de Reyno todos los de dicha nación acuden á cocerse a un horno y aunque para otras cosas admiten algunas personas pobres de los Catholicos paraque les ayuden á trabajar quando an de matar se esconden de ellas y no admiten que los ayuden sino á la de su misma Nación.

23: Que hacen fiesta y guardan todos los dias del Sabado y si trabajan algo en lo publico no es tanto como acostumbran en los demás dias y dexan de hacer fuego en sus casas y de comer hasta que sea de noche comensando á celebrar la fiesta desde los viernes á visperas con tan gran extremo que hasta los que son cassados se abstienen uso del matrimonio.

24: Que acostumbran andar aquadrillados á modo de turba y lo observan mas señaladamente en los dias de las semanas santas mostrandose muy confusos y su asistencia ordinaria es en huertos.

25: Que no oyen missa los dias de precepto ni reciven los santos sacramentos de la Penitencia ni escuchar dicha con la frecuencia ni puntualidad que acostumbran todos los Catholicos ni tampoco hacen ni en caso de muerta se dexan obras pias de missas ni limosnas en sus testamentos ni se les hacen decir responsos en sus sepulturas y hallandose algunas veces en las Iglesias se singularizan entre todos haciendo notables extremos paraque se entienda que son buenos cristianos y tanpoco se assientan por cofrades de las cofradias de sus Parroquias ni de otras.

26: Que procuran estudiar algo de latinidad y tienen todos Biblias y otros libros de historias antiguas en que se refieren las vidas de los Patriarchas y Profetas y de proposito estudian el testamento viejo de modo que tienen en la memoria todo lo de las dichas Biblias y libros porque no se ocupan en otras lecturas y tienen otros libros que los deste genero ni tampoco los tienen otras personas que los de dicha Nación.

27 : Que en las occasiones que estan enfermos hacen sus deudos con los demás de su Nación muchas juntas y en ellas tratan del modo hora y mas requisitos conque se les an de executar las sangrias y aunque los medicos las manden hacer no las executan sino es que primero se resuelva en las tales juntas y estando para hacerlas miran con gran cuydado y ansia hacia al cielo y a los techos de las casas y sobre todo hacer tantos y tan grandes extremos que parece dan á entender que sus almas consisten en la sangre.

28 : Que sienten mucho de confessarse en las tales occasiones y assi lo refusan hasta que estan para morir y mucho aborrecen tambien el sacramento de la extrema unción y los mas dellos se mueren sin recivir lo y para dissimularlo acostumbran avisar en las Parroquias despues que ya son muertos fingiendo mucho ciuydo dan mucha prissa á los Parrochos por dar les á entender que lleguen á tiempo y aviendo llegado á sus casas y otras veces antes que lleguen con el santissimo sacramento les dicen que se buelvan porque no an sido á tiempo que en aquel punto an acabado de espitar como unos pollitos.

29 : Que en todo el discurso de sus enfermedades ni tampoco en el articulo de la muerte no permiten que les asistan sacerdotes, Religiosos ni otras personas porque no les ajuden ni vean morir y mueren todos teniendo los vueltos a la pared y no quieren admitir visitas de las personas que son Catholicas aunque ayan tenido y tenga mucha amistad y correspondencia con ellos.

30 : Que tienen dos personas que son de la misma Nación un hombre para coser y amortajar a los hombres y una muger para las mugeres y á todos cosen y amortajan en telas de lienco nuevas y si algunos dellos por su pobreza no las tienen se las compran de limosna entre los demás y en las casas que an muerto no dexan entrar hasta despues de muchos dias sino es a los de su propia Nación aunque de los demás fuera della tengan mucha amistad no se lo permiten.

31 : Que quando llevan á enterrar los cuerpos de los difuntos de su dicha Nación van dos ó una guarda que no los pierde de vista hasta que los ferteros (?) los an cubierto de tierra y tapiado y despues se van las dichas guardas y a los deudos de los diffuntos dicen ciertas palabras que los testigos.

32 : Que para enterrarse tienen en los Conventos de San Francisco y de Nuestra Señora del Carmen desta dicha Ciudad puestos señalados con diferentes requisitos de los que acostumbran y tienen todos los demás naturales deste Reyno porque estos se entierran dentro de las Iglesias en vasos que tienen ya hechos y los de dicha nación se entierran fuera de las Iglesias entierra virgen y endescubierto de modo que se pueda llover y junto á canal de agua corriente que solo ellos guardan y observan esto con todo los demás que queda dicho en los capitulos precedentes singularizandose sobre todo y contraveniendo a lo que comunm.te se acostumbra guardar y hacer por todos los demás naturales deste dicho Reyno.

33 : Que todo lo arriba dicho es publico y notorio y que dello an resultado y resultan muchos y graves escandalos y ofensas contra Dios Nuestro Señor en menosprecio de la ley evangelica y del exercicio del Santo Oficio y de cada dia es cierto que se iran aumentando con otros mas graves y perniciosos crimines é inconbenientes á que no es justicia que se de lugar y assi pido y sup.co á VS mande que con todo recato y secreto se reciva in-

form^{on} al tenor de los sobredichos cap^{os} examinando los testigos que para este efecto presento contra todos los de dicha Nación pues hacen un mismo cuerpo y estan ya testificados en los testificadores antiguos y tambien en los corrientes y no solo en comun sino en particular y de todo hago presentación y pido que se hagan todas las demás diligencias necesarias (por puestas toda dilación?) con todo el secreto y puntualidad que se requiere para poder conseguir el fin mas principal y tan importante al servicio de Dios, y a la conservación y defensa de la religion Christiana y mayor bien de los reynos de su Magestad executando las personas y bienes de los que resultaren culpados en tan grandes crimines y delitos todas las demostraciones publicas y exemplares de derecho de als (?) . . . hubiere lugar conforme á estilo é instrucciones del Santo Oficio para que a ellos sirva de castigo y a otros de exemplo y a mi se me administre entero cumplimiento de justicia que sobre todo pido *omni meliori modo juribus facias* etc., y en lo necessario . . . etc.

Don Juan de Fontamar.

APPENDIX V

VICISSITUDES OF THE CONVERSOS IN THE SEVENTEENTH CENTURY

(from *Anales Judaicos de Mallorca*[1])

Tragico fué para los Hebreos de Mallorca el desenlace, que tuvo en este siglo el drama a que dieron principio en el siglo 15. La escena del acto que voy a bosquejar tiene cuatro cuadros: el primero tuvo lugar en un huerto extramuros de Palma, donde se reunian los Judios mal convertidos para celebrar las ceremonias de su ley; el segundo paso en las carceles de la Inquisición; el tercero dentro de la Iglesia de Santo Domingo; y el último en la falda de la colina sobre la que se ostenta magestuosamente el anciano castillo de Bellver.

La hipocrita y pérfida intención con que los Judios del Call entraron en el gremio de la Iglesia Catolica para evadirse del castigo que les tenia preparado la Justicia, segun queda referido en el siglo 15, ya estado, va a demostrarse con el suceso que compendiadamente voy a referir, valiendome de las frases mismas de los autores contemporaneos que tengo a la vista. No que poca maña el saber ocultar por mas de dos siglos, bajo el aparente velo de la fé, la obstinación mas decidida á favor de la ley de Moises. Sin ser buenos Judios eran malos Cristianos, y solo amontonaban sacrilegios á sacrilegios, repetiendo los actos mas positivos de cristiana ortodocsia.

Ellos eran los que mas frecuentaban las fiestas y aun sacramentos, sin dar lugar a la piedad inocente de los fieles a formar juicio de su malicia, tan sebosada con capa de aparente virtud. La poca cautela de un muchacho dió margen a que se descubriese una oculta Sinagoga que tenian los Hebreos bautizados en un huerto cercano a la ciudad de Palma, entre las dos puertas que llaman de San Antonio y Pintada. Alli fueron sorprendidas en 1678 docientas doce personas en el acto de judaizar y teniendo noticia de ello el Tribunal de la Inquisición empezo sus pezquizas en averiguación de los autores y complices de aquel delito; y en 16, 23 y 30 de Abril y 3 de Mayo del año siguiente fueron penitenciados los reos confeses y convictos y confiscados sus bienes en cantidad de un millon cuatrocientos noventa y un mil docientos setenta y seis pesos. La Sinagoga fué demolida, y su area sembrada de, sal y junto a ella se levanto un pilar, sobre el cual se puso una lapida de tres palmos de alto y cuatro de ancho en la que se gravo la siguiente inscripción:

Año 1679 fué derribado, arado y sembrado de sal este huerto de orden de la Inquisición par enseñarse en la ley de Moises, nadie la quite, ni rompa esta columna en tiempo alguno, para de excomulgacion mayor.

En una nota que tengo presente se advierte, que con motivo de la nueva fortificación, que despues se hizo en Palma se quitó lugar donde se colocara al principio la sobre dicha inscripción, y se puso fijada en un angulo entrante da la escalera al Palacio de la Inquisición. No era la derecha donde permanecio hasta la extinción del Tribunal en 1812.

---

[1] The spelling and punctuation appear here as in the original record, from which this is a faithful transcription.

190

Queriendo desvanecer la memoria de un suceso, que tanto afectaba a los descendientes de los nuevos conversos, compró la lapida Bartolomé Forteza Mochina y la hizo trasportar a un predio llamado "Son Amatle" y borradas las letras hizo servir la piedra de poyo; pero restablecido el Santo Oficio en 1814 se le obligo a restituir aquella a su primitivo lugar, la cual desapareció en la demolición del precitado Palacio en 1822. Daremos aqui aunque en miniatura una reseña de numero de autos públicos que se celebraron y de los individuos que fueron penitenciados en cada uno de aquellos.

Los reos que salieron en el primer fueron 50; a saber 26 hombres y 24 mujeres y el teatro para la función fué la Iglesia de Padres Predicadores; en el segundo auto fueron 52 reos, 25 hombres y 27 mujeres; en el tercero fueron sentenciados 62 reos; 29 hombres y 33 mujeres; en el cuarto fueron penitenciados 49 reos y entre ellos 23 muchachos de 13 a 17 años; a estas se les quitó el San Benito tan luego como se concluyo la función y a todos los demás se les impuso carcel, a unos perpetua y a otros temporal. Y finalmente en 28 de dicho mes de Mayo del año precitado, Domingo de la Santisima Trinidad, se celebro un nuevo auto en que salieron 13 judaizantes, que fueron sin duda los residuos de la gavilla criminal, y por ser los menos delincuentes, fué tambien leve la pena. Para tener a los nuevos reconciliados en un punto centrico de la Ciudad, donde pudieron ser observados sus costumbres y acciones, tanto por los cristianos viejos como por el Tribunal da la Inquisición, se les obligó a vivir en un barrio llamado la calle d'es Saxell y que todos Domingos y dias de fiesta pasaren en comunidad, accompañados del alguacil de dicho tribunal, á oír la misa mayor en la Iglesia Catedral.

No tuvieron enmienda los Hebreos reconciliados con la Iglesia; porque sin temor a los castigos con que se les habia conminado, no tardaron en reincidir con un invariable tema, y habiendose sabido de positivo que bajo las formas exteriores de una cristiana piedad abrigaban la mas constante adhesion a su antigua y caduca ley, fueron sumariados por la Inquisición. Mas secelosos ó avisados los Hebreos determinaron de abandonar la Isla de Mallorca, contratando para dicho efecto con el capitan de un buque Inglés, que a la razon se hallaba en el puerto de Palma. Aviendo sobre el ajuste, se embarcaron los mas principales en la noche del 2 [sic] de Marzo del año 1688; pero cuando mas se congratulaban Rafael Valls con los suyos, de que el Dios de Abraham les habia librado de las llamas de la Inquisición, como lo hizo en otro tiempo con los tres niños que estaban dentro del horno de Babilonia, se altero el mar, bramaron los vientos y el granizo y los relampagos sustituyeron a la bonanza que habia reinado en todo aquel dia. Un alguacil, enviado por el Tribunal de la Fé, para hacer presa de los transfugos, fue el angel, que Valls y Onofre Tarongi habian profetizado a los suyos les embiaria el Señor para librarles de sus enemigos, llevandoles de la mano para que las piedras no lastimasen los pies de los verdaderos creyentes, hasta conducirlos al puerto seguro de salvacion. Muy a su pesar vieron que se les salian fallidas sus esperanzas y que en vez de asilo que se prometieron, entraron aquella misma noche en las carceles de la Inquisición y la mañana siguiente pasaron a hacerles compania muchos de sus correligionarios, que no tan animosos como aquellos ó quiza mas pegados a sus intereses, no quisieron abandonar el pais donde habian medrado.

Tres años cabales se pasaron sustanciandose las causas de aquellos infelices y conducidas, voladas y consultadas, ochenta y ocho de ellos, el

mismo dia 7 de Marzo de 1691, fueron conducidos por entre innumerable
gentio de todo secso, estado y edad, desde la Inquisición hasta el Templo
de Santo Domingo 25 reos, cerrando la procession los Muy Illustres Inquisidores, asistidos de una gravísima comitiva de Reverendísimos calificadores y familiares noblisimos que habiendo tomado todos lugar en sus puestos y comenza de la misa segun costumbre, se pasó leer las sentencias a los
reos. Estas fueron de galeras en algunos, de carcel perpetua ó temporal,
de destierro, confiscación de bienes y multas en otros.

En el segundo auto que tuvo lugar en la sobre-dicha Iglesia el 1° de
Mayo del citado año, aparecieron 21 judios de uno y otro secso, que fueron
relajados despues al brazo secular para ser quemados vivos; pero como algunos de ellos se convirtieron, se les arrojo a las llamas despues de muertos
garrote. La novedad y calidad del suceso atrajo a la capital de las Baleares
un gentio immenso, y el Tribunal de la Inquisición no dejó por su parte de
tomar todas las precauciones necesarias para dar autoridad á aquel auto y
mantener el orden público Uno de los que asistieron a él tuvo especial en-
cargo de dar publicidad a aquel mas ó por medio de la prensa, del cual su
tomado la siguiente narración:

Por los ultimos de Abril tomada la resolución en el Tribunal
para celebrar el segundo auto y relajar en el, aunque particular, contra la costumbre inconcusa, los reos a la justicia y brazo
secular y dados las comisiones oportunas se paso a participar el
acuerdo al Ilustre Señor Marques de la Casta, Virrey y Capitan
General de este Reyno, al Ilustrisimo y Reverendisimo Señor Don
Pedro de Alagón Arzobispo, Obispo de esta Ciudad, al Muy Ilustre
Señor Conde de Santa Maria de Formiquese, como Procurador
mas antiguo de la Cofradia de San Jorge, consistente del brazo
militar de este Reyno que hoy mexetinamente lo gobierna como
Lugar-Teniente interino de Virrey y Capitan General no solo por
la naturaleza del ofiicio de Procurador Real, sino por especial
denominación de S. M. que para calificado abandono de sus meritos, quiso hacerle esta singular demonstración de soberano agrado,
al Ilustrisimo Señor Obispo de Oropi como Decano del Cabildo,
al Muy Ilustre Señor de Bellpuig entonces Jurado in capite de
esta Ciudad, para que como cabeza de sus gremios participara cada
uno al suyo. Asi mismo participo dicho acuerdo a la Real Audiencia y al Muy Ilustre Señor Diego Hiñau y Muñoz su Regen-
te, noticiando a todos que el día primero de Mayo estaba destinado para el auto. Pasaron algunas sutilezas sobre los mas deli-
cados ápices de la etiqueta, como en cosa tan nueva entre los tribunales de Santo Oficio y de la Real Audiencia, que facilitó y
ajustó y compusó el celo comun de la eczaltación de la Fé, y la pru-
dencia y discreción de quien manejó estos negocios, y habiendose
entendido por parte del Procurador Real, que habia de haber algunos relajados a la justicia y brazo seglar, mando levantar un
brasero de 80 pies en cuadro y 8 en alto y disponer en el a buena
proporción 25 palos con su tablita para asiento de los que habian de
morir a garrote y prevenir la leña necesaria para tan. grande
hoguera. Eligió para este un campo yermo que se ensancha es-
pasioso entre el Lazareto, que esta sobre la orilla del mar, y las
faldas del collado que llaman del Castillo de Bellver, asi por la

capacidad del puesto como por la distancia de la Ciudad, para que no se sintiera la pesadumbre del humo. Aunque otros glosaban habia sido oculta la Providencia Divina que suavemente disponia para desengaño de los reos, muriesen casi en el propio lugar que habian escogido para el embarco de la fuga.

Seria demasiado prolongo si se habia de continuo el texto literal; por lo mismo en beneficio de la brevedad lo extractaré, diciendo:

Que los reos fueron llevados a la Iglesia de Santo Domingo, que alli se les hicieron las sentencias, para cuya ejecución fuerón entregados a uno de los Jueces de la Real Audiencia, que residia sobre un magnifico tablado, levantado al efecto en la Plaza de Corte. Desde este punto fueron conducidos los sentenciados al lugar del suplicio, montados en jumentos, a cuyo sitio llevaron muy cerca de las cinco de la tarde, y reconciliados de nuevo fueron ejecutados a presencia de mas de 30,000 almas que se habian reunido al efecto.

El tercer auto se celebró en la predicha Iglesia de Santo Domingo el dia seis del mismo mes de Mayo con la pompa y autoridad que los precedentes, saliendo en el 15 hombres y 3 mujeres que fueron condenados a saber: Rafael Valls, mayor, Rafael Benito Tarongi y Catalina, hermana de este, a ser quemados vivos, y los restantes a la pena de garrote en el mismo brasero para despues ser quemados en él. Como habia algunos fugitivos, fueron quemadas cinco estatuas que les representaban, y dos cajones con los huesos de otros tantos Judios ya difuntos.

Me difundrá mas de lo que me, he propuesto, si me pasaba en detallar los masos acaecidos con los pertinaces, sobre los que corren aun en Mallorca varios anecdotas, siendo muy vulgar el refran de *"Felet no't dons,"* que equivale a *"Rafaelito no te desapartido,"* le cual se usa cuando uno esta obstinado en su opinion. Tal era la protervidad de Catalina Tarongi, que todo el tiempo que camina al suplicio, despreciando las voces de los sacerdotes que la asistian, gritaba de continuo animando a su hermano Rafael: *"Felet no't dons que no mos cremerán a noltros, si no á sa roba,"* confianza que no la abandono hasta que las llamas empezaron a devorar sus carnes, pues entonces gritaba desesperada que la sacaran del incendio.

El cuarto y ultimo auto celebrado en este siglo tuvo lugar en el susodicho templo de Frailes Predicadores el dos de Junio [sic] del memorado año; en el fueron relajados en persona á la justicia ordinaria dos mugeres por judaizantes reincidentes a las que se les impuso la pena capital en garrote y ser despues entregadas a las llamas. Hizose lo propio con una estatua de un ausente fugitivo; tres fueron los reconciliados en estatua por haber muerto en los carceles durante el curso de la causa con señales de arrepentimiento y quince penitenciados que adjuraron personalmente de Levi, cuyos nombres con el de los demás reos contenidos en esta y demás autos precedentes se pondrian por su orden en el siguiente siglo.

En once de Setiembre de 1695 se celebró otro auto de fé, en el que fueron quemados en estatua diez Judios de ambos secsos en cuya ejecución se dió fin a la escena tragica de este siglo.

APPENDIX VI

PRAYERS

1.

[1]En vuestras manos, Señor, encomiendo el alma mia, mi espíritu, mi entendimiento, el mirar, el hablar, todo quanto, Señor, en mi tengo.

Vos, Señor, me habéis hecho. Señor de toda verdad, vuestras manos me hicieron desde la cabeza hasta los pies. Dadme, Señor, entendimiento para que os conozca, y obrar pueda vuestros mandamientos.

Señor, vos me habéis hecho de nada formada. Si os plaze sea como mandaréis. Muchos son mis pecados, y como mala he cometido mil males é imaginaciones; por eso no me dejés, clementísimo Dios. Hínchame, Señor, del Espíritu Santo. Mira, Señor, que vos dijisteis que todos los invocaren serán salvas. Pues yo, en el tiempo de la tribulación, de la angustia y tentación, a vos invoco, Señor. Libradme y ayudad, y en todo defendedme del día de mis angustias y pecados. Pues vos solo, Señor, me podéis librar y salvar en el día y en la noche. Hazedme tan innumerable gracia que siempre con vos sea mi vivir. Assí siempre vos alaban. A vos siempre vendeciré, y á vos, Señor, adoraré sobre todas' las cosas de este mundo, á vos serviré y á vuestra voluntad, hasta el fin y último del Padre, in secula seculorum.   Amen.

In Thy hands, O Lord, I commit my soul, my spirit, my knowledge, my sight, my speech, and everything, O Lord, that I have within me.

Thou, O Lord, hast made me. Lord of all truth, Thy hands have fashioned me from head to foot. Grant me understanding, O Lord, that I may know Thee and be able to fulfill Thy commandments.

O Lord, Thou hast created me out of nothingness. If it pleaseth Thee, may it be as Thou hast commanded. Many are my sins, and as a wicked person I have committed a thousand evil deeds and thoughts. Yet do not abandon me, O most merciful God. Fill me, O Lord, with the Holy Spirit. Behold, O Lord, Thou hast said that all who call upon Thee shall be saved. Therefore I implore Thee in the time of tribulation, sorrow and temptation. Free me and help me, and above all protect me from the day of my anxieties and sins. For Thou alone, O Lord, art able to save me in the day and in the night. Grant me such boundless grace that I may abide with Thee forever. Thus they always praise Thee. I shall always bless Thee, and Thou, O Lord, I shall adore above all things of this world. I shall serve Thee and I shall do Thy will unto eternity . . . .   Amen.

2.

Bendito tu Adonay, nuestro Dios, Rey del mundo, que formó el hombre con sabiduría, y crió en el orados, orados, huecos, huecos. Descubiertos y sábio delante çilla de tu trono que si serasse uno dellos, ó si se abriesse uno

---

[1] I have not changed the spelling of the words, choosing rather to transcribe literally from the documents. In some cases, I have found it necessary to add or slightly modify words in order to make the text intelligible. These changes are indicated by [ ].

dellos, no [sería] posible sustenarse [por] una hora. Bendito tu Adonay, melcian toda criatura, y maravillas para hazer.[2] Yo con muchedumbre de tu merced, vendré a tu cassa a humillarme a Palacios de tu Santidad, y con temor todos criados de arriba á abaxo.

Blessed art Thou, O Lord our God, King of the universe, Who hast formed man in wisdom, and hast created in him many orifices and vessels. It is revealed and known before Thy throne, that if one of them be closed or one of them be opened, it would be impossible to exist even for a short while. Blessed art Thou, O Lord, Who healest all flesh, and workest wonders. As for me, I will come into Thy House, in the abundance of Thy lovingkindness, to humble myself before Thy holy Temple,[3] and with the fear of all servants from above to below.

3.

Padre nostre poderos
que tot jorn feu maravelles
aijau pietat, gran deu, de nos
y de vostres simples ovelles
qui son fiblades de abelles
en tan gran afligiment.
Tu qui ets poderos, Deu eternal
vúlleste apiedar de elles
santificat sia al teu sant nom
arais tota vegada
monstra'ns Senyor lo teu llum
no le'm tengas amagada
si la nostra gent passada
per algun temps ha errat
de Tu, Senyor, es perdonat;
asi ho diu la ley sagrada
Tu, gran Deu, qui en lo cel
estas en la tua santa cadira
pietat, gran Deu, de nos,
y el poble qui suspira.

Our Almighty Father
Who daily worketh miracles,
Take pity upon us, O great God,
And upon Thy innocent flock
Who are stung by bees
With such great affliction.
Thou Who art powerful, God eternal,
Be willing to have pity upon them.
Blessed be Thy holy name
Now and forever.
Show us Thy light, O Lord,

---

[2] Up to this point, this prayer is from the morning ritual. Cf. Singer's *Authorised Daily Prayer Book*, pp. 4, 5.

[3] These lines are the familiar ones recited upon entering a synagogue. Cf. Singer, *op. cit.*, p. 2.

Hide it not from us.
If our ancestors
Had sinned for a time,
Thou, O Lord, didst pardon them;
Thus saith the Scriptures
Thou great God, Who in heaven
Art in Thy holy throne,
Have pity upon us, great Lord,
And upon Thy suffering people.

4.

En nombre de Dios, y Dios delante y paz [como una] guía, alabado y glorificado sea aquel gran Dios de Israel, que a criado la noche y el día; (el angel St. Raphael bendito, quando guia al hixo de Tobías, el viage que havian de hacer en un año, hicieron en veinte y dos días, por voluntad de aquel gran Dios de Israel; fué buelto los bienes y la vista a Tobías le fué dada Sara por Santa y buena compañía como assí es verdad y no es falso). Gran Dios de Israel, [mostradnos el camino y sea nuestra guía] que [podamos] amar y servir con alegría ahora y siempre. Amen.[4]

In the name of God, and God before and peace as a guide, praised and glorified be that great God of Israel, Who hath created day and night; (blessed angel St. Raphael when conducting the son of Tobit, the voyage that they were to make in a year and a day they made in twenty-two days, through the kindness of that great God of Israel; his wealth and sight were returned to Tobit, and Sarah was given to him as a good and holy companion, as it is true and not false) Great God of Israel, show us the way and be our guide, that we may love and serve Thee with gladness now and forever. Amen.

5.

Grande eres, O Señor, Dios de Israel, y el tu Reyno dura por todos los siglos. Tu eres que azotas y el que salvas, sin que ninguno pueda huír de tu bendita mano. Alabad al Señor, o hijos de Israel, delante de todas las gentes, porque le deis á conoser á todos los del mundo que no hay otro

[4] Another rendering of this prayer in Catalan follows
Deu en avant y pau en vía
alabat sia aquell gran Deu
de Israel qui embía
los angels del cel,
sian la mia guardia y guía
Mon Senyor, St Raphael
qui va guiar aquel St Tobías
viatje que havia de hazer
en un año va fer
en vint i dos días
per voluntat de aquel gran Deu
li va tornar los bens
y la visto lo meu gran Deu;
axi com aso es
veritat i no falsía
los angels del cel sían
en la mia guardia y guía
(de si es i de be?)
sobre Deu Senyor moria.

Dios sino es el   Pues yo en la tierra de la captividad mostraré (porque su
Magestad en la gente peccadora). Por tanto, o peccadores, convertíos a
Dios, que [demostrará a] vosotros misericordia.

Great art Thou, O Lord, God of Israel, and Thy Kingdom endureth
throughout all ages. Thou art He Who punisheth and healeth; no one
can escape from Thy blessed hand   Praise the Lord, O sons of Israel, before all the people, so that the whole world may understand that there is
no other God beside Him. For I shall manifest it in the land of captivity
(because His majesty is with the sinful people)   Therefore turn to God,
O ye sinners, for He shall show mercy unto ye.

6.

Vos que no tenéis fe en el Dios de Israel y en su santa ley, que es Dios
omnipotente que havía criado la gloria el cielo, y la tierra, y todas las cria-
turas, y le havía dado el ser que tiene. Assí que no havía de poner duda en
su santa ley haviendo la dado por su santa boca   .   Oida de todo el
mundo porque no fuesse ignorado por ninguno. Que quando Dios dió la
ley, havían mirado nuestras padres antepassados prometiendo a Dios, Nuestro Señor, que por ellos, y por los suyos, los [escrivieran y adoraran],
assí que [ellos] estarian obligados á adorar á Dios y guardar sus preceptos
y mandamientos.

Ye who have no faith in the God of Israel and in His holy Law, [know]
that He is God omnipotent and hath created heaven and earth and all mankind, and hath given him the form which he hath. There hath been no
doubt in His holy Law, since He hath given it through His holy mouth
    .   .   .   Hearken thereto, that it may not be forgotten by anyone, for
when God gave the Law, our forefathers esteemed it and promised God,
our Lord, that for themselves and for their descendants they would write
and adore them (the commandments?), and thus they would be obliged
to praise God and keep His precepts and His commandments.

7.

Tu gran Dios que has criado el cielo y la tierra, y á mí, y á toda criatura, seas glorificado, y alabado tu santo nombre. [Tu] me has guardado
esta noche, y me has dejado ver la luz del día; me des buenos días y buenos
años, por tu Divina Bondad. Seas mi guarda y ayuda y socorre mis neces-
sidades con tu santo remedio. Tengas misericordia de mí, y perdon de mis
peccados, (y assí lo espero de tu divina bondad por gloria tuya). Me hagas
gracia para alcanzar al fin de mis días tu Santa gloria en que serás alabado
y glorificado para siempre. Amen.

Thou great God Who hast created heaven and earth, and me, and all
mankind, may Thy holy name be glorified and praised. Thou hast preserved
me this night and hast permitted me to see the light of day. Because of
Thy lovingkindness, grant me good days and good years. Be Thou my
Guardian and Helper and support my needs with Thy holy resources.
Have pity upon me, and pardon my sins, (and thus I shall await Thy
glory through Thy lovingkindness). Grant me grace that I may reach the

end of my days, and that Thy holy name may be praised and extolled forever. Amen.

8.

Bendito el bien hacedor, [alabado] á su Pueblo de Israel en [el] día de Sábado (de santidad hasta que aquí). Bendito el, bendito su nombre, y bendita su memoria para siempre de siempre.

Bendito tu Adonay, nuestro Dios, Rey del mundo, y Rey el grande, el Santo Padre, el Piadosso, lloada en boca de su Pueblo; afermoticado en lengua de todos sus buenos, y sus siervos . . . y con cánticos de David tu siervo. Te lloadémos, engrandecerémos, te alabarémos, te glorificarémos, te enaltezerémos, y nombrarémos tu nombre, nuestro Rey, nuestro Dios, único vivo de los mundos Alabado y glorificado sea tu nombre siempre de siempre Bendito tu Adonay, nuestro Dios, Rey alabado con alabamiento.[5]

Blessed be the Creator, praised by His people Israel on the Sabbath day (   ). Blessed be He, blessed be His name, and blessed be His memory forever and ever.

Blessed art Thou, O Lord our God, King of the universe, almighty and holy God, the most merciful Father, praised by the mouth of His people, lauded by the tongue of all His loving ones and His servants. We also will praise Thee, O Lord our God, with the songs of David Thy servant, with praises and psalms we will laud, magnify, praise, glorify and extol Thee, and proclaim Thy name, our King, our God, Thou the only One, the sole life of all worlds. Praised and glorified be Thy name forever and ever. Blessed art Thou, O Lord our God, a King extolled with praises.

9.

De la noche bendecid á Adonay, todos siervos, á Adonay los estantes en cassa de Adonay; en las noches alcad vuestras manos con santidad, y bendecid á Adonay. Bendígate Adonay de Sión; hazador de [los] cielos y tierra; Adonay Sabaoth, con nos emparo; por nos Dios de Jacob, siempre Adonay Sabaoth. Biena venturado el hombre que confía en tu Adonay. Salva el Rey, y nos responderás en día de nuestro [llamamiento]. Y al piadoso perdonará pecado (y multiplicará para amáncar su íra, y no haca acorda toda su saña).

Praise God in the night, all ye servants in the house of the Lord; in the night seasons raise your hands with holiness, and praise the Lord. May the God of Zion, the Creator of heaven and earth, bless thee. The Lord of Hosts Who hath protected us, for us the God of Jacob is always the Lord of Hosts. Blessed be the man who trusts in Thee, O Lord. The King saveth, and Thou shalt answer us when we call. Thou shalt forgive the pious his sin (   ).

---

[5] Follows closely the prayer in the morning ritual which begins: "Baruch sheomar vehayah" ("Blessed be He Who spake"). Cf. Singer, *op. cit.*, pp. 16, 17.

10[6]

El uno: el Gran Dios de Israel,
Los dos: Moysen y Aarón,
Las tres: Abram, Isach y Jacób,.
Los quatros maridos de Israel,
Los cinco libros de la ley,
Los seis días del Sábado,
Los siete días de la semana,
Los ocho días de la circumcisión,
Los nueve meses de la preñada,
Los diez mandamientos de Dios,
Las once estrellas del cielo,
Los doze tribus de Israel,
Las treze palabras que dijo Dios omni-
potente a Moyses . . . . Amen. Amen.

One: the great God of Israel,
Two: Moses and Aaron,
Three: Abraham, Isaac and Jacob,
The four patriarchs of Israel,
The five books of the law,
The six days before Sabbath,
The seven days of the week,
The eight days before circumcision,
The nine months of pregnancy,
The ten commandments of God.
The eleven stars of heaven,
The twelve tribes of Israel,
The thirteen words which God Almighty
spoke to Moses . . . . Amen. Amen.

11.

Ruega Moysen á Dios por la casa de su suegro, que le imbiasse un hombre que se juntasse con ellos.
Bendito sea el varon que en Dios pone la esperança,
Pues dió á Faraón una tan justa vengansa.

Moses prayed to God for the household of his father-in-law that He might send a man who would unite himself with them.
Blessed be the man who places his trust in God,
Since He took such just vengeance upon Pharaoh.

12.

Alabad á nuestro Dios, altas alturas del cielo que en los cielos habi-tando. Qualquiera alabanza es buena. Alabadle sol y luna. Y á su mag-

---

6 In one place(AHN *Proc. de Fe,* legajo 1710, 3, fol. 11) this prayer begins: "Qui sabes y entregues qui es deu alt en cel alabat sie el seu santa-nom . . . Amen, Amen."

nificencia todos le alaben, todos le bendigan el nombre del Señor (dulce maravilla).[7]

O ye heights of heaven, praise our God Who dwelleth on high. Any praise is befitting. Praise ye Him, sun and moon. Let all praise His magnificence. Let all bless the name of the Lord. . . .

13.

Gran Dios de Israel, vos que aveis hecho camino en la mar y en la tierra, ayais merced y piedad por ser vos quien sois.

Great God of Israel, Thou Who hast made a path on land and on sea, have mercy and pity because of What Thou art.

14.

Dios que me haveis criado, seais glorificado. Dios mio, Dios mio, Dios mio, seais glorificado, que el vuestro nombre sea alabado.

O God, Thou Who hast created me, be Thou glorified. My God, my God, my God, be Thou glorified, and may Thy name be praised

15.

Señor, por ser vos quien soys, libre á fulano (nombrando lo) del peligro en que se halla, y asistal, para que [sea] feliz por [ello].

O Lord, because of What Thou art, free (naming the person) from the danger in which he (or she) finds himself (or herself) and assist him, so that he may be happy for it.

16.

Busca á el gran Dios de Israel, sin tardarte á arrepentir, [por]que el te saldrá á recibir si tu le buscas á el, aunque tarde hayas venido, la culpa no te acobarde, porque nunca llega tarde el que viene arrepentido.

Seek after the great God of Israel without delaying your repentance, for He will come forth to receive you if you search after Him. Although you may be delayed, let not your sin terrify you, for he who hath repented is never late.

17.[8]

Vengo á umillarme en tu Palacio Real con tu santidad. [Tu] me oyrás de piedad, de compasión. [Tu] me oyrás de voluntad. [Tu] me oyrás de misericordia. [Tu] me oyrás con lo que quizieras, con tu voluntad por la salud de Israel.

---

[7] Some of these prayers are strongly influenced by the Psalms, many containing lines or ideas taken from the Psalms For example, here are lines similar to those of Psalm 148, 1-3.

[8] The first line of this prayer bears striking resemblance to the last line of Prayer 2, *supra* p. 192

I come to humble myself in Thy holy Temple. Thou wilt hear me out of pity, out of compassion. Thou wilt hear me out of willingness. Thou wilt hear me out of mercy. Thou wilt hear me out of what Thou mayest desire—out of Thy love for the salvation of Israel.

18.

BENEDICTIONS

a.

Bendito tu Adonay, nuestro Dios, Rey del mundo, que nos santificó en sus mandamientos y nos encomendó sobre limpieza de manos (ó cara).

Blessed art Thou, O Lord our God, King of the universe, Who hast sanctified us with His commandments and hast commanded us concerning the washing of the hands (or face).

b.

Bendito tu Adonay, nuestro Dios, Rey del mundo, que nos santificó en sus mandamientos y nos encomendó la degolladura.

Blessed art Thou, O Lord our God, King of the universe, Who hast sanctified us with His commandments and hast commanded us concerning the cutting of the throat.

c.

Bendito tu Adonay, nuestro Dios, Rey del mundo, que nos santificó en sus mandamientos y nos encomendó la cobertura de la sangre.

Blessed art Thou, O Lord our God, King of the universe, Who hast sanctified us with His commandments and hast commanded us concerning the covering of the blood.

19.

Fragments of Prayers

a.

Señor de los mundos, Dios de los Dioses, Señor de los Señores, Señor de los perdones, Dios de nuestros padres . . . .

Lord of all worlds, God of gods, Lord of lords, Lord of forgiveness, God of our fathers . . . .

b.

Gran Señor, Dios de Abram, Dios de Jacob, el Dios grande, el poderoso, el [valiente], el Dios de las batallas, el Dios de los exércitos. . . .

Great Lord, God of Abraham, God of Jacob, the great God, the almighty, the valiant, the God of battle, the God of hosts. . . .

c.

Dios mio, tén de mi misericordia según la muchedumbre de la tuya
. . . El pelicano en soledad criado, triste como lechuga, en las tinieblas,
cerrada del ilusiones y tinieblas. . . .[9]

My God, have mercy upon me, according to Thine abundance (of
mercy) . . . The pelican, sad like an owl, reared in the solitude and in
the utter darkness, encircled by illusions and by mists. . . .

d.

Tu omnipotente Dios [permítame] gozar la luz del día con libertad
para serviros y alabaros.

O Thou omnipotent God, allow me to enjoy the light of day, with
freedom to serve and to praise Thee.

e.

Alabado sea Dios que me dexado para ir á mi hija sin peligro . . . .[10]

Praised be God Who has permitted me to go to my daughter without
mishap . . . .

f.

De la más suprema altura, pues entre nos abaxastes, por guiar ·la
criatura, y quitar nuestra tristura Angel Raphael llamado como mancebo
abaxastes del cielo a nuestro suelo—a donsellas days marido, divino cas-
samentero, de virtud soys infinito.[11]

---

[9] This represents the beginning and the end of a prayer. The middle portion has
not been preserved.

[10] Said upon departure (AHN *Rel. de Causas de Fe,* libro 1, 865, fol. 406).

[11] This prayer defies translation. It is obviously a number of fragments thrown to-
gether. Many of these prayers are, in fact, only fragments of prayers remembered
by the Conversos. (AHN *Proc. de Fe,* legajo 1713, 1, fol. 263v).
Some of these prayers will doubtless make a small contribution to the meagre
Marrano liturgical and devotional material already collected in: Kayserling,
Sephardim, pp. 142-4, 156-61; Schwarz, *Os Cristãos-Novos em Portugal no Século
XX;* Slousch, *Haanusim Beportugal,* p. 136ff.; "Tradições cripto-judaicas: O
manuscripto de Rebordêlo," in *Ha-Lapid O Facha* (the official organ of the Marranos of Portugal), Oporto, II, 1928: no. 10, 4-8; no. 11, 6-8; no. 12, 4-6; "Tradições cripto-judaicas: O manuscripto de Perpetua da Costa," *Id.,* III, 1928: no. 21,
6-8; no. 22, 6-8.

BIBLIOGRAPHY

BIBLIOGRAPHY

I

MANUSCRIPT SOURCES

Anales Judaicos de Mallorca (Escritos con imparcialidad sobre los documentos é historia de dicha Isla), Burdeos, 1847, (138 unnumbered fols.). In the private library of the late Don Francisco Villalonga y Fabregues, Palma, Majorca. (A copy of the *Anales* is in the Archivo General Histórico, Palma: vol. IX of Bartolomé Pascual's *Miscelan*).

Apuntes para la historia General del Santo Oficio de Mallorca, es decir, del Tribunal de la Inquisición, (1° de Enero de 1851), 18575, 25, Cuerpo de Manuscritos, BN.

Brebe descripción y noticia del Auto general de fee que celebró el Tribunal del Santo Officio en la Ciudad de Mallorca el dia 13 de henero del año 1675, (fols. numbered 78-96), JTS.

Cartas, Inquisición de Mallorca, AHN.
   legajo 1, 2249: Expedientes y memoriales de los años 1603 á 1644.
   legajo 1, 2250: Expedientes y memoriales de los años 1650 á 1699.

Cartas, Inquisición de Mallorca, AHN.
   libro 1, 857: libro 15 de Cartas de la Inqn. del Reyno de Mallorca, al Consejo de Inqn. desde el año 1687 á 1692.
   libro 1, 858: libro 16 de Cartas, *Id.*—1693 á 1697.
   libro 1, 859: libro 17 de Cartas, *Id* —1680 á 1752.

Competencias de la Inquisición de Mallorca, Consejo de Aragon, legajo, 1512, ACA.

Documentos historicas referentes á la Isla de Mallorca durante el siglo XVIII, 293 fols., Cuerpo de Manuscritos, BN.

Etiquetas y tratamientos entre el Virrey de Mallorca, Real Audiencia y otros tribunales, Consejo de Aragon, legajo 1513, ACA.

Inventario de las Noticias Instrumentales del Reyno de Mallorca, Don Antonio Fernandez de Córdóba:
   I. Hasta 31 Octubre de 1773, 2 vols , Est. 21, gr. 5a, no. 88, AH.
   II Desde Mayo 1782 hasta 15 de Julio, 1785, Est. 27, gr. 4a, no. 122, AH.

Juntas de Hazienda, Inquisición de Mallorca, AHN.
   libro 1, 867: libro 1° desde el año 1623 hasta el de 1680. (354 fols.)
   libro 1, 868: libro 2° desde el año 1681 á 1685. (652 fols.)
   libro 1, 869: libro 3° desde el año 1686 á 1691. (479 fols.)
   libro 1, 870: libro 4° desde el año 1692 á 1697. (525 fols.)
   libro 1, 871: libro 1°. Tocante a la Hacienda de la Inqn. de Mallorca tantes de lo que pueden importar los bienes confiscados: las casas y rasales, y sus cargas. Separacion de la hacienda libre y litigosa. Diferentes Decretos del Consejo, Juntas de hacienda y Informes del Contador General. (492 fols.)
   libro 1, 872: Various documents from 1606 on. (unnumbered fols.)

Libro Becerro (ó Cabrea Mayor). "Hecho por el Dr. Iuan Vaquer, pro. Abogado de presos de Fee y Archivero del Santo Officio de la Inquisición de Mallorca. En que se hallan continuados todos los bienes sitios y censos confiscados en el año MDCLXXVIII y 1691." In the private library of Don Francisco Villalonga y Fabregues, Palma. Also, AHN, 1, 64. (730 fols.)

Libro Becerro del Santo Officio de Mallorca. "Contiene la hacienda antigua, qua ya posseia desde su fundación; las cassas que despues se le agregaron, y los censos sobre la Universidad, Villas, Gremios, y Alquilar que antes fueron tocantes á las confiscaciones de los Reos reconciliados, y relaxados en la complicidad de Judayzantes del año passado de 1678, sucitada en el de 1688, y se mandaron aplicar para la dotacion de el dho. Santo Oficio. Hecho de orden y comission del Exmo. Sr. Arzobispo de Valencia, Inquisidor General y Señores del Consejo de la Santa General Inquisición. Por el Dr. Pedro Juan Vaquer, presbo. Abogado de presos de fee y Archivero, que haze offo. de Contador del dho. Santo Oficio y lo concluyo en el año del 1700," AHN, 1, 65, (622 fols.)

Libro Becerro del Santo Officio de la Inqn. del Reyno de Mallorca. "Contiene los Censos que pagan diferentes personas particulares, y antes fueron tocantes á las Confiscaciones de Judayzantes del año passado de 1678. Sucitada en 1688; y se mandaron aplicar (con los Corridos que estaban debiendo hasta el año de 1697) para la dotacion del dicho Sto. Officio; Juntamente son los Censos, que pagan la Universidad, Villas y Gremios del dho. Reyno, y los de Alquilar, Contenidos por sus Clases en la Primerra Parte de este dicho libro Bezerro. Hecho De Orden, y Comission del exmo. Sr. Arbpo. de Valencia Inqr. General, y SS. del Consexo de la Sta. General Inqn. Por el Dr. Pedro Juan Baquer, Pro. Abogado de Presos de Feé, y Archivero que haze Officio de Contador de dicho Sto. Officio, y lo Concluyo en el año de 1701. Segunda Parte." In the private library of Don Francisco Villalonga y Fabregues. Also, AHN 1, 66. (632 fols.)

Notas sobre la Inquisición en Mallorca y papeletas bibliograficas de algunos libros, 18574, 46, Cuerpo de Manuscritos, BN.

Origen de la Inquisición de Mallorca, 18574, 45, Cuerpo de Manuscritos, BN.

Otros Negocios Notables de Mallorca, Consejo de Aragon, ACA.
    legajos: 966, 967, 968, 969, 970, 971, 972, 973, 974, 975 (primera parte), 1502, 1503, 1504, 1505, 1506, 1507, 1508, 1509, 1510, 1511.

Pleitos Civiles, Inquisición de Mallorca, AHN.
    legajo 1: hasta el año de 1609.
    legajo 2: hasta el año de 1689. Copia del Proceso Criminal de fee hecho en el Santo Oficio de la Inqn. de Mallorca, a instancia del Sr. Fiscal contra Isabel Cortes. (32 fols.)
    legajo 2, 11: Copia del Processo Criminal contra Francisca Marti, viuda de Francisco Marti, alias Verdet. (41 fols.)
    legajo 2, 12: *Id.,* contra Leonor Cortes, muger de Joseph Marti de Francisco, alias Bruy. (66 fols.)
    legajo 2, 13: Adición de Processo de Francisca Tarongi, dfa., muger de Bartholome Aguilo. (16 fols.)

legajo 2, 14: Sumaria Informacion contra la Memoria y Fama de Leonor Marti, dfa., primera muger de Bartholome Tarongi, alias el Conde. (45 fols.)

legajo 3, A, 111: 1690.

legajo 4, A, 112: 1691.

legajo 5, A, 113: 1692.

legajo 6, A, 114: 1693.

legajo 7, A, 115: 1694. Processo entre el Procurador del Real Fisco con Pedro Juan Fuster de la ciudad de Mallorca.

legajo 8, A, 116: 1695.

legajo 9, 14: 1696. Relacion de los pleytos pendientes en el tribunal de la Judicatura de bienes confiscados de la Inquisición de Mallorca, en que el Fisco asido convenido y en los concursos a los bienes de los reos reconciliados en las sentencias de ellos, reservio el Juez Sentencias en otro Juicio.

legajo 9, A, 117: 1725, onward. Processo entre Miguel Alexos Cortes y Joseph Alexandro Cortes. El Procurador del Real Fisco de la Inquisición de Mallorca sobre las dastergua parte de la herenzia de Raphael Geronimo Cortes que pide a la confesante de Leonor Marti, muger de dicho Raphael.

Processos Criminales, Inquisición de Mallorca, AHN.

legajo 2, 18: Cargos y Respuestos del Sr. Inqor. Ldo. Don Francisco Rodriguez Cossio y el voto, 1680.

legajo 3, 15: Auttos contra Diego Leal del Seronde, Secretario de Santo Oficio por aver ido a un Bayle el Domingo que se contaron 29 de Henero de 1679 an compania de una Doncella que tiene en su casa con titulo de pariente, siendo assi que á muchos meses falta del tribunal con motivo que estar enferma, 1699.

legajo, 3, 16: contra Don Diego Leal por haver abierta la primera cubierta de una carta delexmo. Sr. Inqor. General y palabras que sobre ello tubo con dicho Sr. Fiscal.

legajo 4: 1700.

legajo 5: 1701.

legajo 6: 1702.

legajo 9: 1703.

legajo 10: 1704.

Processos Criminales de Fe, Inquisición de Mallorca, AHN.

legajo 1705, 6, pieza 1: Pedro Juan Simon Forteza, dfo. (63 fols.)
pieza 2: *Id.* (58+6+10+10 fols.)

legajo 1705, 7: Pedro Juan Aguilo, hijo de Pedro Juan. (82 fols.)

legajo 1705, 15, pieza 1: Pedro Onofre Cortes de Guillermo, 1687. (240 fols.)
pieza 2: *Id.* (34 fols.)
pieza 3: *Id.*, 1685. (17 fols.)
pieza 4: *Id.*, 1677. (5 fols.)
pieza 5: *Id.* (8 fols.)

legajo 1705, 16: Pedro Juan Forteza de Christoval, alias Menyus, dfo., 1691. (59 fols.)

legajo 1705, 17: Pedro Juan Marti, dfo., 1692. (98 fols.)

legajo 1705, 18, pieza 1: Pedro Miguel Marti, dfo., 1693. (28 fols.)
pieza 2: *Id.,* 1683. (58 fols.)

legajo 1705, 26: Quiteria Marti, viuda de Bernardo Aguilo, alias Zorra, 1689. (85 fols.)

legajo 1706, 9: Geronima Pomar, muger Pedro Juan Miro, de la villa de Arta, 1688. (82 fols.)

legajo 1706, 10: Gabriel Melchor Marti, 1678. (40 fols.)

legajo 1706, 11, pieza 1: Gabriel Cortes, hijo de Agustin Cortes mayor, 1688. (122 fols.)
pieza 2: *Id.,* 1690. (48 fols.)

legajo 1706, 17, pieza 1: Gabriel Nicolas Marti, 1689. (138 fols.)
pieza 2: *Id.,* 1690. (11 fols.)

legajo 1706, 18, pieza 1: Geronimo Cortes, hijo de Gabriel Cortes, 1690. (83 fols.)
pieza 2: *Id.,* 1691. (23 fols.)

legajo 1706, 19: Guillermo Thomas Terongi, 1689. (161 fols.)

legajo 1706, 20: Gabriel Piña, alias Cap de Olleta, 1688. (78 fols.)

legajo 1706, 21, pieza 1: Geronimo Diego Cortes, dfo. (27 fols.)
pieza 2: *Id.,* 1692. (76 fols.)

legajo 1707, 11: Isabel Marti, muger de Juan Baptista Marti, alias Berdet, 1688. (150 fols.)

legajo 1707, 12: Catalina Bonin, muger de Raphael Agustin Pomar, 1688. (148 fols.)

legajo 1707, 13: Gabriel Cortes, alias Morrut, 1720. (127 fols.)

legajo 1707, 14, pieza 1: Isabel Marti, muger de Bartholome Terongi, alias el Conde, 1689. (111 fols.)
pieza 2: Isabel Cortes, muger de Francisco Marti, alias Verdet, 1689. (100 fols.)

legajo 1707, 15: Isabel Marti, muger de Pedro Balthasar Marti, alias el Hereu, 1689. (93 fols.)

legajo 1707, 16. Isabel Aguilo, muger de Pedro Juan Aguilo, 1689 (164 fols.)

legajo 1707, 17, pieza 1: Isabel Marti, viuda de Agustin Antonio Cortes, 1689. (80 fols.)
pieza 2: *Id.,* 1691. (31 fols.)
pieza 3: *Id.* (11 fols.)

legajo 1707, 18: Isabel Forteza, doncella, hija de Raphael Diego Forteza, 1678. (20 fols.)

legajo 1707, 19: Isabel Cortes, muger de Miguel de Francisco, 1677. (6 fols.) (attached to same case: 4+6 fols.)

legajo 1708, 2, pieza 1: Ana Cortes, muger de Juanot Sureda, 1689. (90 fols.)
pieza 2: *Id.,* 1677. (89 fols.)

legajo 1708, 3: Ana Marti, doncella, hija de Raphael Marti menor, alias del Arpa y de Catalina Pomar, 1688. (187 fols.)
pieza 2: *Id.,* 1691. (26 fols.)

legajo 1708, 4, pieza 1: Ana Valls, doncella, dfta., hija de Raphael Valls, mayor, 1693. (37 fols.)
pieza 2: *Id.,* 1678.

legajo 1708, 5, pieza 1: Ana Sureda, muger de Juanot Sureda, 1677. (7 fols.)

  pieza 2: *Id.*, 1677. (6 fols.)

legajo 1708, 16: Alonso, alias Jacob Lopez, natural de la villa de Madrid, 1672. (33 fols.)

legajo 1708, 20: Ana Cortes, muger de Gabriel Joseph Cortes, alias el consul, 1688. (38 fols.)

legajo 1708, 21: Agustin Cortes de Alfonso, alias Formatge, 1689. (141 fols.)

legajo 1708, 22: Ana Marti, viuda de Agustin Salvador Cortes, 1688. (162 fols.)

legajo 1708, 23, pieza 1: Ana Aguilo, muger de Raphael Cortes de Gabriel, 1689. (50 fols.)

  pieza 2: *Id.*, 1691.

legajo 1709, 1, pieza 1: Raphael Diego Forteza, dfo., alias el Pages, 1691. (12 fols.)

  pieza 2: Juan Antonio Cortes de Joseph y Catalina Aguilo, su muger, sus hijos y otros familias reconciliados por el Santo Oficio y aora son Judios en la cuidad de Nissa del Ducado de Saboya, 1688. (10 fols.)

  pieza 3: los descendientes de Judios que estan en la Calle de Sayel, y Agustin Cortes y otros de dicha Calle por observantes Judaycas, 1674. (35 fols.)

legajo 1709, 2: Raphael Joseph Cortes de Agustin, alias Filoa, 1688. (177 fols.)

legajo 1709, 3: Raphael Agustin Pomar, alias Xotento, 1688. (224 fols.)

legajo 1709, 4, pieza 1: Raphael Marti, menor, alias del Arpa, dfo., 1692. (74 fols.)

  pieza 2: *Id.*, 1693. (53 fols.)

legajo 1709, 5: Raphael Forteza de Baptista, alias el Rey, 1690. (27 fols.)

legajo 1709, 6: Raphael Ennrique Cortez, 1688. (103 fols.)

legajo 1709, 7, pieza 1: Raphael Bonin de Joseph, 1688. (63 fols.)

  pieza 2: *Id.*, 1691. (15 fols.)

legajo 1709, 8: Raphael Geronimo Cortes, dfo., 1681. (19 fols.)

legajo 1709, 9: Raphael Joseph Aguilo, 1683. (7 fols.)

legajo 1709, 10, pieza 1: Raphael Forteza, 1682. (13 fols.)

  pieza 2: Gabriel Piña, 1690. (9 fols.)

legajo 1709, 13: Raphael Henrique Cortes, hijo de Gabriel Joseph Cortes, alias el Consul, 1692. (15 fols.)

legajo 1709, 14: Raphael Christoval Forteza, alias Menyus, dfo., 1678. (67 fols.)

legajo 1710, 1, pieza 1: Honofre Cortes de Agustin, 1690. (129 fols.)

  pieza 2: Onofre Joseph Cortes, alias Moyanet, 1690. (77 fols.)

legajo 1710, 2: Isabel Terongi, muger de Augustin Cortes de Raphael, alias Brugea, 1688. (211 fols.)

legajo 1710, 3: Isabel Marti y Cortes, muger de Raphael Joseph Marti, 1679. (24 fols.)

legajo 1710, 4, pieza 1: Isabel, muger de Miguel Alexos Cortes, 1690. (47 fols.)
pieza 2: *Id.*, 1689.

legajo 1710, 5: Juana Bonin, muger de Raphael Forteza, 1690. (49 fols.)

legajo 1710, 6: Juana Cortes, viuda de Bartholome Forteza, alias Menyus, 1688. (162 fols.)

legajo 1710, 7, pieza 1: Juanot Forteza, 1689. (47 fols.)
pieza 2: *Id.*, 1691. (10 fols.)

legajo 1710, 8, pieza 1: Juana Ana Marti, muger de Raphael Nicolas Forteza, 1678. (54 fols.)
pieza 2: *Id.*, 1690. (60 fols.)

legajo 1710, 9, pieza 1: Juanot Cortes, hijo de Pedro Onofre Cortes de Guillermo, 1688. (178 fols.)
pieza 2: *Id.*, 1683. (10 fols.)

legajo 1710, 10: Joseph Andres Cortes, hijo de Juan Antonio Cortes de Joseph, 1678. (20 fols.)

legajo 1710, 11: Juanot Sureda, 1677. (30 fols.)

legajo 1710, 12: Joseph Aguilo, hixo de Onofre Aguilo de Pedro y de Theresa Cortes, 1688. (131 fols.)

legajo 1710, 13: Juanot Marti, 1689. (155 fols.)

legajo 1710, 14: Juana Aguilo y Forteza, muger de Raphael Aguilo, 1678. (26 fols.)

legajo 1710, 15: Juan Antonio Pomar, 1679 y 1688. (67 fols.)

legajo 1710, 16: Jacinta Cortes, hija de Juan Antonio Cortes de Joseph, 1678. (unnumbered fols.)

legajo 1710, 17: Onofre Cortes de Melchor, alias Don Juan, 1689. (56 fols.)

legajo 1710, 18, pieza 1: Onofre Joseph Cortes, hijo de Isabel Cortes, viuda Moyaneta, 1688. (104 fols.)
pieza 2: Onofre Cortes de Augustin. (412 fols.)

legajo 1711, 7, pieza 1: Francisca Marti, viuda de Francisco Marti, alias Verdet, 1690. (33 fols.)
pieza 2: *Id.*, 1678. (38 fols.)

legajo 1711, 8: Francisca Forteza, muger de Bartholome Joachin Marti, alias el hereu, 1690. (30 fols.)

legajo 1711, 9: Francisca Cortes, muger de Onofre Aguilo de Onofre, 1688. (344 fols.)

legajo 1711, 10: Francisca Forteza, muger de Bartholome Joachin Marti, alias el hereu, 1690. (96 fols.)

legajo 1711, 11, pieza 1: Francisca Cortes, muger de Gabriel Cortes de Agustin, alias Capalt, 1688. (80 fols.)
pieza 2: *Id.*, 1678. (17 fols.)

legajo 1711, 12, pieza 1: Francisca Terongi, muger de Bartholome Aguilo, 1691. (25 fols.)
pieza 2: *Id.*, 1691.
pieza 3: *Id.*, 1690. (176 fols.)

legajo 1711, 15: Francisca Aguilo, hija de Bartholome, muger de Raphael Henrique Cortes, 1692. (11 fols.)

legajo 1711, 18: Francisco Aguilo, 1692. (70 fols.)

legajo 1711, 19: Francisca Forteza, viuda de Miguel Geronimo Terongi, 1689. (63 fols.)

legajo 1711, 20: Francisco Joseph Terongi, hijo de Raphael Joseph Terongi, alias Felos, 1688. (136 fols.)

legajo 1712, 1: Onofre Cortes de Agustin, 1691. (13 fols.)

legajo 1712, 3: Testimonio de lo que consta por los processos de la complicidad de los Judaycantes de la calle del Sayel, Bolseria y Plateria, en quanto de los escrutinios de los susdhos., 1680. (7 fols.)

legajo 1712, 9: Juan Antonio Cortes de Joseph, 1678-9. (37 fols.)

legajo 1713, 1: Isabel Bonin, muger de Raphael Valls, mayor, 1688. (268 fols.)

legajo 1713, 2: Isabel Terongi, viuda de Francisco Aguilo, 1690. (57 fols.)

legajo 1713, 3, pieza 1: Isabel Marti, hija de Raphael Marti, menor, 1688. (240 fols.)

pieza 2: Adicion y Diligencias hechas en virtud de Autos de los Señores del Consexo de 17 de Noviembre del año pasado de 1690-1. (13 fols.)

legajo 1713, 9: Theresa Cortes, viuda de Onofre Aguilo de Pedro, 1688. (281 fols.)

legajo 1713, 12: Violante Marti, viuda de Onofre Cortes, 1690. (93 fols.)

legajo 1713, 13, pieza 1: Ursula Forteza, muger de Gabriel Pomar de Miguel y hija de Raphael Forteza de Baptista, alias el Rey, 1692. (60 fols.)

pieza 2: Id., 1690. (64 fols.)

legajo 1713, 14: Violante Forteza, muger de Raphael Cortes de Augustin, 1688. (173 fols.)

legajo 1714, 2: Onofre Aguilo de Onofre, 1689. (104 fols.)

legajo 1714, 10: Augustin Cortes, mayor, dfo., 1689. (132 fols.)

legajo 1714, 11, pieza 1: Leonor Valls y Pico, muger de Juan Pico, 1689. (45 fols.)

pieza 2: Leonor Forteza y Valls, viuda de Gregario Forteza, 1690. (43 fols.)

pieza 3: Leonor Cortes, muger de Joseph Marti de Francisco, alias Bruy, 1689. (66 fols.)

pieza 4: Leonor Marti, viuda de Raphael Geronimo Cortes, 1690. (84 fols.)

pieza 5: Leonor Marti, dfa., muger de Bartholome Terongi, alias el Conde, 1678. (45 fols.)

pieza 6: Id., 1693. (39 fols.)

legajo 1715, 5, pieza 1: Raphael Joachin Valls, 1722. (36 fols.)

pieza 2: Id., 1724 y 1728. (262 fols.)

legajo 1715, 12, pieza 1: Jacobo Cardozo Nuñez, Samuel Nahon y Salomon Nahon, 1720 y 1722. (78 fols.)

pieza 2: Autos en Razon de tres Hebreos apresados por los Armadores de Ibiza en embarcación de Moros y presos en aquella Isla, 1719.

legajo 1715, 12, pieza 3: Sobre lo que en el memorial incluso repre-
senta y pide Jacobo Cardozo Nuñez, que se
hallo en la fortaleza de Iviza; me consultará el
Consejo de Inquisizión, lo que sele ofreciere
y pareciere, en San Lorenzo á 8 de Octubre
de 1719. (unnumbered fols.)

Processos de Fe, Inqn. de Mallorca, JTS.
legajo 3, 18: Isabel Cortes, viuda de Raphael Joseph Cortes, alias
la Moyaneta. (253 fols.)
legajo 3, 19: Isabel Pomar, viuda de Raphael Marti del Arpa. (109
fols.)
legajo 6, 2: Isabel Pomar y Bonin. (237 fols.)

Relaciones de Causas de Fc, Inqn. de Mallorca, AHN.
libro 1, 860, años 1579-1606 (312 fols.)

861	1607-1631	(478 fols.)	
862	1632-1644	(504 fols.)	
863	1649-1660	(524 fols.)	
864	1661-1689	(452 fols.)	
865	1689-1690	(425 fols.)	
866	1693-1698	(399 fols.)	

legajo 1716, 1, años 1621-1622 (6 fols.)

2	1627	(unnumbered fols.)
3	1717, 1718, 1719	(46 fols.)
4	1720	(38 fols.)
5	1726	(30 fols.)
6	1727	(19 fols.)
7	1728	(27 fols.)
8	1730	(31 fols.)
9	1731	(unnumbered fols.)
10	1732	(unnumbered fols.)
11	1736	(73 fols.)
12	1738	(unnumbered fols.)
13	1739	(unnumbered fols.)
14	1740	(unnumbered fols.)
15	1742	(unnumbered fols.)
16	1743	(56 fols.)
17	1744	(unnumbered fols.)
18	1745	(30 fols.)
19	1746	(21 fols.)
20	1747	(unnumbered fols.)
21	1748	(unnumbered fols.)
22	1749	(unnumbered fols.)
23	1750	(unnumbered fols.)
24	1751	(unnumbered fols.)
25	1752	(24 fols.)
26	1753	(unnumbered fols.)
27	1755	(unnumbered fols.)
28	1756	(32 fols.)
29	1757	(36 fols.)
30	1758	(unnumbered fols.)
31	1760	(unnumbered fols.)

32	1761	(10 fols.)
33	1762	(unnumbered fols.)
34	1763	(unnumbered fols.)
35	1764	(9 fols.)
36	1765	(unnumbered fols.)
37	1768	(19 fols.)
38	1771	(20 fols.)

Tratado del Origen de las Sinagogas, y Judíos de esta Isla de Mallorca, de su combersion, y reincidencias al Judaismo y de los buelos que han intentado á impulsos de sus combeniencias, y riquezas de que abundan, Palma, October 31, 1773. I-IV Sections of 22, 14, 25, 34 *capitulos,* respectively. (In the private library of the late Don Francisco Villalonga y Fabregues, Palma. A copy is in the possession of Elkan N. Adler, Esq., of London.)

Votas y Sentencias, Consejo de la Inqn., AHN.

libro 1, 1160: Libro Segundo de Votos de la Corona de Aragon desde el año de 1652 hasta el de 1685. (310 fols.)

1161: Libro Quarto de Votos de autos en Causas de Fe del Consejo de su Magestad de la Santa general Inqn. desde el año de 1685 hasta fin de 1690. (388 fols.)

1162: *Id.,* 3 Dic. 1709—20 Sept. 1731. (341 fols.)

1163: *Id.,* 22 Sept. 1731—15 Enero 1745. (unnumbered fols.)

1164: Id., 21 Enero 1645—22 Oct. 1756. (unnumbered fols.)

II

Printed Sources

Abrahams, Israel, *Jewish Life in the Middle Ages,* (Ed. by Cecil Roth), London, 1932.

Acton, Lord (John Emerich Eduard Dalberg-Acton), *Correspondence,* London, 1907.

Adler, Elkan Nathan, "Auto de Fé and Jew," *JQR,* XIII, 1901, 392-437. *Auto de Fé and Jew,* London, 1908.

Aguiló, Estanislao, "Ordenes de Jaime II que los judios moren todas dentro del Calle," *BSAL,* VII, 1897-8, 18.

Albertí, Arnaldo, *Repetitio nova, sive commentaria rubricae et C. I. De Hereticis,* Valencia, 1534. *Tractatus de Agnoscendis assertionibus catholicis et haereticis,* Palermo, 1554.

Alomar, Gabriel, "Prologue" to Sand, George, *Un Invierno en Mallorca,* Palma, 1932.

Altamira y Crevea, Rafael, *A History of Spanish Civilization,* 2 vols., London, 1930. (Abridged version of *Historia de España y la Civilización Española,* 4 vols., Barcelona, 1913.)

Amador de los Rios, José, *Historia Social, Politica, y Religiosa de los Judios de España y Portugal,* 3 vols., Madrid, 1875-6.

Amengual, Juan José, *Gramatica de la lengua mallorquina,* Palma, 1872. *Nuevo Diccionario mallorquin-castellano-latino,* Palma, 1858-78.

Asaf, Simhah, "Anuse Sefarad Uportugal Besifrut Hateshuvot," *Zion,* Book V, 1932, 61-88.

Baer, Fritz, *Die Juden im christlichen Spanien,* Berlin, 1929.

Bernaldez, Andrés, *Historia de los reyes Catolicos D. Fernando y Isabel,* 2 vols., Sevilla, 1870.

Binimelis, Juan, *Nueva Historia de la Isla de Mallorca y de Otras Islas a ella adyacentes,* 2 vols., Palma, 1927.

Blasco-Ibáñez, Vicente, *Los Muertos Mandan,* Valencia, 1916. (English tr.: *The Dead Command,* Frances Douglas, New York, 1919.)

Bover de Roselló, Joaquin María, *Biblioteca de Escritores Baleares,* 2 vols., Palma, 1868.

Braunstein, Baruch, "Jews in Many Lands—The Island of Majorca," *B'nai B'rith Magazine,* March, 1934.

Breve Reseña de la Historia de Mallorca, Palma-de-Mallorca, 1929.

Campaner y Fuertes, Alvaro, see, *Cronicon Mayoricense.*

Castro, Adolfo de, *Historia de los Protestantes Españoles,* Cadiz, 1851. (English tr.: *The Spanish Protestants and Their Persecution by Philip II,* Thomas Parker, London, 1851.)

Catálogo de las Causas contra la fe seguidas ante el tribunal del Santo Oficio de la Inquisición de Toledo y de las informaciones genealogicas de los Pretendientes a Oficios del Mismo, (con un Apendice en que se detallan los fondos existentes en este Archivo de los demas tribunales de España, Italia y America), Padre Fresca, S. J., y Don Miguel Gomez del Campillo, Madrid, 1903.

Catálogo de las Informaciones Genealogicas de los Pretendientes a Cargos del Santo Oficio, Valladolid, 1928.

Chevalier, Ulysee, *Répertoire des source historiques du moyen âge, Topobibliographie,* 2 vols., Montbeliard, 1894-1903.

Cortada, Juan, *Viaje á la Isla de Mallorca,* Barcelona, 1845.

Coulton, G. G., *The Inquisition,* New York, 1929.

Cronicon Mayoricense, Noticias y relaciones históricas de Mallorca desde 1229 á 1800, Alvaro Campaner y Fuertes, Palma de Mallorca, 1881.

Danvila y Collado, Manuel, *La Expulsión de los Moriscos Españoles,* Madrid, 1889.

Dunlop, John, *Memoirs of Spain during the Reigns of Philip IV and Charles II, from 1621-1700.* 2 vols., Edinburgh, 1834.

Emanuel, Charles H. L., *A Century and a Half of Jewish History,* London, 1910.

Epstein, Isidore, *The Responsa of Rabbi Simon B. Zemah Duran as a Source of the History of the Jews in North Africa,* London, 1930.

Estrugo, Jose M., *El Retorno a Sefard,* Madrid, 1933.

Evans, Austin P., "Social Aspects of Medieval Heresy," in *Persecution and Liberty,* New York, 1931, 93-116.

Fajarnés, Enrique:
"Cartas Reales sobre las laudemios de los bienes confiscados á los judios de Mallorca (siglo XVII)," *BSAL*, VIII, 1899-1900, 94.
"Disposiciones de Alfonso III de Aragon sobre los judios de Mallorca (1288-9)," *BSAL*, VIII, 1899-1900, 6.
"El Santo Oficio y los compradores de bienes de judaizantes (1680)," *BSAL*, VIII, 1899-1900, 34.
"Emigración de los judios y conversos de Mallorca después de la matanza del Call (1392)," *BSAL*, VIII, 1899-1900, 55-7.
"Ferrer Cresques, Médico judio mallorquin del siglo XIV," *BSAL*, VII, 1897-8, 328.
"Fundación de la Cátedra de Hebreo en Mallorca (1692)," *BSAL*, VII, 1897-8, 33.
"Juseff-ben-Barahon, Rabí de la escuela de los judios de Mallorca; su familia y sus bienes (1392)," *BSAL*, VII, 1897-8, 376.
"La Aljama hebraica de Mallorca en el siglo XIV," *BSAL*, VIII, 1899-1900, 39-40.
"Licencia de vender carnes en la casa de la Inquisición para los presos en las cárcelas secretas (1678)," *BSAL*, VII, 1897-8, 388.
"Los Bienes de los Judíos y Conversos de Mallorca después del Saqueo del Call (1391-3)," *BSAL*, VIII, 1899-1900, 441-4.
"Los Judíos Mallorquines bajo la protección real (1393), *BSAL*, VIII, 1899-1900, 31.
"Ofrecimientos á los conversos de Valencia para poblar Mallorca (1463)," *BSAL*, VIII, 1899-1900, 51.
"Pregó Prohibint Fer Dany Al Call dels Jueus de Mallorca (1393)," *BSAL*, VIII, 1899-1900, 381.
"Primeras Disposiciones de Pedro IV de Aragon Sobre los Judíos de Mallorca,".*BSAL*, VIII, 1899-1900, 203-4.
"Sobre la venta de ropas que fueron de los judios mallorquines (1679)," *BSAL*, VII, 1897-8, 412.
"Un pregón contra los judaizantes de Mallorca (1393)," *BSAL*, VIII, 1899-1900, 64.
Fernandez y Gonzalez, Francisco, *Instituciones Jurídicas del Pueblo de Israel en los Diferentes Estados de la Península Ibérica desde su Dispersion en Tiempo del Emperador Adriano hasta los Principios del Siglo XVI*, Madrid, 1881.
Fita, Fidel, *Datos Historicos por la España Hebrea*, 2 vols., Madrid, 1890.
"Los Judios Mallorquines y el Concilio de Viena," *BAH*, XXXVI, 1900, 232-58.
Fita, Fidel, and Llabres, Gabriel, "Privilegios de los Hebreos Mallorquines en el Codice Pueyo," *BAH*, XXXVI, 1900, 15-35, 122-48, 185-209, 273-306, 369-402, 458-94.
Furio y Sastre, Antonio de, *Memorias para Servir a la Historia Eclesiastica General Politica de la Provincia de Mallorca*, Palma, 1820.
Garau, Francisco, *La Fee Triunfante en Quatro Autos Celebrados en Mallorca*, Palma, 1931.
Geddes, Richard, *History of Expulsion of the Moriscos*, (vol. I of Miscellaneous Tracts), London, 1714.

Gottheil, Richard, "Gleanings from Spanish and Portuguese Archives," *JQR*, XIV, 1901, 80-95.

Grasset de St. Sauveur, André, *Voyage dans les îles Baléares et Pithiuses, fait dans les annees 1801, 2, 3, 4, 5,* Paris, 1807. (Eng. tr.: *Travels through the Balearic and Pithusian Islands, performed between the years 1801, and 1806,* vol. VIII of *A Collection of Modern and Contemporary Voyages and Travels,* London, 1808.)

Hamilton, Earl J., *American Treasure and the Price Revolution in Spain, 1501-1650,* Cambridge, Mass., 1934.

Hamy, M. E. T., "Cresques lo Jeheu: Note sur un Géographe Juif Catalan de la fin du XIVe. siecle, *"Bulletin de Geógraphie, Historique et Descriptive,* no. 3, 1891.

Herculano, Alexandro, *Da Origem e Estabelecimento da Inquisição em Portugal,* 3 vols., Lisbon, 1854-9. (Eng. tr. by John C. Banner in *Stanford University Publications,* I, 1926, 189-632).

Historia General del Reino de Mallorca, Juan Dameto, Vicente Mut, y Gerónimo Alemany. Segunda Edición, Corregida É Ilustrada con Abundantes Notas y Documentos, y Continuada Hasta Nuestros Dias. por Miguel Moragues y Joachin María Bover, 3 vols., Palma, 1840-1. (Abridged tr.: *The Ancient and Modern History of the Balearick Islands; or of the Kingdom of Majorca,* Colin Campbell, London, 1716.)

Hume, Martin A. S., *Spain, Its Greatness and Decay (1479-1788),* (in the *Cambridge Historical Series),* Cambridge, 1899.

Infante, Eduardo, *Jorge Aguiló ó Misterios de Palma, Novela de Costumbres Mallorquines,* 2 vols., Palma, 1866.

Instrucción, que han de guardar los Comisarios del Santo Oficio de la Inquisición, en las Causas y Negocios de Fé, y los demás que se ofrecieron, 17 pp., n. d.

Instrucción, y Regla Que Han De Observar Los Ministros de el distrito de esta Inquisición de Toledo y demás personas á quienes por ella se cometiere el examen y declaración de los Hereges que vinieren pidiendo ser admitidos a el Gremio de nuestra Santa Madre Iglesia Catolica, Apostolica Romana ó Reconciliados con ella, 4 fols., n. d.

Jacobs, Joseph, *An Inquiry into the Sources of the History of the Jews in Spain,* London, 1894.

James I, Chronicle of, King of Aragon, surnamed the Conqueror, (written by himself), tr. by John Forster, 2 vols., London, 1883.

Juicio de la Prensa Española sobre la Cuestion Social Mallorquina Y Sobre el Libro de Polemica titulado Estado Religiosa y Social de la Isla de Mallorca, Palma, 1878.

Kayserling, M., "Auto de Fé and Jews," *JQR*, XIV, 1901, 136-40.
  Biblioteca Española-Portugueza-Judaica, Strasbourg, 1890.
  "Die Juden auf Mallorca," *Jahrbuch fur die Geschichte der Juden und des Judenthums,* I, 1860, 67-100.
  Die Juden in Navarra, den Baskenlandern und auf den Balearen, Berlin, 1861.
  "Notes sur l'histoire des Juifs de Majorque," *REJ*, XLIV, 1902, 297-300.
  Sephardim: Romanische Poesien der Juden in Spanien, Leipzig, 1859.

Lacroix, Paul, *Military and Religious Life in the Middle Ages at the Period of the Renaissance,* London, 1874.

Lardizabal y Uribe, Miguel de, *Apología por los Agótes de Navarra, y los Chuetas de Mallorca, con una breve digression á los Vaqueros de Asturias,* Madrid, 1786.

Lea, Henry Charles, *A History of the Inquisition of the Middle Ages,* 3 vols., New York, 1887-8.
  A History of the Inquisition of Spain, 4 vols., New York, 1906-7.
  The Moriscos of Spain: Their Conversion and Expulsion, Philadelphia, 1901.

Levi, Israel, "L'Inventaire du Mobilier et de la Bibliotheque d'un Médicin Juif de Majorque au XIVe siecle," *REJ,* XXXIX, 1899, 242-60.

Levin, D., "Der Chueta," [A Poem], *Populär-Wissenschaftliche Monatsblatter,* November, 1884, no. 11.

Lewin, A., "Die Neuchristen auf der Insel Mallorca," *Jüdisches Litteratur-Blatt,* (Madgeburg), XII, 1883, 105-6, 109-10, 113-4, 117-8.

Lindo, E. H., *The History of the Jews of Spain and Portugal,* London, 1848.

Llabres, Gabriel, "La Conversion de los Judios Mallorquines en 1391," *BAH,* XL, 1902, 152-4.
  "Los Judios Mallorquines: Colección Diplomatica desde el año 1247 hasta 1387," *BAH,* XXXVI, 1900, 13-15.

Llebrés y Moporter, Juan, (pseudonym for Morell, Juan), *Memoria instructiva sobre el estado actual de la isla de Mallorca,* Madrid, 1787.

Llorente, Juan Antonio, *Histoire Critique de L'Inquisition D'Espagne,* 4 vols., Paris, 1818.
  Memoria Historica sobre cual ha sido la opinion nacional de España acerca del Tribunal de la Inquisición, Madrid, 1812.

Loeb, Isidore, "Le Nombre de Juifs de Castile et D'Espagne Au Moyen Age," *REJ,* XIV, 1887, 161-83.
  "Notes sur l'Histoire des Juifs en Espagne," *REJ,* XIV, 1887, 259-61.

Madariaga, Salvador de, *Spain,* New York, 1931.

Maycock, A. L., *The Inquisition from its Establishment to the Great Schism,* London, 1927.

Mendoza y Bovadilla, Francisco, *El Tizon de la Nobleza,* Barcelona, 1880.

Menendez y Pelayo, Marcelino, *Historia de los Heterodoxes Españoles,* 3 vols., Madrid, 1880-1.

Merriman, R. B., *The Rise of the Spanish Empire,* 4 vols., New York, 1918-34.

Michel, Francisque, *Histoire des Race Maudites de la France et de l'Espagne,* 2 vols., Paris, 1847.

Morel-Fatio, Alfred, "Notes et Documents pour Servir a L'Histoire des Juifs des Baléares sur la Domination Aragonaise du XIIIe au XVe siecle," *REJ,* IV, 1882, 31-56.

Nos Los Inquisidores Apostolichs contra la Heretica Pravitat y Apostasia en la Ciutat, Diocesi, y Regne de Mallorca, JTS. (6 fols.)

Oliver, Miguel Santos, *Mallorca durante la primera Revolución. 1808 á 1814,* Palma, 1901.
  Hojas del Sábado, Barcelona, 1908.

Olmo, Joseph del, *Relacion Historica del Auto General de Fe que se Celebro en Madrid este año de 1680,* Madrid, 1680.

Ordinacions y Sumari Dels Privilegis, Constetuts, y Bons Usos del Regne de Mallorca, Palma, 1663.

Paramo, Luis de, *De Origine et Progressu Officii Sanctae Inquisitionis,* Madrid, 1598.

Paz, Julian, "Reclamaciones de los Mallorquines Llamados de LA CALLE sobre su condicion Social," *RABM,* XVI, 1907, 184-200.

Paz y Melia, A., *Catálogo Abreviado de Papeles de Inquisición,* Madrid, 1914.

Petrie, Charles, *Spain,* (no. V in *Modern State Series,* R. B. Mowat, Gen. Ed.), London, 1934.

Piferrer, Pablo and Quadrado, José Maria, *Islas Baleares,* 2 vols., Barcelona, 1888.

Pons, Antoni, "Dels Dies Terribles, 1793-1799," *La Nostra Terra,* (Palma de Mallorca), Any VI, 1933, 364-72

Portocarrero, Iuan Dionisio, *Sobre la Competencia de Jurisdición, de que se trata, entre la Inquisición y Ministros Reales de Mallorca,* Madrid, 1624.

Prescott, William H., *History of the Reign of Ferdinand and Isabella, the Catholic, of Spain,* 2 vols., London, 1851.
    History of the Reign of Philip the Second, King of Spain, 3 vols., London, 1855-9.

Puerta Vizcaino, Juan de la, *La Sinagoga Balear ó Historia de los Judios de Mallorca,* Valencia, 1857.

Puigblanch, Antonio, (under the pseudonym of Jomtob, Natanael), *La Inquisición sin Mascara; ó-Disertacion en que se prueban hasta la evidencia los vicios de esto tribunal y la necessidad de que se suprima,* Sevilla, 1813.

Pulgar, Hernando de, *Cronica de los reyes católicos Fernando y Isabel de Castilla y de Aragon,* Valencia, 1780.

Quadrado, José Maria, *Forenses y Ciudadanos, Historia de las disensiones civiles de Mallorca en el siglo XV,* Palma, 1847.
    "La Juderia de la Capital de Mallorca en 1391," *BAH,* IX, 1886, 294-312.

Rahola, Carles, *Els Jueus a Catalunya,* Barcelona, 1929.

Ramis de Ayreflor y Sureda, José, *La Nobleza Mallorquina, Singularmente en el Siglo XVII,* Palma, 1922.

Reales Cedulas de Don Carlos III, Libro XII, Ley VI, Titulo I, Madrid, 1788.

Régné, Jean, *Catalogue des actes de Jaime I, Pedro III, et Alfonso III, rois d'Aragon concernant les Juifs (1213-1291),* Paris, 1914.

Relacion de los Autos Particulares de Fe, que se han celebrado en las Inquisiciones de Cuenca, el dia del Apostal San Pedro, 29 de Junio de este año de 1722 en la Iglesia del Convento de San Pablo, orden de Predicadores, de dicha Ciudad; y la de Mallorca, el dia 31 de Mayo de dicha año, en la Iglesia del Real Convento de Santo Domingo, de los Reos que salieron en ellas, y sentencias en que fueron condenados, 7 pp., Library of the Hebrew Union College, Cincinnati.

Relacion De Los Sanbenitos, que se han puesto, y renovado este año de 1755 en el Claustro del Real Convento de Santo Domingo, de esta Ciudad de Palma, por el Santo Oficio de la Inquisición del Reyno de Mallorca, de REOS RELAXADOS, Y RECONCILIADOS PUBLICAMEN-TE, por el mismo tribunal desde el año de 1645, Palma de Mallorca, 1755. (May be found in Garau's *La Fee Triunfante,* Palma, 1931, Apéndice V).

Responsa of Rabbi Isaac Ben Sheshet Barfat, (Teshuvot Rabi Itzhak Ben Sheshet), Constantinople, 1546-7.

Responsa of Rabbi Simon Ben Zemah Duran, (Sefer Hatashbetz), Amsterdam, 1741.

Roth, Cecil. *A History of the Marranos,* Philadelphia, 1932.
"The Religion of the Marranos," *JQR,* XXII, 1931, 1-35.

Sampol y Ripoll, Pedro, *Anuario Bibliográfico, 1897-1902: Apuntes para una biblioteca Mallorquina,* Palma, 1898-1904.

Sánchez, Alonso B., *Fuentes de la Historia Española e Hispano-Americana,* Madrid, 1927.

Schäfer, Ernst, *Beitrage zur Geschichte des Spanischen Protestantismus und der Inquisition im sechzehnten Jahrhundert,* 3 vols., Gütersloh, 1902.

Schwarz, Samuel, *Os Cristãos-Novos em Portugal no Século XX,* Lisbon, 1925.
"The Crypto-Jews of Portugal," *Menorah Journal,* XII, 1926, 138-49, 283-97.

Slousch, Nahum, *Haanusim Beportugal,* Tel Aviv, Palestine, 1932.

Solberg, Thorvald, "Some Notes on the Balearic Islands with Special reference to their Bibliography," in *The Papers of the Bibliographical Society of America,* XXII, 1928, 69-146.

Soler, Tomás Bertran, *Un Milagro y Una Mentira: Vindicación de los Mallorquines Christianos de Estirpe Hebrea,* Valencia, 1858.

Stanhope, Alexander, *Spain under Charles the Second; or Extracts from the Correspondence of the Hon. Alexander Stanhope, British Minister at Madrid, 1690-1699,* London, 1844.

Störmann, Auguste Franziska, *Studien zur Geschichte des Königsreichs Mallorka,* Berlin, 1918.

Tanon, L., *Histoire des Tribunaux de l'inquisition en France,* Paris, 1893.

Taronjí, José, *Algo Sobre el Estado Religiosa y Social de la Isla de Mallorca: Polémica contra las Preocupaciones de Clase,* Palma, 1877.
Una Mala Causa A Todo Trance Defendida, Palma, 1877.

Turberville, Arthur Stanley, *Medieval Heresy and the Inquisition,* London, 1920.
The Spanish Inquisition, London, 1932.

Vacandard, E., *The Inquisition,* (Tr. from the French by Bertrand L. Conway), New York, 1908.

Valera, Juan, "Del Influjo de la Inquisición y del Fanatismo Religiosa en la decadencia de la literatura Española," in *Obras: Disertaciones y Juicios Literarios,* Madrid, VII, 1890, 153-87.

Vidal, Pierre, "Les Juifs des Anciens Comtés de Roussillon et de Cerdagne," *REJ*, XV, 1887, 19-55.

Villanueva, Jaime, *Viage á Mallorca*, vols. XXI and XXII of *Viage Literario a las Iglesias de España*, Madrid, 1851-2.

Walsh, William Thomas, *Isabella of Spain. the Last Crusader*, New York, 1930.

Zaforteza y Musoles, Diego, *Ciutat*, Palma, 1932.

Zimmels, H. J., *Die Marranen in der Rabbinischen Literatur*, Berlin, 1932.

Zurita, G., *Anales de la Corona de Aragon, 7* vols., Saragossa, 1610-21.

INDEX

INDEX

CPSIA information can be obtained
at www.ICGtesting.com
Printed in the USA
BVHW051428261221
624765BV00005B/241